The Heart of Yoknapatawpha

The Heart of

Yoknapatawpha

BY

JOHN PILKINGTON

UNIVERSITY PRESS OF MISSISSIPPI

JACKSON

1981

Library of Congress Cataloging in Publication Data

Pilkington, John, 1918–
  The heart of Yoknapatawpha.

  Includes bibliographical references.
  1. Faulkner, William, 1897–1962—Criticism and interpretation. I. Title.
PS3511.A86Z9463   813'.52   80-29686
ISBN 0-87805-135-X

TO

L.K.P. AND C.K.P.

Contents

Preface

WITH THE WRITING of *Sartoris* and its publication in 1929, William Faulkner discovered the immense fictional possibilities inherent in the hill country of north Mississippi, where he had been born and reared. Between this date and 1942, when *Go Down, Moses* was published, Faulkner wrote the novels upon which his enduring fame must always rest. Afterwards, his powers would slowly diminish; and although his second-best writing was still very, very good, he would never again reach the levels of excellence he had shown in *Sartoris*, *The Sound and the Fury*, *As I Lay Dying*, *Sanctuary*, *Light in August*, *Absalom, Absalom!*, *The Unvanquished*, *The Hamlet*, and *Go Down, Moses*. These works lie at the heart of Faulkner's Yoknapatawpha saga, and they form the subject of this study.

The immense amount of critical exegesis and commentary that these nine novels have prompted has been staggering. Prior to 1950, when Faulkner received the Nobel Prize for Literature, almost no criticism of his work was available in hard-cover. Since that time, the Faulkner "industry" has been such that the academic community has scarcely been able to keep up with the dissertations, articles, and books dealing with almost every conceivable aspect of Faulkner's writing. The 1960s, especially, witnessed a great outpouring of Faulkner studies, a number of which, like the present volume, surveyed all or most of Faulkner's major works; and in the 1970s numerous dissertations, which often later appeared in hard-cover, examined in detail particular novels, while other books treated Faulkner's writing from philosophical and theoretical points of view. In the light of thirty years of intense examination by literally hundreds of critics, one might reasonably wonder if anything else remains to be said about the fiction of William Faulkner.

Preface

This book rests upon the premise that not only does something else remain to be said, but also that so long as Faulker's writings continue to speak to man's problems and to help man understand his perplexities and humanity, there will always be something more to be said. The conclusions of the general surveys made in the 1960s, valuable as they were and remain, must be modified by new perspectives made inevitable through the lapse of time, by the advance of knowledge about Faulkner's biography, and by the research now available in specialized studies which in themselves are necessarily fragmentary but influence the overall estimate of Faulkner's work. To phrase the matter directly, fifty years after *Sartoris* and almost forty after *Go Down, Moses*, Faulkner's readers, entering the 1980s, should take a fresh approach to those novels that form the heart of the Yoknapatawpha fiction in the light not only of what has been said but also to discover what Faulkner has to say to the present.

This examination of Faulkner's work focuses upon the individual novels and upon their relationships to the totality of Faulkner's contribution. Criticism of the kind practiced here should always acknowledge its debts to earlier studies, but criticism of criticism must be kept to a minimum. My objective is to present balanced, even-tempered, perhaps slightly conservative studies of nine of Faulkner's best novels. I have endeavored to write from the perspective of literary history and from within the framework of the novels to reveal the close relationships among them; to explicate certain passages, notably in *The Sound and the Fury*, *Absalom, Absalom!*, and *Go Down, Moses*, which have always been and remain perplexing to many readers; and to reach conclusions about the overall significance or implications of Faulkner's novels. In meeting these objectives, I have sought to support my interpretations with abundant quotations and citations from the novels themselves.

In general, critics dealing with Faulkner's work in the period under discussion have concentrated upon his uniqueness. Attention has been directed primarily to such literary concerns as his efforts to render psychological states or processes, his use of myth, the qualities of his literary style, and his innovations in narrative techniques. Much less has been said about his kinship with his fellow writers, particularly in the 1920s. The importance of the strictly literary or artistic aspects of his work, of course, should not be minimized, but for most readers these matters are secondary to Faulkner's commentary upon the humanity of man in the twentieth century. In any assessment of Faulkner's ultimate contribution to American literature, the critic must recognize that in his novels of the late 1920s and 1930s Faulkner handled themes that other writers had initiated earlier in their fiction. Faulkner's affinities with such writers as Sherwood Anderson, Edgar Lee Masters, Ellen Glasgow, Sinclair Lewis, F. Scott Fitzgerald, Ernest Hemingway, and others cannot be overlooked. The general nature of these relationships can readily be identified but need not be examined here in detail.

When Faulkner began to write in the 1920s, American literature contained a number of sharply defined configurations to which he responded. Sherwood Anderson's theories about a new looseness of form in the novel—ideas which owed something to Edgar Lee Masters and found illustration in *Winesburg, Ohio*—clearly exerted an influence upon Faulkner's concept of the novel. In 1925, the year in which Faulkner was most closely associated with Anderson, Ellen Glasgow published *Barren Ground*, one of a long series of novels in which she endeavored to explore the history of Virginia from about the time of the Confederacy to modern times. When Faulkner decided to examine the history of north Mississippi in his Yoknapatawpha novels, he had her example before him. In this important mid-year of the decade, Faulkner could also have read Theodore Dreiser's *An American Tragedy*, notable for containing Dreiser's fullest and most powerful statement of naturalism and his attack upon the administration of justice and organized religion in America. Faulkner would utilize these themes in several novels, perhaps the best examples being *As I Lay Dying* and *Sanctuary*. In Fitzgerald's *The Great Gatsby* and in Hemingway's *In Our Time*, both of which appeared in this same remarkable year of the American novel, Faulkner could have read the outpouring of the disillusionment of the Lost Generation, ideas that colored *Sartoris*, *The Sound and the Fury*, *Sanctuary*, and probably *As I Lay Dying*. In Sinclair Lewis' *Babbitt* (1922), Faulker might have seen a precursor of his own Jason Compson; and in Lewis' *Elmer Gantry* (1927), he could have viewed examples of religious bigotry that anticipated his own Doc Hines and Simon McEachern. The similarities between Faulkner's themes and those of his contemporaries demonstrate convincingly that despite the rather narrow focus of his fiction upon life in north Mississippi, Faulkner was very much a part of the pattern of the national literary scene and responded to the same subjects that occupied writers in other parts of the country. To a degree, Faulkner's Yoknapatawpha was a literary microcosm of the 1920s.

Although he was ever willing to seize upon any material wherever he found it, Faulkner can never be called an imitator. The ideas or themes he took from others he so thoroughly assimilated into his own thinking that they emerged with a singular Faulkner stamp that marked them for his own. Thus, the record shows that Faulkner began the great years of his literary work, the period between *Sartoris* and *Go Down, Moses*, by choosing to deal with many of the subjects favored by his contemporaries. In *Sartoris*, *The Sound and the Fury*, *As I Lay Dying*, and *Sanctuary*, one can observe his identification with many of the major problems that confronted America after World War I. At the same time, he was also beginning his measurement of Southern history from the Civil War to his own time in north Mississippi. In that assessment, the deterioration of great Southern families and the perversion of traditional American virtues became new and prominent features of his work. With *Light in August* and *Absalom, Absalom!*, Faulkner began to emphasize the need for man to tolerate the burden of his humanity and to assert the difficulties that lie in the way of the discovery of historical truth. Probably more than any other American novelist, Faulkner understood the movement of American history and the vital role of history in man's understanding, if not always justification, of his present. These elements of his work came to fruition in *The Unvanquished*, *The Hamlet*, and *Go Down, Moses*—novels in which he increasingly emphasized his conviction that man can never realize his freedom by living to himself alone. In these novels, especially, Faulkner insisted upon the dignity of every man whatever his color or condition in life; he continually affirmed that the poor, the sick, the elderly, the young, the mentally retarded, even the criminal, have yet their claim to the rights of man.

Faulkner believed that freedom, in America or in any other country, can only be attained in the context of the community. He recognized that two forces primarily inhibit man's realization of his freedom in society: his failure to recognize the humanity, the equality, the rights, the needs of others; and his vulnerability to the temptations of greed. More vividly and more persuasively than the works of any other American novelist, Faulkner's fiction reveals the depth to which the human spirit can be eroded by an insatiable greed for material possessions that is the besetting sin in modern times. Like Shakespeare, Milton, Hawthorne, Melville, and Whitman, Faulkner warned man against the evil that lies within himself but believed in man's potential for right living within the context of human brotherhood. These are the timeless truths that lie at the heart of Faulkner's Yoknapatawpha.

Acknowledgments

FROM THE BEGINNING of this study of William Faulkner's best fiction, I have been indebted to literary historians and critics who have sought diligently over the past three decades to assist readers of his novels to appreciate his contribution to the literature of the twentieth century. With no intention of slighting any of these perceptive writers by not referring to them by name, I wish to mention especially my appreciation of the biographical research of Joseph Blotner and the critical studies of Cleanth Brooks, Melvin Backman, Warren Beck, Carvel Collins, Michael Gold, Elizabeth Kerr, James Meriwether, Michael Millgate, William Van O'Connor, Lewis Simpson, Olga Vickery, and Hyatt Waggoner.

Without permission to publish material from Faulkner's fiction, letters, and other writings, this volume would lose much of its effectiveness. For permission to publish excerpts from Faulkner's novels and his nonfiction writings, I am grateful to Mrs. Jill Faulkner Summers; for permission to publish quotations from Faulkner's novels and *Selected Letters of William Faulkner*, I thank Random House, Inc.; and for permission to publish material from *Faulkner in the University*, I express my appreciation to the University Press of Virginia.

Although in the notes and references I have acknowledged help from many scholars, the contributions of my friends and colleagues cannot be identified in this manner. I refer particularly to Robert W. Hamblin, Gerald W. Walton, Evans B. Harrington, and W. Gordon Milne, who read the manuscript and made helpful suggestions, and to Ann J. Abadie, Vasser Bishop, Chester A. McLarty, and Charles E. Noyes.

Acknowledgments

Throughout the years in which I have studied and enjoyed the novels of William Faulkner, I have been fortunate to have the help of my wife, Lillian, and my son, Kirk, who have supported my work with endless patience, good humor, and understanding.

The Heart of Yoknapatawpha

CHAPTER I

The Poles
of Historical Measurement

Sartoris

TWO WEEKS after he had finished the manuscript of his third book and dated it 29 September 1927 on page 583, William Faulkner wrote his publisher, Horace Liveright: "I have written THE book. . . . I believe it is the damdest best book you'll look at this year, and any other publisher." When Liveright rejected the manuscript, Faulkner, shocked yet still confident, answered, "I still believe it is the book which will make my name for me as a writer." [1] To a degree, the argument over the merits of the work continues and relates not to one novel but two. In 1927 Faulkner entitled his lengthy manuscript "Flags in the Dust." When it was finally published by Harcourt, Brace, and Company on January 31, 1929, the title had been changed to *Sartoris*; and the manuscript had undergone substantial cutting—some might say tinkering—by Ben Wasson, Faulkner's literary agent. The circumstances are sufficiently pertinent to the study of the novel to warrant a brief account of them.

Very likely, the source of Faulkner's optimism about his book was his discovery that he could insert contemporary issues and ideas into an intensely local Mississippi setting. In other words, he had discovered Yoknapatawpha, and the discovery convinced him of the inexhaustible fund of stories that could be developed out of north Mississippi. Even as he wrote, he saw the emerging work as a turning point in his career. Looking at the finished manuscript from an entirely different point of view, Horace Liveright could not share his author's enthusiasm. Liveright wrote, bluntly, that the work lacked plot, character development, dimension, and cohesiveness; and virtually all of the other publishers to whom the novel was submitted voiced similar objections. Finally, Ben Wasson persuaded Harrison Smith, an editor at Harcourt, Brace, to recommend it favorably to Alfred Harcourt. The firm decided to publish the manuscript only if it were cut substantially. Faulkner, then absorbed in another novel and, to say the least, unenthusiastic about the cutting, agreed for Wasson to undertake the revision. The story is told that late in September, 1928, Faulkner sat in Wasson's apartment in New York, writing *The Sound and the Fury*, while his friend and literary agent transformed "Flags in the Dust" into *Sartoris*. No one knows how or exactly when the change of name occurred. Roughly, one-fourth of the original manuscript, or about twenty thousand words, was excised. Although Wasson seems to have performed the major portion of the cutting, Faulkner also made revisions and probably approved the final typescript from which the printer set type for the book.[2] Unfortunately, this "setting" copy of *Sartoris* and the galley proof sheets have been lost.

Although Faulkner disliked the stripping of his novel, Ben Wasson's knife moved with direction. Wasson correctly understood that the focus of the novel should be upon the young Bayard Sartoris. Accordingly, he pruned away much of the material Faulkner had used to define the roles of Narcissa and Horace Benbow. Likewise, Wasson removed many of the pages relating to Belle Mitchell, Byron Snopes, and Virgil Beard. By thus sharpening the emphasis upon Bayard, Wasson tightened the form of the novel, but in the process he diminished the contrast between Horace and Bayard and notably reduced the attention given to the Yoknapatawpha community, which forms the baseline of the action. Most of the Sartoris material remained as Faulkner wrote it; the real cost to the work lay in the loss of the antithesis and balance provided by the Benbows.

Among his papers, Faulkner kept the autograph manuscript and a large quantity of typescript material that apparently represents various stages in the composition of the original *Flags in the Dust*. Faulkner's practice seems to have been to compose segments of his book in longhand and then type them, revising and adding as he typed. Before the final typescript was made, Faulkner often inserted further changes which sometimes involved the rearrangement of scenes as well as alterations in content. After his death, the manuscript and the typescripts were deposited in the Alderman Library of the University of Virginia. From them Douglas Day and Albert Erskine in 1973 published a "restored" version of the novel under the original title *Flags in the Dust*. Although it undoubtedly contains material by Faulkner associated with the original book Faulkner offered to Liveright and later to Harcourt, no one can absolutely say that *Flags in the Dust* now represents what Faulkner originally intended to be published. Although some of Faulkner's admirers prefer it to *Sartoris*, *Flags in the Dust* does exhibit weaknesses that Liveright, Harcourt, and several other publishers, as well as Ben Wasson and finally Faulkner himself, identified before Wasson and Faulkner began the work of cutting. In many respects, *Sartoris* remains the better book. Moreover, throughout Faulkner's lifetime, *Sartoris* was at least tacitly acknowledged by the novelist himself to be his third novel. In 1958 he recognized its claims by suggesting that it held "the germ of my apocrypha in it."[3]

Two brief fragments that are part of the surviving manuscript material of *Sartoris*, as well as Faulkner's later account of the writing of the novel, may help to identify the essential core of the work and the novelist's intentions. The two fragments seem to be the beginning of a short story. The first consists of five pages relating to the death of Evelyn Sartoris. In it a man arrives at a squadron office at an aerodrome near Arras and orders a drink for everyone present. He tells Evelyn Sartoris that there is someone named Sartoris in a replacement squadron recently arrived at the wing headquarters. Evelyn knows at once that this Sartoris must be his brother Bayard. The two men have not seen each other for eighteen months. Unable to get to headquarters that night, Evelyn arranges to rendezvous with Bayard the next morning over Arras; and the brothers communicate with each other by gestures. At this point, Faulkner interrupts the action to provide a short account of the two brothers. They are twins and between them there is more affection than there has ever been among other men of the Sartoris family. Evelyn has broken his leg in an accident suffered while he was trying to loop a Bristol scout plane too close to the ground. Meanwhile, Bayard was ordered to Memphis to train American pilots. He has married "Carolyn" White and returned to duty in England. Here Faulkner resumes the narrative of the brothers' rendezvous. As they meet the enemy, Bayard sees Evelyn's plane hit and set on fire by a machine gun burst from a German fighter. As the sun breaks through the clouds and reveals the stricken plane, Evelyn jumps from the cockpit, thumbs his nose at his brother, and salutes the German who has shot him down. The fragment ends at this point.

In the second fragment, which consists of two pages, Evelyn's name has been changed to John. Mississippi, which had been only casually mentioned in the first fragment, becomes a prominent part of the locale; and Bayard's marriage takes on marked prominence. By the time he wrote these pages, Faulkner may have begun to see that the center of his story would be not the death of John (Evelyn) but Bayard's reaction to John's death and that the locale would be Mississippi.[4] This conjecture about the inception of the novel gains support from Faulkner's account of the composition of *Sartoris*.

In an essay written about two years after *Sartoris* was published, Faulkner recalled that he began to write with the intention of re-creating in a book the world and feeling of his youth, a world and feeling that he believed would pass from him as he grew old. "So I began to write, without much purpose, until I realised that to make it truly evocative it must be personal, in order to, to not only preserve my own interest in the writing, but to preserve my belief in the savor of the bread-and-salt."[5] The passage seems almost a gloss upon Faulkner's tentative short story about the death of Evelyn Sartoris. One wonders if Faulkner was referring to his realization that the incident over Arras was not the right material but that Bayard's reaction to the war experience, set in north Mississippi, provided a means to utilize the personal, even biographical material that he wished to include. At that moment, Faulkner began to write with direction and purpose. "So I got some people," continued Faulkner, "some I invented, others I created out of tales I learned of nigger cooks and stable boys of all ages between one-armed Joby, 18, who taught me to write my name in red ink on the linen duster he wore for some reason we have both forgotten, to old Louvinia who remarked when the stars 'fell' and who called my grandfather and my father by their Christian names until she died. . . . Created I say, because they are composed partly from what they were in actual life and partly from what they should have been and were not: thus I improved on God, who, dramatic though He be, has no sense, no feeling for, theatre." These statements could hardly be more revealing.

In defining the "personal" aspect of *Sartoris*, Faulkner alluded only to the locale and the characters that had their origin in his Mississippi youth. About the more truly "personal" relationship between the characters of his fiction and Faulkner himself, as well as his family, he said very little. But Faulkner's silence upon these points does not mean that much of

Sartoris was not grounded in Faulkner's own experiences, that is, his biography. Although the relationship between fiction and autobiography is a matter that has concerned novelists from the very beginning of the novel, Faulkner's contemporaries seem particularly occupied with it. Theodore Dreiser's huge spread of eight major novels, for example, reads like a monumental autobiography turned into fictional disguise. Thomas Wolfe, whom Faulkner ranked among the finest writers of his time, once wrote that "my conviction is that all serious creative work must be at bottom autobiographical, and that a man must use the material and experience of his own life if he is to create anything that has substantial value."[6] Wolfe did not mean, of course, that a writer could not take imaginative liberties with his own experience, but he did mean that essentially a writer's experience, both actual and vicarious, and his reflections upon that experience lie at the heart of serious fiction. The works of such writers as Sherwood Anderson, F. Scott Fitzgerald, Ernest Hemingway, as well as those of Dreiser and Wolfe, provide abundant illustration of the validity of this premise for American literature in the 1920s and 1930s. The frequently insolvable problem for the reader interested in establishing this relationship, however, lies in determining the precise autobiographical content of a given work. Often the biography may illuminate the work, but any effort to establish the biography from the fiction is always fraught with risks too great to be taken.

Readers of Faulkner's fiction, nevertheless, can scarcely escape the conclusion that the fiction he wrote during the last years of the 1920s into the decade of the 1930s took form and content from the tenor of thought that characterized the most gifted artists of his generation. Like many of his contemporaries, Faulkner responded to ideas that had been voiced in the 1890s (but not given wide circulation until at least a decade later) by Henry Adams. Literary historians have long recognized that Adams was the source of many beliefs and attitudes that came to full expression during the 1920s. In both *The Education of Henry Adams* and *Mont Saint-Michel and Chartres*, Adams had reacted to the age-old need of man to achieve a synthesis of his individual acts or experiences (or thoughts) with his perception of the past. Implicitly, Adams understood the need for history in the life of every man; without it the present becomes meaningless and activity futile. In other words, unless the individual can place his present in context with his concept of the past (history or time), purposeful conduct directed towards a future becomes pointless. In his analysis of the thirteenth-century Gothic cathedral, Adams realized that its basic support was neither stone nor vaulting but faith. "Never let us forget," he wrote in the final paragraph of his book, "that Faith alone supports it, and that, if Faith fails, Heaven is lost."[7] The remark, as Adams knew, has far wider implications than its immediate context would seem to warrant. Adams failed, or thought he failed, to achieve a unified or integrated experience, largely because he viewed the march of history as movement from unity to multiplicity; but his search for the integration of experience, his measurement of motion between two historical points, and his analysis of the deadening forces in modern life became his legacy to many of the major writers of the first half of the twentieth century. To the magnificent canon of literature in which their searchings are embedded, William Faulkner contributed *Sartoris, The Sound and the Fury, As I Lay Dying*, and *Sanctuary*.

Like Adams, Faulkner chose to examine the life experience from two poles of history. In place of Adams' choice of the thirteenth and twentieth centuries as measuring points for history, Faulkner chose the Civil War and World War I. For the most part, he paid scant attention in his fiction to the years that intervened between the two poles. During one of his seminars at the University of Virginia, a student asked him why he "sort of skipped over one generation of the Sartoris family between the old Bayard and the young Bayard." Faulkner's answer underscores his deliberate choice of historical poles for *Sartoris*. Answered Faulkner, "Well, the twins' father didn't have a story. . . . From '70 on to 1912–14, nothing happened to Americans to speak of. This John Sartoris . . . lived at that time when . . . nothing happened to him."[8]

Faulkner's reply coincides with his use of his own family in his fiction. Faulkner's great-grandfather, Colonel William Clark Falkner (the old "Colonel," 1825–1889) became the benchmark of the past from which the novelist measured motion (progression) to his own time. The generations of his family between these two poles seemed to Faulkner much less exciting and therefore less suitable for fiction in comparison with the epic figure from whom they descended. By any standard, William Clark Falkner lived a full, tumultuous life. Although he fought in the Mexican War and the Civil War and lived through Reconstruction, the pivotal, climactic event of his life was the Civil War. At some point early in the novelist's career, probably as he was writing *Sartoris*, Faulkner perceived that in the old Colonel the major historical event and the personal experience could be made to coincide so that either one could be used to illustrate the other. Between the two wars and between the old Colonel and the young Bayard (Faulkner's own generation), the middle years were visualized by Faulkner as a time of consolidation, important but lacking in dramatic interest. Working thus from the two poles of history, the Civil War and World War I, dramatized respectively in the old Colonel and the young Bayard (but also in Quentin Compson of *The Sound and the Fury*, perhaps Horace Benbow in *Sanctuary*, and other characters in other novels), Faulkner endeavored to integrate the past into the present experience. Most likely, in *Sartoris* and in many other novels, he was never completely satisfied with the results; but he never ceased his efforts to synthesize or integrate the experience of the past with that of the present.

Before one examines the historical bases or the two historical poles of *Sartoris*, he must distinguish between the professional historian's and the artist's handling of history, a distinction crucial in any appraisal of Faulkner's concern with history. The compulsion of Adams and Faulkner to integrate the past with the activity and outlook of the present is the personal, privately felt, individual desire of the creative artist endeavoring to make history illuminate his own times. Theirs is essentially an act of the creative imagination. Upon this question of the imagination rests much of the issue.

Many otherwise perceptive readers in the twentieth century still believe that history is a matter of irrefutable, established facts that do not change and bind the historian irrevocably to their recital. Generations of Americans have had their views of the American past fixed for them by historians writing textbooks for the primary and secondary schools and colleges, and each generation for the most part has remained unaware that the American past in those textbooks has changed again and again over the years. Implicitly, most readers continue to believe that historians are impartial scholars seeking the unbiased, objective discovery of truths that do not change. Likewise, probably a majority of readers incline to accept tacitly a theory of progress which assumes that because of modern research the most recent history of any period in the past is the best, truest history ever written. After all, the reader thinks, the author has had the advantage of the greatest amount of data as well as the work of all previous historians. Somehow the most recently published history—unless new data are found—is assumed to have carried a given subject about as far as it can be taken. Any professional historian, of course, knows the fallacies of these premises.

Regardless of the data on hand, each historian, as an individual writer, before he begins to write, must answer the crucial question: what was the past like? He turns around from his place in the present much like the person watching the road receding from the back of a moving automobile—an analogy Jean Paul Sartre made of Faulkner's world vision.[9] The present is all around the historian. Consciously or unconsciously, the historian in writing the past does apply Adams' principle of the polarity of history, that is, the historian inevitably views the interpretation of the past in terms of his perspective on the present. His need to fashion history to fit the present produces the continual revision of the past which he re-creates in every volume he writes. As Emerson once remarked, each generation must write its own books. Americans have seen their past explained by the influence of the frontier, by the economic motives of the Founding Fathers, by the geography of the nation's diverse regions, by the nation's role as a melting pot of diverse nationalities, by the Civil War, and by various other suggested forces. Currently, American historians are busily rewriting American history but are by no means united on such matters as the nature of slavery, the contributions of the Negro to American culture, and the Civil War and Reconstruction. In the long run, the "hard-core" data, that is, facts like the date of Lincoln's death or the number of dead at Gettysburg, do not determine history; rather, the imaginative re-creation of the past, which the historian fashions out of his need to explain, justify, or support the present, determines history.

As a writer of serious fiction and a man deeply concerned with understanding the plight of man in the twentieth century, William Faulkner's approach to his material offers a parallel to that of the historian. The difference between them is more in degree than in kind. Today no writer of fiction would dare alter the hard-core facts of history, because the reviewers would immediately discredit him. Sir Walter Scott's notorious anachronisms, for example, are no longer tolerated as good fiction. But the fictional writer can render his historical legend more figuratively and emotionally than the professional historian, and the artist can limit much more severely or selectively than the historian the topics to be included. Most important, a novelist like Faulkner can deal more effectively than the historian with all aspects of an individual's life; and, if he wishes, he may even omit the historical force or the political event. In the end, the writer's concern, as Faulkner understood, is with the personal life, the private life, often the inner consciousness, of the individual within the historical context. Despite these differences in emphasis, however, the essential treatment of the past as a gloss, or commentary, or explanation, or justification of the present remains common to both writers. In this sense, William Faulkner may be viewed as a historian concerned with the shaping of the legend that is history if not to justify at least to construct a view of Southern history that would provide for him a satisfying context for the agonies and ecstasies of life as he experienced it from day to day in the South. A pervasive concern with the historical past as related to the living present informs the best of Faulkner's fiction.

As an important aspect of his interest both in his personal past and in the history of his region, Faulkner possessed a keen awareness of his family's genealogy. For him, as for thousands of other Southerners, the family Bible was a cherished possession in which genealogical entries were to be kept accurate and current; it passed from father to son, from generation to generation. The "huge, brass-bound Bible," [10] in which old Bayard makes entries in *Sartoris*, its fly-leaves containing columns of names and dates that "rose in stark and fading simplicity, growing fainter and fainter where time had lain upon them" (p. 92) could be duplicated in many a household throughout the South. In 1859, when Faulkner's great-great-great-uncle, John Wesley Thompson, joined the Book and Tract Society of the Memphis Conference of the Methodist Episcopal Church South, he received a "genealogical family Bible and case." In his will, he provided that the Bible should descend in the family through the eldest son. William Faulkner inherited this Bible at the death of his father on August 7, 1932, and in it made new entries in some of the genealogical tables, characterized by Faulkner's biographer as "literally hundreds of pages bound into the Bible between the Old and New Testaments." [11] In the South, a man's knowledge of his ancestors helped him to answer the question Who am I? It gave him a sense of continuity. The family reputation defined his position in the community. The comment in *Sartoris*—"the man who professes to care nothing about his forebears

11

is only a little less vain than the man who bases all his actions on blood precedent"—falls considerably short of rendering Faulkner's absorption in family tradition, family legends, family stories, and, particularly, the career of Colonel William Clark Falkner, the novelist's great-grand-father. As even the briefest comparison of their lives will show, the similarities between the Colonel and Faulkner's fictional Colonel John Sartoris are so close that the novelist's imaginative use of his ancestor as the prototype or model for this character in *Sartoris*, *The Unvanquished*, and elsewhere is really beyond dispute. The great-grandfather anchors one of the historical poles in Faulkner's fiction.

According to family tradition, the first Falkners (William Faulkner changed the spelling) in this country landed before the Revolution at Charleston, South Carolina, from Scotland.[12] (Many of the older Sartorises are said to have moved westward to Mississippi from the Carolinas.) About the time of the conflict, one of them moved to a North Carolina county near the Tennessee border, where he settled and reared a family, including two sons, Joseph and John. Joseph married Caroline Word and sometime later began to move westward. On July 6, 1825, in Knox County, Tennessee, their son, William Clark Falkner, was born, and sometime afterward they reached their destination, Sainte Genevieve, Missouri, on the Mississippi. About 1840 William Clark Falkner left his home in Missouri and walked south through Tennessee into Mississippi.

William Faulkner probably thought that his ancestor was seeking his aunt, Justiania Dickinson Word, and her husband, John Wesley Thompson, first in Ripley and then in Pontotoc, where Thompson was in jail for murder. After the uncle was acquitted, he and his nephew returned to Ripley. Although parts of this account cannot be documented, by June, 1845, William Clark Falkner was established in Ripley and living in the household of his uncle John Wesley Thompson, whose life was marked by incidents of physical violence, criminal trials, and political activity.

By the outbreak of the Mexican War, Falkner was practicing law. He became a first lieutenant in Jefferson Davis' 1st Mississippi Volunteer Regiment and fought in the engagements near Monterrey. Probably embarked on a private affair, he was found by a search party with his left foot shattered and the first joints of three fingers on his left hand blown away. In April, 1847, he returned to Mississippi on convalescent leave, and on

July 9, 1847, he married Holland Pearce. Although he returned to Mexico, he soon resigned from the army because of his wounds.

Back in Ripley, Falkner began an eventful career. Financed in part by his wife's dowry, he bought land and became a planter. On September 2, 1848, a son, John Wesley Thompson Falkner, was born. A short time later, Falkner was involved with Robert Hindman in a fight that ended in the latter's death. Although Falkner was acquitted of murder on grounds of self-defense, Robert's brother Thomas and their father, General Thomas C. Hindman, Sr., continued to harass Falkner. Shortly after this incident, Holland Pearce Falkner died, and Falkner asked his uncle, John Wesley Thompson, to adopt their son. In 1851 Falkner again became involved in violence with the Hindmans. He was indicted for murder after he shot Erasmus W. Morris, a Hindman partisan. The prosecuting attorney in the case was Thomas C. Hindman, Jr., brother of the Hindman whom Falkner had killed earlier. Falkner was acquitted at the trial but immediately afterward narrowly escaped being killed by General Hindman. The year 1851 was also eventful for Falkner in that he published his first volume of poetry, *The Siege of Monterey*, and his first novel, *The Spanish Heroine*. In October of this year, he married Lizzie Vance of Pontotoc, by whom Falkner was to have eight children. In 1857, the Hindman feud broke out once more. After one of Falkner's friends attempted to shoot General Hindman, a duel between Hindman and Falkner was arranged; but just before it was scheduled to take place, Falkner's friends negotiated a settlement.

Since William Faulkner's novels contain many references to Colonel Sartoris' exploits in the Civil War, William Clark Falkner's role in the war becomes of particular interest to Faulkner's readers. After the secession of Mississippi on January 9, 1861, Falkner became captain of a company called the Magnolia Rifles. In April the company entered the Confederate service, and in May it was merged into the 2nd Mississippi Infantry Regiment. Falkner was elected colonel before the regiment joined General Joseph E. Johnston's Army of the Shenandoah at Harpers Ferry. Faulkner's biographer writes that Falkner worked hard to train his troops into an excellent fighting force. In July, 1861, the Confederates under Johnston, Brigadier General Pierre G. T. Beauregard, Brigadier General Thomas Jonathan (Stonewall) Jackson, Colonel J. E. B. Stuart (commanding the First Virginia Cavalry), and other field officers opposed the Federal troops at Manassas Junction and nearby Bull Run. The main battle was fought on July 12, and in it Colonel Falkner distinguished himself. His regiment was assigned the task of reinforcing the left flank of Confederate cavalry under "Jeb" Stuart. According to an account in the Memphis *Appeal*, "Col. Wm. C. Faulkner [*sic*] of the Second Mississippi regiment, and all the brave men of his command, won immortal honor. The colonel, who was ever in the van of the battle, received a slight wound in the face, and had two horses felled under him. When the second horse fell under him, he was thrown violently against a stump, and for some moments lay senseless. Recovering, he again mounted and went forward to engage the foe."[13] The writer for the *Appeal*, a battlefield correspondent with the Confederate forces, added: "Gen. Beauregard, who had been watching his gallant conduct, shouting to him as he went, 'Go ahead, you hero with the black plume; *history shall never forget you!*'" After the battle, which ended in a rout of the Union troops, another dispatch to Mississippi included the comment: "The victory is ours. Colonel Falkner of 2nd Mississippi Regiment, charged and took four pieces of [Col. William Tecumseh] Sherman's battery. His loss was a hundred killed and wounded."[14] The Colonel's military exploits and the fame they brought him became part of the Faulkner family's fund of stories told William Faulkner in his boyhood and not forgotten by him when he became a writer. Had not these events occurred, both *The Unvanquished* and *Sartoris* would not have been written as they were.

The remainder of Colonel Falkner's military career seems anything but spectacular. In April, 1862, the men of his regiment held another election of officers. Falkner was defeated by a margin of thirteen votes, and the command passed to John M. Stone. The army commander (Johnston) and the brigade commander (Brigadier General W. H. H. Whiting) wrote on his behalf to the Confederate secretary of war, but to no avail. Falkner returned to Mississippi. At once he raised a regiment of Partisan Rangers, whom he is said to have equipped with horses and material captured from the Yankees. With his force he harassed the Federal troops in Tennessee and Mississippi. On one occasion he covered General Earl Van Dorn's retreat from Tennessee; and on another Falkner defeated a force of Federal troops at Corinth. In October, 1862, the Confederate secretary of war ordered the disbanding of all Partisan Ranger units and sent conscription officers to enlist Falkner's men. During the winter of 1862–1863, Grant moved into Lafayette County, stopped in Oxford while Sherman encamped at nearby College Hill, and departed after burning cotton gins, gristmills, and several homes. In January, 1863, Falkner was given permission to reorganize his regiment. He established his headquarters at Coldwater, thirty-five miles south of Memphis, and in April drove a detachment of Federals back to Memphis. A short time later, the Union colonel, B. H. Grierson, made a cavalry raid through Mississippi; and just south of Hernando (about twenty-five miles south of Memphis), the cavalry of Grierson's supporting force inflicted heavy losses on Falkner's regiment. By the end of the month, Falkner had been replaced and his military career was virtually over. In October, 1863, he formally resigned. According to tradition, in 1864 he rode with Major General Nathan Bedford Forrest. After the Union debacle at Brice's Cross Roads, Sherman ordered Major General Andrew J. ("Whiskey") Smith to pursue and destroy Forrest. When his troops occupied Ripley, Smith burned Falkner's house. Later, in another effort to defeat Forrest, who had surprised the Yankees in Memphis, Smith entered Oxford, burned the courthouse, the buildings on the square, and the home of Jacob Thompson (scarcely a hundred yards from the house William Faulkner would occupy for the last three decades of his life).

No one knows precisely what Colonel Falkner did from the time of his resignation in 1863 until the end of the war. Some accounts say he fought with Forrest; others indicate that Falkner engaged in blockade running. Whatever occupied him, the fact is that at the end of the war he was in better circumstances than most Confederate soldiers, more than a third of whom in Mississippi did not even survive the war. Even before he rebuilt his home, he began to plant crops and consolidate his financial position. He wrote a play, *The Lost Diamond*, which vastly pleased the people of Ripley. With other men of his station, he moved to keep the freedmen, carpetbaggers, and scalawags from political office. On May 13, 1871, with R. J. Thurmond and others, Falkner obtained a charter for the Ripley Railroad Company; on September 18, 1871, he became president of the railroad.

Originally, the railroad was planned to connect Ripley with the Memphis and Charleston Railroad at Middleton, Tennessee, about five miles north of the Tennessee border. In 1872 the legislature changed the name of it to the Ship Island, Ripley and Kentucky Railroad Company, and backers anticipated that it would ultimately connect lower Illinois with the Gulf of Mexico. Earlier the legislature had offered a bounty of $4,000 per mile to any company completing at least twenty-five miles of track by September 1, 1872. Although the Ripley Railroad, known in Mississippi as the "Doodlebug Line," was operational before the deadline, the legislature refused to pay the bounty because the track was narrow-gauge instead of standard width. As a result, the bonds sold to finance the construction were defaulted, and a New York company became trustee of the railroad. In 1877 Richard J. Thurmond purchased the bonds and shortly afterward sold half of his interest to Falkner. The two men, however, quarreled frequently.

Meanwhile, Falkner was active as a planter, a politician, and a writer. In 1880 he contributed the first installment of his novel, *The White Rose of Memphis*, to the Ripley *Advertiser*. Anyone interested in Colonel Falkner should read this novel, since much of it relates to his life and the problems of Southern communities during Falkner's lifetime. Even before the serial publication was completed, it was issued in book form by a New York publisher. In 1882, encouraged by the popular success of *The White Rose of Memphis*, Falkner published another novel, *The Little Brick Church*, but it was never so successful as the earlier work. Two years later, after a trip to Europe, he wrote a travel book entitled *Rapid Ramblings in Europe*, which enjoyed a modest success nationally and a popular success locally.

The railroad, however, continued to interest Falkner. So early as 1881 he became vice-president of the New Orleans and North Eastern Railroad, controlled by W. H. Hardy, who envisioned a railroad through the center of Mississippi that would link with the Ship Island, Ripley and Kentucky road. In 1886 Falkner bought out Thurmond's interest in the road and began to extend it southward from Ripley towards Pontotoc. For labor, he leased convicts from the state. On July 4, 1888, the first locomotive chugged into Pontotoc pulling cars filled with Falkner's admirers. The road was now completed from Middleton, Tennessee, to Pontotoc, Mississippi, sixty-three miles. The two trains each day (one pulled by a locomotive named *The Colonel W. C. Falkner*) made the trip in about five hours.

The success of the road encouraged Falkner to invest even more heavily in railroads. In the summer of 1889 he acquired at foreclosure sales both the Ship Island, Ripley and Kentucky and the Gulf and Ship Island companies. Falkner went to New York to seek financial help to merge the two roads. Meanwhile, he was also running for the legislature. Among those supporting his opponents was his former partner, Richard J. Thurmond. Although still in New York on election day, Falkner won the nomination by more than four hundred votes. While in New York, he commissioned the statue of Carrara marble that was to become his monument and that his great-grandson would describe vividly in the final pages of *Sartoris*.

Falkner's relationship with his former partner, Thurmond, became steadily worse. Believing that Thurmond planned to kill him, on October 25, 1889, Falkner asked his attorney, Thomas Spight, to draw his will. On November 5, Falkner, unarmed, stopped near Thurmond's office to speak with a friend. Suddenly, Falkner turned to see Thurmond's pistol pointed at his head. Thurmond fired, and Falkner fell, losing his pipe as he struck the pavement. Within a short time he died. In February, 1890, Thurmond was tried for manslaughter and acquitted.

The foregoing account of William Clark Falkner's life, though far too brief to deal fully with this man's remarkable biography, includes the most important events in his career. One can never be certain, of course, that William Faulkner knew all of these matters or that he did not utilize other accounts not now available to his biographer. But for the most part these biographical data about Colonel Falkner represent the historical facts upon which his great-grandson based an imaginative representation of his ancestor. In analyzing Faulkner's use of this material, readers must also take into account the fictional source of any information related in a novel. For example, old man Falls, talking to old Bayard, recalls the major events of Colonel John Sartoris' (that is, Colonel Falkner's) life; but is old man Falls a trustworthy informant? In like manner, Aunt Jenny tells the story of the anchovy raid conducted by her brother and Jeb Stuart, but the reader must include Aunt Jenny herself in determining the degree of credence and significance to be given the story. Despite this word of caution, the fact remains that in *Sartoris*, as in *The Unvanquished*, the character of Colonel John Sartoris stands as one pole of history from which Faulkner measured *motion* (a word used by both Faulkner and Adams) to the present, that is, World War I. Before drawing any conclusion about this pole of history, however, readers should examine the other pole, Faulkner's presentation of World War I, and the reality behind it.

Faulkner's direct involvement in World War I was slight. Motivated in part by an unhappy love affair, he enlisted as a cadet in the Canadian branch of the Royal Air Force and saw service from July to early December, 1918. His training seems to have been wholly confined to ground school, and despite stories he later told in Oxford about his flying exploits, no evidence exists to show that during his military duty he ever learned to fly or even flew in a military airplane. But the war, especially the war in the air, the planes, and the men who flew them powerfully gripped his imagination. As a cadet in ground school, he drew pictures of the RAF instructors, who often were combat pilots ordered to training duty because of wounds or combat fatigue. On one occasion he began a poem entitled "Ace," in which he described the pilot "huge through the morning / In his fleece and leather, gilds his bright / Hair and his cigarette." [15] He made sketches of various types of planes and compiled lists of military aircraft, including the glamorous and frequently fatal Sopwith Camel (in Faulkner's training school there was none of this type). Even after the war ended and pilot training virtually ceased, he wrote home to his mother that he had made flight after flight, including four hours of solo flying time; and after he returned to Oxford, he told stories about celebrating the armistice with daring feats of flying. In one story he claimed that he had taken up "a rotary-motored Spad with a crock of bourbon in the cockpit, gave diligent attention to both, and executed some reasonably adroit chandelles, an Immelman or two, and part of what could easily have turned out to be a nearly perfect loop." [16] Instead, asserted Faulkner, he flew through the roof of the hangar and "ended up hanging on the rafters." These stories had no basis in actual fact, but they illustrate the powerful influence that the romance of flying and the glamor of aerial combat exerted on Faulkner's imagination. Yet, when Faulkner returned to Oxford in December, 1918, there was little to suggest that his war experiences had either blighted his life or left him with an overwhelming pessimism and disillusionment.

He did return home, however, without a specific commitment to a career objective; and for considerable time thereafter he had no well-defined occupational goal. If he had any discernible leaning, it was probably towards writing poetry. He published a few poems before enrolling for a year in the University of Mississippi as a special student (he had not been graduated from high school). But formal academic education did not interest him. In 1921, at the invitation of Stark Young, Faulkner went to New York, where he met Elizabeth Prall, soon to be the wife of Sherwood Anderson. Back in Oxford, Faulkner became postmaster and scoutmaster, had long discussions about writing, poetry, philosophy, and art with Phil Stone, and completed a manuscript of poetry entitled "The Marble Faun." After resigning the job in the post office and leaving the scout troop, he went to New Orleans where Elizabeth Prall introduced him to her husband, Sherwood Anderson. For most of the first six months of 1925, Faulkner lived in New Orleans, enjoying his friendship with Anderson and writing *Soldiers' Pay*, short stories, and sketches. The period was crucial for Faulkner because during this time he learned a great deal about writing from Anderson and matured rapidly as man and as artist. By July, when he sailed for Europe, the Four Seas Company of Boston had published Faulkner's slender volume of verse entitled *The Marble Faun*. In the next few months, he would shift his work steadily away from poetry to fiction.

Faulkner's six months of travel in Europe virtually completed his education for writing. With his friend William Spratling, Faulkner enjoyed the leisurely three-week voyage by freighter to Genoa, but there they separated. He went to Rapallo, where Max Beerbohm had lived and Ezra Pound was living. By train, he journeyed to Milan, tramped around the beautiful Italian lake country, and then moved on to Switzerland. At Montreux, he admired Mont Blanc and Lake Geneva. By the middle of August, he was in Paris, living in the Latin Quarter, where Gertrude Stein, Alice B. Toklas, Sylvia Beach, Ernest Hemingway, John Dos Passos, F. Scott Fitzgerald, and others of the Lost Generation had lived. Faulkner quickly settled down to a routine of writing and sightseeing. At times he worked on a novel called "Elmer" (never published) and another work that would become *Mosquitoes*. On other occasions he would write travel sketches, short stories, and poems. Day after day he explored the places tourists visit, among them the Eiffel Tower, the Place de l'Étoile, the Arc de Triomphe, the tomb of Oscar Wilde, the Panthéon, and the Hôtel des Invalides. Often he sat on a bench in the Luxembourg Gardens and watched children at play and an old man sailing a toy boat—a scene he rendered vividly when he described Temple Drake and her father at the conclusion of *Sanctuary*.[17] He liked to dine at the sidewalk café of the Deux Magots on the Left Bank. Again and again he visited the Louvre, where he admired the Winged Victory, the Venus de Milo, and the Mona Lisa. In letters home, he expressed fondness for the paintings of Degas, Manet, Cézanne, Matisse, and Picasso. Despite his concern with writing, the only literary man he later remembered seeing was James Joyce, but Faulkner did not meet him.

Although seven years had passed since the Armistice, evidences of the war were still abundant. Faulkner was impressed by the long lists of names of the dead inscribed on monuments. Even more impressive were the veterans he encountered on the streets; in a letter he noted, "so many many young men on the streets, bitter and gray-faced, on crutches or with empty sleeves and scarred faces."[18] The really grim reminders of the war, however, were not in Paris. In September, Faulkner made a walking trip into the French countryside near Montdidier, Compiègne, and Amiens, where, during the last months of the war, the Germans made a desperate assault and half a million men died. Of the area beyond Montdidier, Faulkner wrote that "it looks as if a cyclone had passed over the whole world at about six feet from the ground. Stubs of trees, and along the main roads are piles of shell cases and unexploded shells and wire and bones that the farmers dig up." Near Compiègne, not far from where Marshal Foch had signed the Armistice, Faulkner remarked: "Walking through the war-zone. Trenches are gone, but still rolls of wire and shell cases and 'duds' piled along the hedge-rows, and an occasional tank rusting in a farm yard. Trees all with tops blown out of them, and cemeteries everywhere."[19] Students of Faulkner's work would like to know how to evaluate these comments. What was the depth of Faulkner's response to the war as he looked at the battlefields of France? Little other evidence exists, and one must remember that these were letters written for his family to read. In context of the letters themselves, his words do not seem those of a man overwhelmed by the tragedy of war, but he may have felt much more than he wrote. Here in France, seven years after the Armistice, Faulkner came closer than ever before to the fighting in World War I. That these scenes made a lasting impression upon him is suggested by his use of them more than twenty-five years later in a novel (*A Fable*) dealing with the war in France. Readers of his fiction would like to know the personal significance for him of this journey to Amiens and how much it influenced his portrayal in *Sartoris* of those who returned from combat.

Faulkner's experiences in Canada during the war and in France seven years later constitute his most direct contact with the conflict. In evaluating his attitudes, however, one must not forget the vicarious experiences that came to him through literature. His writing during these years, in letters, sketches, poems, and fiction, provides abundant evidence of his admiration for such contemporary writers as T. S. Eliot, Ezra Pound, Ernest Hemingway, John Dos Passos, and F. Scott Fitzgerald. These men represented a special group of artists, identified and named by Gertrude Stein as the Lost Generation. For them the war had been a crucial experience, and their response to it had been a determining factor in their attitude towards the quality of human life in the twentieth century.

Gertrude Stein's famous assertion to Ernest Hemingway, "You are all a lost generation," which he had printed on the back of the dedication page of *The Sun Also Rises*, was intended to characterize a group of intellectuals who returned from the carnage of World War I broken in spirit and unable to act purposefully because they had lost faith in the value of any action. In Henry Adams' words, faith for them had failed and heaven had indeed been lost. T. S. Eliot's poem *The Waste Land* with its agonized cry for the grace to bring faith and its background of the Fisher King wounded in the genitals and thereby unable to reproduce; his "Love Song of J. Alfred Prufrock," to whom the mermaids no longer sing; and his characterization of the "hollow men" who ended their lives in the wasteland of the present "not with a bang but with a whimper"—all of these were expressions of the spiritual despair of the Lost Generation. In fiction, Ernest Hemingway's *The Sun Also Rises*, published in 1926, seemed to many the most disillusioned of all the disillusioned books of the Lost Generation. In it, Jake Barnes, wounded, like the Fisher King, in the genitals, answers a prostitute's question, "You sick?" by saying, "Yes." There is no cure for the sickness of living. Life is an eternal round of daily nothingness. In Hemingway's "A Clean Well-Lighted Place," the same attitude is expressed. Men sleep with the lights on because they fear the dark, fear to close their eyes to dream about the horrors of war. Literature based upon this attitude of futility and doom seems to deserve the title Lost Generation.

Although a "typical" Lost Generation writer did not exist, the lives of many of the writers seem to fit a pattern. Few of them, for example, served in the combat ranks; instead, they entered the ambulance or military transport service in France or Italy. As ambulance drivers, they enjoyed great freedom of movement. They saw the war from the windows of their vehicles, watched the progressive devastation as the fronts moved, and heard day after day and through the long nights the cries of the wounded and dying. Though they never climbed out of the trenches to go "over the top," they saw more of the fighting than most soldiers, and some, like Hemingway, were even wounded. After the war, these men returned to the states, only, as they said, to fight and lose the battle of America. Spiritually exhausted and depressed by the war and defeated at home by the combined forces of prohibition, labor troubles, unemployment, and general unrest, they drifted back to Europe as expatriates, self-exiles. They gathered in Paris at the home of Gertrude Stein and her companion Alice B. Toklas and in the Shakespeare bookstore of Sylvia Beach.

Literary historians, however, distinguish a second group of "exiles" who belonged to a younger generation, who were not really scarred by war, and who came to Paris in the middle or late 1920s.[20] For the most part, these men were not rebels, they had no great disillusionment to drown, and some were neither writers nor artists. But they often settled in the Latin Quarter, where the earlier group had lived, and imagined themselves lost and spiritually bankrupt. For them disillusionment became a romantic pose, and very few ever produced enduring art. In some ways, they were similar to many others of the generation who, like the Yale Whiffenpoofs, liked to think of themselves as "doomed [damned?] from here to eternity." The difference between the two groups is that between those who suffered from being lost and those who enjoyed the experience—the reality versus the romance.

Faulkner had more affinities with the earlier exiles than with the later group. To be sure, he had had no firsthand experience at the front, but the evidence from his biography indicates that he vicariously participated with great intensity in the war in the air. Unquestionably, he shared the aimlessness and lack of direction of those who after the Armistice came home with no particular vocation in mind and once home found nothing to challenge them; and he finally made his pilgrimage to Paris and the fronts which the others had witnessed while the actual fighting was taking place. The depth and extent of his commitment to the intellectual and emotional disillusionment of the real Lost Generation writers, however, remains in the realm of conjecture. Readers of his fiction cannot but wish that more specific information were available about his attitude towards the plight of man in modern times as he worked on the manuscript of *Sartoris* in 1927. To what extent was he committed to the disillusionment vividly dramatized by Jake Barnes, Alfred Prufrock, and others? In terms of *Sartoris*, to what degree is young Bayard a reflection of his creator? Answers to such questions would help materially the reader's understanding of the strengths and weaknesses of the novel. In the absence of positive answers, inferences must be made with great caution.

To understand *Sartoris*, Faulkner's readers, as has been suggested, must bear in mind the relationships between the biographical facts about Colonel William Clark Falkner and those of the fictional character Colonel John Sartoris; the connection, if any, between Bayard Sartoris' war experiences and attitudes and those of William Faulkner; and, finally, the inferences to be made from a comparison between the present of 1919 and the past of the Civil War as revealed in the Sartoris family and, to a lesser degree, Horace Benbow, Buddy MacCallum, and Caspey Strother. This last measurement of the poles of history remains the central challenge of the novel.

So far as a connection exists between the actual life of William Clark Falkner and the fictional life of John Sartoris, the account given earlier establishes the fact that the resemblance is so close that one could scarcely deny that Faulkner used his ancestor as the model for Colonel Sartoris. In one of his question-and-answer sessions at the University of Virginia, he admitted that the dependence was such that he would have to go through the novel "page by page" to determine the precise extent of his indebtedness. Faulkner added, however, that part of Colonel Sartoris' character was shaped by his imagination. In other words, like the historian, Faulkner was using the data at hand as a base and fleshing it out with his imagination, that is, adding his interpretation to the facts of history.

The result, in the nineteenth century, is an account of two brothers, John and Bayard Sartoris. Fifteen years younger than John, Bayard (also called Carolina Bayard) died in the famous anchovy raid by a shot from a cook's derringer. According to Aunt Jenny, the Confederate general Jeb Stuart "always spoke well of Bayard. He said he was a good officer and a fine cavalryman, but that he was too reckless" (p. 18). And the omniscient author added that "Bayard Sartoris' brief career swept like a shooting star across the dark plain of their mutual remembering and suffering, lighting it with a transient glare like a soundless thunder-clap, leaving a sort of radiance when it died." In the same scene John Sartoris repeats the assertion that his brother was "wild." "Reckless," repeats the Scotsman. Then Aunt Jenny remembers that Bayard had "a strange sense of humor." Finally, she concludes her story, "and her voice was proud and still as banners in the dust" (p. 19). The Carolina Bayard's career and Faulkner's romantic, emotionally charged evocation of it emerge clearly from the brief account. Little else is added to this characterization of Bayard.

Of greater importance to the novel is the character of Bayard's brother, Colonel John Sartoris. Old man Falls recalls that John took his regiment to Virginia but was demoted by his men in an election of officers "because he wouldn't be Tom, Dick and Harry with ever' skulkin' camp-robber that come along with a salvaged muskit and claimed to be a sojer" (p. 20). The reader infers that Sartoris had very little of the plebian about him. Old man Falls also remembers with some pride the incident of Sartoris' escape from the Yankees (a slightly different version is told in *The Unvanquished*). The account features the Colonel's bravery, daring, and resourcefulness. But old man Falls also remembers the Colonel's struggle to build the railroad. "That 'us when hit changed. When he had to start killin' folks. Them two cyarpet-baggers stirrin' up niggers, that he walked right into the room whar they was a-settin' behind a table with they pistols layin' on the table, and that robber and that other feller he kilt, all with the same dang der'nger" (pp. 22–23). (Faulkner would later retell this incident from different points of view in *Light in August* and *The Unvanquished*.) Old man Falls passes judgment upon this part of the Colonel's life: "When a feller has to start killin' folks, he 'most always has to keep on killin' 'em. And when he does, he's already dead hisself." And again the omniscient author comments: "It showed on John Sartoris' brow, the dark shadow of fatality and doom." The passage concludes with Sartoris' assertion "And so . . . Redlaw'l kill me tomorrow, for I shall be unarmed. I'm tired of killing men." Faulkner's comment on Sartoris' death has important implications. The next day John was dead, "as though he had but waited for that to release him of the clumsy cluttering of bones and breath, by losing the frustration of his own flesh he could now stiffen and shape that which sprang from him into the fatal semblance of his dream." One scarcely needs to underscore the emphasis in the character portrait: aristocratic pride, action, bravery, daring, resourcefulness in the Civil War but later, during Reconstruction, under other circumstances, violence, the "shadow of fatality and doom" upon his brow, his seeking his own death, and the "fatal semblance of his dream."

To this account, for the sake of completeness even though it adds little to old man Falls's memories, the last-act pronouncement of the author upon Colonel John Sartoris must be appended. The passage is widely known and greatly admired by readers of Faulkner's works. Miss Jenny stands looking at his marble statue:

> He stood on a stone pedestal, in his frock coat and bareheaded, one leg slightly advanced and one hand resting lightly on the stone pylon beside him. His head was lifted a little in that gesture of haughty pride which repeated itself generation after generation with a fateful fidelity, his back to the world and his carven eyes gazing out across the valley where his railroad ran, and the blue changeless hills beyond, and beyond that, the ramparts of infinity itself. The pedestal and effigy were mottled with seasons of rain and sun and with drippings from the cedar branches, and the bold carving of the letters was bleared with mold, yet still decipherable:
>
> COLONEL JOHN SARTORIS, C.S.A.
>
> 1823   1876
>
> Soldier, Statesman, Citizen of the World
For man's enlightenment he lived
By man's ingratitude he died
Pause here, son of sorrow; remember death
>
> This inscription had caused some furore on the part of the slayer's family, and a formal protest had followed. But in complying with popular opinion, old Bayard had had his revenge: he caused the line "By man's ingratitude he died" to be chiseled crudely out, and added beneath it: "Fell at the hand of —— Redlaw, Sept. 4, 1876." (pp. 375–76)

Ever mindful of the need for qualification and the recognition of other interpretations, one may conclude that in *Sartoris* Colonel John Sartoris and his brother Bayard are seen as men whose lives stand out from those of others. They share the family traits of courage, pride, resourcefulness, and, at times, recklessness. About them, however, are intimations of fatality and doom. The Colonel's career during the Civil War is viewed as more attractive than his life afterward when he cannot cope with the new forces unleashed by the war (a suggestion more explicit in *Light in August* and in *The Unvanquished*). Despite his dream of building his railroad and uplifting his people, he can find no other way to effectuate his hopes than through violence; and in the end that way becomes death itself. Although one can say that Sartoris' meeting with Redlaw (Redmond) arises out of a search for death, Sartoris does not seek death because of a conviction of the futility of all purposeful conduct or action (an important point to remember). The possibility cannot be entirely dismissed that his final action, like his son's in "An Odor of Verbena"—both actions arise out of a desire for some "moral house-cleaning"—does much to redeem the Colonel's character.

In the twentieth century, twin brothers, also named John (often called Johnny) and Bayard, could be expected to carry on the Sartoris family. Many of the traits that were prominent in the Colonel and his brother are also visible in the twins, so much so that Miss Jenny confuses anecdotes about Johnny with anecdotes about his grandfather. As boys the twins spend much of their time fighting; and as students at Virginia and Princeton, they continue their reckless pranks. Aunt Sally Wyatt gets them mixed up, but she remembers the episode of the water tank and the balloon ride. The MacCallums were particularly fond of Johnny. One by one they praise him: "fine boy," "feller fer huntin'," "never sulled on a hunt . . . even when he was a little chap," "sho' a feller fer singin'," "gittin' a whoppin' big time outen ever'thing that come up" (pp. 332–33). These anecdotes and comments the reader must combine with the several accounts of Johnny's death to form a concept of his character. In the war, Johnny continues the reckless actions of his youth. He meets his death in a daredevil fight with an overwhelming force of German fighter planes led by a famous German ace, a pupil of Richtofen. The incident has parallels with the anchovy raid of the Carolina Bayard except that it lacks the irony of being shot by a cook.

Readers are puzzled about what interpretation to place upon Johnny's death. Did he deliberately seek his death because he could not face a purposeless existence? The evidence, virtually all of which the reader obtains from Bayard's recitals of his brother's last moments, suggests that Johnny's last patrol was merely another reckless action in a long career of such incidents. The same comment, however, can hardly be made for his brother, Bayard, about whom more details are available.

Although one may question how convincingly the novelist presents Bayard's despair and disillusionment, his haste to visit Johnny's grave underscores the importance of their relationship. One by one Bayard's reckless actions—including the speed with which he drives, his drinking, riding the stallion, and others—arouse the reader to the realization that Bayard has no regard for his own life. At the same time, Faulkner endeavors to make believable Bayard's absorption in Johnny's death. Early in the novel, Miss Jenny exclaims: "Bayard love anybody, that cold devil? . . . He never cared a snap of his fingers for anybody in his life except John" (p. 56). Old Bayard watches his grandson with concern, but as Bayard appears to settle down to the farm routine, the old man voices "his growing belief that at last young Bayard had outworn his seeking for violent destruction" (p. 204). Yet, as summer came and the pressure of farming relaxed, Faulkner writes: "it was like coming dazed out of sleep, out of the warm, sunny valleys where people lived into a region where cold peaks of savage despair stood bleakly above the lost valleys, among black and savage stars" (p. 205). Although many readers have difficulty visualizing "cold peaks of savage despair" and "black and savage stars," Faulkner's intent is to remind one that Bayard continues to suffer inwardly. And during his convalescence from one of his accidents, he learns "to lie, usually with his eyes closed, voyaging alone in the bleak and barren regions of his despair" (p. 218).

Midway in the novel, the references to Bayard's despair become more frequent. Bayard's marriage proves a failure because Narcissa finds all too often that "he had left her for the lonely heights of his despair," and in their kisses, she tastes "fatality and doom" (p. 289). At night they would lie "holding to one another in the darkness and the temporary abeyance of his despair and the isolation of that doom he could not escape" (p. 289). At the MacCallum farm, Bayard acknowledges to himself that he is "*afraid to face the consequences of your own acts*," and something inside him declares, "*You did it! You caused it all; you killed Johnny*" (p. 311). At night in his imagination he revisits the scene of Johnny's death. Finally, like Johnny before him, Bayard finds death in an airplane.

Interpretations differ, of course, and they should, but not all readers have felt that Bayard's despair is wholly convincing. Given the facts of

Johnny's death as Faulkner narrates them, one cannot but believe that Bayard should have been able to "get a hold of himself," assuage his grief, and find a satisfactory, purposeful objective in life around which to orient his conduct or activity. Narcissa makes the point when she says, "He doesn't love anybody" (p. 298). Bayard's self-centeredness and his lack of self-discipline are responsible for his plight. Moreover, it is not so much because of the war that he cannot cope with life as it is because of his inability to recognize his responsibilities to his wife, his unborn child, his family, and, finally, to his fellowmen. He reminds one of Matthew Arnold's indictment of the aristocracy: having the talents and place of leadership, he refuses to lead. Against the sufferings that are the common lot of man, he can only "curse God and die."

Using John Sartoris in the nineteenth century and his grandson Bayard in the twentieth, Faulkner measures the progression of the Sartoris family between these two points of history. If one must choose between them, the Colonel comes off best, because the motion is all downhill from him. In Bayard's generation, the Colonel's courage, his pride, and the recklessness so evident in the Carolina Bayard's anchovy raid remain; but the will-to-do, the belief in the rightness, significance, or purposefulness of his life, and the sense of responsibility towards others have petered out in his grandson. After Johnny's death, Bayard never grows up to responsible adulthood. Since the family has gone to seed, perhaps Narcissa is justified in refusing to name her baby either John or Bayard. The motion in time (history), Faulkner has described, measured, even documented; but most readers want something more, some explanation of the causes of the Sartoris decline.

Faulkner has implied that the Sartoris pride, recklessness, and self-centeredness have increased in the later generations and that in Bayard these traits have combined with his guilt feelings over the death of his twin brother. As the incident of Johnny's death is related, Bayard's guilt feelings seem hardly justifiable except to the degree that everyone is his brother's keeper. Certainly, he could be expected to outgrow them. Perhaps aware of the slightness of this explanation for Bayard's despair and self-destruction, in the final pages of the novel Faulkner offers another suggestion that may impress the reader almost as an afterthought. When Narcissa announces her decision not to name the baby John (or Bayard) but Benbow Sartoris, Miss Jenny replies, "Do you think you can change one of 'em with a name?" Immediately, Faulkner writes:

28

The music went on in the dusk softly; the dusk was peopled with ghosts of glamorous and old disastrous things. And if they were just glamorous enough, there was sure to be a Sartoris in them, and then they were sure to be disastrous. Pawns. But the Player, and the game He plays . . . He must have a name for His pawns, though. But perhaps Sartoris is the game itself—a game outmoded and played with pawns shaped too late and to an old dead pattern, and of which the Player Himself is a little wearied. For there is death in the sound of it, and a glamorous fatality, like silver pennons downrushing at sunset, or a dying fall of horns along the road to Roncevaux. (p. 380)

Faulkner has used the words *fatality* and *doom* earlier in association with the Sartorises, but he has made no suggestion of a power outside them using them as pawns in a game. Here in this highly poetical and romantic passage, there is a suggestion of a predestined fate that the Sartorises may not escape. Perhaps the novelist meant that the Sartoris traits were in the blood and would always produce the same disastrous results. He may also have been making here an early statement of his tragic view of man. Faulkner may have intended the phrase "death in the sound" of the Sartoris name to lead into the Keatsian ending: "beyond the window evening [death] was a windless lilac dream, foster dam of quietude and peace."

The role of Horace Benbow, as has been noted, was shortened significantly by Ben Wasson in the transformation of the manuscript of "Flags in the Dust" into *Sartoris*. Faulkner apparently intended Horace as a foil to Bayard and to a degree did establish the contrast. Whereas Bayard comes back from the war almost frantically engaging in ceaseless activity with racing cars, wild stallions, and airplanes, Horace returns to blow delicate glass vases. Whereas Bayard lies in bed and dreams of "cold peaks of savage despair," Horace lies in bed while that "wild, fantastic futility of his voyaged in lonely regions of its own beyond the moon, about meadows nailed with firmamented stars to the ultimate roof of things, where unicorns filled the neighing air with galloping, or grazed or lay supine in golden-hoofed repose" (p. 179). Moreover, Horace's fondness for his sister, bordering on incest, offers a parallel to Bayard's love of his twin brother Johnny. And in a reverse kind of image, Horace is just as lacking in purposeful conduct and just as self-centered as Bayard. More than one reader has noted that Horace's affair with Belle Mitchell, the woman with a "backstairs nature" (p. 256), becomes as self-destructive as Bayard's fatal flight in the experimental airplane.

29

In *Sanctuary*, Faulkner would present a slightly different Horace who faintly reminds the reader of Hamlet's melancholy disillusionment at the realities of life; but in *Sartoris*, Horace appears less admirable than Bayard. The war seems not to have been a crucial, shattering experience for Horace. Intelligent, perceptive, and sensitive, he is not a man of action. While Bayard fights the war in the air, Horace serves as an officer in the Y.M.C.A. After the war, life becomes a series of compromises, each one of which erodes further his principles until the endless repetition of compromises leaves him a pathetic, hedonistic esthete. Literary analogues for him are abundant. Perhaps the closest are such characters as Amory Blaine, Anthony Patch, and others whom F. Scott Fitzgerald described as the "sad young men." Readers have been reminded of Eliot's Prufrock and predicted that Horace would end his life, like Eliot's hollow men, "not with a bang but a whimper." In some measure, Horace belongs to those who, in Thoreau's words, live lives of "quiet desperation." In Henry Adams' terms, Horace had better cards to play in the game of life than he ever used.

Two minor characters who have been to war and returned deserve mention. On a serious level, Caspey Strother, the "uppity" Negro, voices his race's complaint, to be raised with increasing frequency after World War II, that if the Negro could be called upon to defend the country abroad in time of war, he was certainly entitled to all the privileges of citizenship at home. On another level, Caspey's fantastic claims of Negro victories in the war add humor to the otherwise grim plot line of the novel. Farther along in *Sartoris*, Faulkner writes that Caspey "more or less returned to normalcy" (p. 199), working in the shade while Miss Jenny was watching him and then retreating to the creek bank to fish during the remainder of the afternoon.

Faulkner has been criticized for his treatment of Negro characters in *Sartoris*. The verbal exchanges between Miss Jenny and Simon, Isom, and others, as well as the handling of Caspey, have been viewed as placing the Negroes in traditional stereotype roles. Moreover, attention has been called to Faulkner's use of the word *nigger* in the passage on the mule (pp. 278–79), perhaps the only occurrence of the word outside of dialogue in all of Faulkner's fiction. Without even attempting to defend him from these criticisms—and a defense could be made—one has only to point to the splendid examples of Faulkner's understanding of the

Negro and white-Negro relationships. Among them one should include the scene in which Bayard rides around Jefferson with the Negro musicians and drinks with them from the breather-cap. Perhaps even superior is the scene in the Negro sharecropper's cabin where Bayard eats Christmas dinner. And some of the incidents involving Simon, especially the church treasury episode, should be mentioned. To contend, however, that white-Negro relations are a major theme in the novel would be a mistake; they contribute but are subordinate to the Bayard-Horace plot line.

Also significant but subordinate is the account of Bayard's brief sojourn with the MacCallum family. This splendidly conceived episode precedes and parallels Bayard's Christmas dinner with the Negro family. It is the first of Faulkner's accounts of men living and hunting in the big woods and often reminds readers of the atmosphere of "The Bear" in *Go Down, Moses*. For others, it seems to have a remote kinship with Hemingway's account of the visit of Jake Barnes and Bill Gorton to the Pamplona fishing camp in *The Sun Also Rises*. Like the characters in Hemingway's novel, Bayard finds a temporary peace among the surroundings of nature and with the MacCallum family whose simple life in the woods has dignity, affection, and warmth.

Buddy MacCallum, the youngest of the six sons, has fought in the war, won a "charm" or medal for gallantry, and returned to live in the woods as hunter and farmer. Although he may lack Bayard's education and sophistication, Buddy is neither so hounded by guilt nor so self-centered that he cannot fulfill his responsibilities to his family with simple affection. He is not one of Fitzgerald's sad young men. Somehow Buddy has escaped the laziness of Caspey, the death-seeking recklessness and guilt feelings of Bayard, and the deadening hedonism of Horace. Instead, he illustrates the right relationship of man to nature and presages a theme that will surface repeatedly in Faulkner's novels.

Most students of Faulkner's work agree that *Sartoris* is not wholly successful. Its defects are plain. Like many young writers, Faulkner tried to crowd too much into one book—two wars sixty years apart, several generations, all kinds of characters, airplanes, racing cars, wild stallions, fox hunts, possum hunts, Christmas, Thanksgiving, sorghum making—the list seems endless. Moreover, he often failed to bring subordinate incidents to satisfactory conclusions. Examples that come readily to mind are Narcissa's letters, Horace's affair with the young tennis player, and Horace's involvement with Belle Mitchell. Readers often complain of the purple passages, vague metaphors, and overly romantic descriptions of nature.

More serious are the weaknesses in the conception and portrayal of character. The success of the novel depends largely upon the credibility of Johnny's character, upon the relationship between Johnny and Bayard, and, most importantly, upon Bayard's despair. Although readers must decide these matters for themselves, many have felt that in the crucial instances of theme, plot, and character portrayal, Faulkner has been less than convincing. As a twentieth-century example of the daredevil Sartoris recklessness, Johnny may be acceptable; but Bayard all too often appears to be merely an immature, romantic, and neurotic young man, a special case, too limited to be representative either of the Sartoris family traits or the plight of modern man. The difficulty is that the novelist has not made the failure of Bayard's life an inevitable or necessary failure or the inexorable result of character traits handed down through generations of Sartorises. Faulkner offers no compelling or convincing reason for Bayard's death wish, and the reader is tempted to speculate that the reason may lie in the absence of an intensely felt relationship between Bayard's attitudes and those of his creator. One remembers Faulkner's statement, already quoted, that "to make it truly evocative it must be personal." The failure to treat Bayard successfully causes Faulkner to fall somewhat short of measuring the two poles of history; consequently, the comparison of Bayard with Colonel John Sartoris has less significance than Faulkner apparently intended. Faulkner would try again, and in *The Sound and the Fury* he would handle Quentin Compson with much greater success than he portrayed Bayard Sartoris.

Despite these reservations, one must appraise *Sartoris* as an important novel in Faulkner's career. In it he first found the material that would become the substance of his fiction for the remainder of his life. He saw that he could apply the matter—and even the method—of modern fiction writers like James Joyce and Joseph Conrad to his own home area of north Mississippi. Likewise, he learned that he could enrich his fiction by drawing upon the wealth of his reading. He could make, for example, Keats's "Ode on a Grecian Urn," Eliot's poetry, classical mythology, and the Bible illuminate the stories about his ancestors and the tales of backwoods Mississippi. Even at this early stage in his career, he may also have understood that he could make his own local region a microcosm not only of the South but also of Western man. Finally, in writing *Sartoris*, Faulkner learned how the past could be made to illuminate the problems of the present and how the polarities of history could be made to measure motion and the quality of life.

CHAPTER II

The Collapse of Family

The Sound and the Fury

ALTHOUGH no one can know William Faulkner's thoughts as he finished *Sartoris* and began to consider material for his fourth book, first to be called *Twilight* and later *The Sound and the Fury*, certain similarities between the two novels suggest that he had by no means dismissed the subjects and themes he had treated in *Sartoris*. His concern with history, for example, would continue in the new work, except that on this occasion he would move the poles much closer together than he had earlier; in fact, he would deal primarily with two generations: one that came to maturity in the 1890s, the generation skipped in *Sartoris*, and the other the generation of the 1920s that he had used in the earlier work. The Compsons of *The Sound and the Fury* would relate, of course, to earlier and certainly more distinguished members of the family, but the emphasis would be on the two living generations. Time (history) would be even more crucial in *The Sound and the Fury* than it was in *Sartoris*.

The slow deterioration down the long corridors of the generations, observable in *Sartoris*, becomes more pronounced in *The Sound and the Fury*. At the end of *Sartoris*, the family survives in the baby Benbow, who, despite his first name, cannot escape his Sartoris heritage. At the conclusion of *The Sound and the Fury*, however, the Compson decay has become total. Not a single member of the family lives to perpetuate the house of Compson. Meanwhile, in the plight of young Quentin Compson, who, having lost his faith in all purposeful action, has jumped off a bridge, the reader remembers the despair and self-destructive urge of young Bayard. Quentin is yet another portrait of the sad young men in the Lost Generation.

Faulkner's narrowing of the focus from an event that had its origin in another country against a background of a vast world struggle to the inner consciousness of a youth troubled with sexual relationships recalls Herman Melville's narrowing of his focus from Ahab's dark battles in the far Pacific with leviathan personifications of cosmic evil to Pierre Glendenning's tortured struggles with the ambiguity of family sexual relationships. The similarities of Faulkner's work with Melville's themes, as well as the relationship between *The Sound and the Fury* and *Sartoris*, also find reflection in the development of the half-realized incestuous relationships between Horace and his sister Narcissa in the earlier novel and between Quentin and his sister Candace (Caddy). Indeed, from some aspects, *The Sound and the Fury* becomes a second treatment of the same basic theme that Faulkner had explored in *Sartoris*, a theme to which he would also return in *Absalom, Absalom!*. The recurrence of these basic motifs establishes the continuity of Faulkner's thought and artistry.

In virtually every respect, however, *The Sound and the Fury* is a better novel than its predecessor. The difference is that observable between an acceptable but many-blemished novel and a masterpiece, one of the great novels of all time. Emotionally, philosophically, and artistically, Faulkner developed so rapidly during the months he worked on the Compson story that one hardly can account for the seemingly instantaneous growth. Like Keats and Byron, overnight he changed from an average writer to a genius. The apprentice became the master, but in the process he began to place far greater demands upon his readers, demands that baffled many of his early admirers and turned away others not so kindly disposed. Even now, understanding, or even reading, *The Sound and the Fury* is no easy undertaking. Most readers require help, and some help can be obtained from Faulkner's various accounts of the genesis of his novel.

Faulkner was aware from the very beginning that readers would find his novel rough going, particularly the first two sections. Like T. S. Eliot's *The Waste Land*, the Benjy section (and parts of Quentin's narration) is so close to being incomprehensible that many readers never get past it. Probably no one could fully understand Benjy's monologue upon first reading; even now, more than forty years later, there is uncertainty about portions of it. As will be discussed later, Faulkner considered various devices to help the reader (for example, italics, colored ink, a summary or "appendix"). Some critics have suggested that one might profitably read the novel backwards, that is, the last section first, then the third part, second, and finally the first. This suggestion arises from the premise that the four sections of the novel recount essentially the same story and become progressively easier for the reader to grasp. To read the novel in this manner, however, distorts Faulkner's artistic objectives. His own comments about the inception of the novel provide a better approach and actually may help the reader.

In 1955, when Faulkner lectured in Japan, and in 1957, when he answered questions from students at the University of Virginia, he talked about the writing of *The Sound and the Fury*. He noted that the novel began "as a short story . . . a story without plot, of some children being sent away from the house during the grandmother's funeral"[1] because they are too young to understand what was happening. While the preparations for the funeral are being made, the children are playing in the branch, and one of them, a little girl, gets her drawers muddy. Upon returning to the house, the children notice something unusual, and the little girl climbs a tree to look in the parlor window. Commented Faulkner, "it began with the picture of the little girl's muddy drawers, climbing that tree to look in the parlor window with her brothers that didn't have the courage to climb the tree waiting to see what she saw."[2] Literally, the tree is a tree of knowledge, and the knowledge to be gained is the knowledge of death inside, but the boys below gain something of the knowledge of sex and life from the sight of the girl's muddy drawers. Later on, the reader's understanding of the tree is enriched by the knowledge that it is a pear tree, whose fruit, shaped like a woman's womb, symbolizes fertility (captured in the Christmas carol of the partridge and the pear tree). In recalling this seminal image of the novel, Faulkner called it an apple tree, almost as fitting a symbol since it is the ancient symbol of Adam and Eve's fall from paradise through their knowledge of the tree of good and evil.[3]

On another occasion Faulkner elaborated his account of the single image that formed the genesis of the novel. "It's more an image. . . . 'Course, we didn't know at that time that one was an idiot, but they were three boys, one was a girl and the girl was the only one that was brave enough to climb that tree to look in the forbidden window to see what was going on. . . . and it took the rest of the four hundred pages to explain why she was brave enough to climb the tree to look in the window."[4] Faulkner stressed the idea of the single image as the germ of the entire work. "It was an image, a picture to me, a very moving one, which was symbolized by the muddy bottom of her drawers as her brothers looked up into that apple [pear] tree that she had climbed to look in the window." But eventually the symbol became important. "And the symbolism of the muddy bottom of the drawers became the lost Caddy, which had caused one brother to commit suicide [later] and the other brother had misused her money that she'd send back to the child, the daughter."

The force of this image apparently never diminished in Faulkner's mind. In each account of it, he added details that emphasize the centrality of the image and shed additional light upon it. "I saw that they [the children] had been sent to the pasture [near the branch] to spend the afternoon to get them away from the house during the grandmother's funeral in order that the three brothers and the nigger children could look up at the muddy seat of Caddy's drawers as she climbed the tree to look in the window at the funeral, without then realizing the symbology of the soiled drawers. . . . For I had already gone on to night and the bedroom and Dilsey [the family servant] with the mudstained drawers scrubbing the naked backside of the doomed little girl—trying to cleanse with the sorry byblow of its soiling that body, flesh, whose shame they symbolized and prophesied, as though she already saw the dark future and the part she was to play in it trying to hold that crumbling household together."[5]

From the several accounts of the image that Faulkner considered the starting point of his novel, one can begin to see how the work took shape in his imagination. Actually, the image seems to have been twofold: one, of children playing in a branch and the little girl getting her underclothes wet and muddy, and the other, of the little girl climbing the tree to look at the funeral of her grandmother. Artistically, the image suggested to Faulkner at the beginning only a short story. In another comment relating to this point, Faulkner noted: "It was, I thought, a short story, something that could be done in about two pages, a thousand words, I found out it couldn't. I finished it the first time, and it wasn't right, so I wrote it again, and that was Quentin, that wasn't right. I wrote it again, that was Jason, that wasn't right, then I tried to let Faulkner do it, that was still wrong."[6] The image and Faulkner's efforts to tell the story he associated with it account for much of the content of the novel.

Essentially, Faulkner did tell the same story four different times. The first telling, which is Benjy's monologue, is dated April 7, 1928, the Saturday before Easter. The second telling, which is Quentin's monologue, is dated June 2, 1910, the day on which he commits suicide. The third telling, which is Jason's narrative, is dated April 6, 1928, Good Friday. And the final account, often called Dilsey's story but actually that of the omniscient author, is dated April 8, 1928, Easter Sunday. Because to Benjy all past time is present, his section is appropriately placed between Good Friday and Easter Sunday. Faulkner gives this part a precise date so that the reader can identify events that Benjy could not be expected to have experienced. From this point of view, only Quentin's section is out of order—for a good reason which will be discussed later. As Faulkner's comments imply, the same events, at least in general, are covered in each of the four accounts. Since for the most part Jason's and Faulkner's accounts are narrated traditionally in straightforward fashion, they present no reading difficulties. The interior monologues of Benjy and Quentin, however, are formidable challenges.

As Faulkner's remarks indicate, he initially proposed to tell the story through the mind of Benjy, who, though a grown man in body, possesses the mind of a three-year-old child. Totally unable to reason, to link cause and effect, Benjy is also without any sense of time (history) other than the present. All events, regardless of how distant past, are equally present to him. Thus, on April 7, 1928, the day of his monologue, events that took place in the early fall of 1898 are in his mental processes *now*—just as vividly *now* as they were thirty years earlier. His mind records as a camera captures a moment in time, and the moments he captures may be summoned again, not in logical sequence of thought but by association of ideas. As the association of ideas triggers different scenes or images, his monologue shifts rapidly without transition (except through this idea association) from one year or day to another. The rapid shifts of the time-frame, more than any of these other matters, bewilder the reader. Faulkner, himself, at one point in the composition, remarked that what he had written was "incomprehensible, even I could not have told what was going on then, so I had to write another chapter [Quentin's story, which proved to be almost as difficult for many readers]."[7]

In his original manuscript, Faulkner helped the reader by indicating a time-shift in Benjy's monologue by means of italics. A change from roman to italic or from italic to roman alerted the reader to a difference in time. At the publisher's office in New York, Faulkner's friend and agent Ben Wasson revised the Benjy section by removing the italics and ordering wider spacing between lines in the text to indicate the time shifts. Faulkner also proposed the use of different colored inks to mark the divisions in time. Both the wide spacing and the colored inks were rejected by the publishers. As he read proof, Faulkner attempted to restore the italic-roman type device; but there is evidence that between Wasson's changes and Faulkner's corrections or attempts at restoration, the present text contains in some places unintended confusion.[8]

In writing Benjy's section, Faulkner also attempted to help his readers to grasp the abrupt changes in scene and time by references to the Negro boys who at different periods cared for the idiot. Benjy's earliest memories around the turn of the century are associated with Versh, who may have been Dilsey's eldest child. T. P., perhaps a younger child of Dilsey, follows Versh; and Luster, who may have been one of Dilsey's grandchildren, looks after Benjy in 1928, the present time of the novel. The chronological order of these "nurses" helps a reader to establish the sequence of events in Benjy's monologue. In addition, present-time sequences may often be identified by the allusions to Luster's search for his lost quarter that will admit him to the carnival show.

Despite these aids to reading, Benjy's interior monologue initially baffled many readers of the novel. As early as 1937, Faulkner considered including in a French edition of his work some kind of list or guide to characters and chronology, a practice Stark Young had adopted a couple of years earlier in the second edition of *So Red the Rose*. (Faulkner's list of characters and chronology for the French edition should not be confused with the "introductions" Faulkner wrote about 1933 for a "new" edition of *The Sound and the Fury*, which was announced but never actually published. These introductions were "lost" for many years but were found—one page being discovered under the stairs in the Faulkner house in Oxford—several years ago. They are now principally important for Faulkner's comments on the inception of the novel.)[9] When, in 1945, Malcolm Cowley proposed to include a section of *The Sound and the Fury* in an anthology of Faulkner's work, the novelist prepared a character-identification guide to the Compson family. "I should have done this when I wrote the book," remarked Faulkner to Cowley but cautioned: "NOTE: I dont have a copy of TSATF, so if you find discrepancies in chronology (various ages of people, etc) or in the sum of money Quentin stole from her uncle Jason, discrepancies which are too glaring to leave in and which you dont want to correct yourself, send it back to me with a note. . . . Let me know what you think of this. I think it is really pretty good, to stand as it is." [10] Despite some rather glaring discrepancies— the most notable is the substitution of a rainpipe for the pear tree— Cowley printed this brief "induction," as Faulkner called it, as an "Appendix" at the end of the Viking *Portable Faulkner*.

Early in 1946 Random House began to negotiate with Faulkner for reprinting *The Sound and the Fury* coupled with *As I Lay Dying* in its Modern Library series. Random House editors wanted the novelist to write an introduction; instead, Faulkner urged them to print the "Appendix" Cowley had used for the *Portable Faulkner*. Calling the Appendix a "new section to go with it" and saying again that he should have written the new piece when he wrote the novel, Faulkner gave specific directions: "When you issue the book, print the sections in this order, print this appendix first, and title it APPENDIX. This will be anachronic but no more so than the other sections." [11] Writing about this decision a few days later to Malcolm Cowley, Faulkner reviewed the whole matter: "I dont want to read TSAF again. Would rather let the appendix stand with inconsistencies, perhaps make a statement (quotable) at the end of the introduction, viz: the inconsistencies in the appendix prove that to me the book is still alive after 15 years, and being still alive is still growing, changing; the appendix was done at the same heat as the book, even though 15 years later, and so it is the book itself which is inconsistent: not the appendix. That is, at the age of 30 I did not know these people as at 45 I now do." [12]

Although the possibility exists that Faulkner simply offered the Appendix as a means of evading the task of writing an introduction, in his correspondence he says plainly that he wanted the "Appendix" to become a part of the novel itself and that he felt its placement at the beginning was consonant with the apparent disregard for traditional chronological order in the sequence of the other sections. He may also have feared that an aftermath or coda would detract from the force and artistic rightness of the novel's concluding paragraph, a passage that must be numbered among Faulkner's most brilliant achievements. He appears to have liked the idea of the novel continuing to develop in the mind of the author. (Years later, in explaining differences between *The Mansion* and the earlier volumes of the Snopes trilogy, he made a very similar statement.) Some critics have felt that the inclusion of the Appendix has damaged the artistic effect of the opening of Benjy's section; others have been grateful for the enrichment it brings to the novel and the assistance it provides the reader. Regardless of the argument, for almost three decades the Appendix has "belonged" with the novel as an integral part of it, and the Modern Library edition has been the one cited by most scholars. Random House has unfortunately reissued the novel at different times both without the Appendix and with the Appendix at the end, thereby disregarding Faulkner's own wishes about its inclusion and position in the work and, incidentally, altering the pagination to which the bulk of scholarship is tied.

The same difficulties that have almost always troubled readers of *The Sound and the Fury* very likely worked against its acceptance by Alfred Harcourt, who had published *Sartoris*. After he rejected the manuscript, the firm of Jonathan Cape and Harrison Smith agreed to publish it and in February, 1929, mailed to Faulkner a contract. It provided an advance of two hundred dollars on royalties and 15 percent thereafter. Early in July, Faulkner read the galley proofs, and on October 7 the firm published the novel, less than three weeks before the stock market panic that marked the beginning of the Great Depression. Despite generally favorable reviews, the first printing of 1,789 copies was sufficient to supply bookstores for almost a year and a half. Throughout his lifetime, Faulkner thought it was his best book, "the one that I worked at the longest, the hardest, that was to me the most passionate and moving idea, and made the most splendid failure." [13] Readers throughout the world have agreed that *The Sound and the Fury* is his best novel, whereas only a handful have regarded it a failure. The few who have thought it unsuccessful have mainly been those who have been unable to surmount the difficulties initially encountered by everyone who reads the book. To help them, as well as to deepen and enrich readers' understanding of the novel as a work of art and a vehicle for Faulkner's thought, scholars and critics over the past five decades have published an impressive quantity of excellent commentary and exegesis. The service they have rendered to both author and reader cannot be overlooked by anyone interested in knowing the best of Faulkner.

Those who approach the novel through the Appendix will find that Faulkner's remarks about the Compson genealogy and his interpretative sketches of various members of the family shed considerable light upon the basic patterns of the great families—the Compsons, Sartorises, and McCaslins—who dominate the Yoknapatawpha stories. The Compsons, like the Falkners (and the McGehees of Stark Young's ancestry), originated in Scotland. For one reason or another (with the McGehees it was the plight of the younger sons in clan McGregor), a male ancestor—in this instance Quentin MacLachan Compson—fled to Carolina after the battle of Culloden in which Bonnie Prince Charlie (the Stuart pretender to the English throne) was defeated. In 1779 this same Compson fled from Carolina to Kentucky with his infant grandson. Quentin MacLachan's son, appropriately named Charles Stuart, after fighting against the American rebels, followed his father westward to Harrodsburg, Kentucky (the Daniel Boone country), turned first schoolmaster, then gambler, then revolutionary when he joined in a plot to seize the Mississippi Valley for Spain. Faulkner describes this Compson as a "sardonic embittered woodenlegged indomitable" [14] man who had a lingering desire to be a classicist schoolteacher.

With Jason Lycurgus Compson, the son of Charles Stuart, Faulkner traces the beginnings of the family in Mississippi and the founding of Jefferson. The history he provides matches very closely that of Oxford, Mississippi. Riding up the Natchez Trace one day in 1811, Jason Lycurgus found employment in the Indian Agency at Okatoba (Oxford), became a partner in the agency, and soon acquired from Ikkemotubbe a solid square mile of land destined to be the center of Jefferson and to be called the Compson mile. (The Compson mile and house have been associated with the Jacob Thompson house and estate almost adjacent to the house William Faulkner was to purchase in Oxford.) As Faulkner writes, the Jefferson (Oxford) community blossomed for a few decades.

In Faulkner's Appendix, the next Compson was Quentin MacLachan, son of Jason Lycurgus Compson and named after the grandfather who fled Scotland after Culloden. He became governor of Mississippi. Probably Faulkner made him a governor to demonstrate that the Compsons had once been men of public prominence, but in narrating the Compson genealogy in *Requiem for a Nun*, Faulkner omits this character, and in *The Town*, he assigns the role to Jason Lycurgus II.

In any event, Jason Lycurgus Compson II marks the beginning of the Compson decline. His generation corresponds to that of Colonel John Sartoris in *Sartoris* and *The Unvanquished*. This statement requires further explanation. To have been a brigadier general in the Confederate army, Jason Lycurgus Compson II, who died in 1900, must have been born sometime between 1813 and 1833. He lived twenty-seven years longer than Colonel John Sartoris (1823–1873). Yet because they both fought in the Civil War, they probably should be considered of the same generation. If this assumption is correct, Faulkner seems either to have left out a Compson generation parallel to that of "old" Bayard Sartoris (1849–1919), son of Colonel John Sartoris, or to have combined the "old" Bayard generation with that of the Colonel into a single lifetime of the Compson brigadier general. Faulkner writes that the brigadier general "failed at Shiloh in '62 and failed again though not so badly at Resaca in '64" (p. 7; p. 408) and implies that he also failed to cope with the rising clan of Snopeses after the Civil War. The important point is that Jason Lycurgus Compson II lived on after the war long enough to mortgage gradually most of the Compson square mile and sell off fragments of it to keep the mortgage on the remainder.

The traits discernible in the Compsons since Quentin MacLachan fled Culloden come to focus in Jason Richmond Compson III or Jason III, the head of the household during the events covered by *The Sound and the Fury*. Although his birth date is uncertain, he died in 1912. The evidence of the Compson decline may be seen externally: the lawn and promenades in ruins, the columns of the portico needing paint, and the boundaries of the estate rapidly shrinking. Jason III ("Mr. Compson"), "bred for a lawyer" (p. 8; p. 409), sits all day in his office "with a decanter of whiskey and a litter of dogeared Horaces and Livys and Catulluses" (p. 8; p. 410). Jason III sells the last sizable parcel of the property "to a golfclub for the ready money with which his daughter Candace could have her fine wedding in April and his son Quentin could finish one year at Harvard and commit suicide in the following June of 1910" (p. 8; p. 410). At this point, Faulkner summarizes the final demise of the Compson family:

[the property] already known as the Old Compson place even while Compsons were still living in it on that spring dusk in 1928 when the old governor's doomed lost nameless seventeen-year-old greatgreatgranddaughter
robbed her last remaining sane male relative (her uncle Jason IV) of his secret
hoard of money and climbed down a rainpipe and ran off with a pitchman in a
travelling streetshow, and still known as the Old Compson place long after all
traces of Compsons were gone from it: after the widowed mother died and
Jason IV, no longer needing to fear Dilsey now, committed his idiot brother,
Benjamin, to the State Asylum in Jackson and sold the house to a countryman
who operated it as a boarding house for juries and horse- and muletraders,
and still known as the Old Compson place even after the boardinghouse (and
presently the golfcourse too) had vanished and the old square mile was even
intact again in row after row of small crowded jerrybuilt individuallyowned
demiurban bungalows. (pp. 8–9; pp. 410–11)

Sometime around 1890 Jason Richmond Compson III was married
to Caroline Bascomb. They had three boys and a girl: Quentin III, who
was born either in 1890 or 1891, probably 1890; Candace or "Caddy,"
who was born in 1892; Jason IV, who was born in 1894; and Maury, who
was born in 1895. Maury was named after Caroline Bascomb Compson's brother Maury Bascomb; but after she discovered her son's retarded
condition, Mrs. Compson changed his name to Benjamin. (Faulkner's
choice of the biblical name was intentional.) Other members of the family called him Benjy.

After the sketch of "Mr. Compson," Faulkner includes accounts of the
Compson children. These sketches are important because they not only
provide additional information about events in the novel and "what happened afterwards," but also they offer Faulkner's own interpretation of
the characters. A careful reading of them yields information about the
earlier generations of the Compsons.

Faulkner's account of Quentin clearly indicates that the novelist
thought that Quentin based his faith in purposeful activity upon a "concept of Compson honor" symbolized by Caddy's virginity and that he did
not commit incest with her (a point disputed by readers who believe that
Quentin and Caddy did have an actual incestuous relationship). Moreover, Faulkner says that Quentin "loved death above all" and anticipated
death as a lover anticipates the surrender of his beloved's body. One can
understand from this comment the much stronger degree of "death
wish" possessed by Quentin than that seen in Bayard Sartoris. A reader

might also remember that Faulkner indicates in the last sentence of this paragraph Quentin's feeling for Benjy—a point often forgotten in discussions of Quentin's character. Since Quentin III is frequently viewed as the pivotal character in the novel, every word in Faulkner's sketch merits the reader's careful attention.

The short sketch of Caddy, containing some of Faulkner's finest and most typical narrative, seems to have been intended to answer questions that had been raised in the minds of readers after the novel was first published. Most apparent of these matters is, of course, the whereabouts of Caddy after 1928; but equally interesting are the accounts of Jason and Dilsey, which are thoroughly consistent with their characters in the novel. Perhaps even more important, however, are Faulkner's remarks about the progressive deterioration and failures in the Compson family as the line descended to Quentin, Jason, and Caddy. At the University of Virginia, Faulkner made a remark indirectly related to this passage. Asked if Quentin's failure came from his father, Faulkner replied: "The action as portrayed by Quentin was transmitted to him through his father. There was a basic failure before that. The grandfather had been a failed brigadier twice in the Civil War. It was the—the basic failure Quentin inherited through his father, or beyond his father. It was a—something had happened somewhere between the first Compson and Quentin." [15] Likewise of great interest to the reader are Faulkner's comments in this section of the Appendix about Caddy and her understanding of her brother Quentin. In the phrase describing Quentin as "incapable of love," Faulkner has made a highly significant statement, and in saying that Caddy was "doomed and knew it" he has introduced a subject that may never fully be resolved but must be discussed after the novel has been read.

When contrasting Jason IV with Quentin, critics have emphasized Faulkner's description of Jason as "the first sane Compson since before Culloden." In this sense, *sane* is not necessarily a complimentary term, as the characterization that follows demonstrates. Although Faulkner writes of Jason "no Snopes," the fact is, as will be seen, Jason has many affinities with the Snopeses. The main point of this section, however, is to supply in Jason's case "what happened after" 1928.

To some readers, the Appendix, if read first, may appear tantalizing, since it narrates fragments of the story and often repeats material in one sketch already mentioned or related in previous sketches. But it is remarkably a piece with the other parts of the novel. Viewed in its totality, *The Sound and the Fury* originally consisted of four primary narrations to a considerable degree independent of each other to which Faulkner later added a fifth and called it Appendix. The story he tells is not complete until the reader has not only finished all of its parts but reassembled them in his own mind. To a degree, Faulkner has almost compelled the reader to create his own "sixth" which for him becomes the truth of the matter.

Regardless of how much help the reader receives in advance, Benjy's interior monologue remains a formidable challenge. Even after decades of study by persistent Faulkner scholars, no definitive exegesis of Benjy's narration has been made.[16] For a full appreciation of his narration, the novelist tacitly asks the reader to accept the supposition that an idiot's mind operates without regard to time but upon the principle of association of ideas. The use of John Locke's theory of the association of ideas in the mind is an old fictional technique that dates back at least to Laurence Sterne's *Tristram Shandy*. Readers of this great eighteenth-century masterpiece are familiar with the device. Faulkner, however, adds to it aspects of Freudian psychology and the timelessness mentioned earlier. The success or failure of the method depends upon whether the reader accepts Benjy as a plausible or believable hypothesis of how an idiot's mind might function. In other words, the test is whether Benjy is an acceptable, "rationally" conceived idiot.

The movement of Benjy's mind from one time or occasion in his life to another seems triggered by his association of ideas; that is, a stimulus present on one occasion will become associated with a similar stimulus on another occasion. Although specific analyses may vary, as many as thirteen specific times, including the present, have been identified, and approximately one hundred "shifts" triggered by associations occur throughout his monologue. In other words, to most readers the narrative in Benjy's section seems at first glance hopelessly scrambled. Although the material can be unscrambled and put into chronological order, any unscrambling should be considered a method of analysis and never a substitute for reading the monologue as Faulkner conceived and wrote it. The sequential ordering of the events in Benjy's monologue that follows is neither designed to rewrite Faulkner's novel nor to present "Faulkner improved." The reader who stops at this point will of course miss completely the novelist's representation of the distorted mind of Benjy and the artistic effect of this initial part of the novel.

Approximately three-fourths of the scene and time changes in Benjy's monologue relate either to the present time (April 7, 1928), or to the death of "Damuddy" in the fall of 1898, or to the occasion of the change of his name from Maury to Benjamin in November, 1900. The predominance of these references suggests the crucial nature of the events that Benjy associates with them and the powerful impression they have made upon him. The juxtaposition of the present time with the very earliest of his associations illustrates in part the difficulties encountered by readers in understanding the text.

In the present time sequences, Luster, Benjy's nurse in 1928, has taken him down to the branch where several boys are playing. He orders Benjy, who has been moaning whenever he hears some golfers looking for lost balls shout "Caddie," into the branch:

> "Now, git in that water and play and see can you stop that slobbering and moaning."
> I hushed and got in the water *and Roskus came and said to come to supper and Caddy said,*
> *It's not supper time yet. I'm not going.*
> She was wet. We were playing in the branch and Caddy squatted down and got her dress wet and Versh said. . . . (p. 37; p. 19)

Benjy's statement "I hushed and got in the water" relates to the present (April 7, 1928). Getting into the water, however, triggers an association with an experience he had in the branch in the early fall of 1898 when he was three years old and Versh was his nurse. Here the abrupt change in time is emphasized by the change to italics. Benjy says that Roskus came and told them to come to supper but that Caddy refused. The image in his mind of Caddy and him in the branch transports him back to the beginning of the scene that concluded with Roskus telling them to come to supper. In other words, the action narrated in italics takes place thirty years before the present time but after the incident that Benjy narrates in the passage beginning "She was wet." Benjy narrates this happening until he says "Caddy smelled like trees in the rain" (p. 38; p. 22) two pages later. At that point, he shifts back to the present time (in italics) before returning to the branch scene in 1898 and repeating the remark about Roskus telling them to come to supper ("Roskus came and said to come

to supper and Caddy said it wasn't supper time yet"—p. 39; p. 22).
Upon first reading, only an extremely alert reader would be able to comprehend the movement of Benjy's mind in these passages and disentangle
the sequence of the incidents.

In the passages relating to 1898, Benjy narrates the incident that
Faulkner said was the genesis of the novel. Essentially this sequence contains four "scenes": the play in the branch, where Caddy gets her dress
wet, takes it off, and Benjy images her as "all wet and muddy behind"
(p. 38; p. 21); the talk at Frony's where the children learn about funerals;
the account of Caddy in the tree watching the funeral in the parlor while
her brothers see her muddy drawers from below; and the bedroom scene
in which Mr. Compson kisses Caddy goodnight and puts his hand on
Benjy's head. Relatively speaking, the material is presented in large
"chunks," possibly because of its central importance to the entire novel.
Benjy's narration of these scenes contains a great deal of foreshadowing of
what is to come, especially hints or suggestions about Jason's character,
Quentin's concern with Caddy's purity, Caddy's unconcern with the nice-
ties of modesty, the stain upon Caddy, the snake under the house, and the
role of Mr. Compson. Even in Benjy's chaotic mind, the events that take
place in the branch followed by those relating to his grandmother's death
held great significance. A Freudian psychologist might say that they
push their way from deep within his subconsciousness to the surface of
his conscious thoughts where they are not past but present: he relives
them (and other experiences throughout his monologue) as if they are
taking place *not* in memory but in the *now*.

In November, 1900, when Benjy was five, another event occurred that
would remain in his mind for the next twenty-eight years—the changing of his name from Maury to Benjamin. His account of the "name-
changing" clusters in the final fifteen pages of his monologue, and like
many other scenes that Benjy summons to his conscious level, they emphasize the disorders and unhappiness in the Compson household. Benjy
"recalls" his crying when Caddy endeavors to explain to him that his
name is now Benjy (pp. 80, 91; p. 74). In perhaps the longest scene
between Benjy and his mother, the unsympathetic Mrs. Compson will
neither permit Caddy to hold him nor Benjy to sit upon her lap. Mrs.
Compson, who dislikes nicknames, cannot calm the boy; only Caddy,
the red and yellow cushion, and the firelight he loves can console him.

Caddy's remark to her mother at the end of the passage reveals the character of this complaining, self-centered woman: "You go upstairs and lay down, so you can be sick" (p. 83; p. 78).

In the name-changing sequence, Dilsey's Christian faith and common-sense understanding of Benjy's needs contrast sharply with Mrs. Compson's callousness. Dilsey has no patience with the name-changing (made by Mrs. Compson to keep the retarded child from bearing her brother's name). *"He aint wore out the name he was born with yet, is he,"* she says. *"Folks dont have no luck, changing names"* (p. 77; p. 71). This passage concludes with a brief exchange between Caddy and Dilsey in which the devoted servant asserts her faith. She knows her name will be *"in the Book. . . . Writ out,"* and though she cannot read, she knows that *"All I got to do is say Ise here"* (p. 77; p. 71). The remark recalls Samuel's answer to the Lord: "Here *am* I" (I Samuel 3:4). Unlike Mr. Compson, Mrs. Compson, Quentin, Caddy, and Jason, for Dilsey faith has not failed; she lives a purposeful life of service, and her heaven is secure.

The few occasions of domestic tranquility in the Compson household stand out impressively in Benjy's monologue. Earlier he "recalled" Mr. Compson kissing Caddy goodnight and patting Benjy on the head. In the name-changing sequence, Benjy relives the scene after supper when the family gathers in Mrs. Compson's room. She lies in bed with a headache. Benjy has his cushion. "Caddy and Father and Jason were in Mother's chair. Caddy's head was on Father's shoulder. . . . and I went and Father lifted me into the chair too, and Caddy held me" (p. 91; p. 88). This fleeting moment of peace and tenderness in the family leaves such an indelible impression upon Benjy that he can summon it up to his consciousness years afterwards.

Benjy's mind, always selective in the scenes it re-creates, focuses on the day before Christmas Eve in 1904, when he is nine. In the care of Versh, Benjy runs down to the gate to wait for the arrival of Caddy from school. They return to the house, but after some debate Caddy and Benjy venture out again, because Uncle Maury secretly wishes Caddy to deliver a letter to Mrs. Patterson, a neighbor, with whom he is having an affair. Benjy traces the route through the fence where Caddy *"uncaught me"* (p. 24; p. 3), across the garden, over the pig pen fence, around the barn in which they can hear Prince, Queenie, and Fancy stomping, and down to the branch, near the area where a pig is being killed, across the branch and up the hill to the Patterson fence where Benjy waits for Caddy to climb over it and deliver the letter to Mrs. Patterson.

More important than the route, however, is the glimpse the passage offers into the life of the Compson family. The sickly, complaining Mrs. Compson views Benjy as a "judgment on me" (p. 25; p. 4)—the reader understands the irony of the word. Benjy worries her (p. 27; p. 7). Meanwhile, Uncle Maury freely helps himself, and often Mrs. Compson, to Mr. Compson's whiskey and uses Caddy to carry his messages to Mrs. Patterson. Perhaps the most significant aspect of this passage is the understanding the reader obtains of Caddy's tenderness toward her retarded brother who can "smell the cold" (p. 26; p. 5) and mistakes weeds for flowers.

The next three events, which take place when Benjy is ten, eleven, and fourteen, relate primarily to Caddy; and they are connected by Benjy's growing but perhaps only instinctive realization that others are competing for her love and tenderness. Only a single passage deals with the events of Christmas, 1905, but each line has significance. Benjy resents Caddy's maturing into a young woman and senses that her hat, what Jason calls her "prissy dress" (p. 59; p. 49), the water in the bathroom (recalling to some readers the branch incident of 1898), and her perfume are signs of change. Her question, "Did you think Caddy had run away" (p. 61; p. 50), appropriately calls attention to Benjy's feelings. Once the hat, the dress, and perfume are gone, Caddy *"smelled like trees"* (p. 62; p. 51). Other remarks indicate that matters in the Compson household have not changed. The children continue to disturb Mrs. Compson as she lies in her room "with the sickness on a cloth on her head," and she wants Benjy out of her sight "so I can have some peace" (p. 60; p. 49). Meanwhile, Jason and Caddy continue to quarrel, and Mr. Compson seeks to bring a measure of stability to the family.

Three brief references to Caddy and Charlie in the swing near the pear tree emphasize Caddy's growing sexual maturity and Benjy's ever sharpening awareness that he is losing her. Just as he has forced her to give up her perfume, he makes her, at least temporarily, give up Charlie. He "recalls" that "Caddy took the kitchen soap and washed her mouth at the sink, hard. Caddy smelled like trees" (p. 67; p. 58). The references to Dan (the dog) and Charlie help readers to identify the incident.

The Collapse of Family

The distance between Caddy and Benjy continues to widen. When he is thirteen (1908), Caddy is considered too old to sleep in the same bed with him, but Dilsey compromises by allowing her to lie down beside him in her bathrobe between the spread and the blanket. About this same time, Uncle Maury sends Benjy, instead of Caddy, to deliver a message to Mrs. Patterson; but on this occasion, Mr. Patterson takes the letter away from Benjy (the reader cannot tell if Benjy wanted to give the letter to Mr. Patterson instead of his wife). The result of this mistake in delivery is a black eye and "fat lip" for Uncle Maury ("His eye was sick, and his mouth"—p. 62; p. 52) and a number of sardonic comments on the incident from Mr. Compson. In the background, Mrs. Compson's false pride in her family lineage and the ever present whiskey decanter underscore the family's problems.

Two passages, when Benjy is fourteen, near the end of his monologue do not so clearly delineate specific events as the other sequences, but plainly they are intended to have certain sexual overtones and to underline the growing separation between Benjy and Caddy that her sexual maturity inevitably brings. As Caddy walks past the door, she sees Benjy looking at her. "I went toward her, crying, and she shrank against the wall and I saw her eyes and I cried louder and pulled at her dress. . . . Her eyes ran" (p. 87; p. 84). They go upstairs, and again "she shrank against the wall, looking at me. She opened the door to her room, but I pulled at her dress and we went to the bathroom . . ." (p. 88; p. 85). For his part, Benjy seems to sense the change in Caddy and to realize that she is again running away from him; and for her part, Caddy's weeping suggests that she is conscious of wrongdoing but unable to stop. The allusion to the bathroom again recalls the branch incident in 1898.

These three scenes treating Caddy's growth to womanhood prepare for her wedding on April 25, 1910. Although in his monologue Benjy says nothing about her illicit pregnancy or the circumstances of her marriage, clearly the event is always a traumatic experience for him often juxtaposed with the funeral of Damuddy. With T. P., who has replaced Versh as the nurse, Benjy watches *the lights coming up the drive* (p. 56; p. 44) as the guests arrive and tastes the *"sassprilluh"* (p. 56; p. 45) that T. P. has found in the cellar. The drink makes him *feel just like a squinch owl inside* (p. 57; p. 46). But the intensity of his feeling does not appear until the brief passage that follows. Benjy climbs on a box and peers in the window (as Caddy had done at Damuddy's funeral): "*I saw them. Then I saw Caddy, with flowers in her hair, and a long veil like shining wind. Caddy Caddy* . . . I clawed my hands against the wall Caddy" (p. 58; p. 47). Against this background of Benjy's despair, Faulkner provides comic relief through the drinking scene. The champagne "sassprilluh," which proves too much for both T. P. and Benjy, makes the idiot cry and the Negro laugh. Even in his drunkenness, Benjy remains aware that Caddy is being separated from him and no longer smells like trees.

T. P. understands far better than Mrs. Compson what the loss of Caddy means to Benjy. A short time after the wedding, Benjy stands at the gate as if waiting for Caddy to return as he had earlier waited for her arrival back from school. "*You cant do no good looking through the gate, T. P. said. Miss Caddy done gone long ways away. Done got married and left you. You cant do no good, holding to the gate and crying. She cant hear you*" (p. 70; p. 62). When Mrs. Compson tells him to quiet Benjy, T. P. responds: "*Aint nothing going to quiet him. . . . He think if he down to the gate, Miss Caddy come back*" (p. 70; p. 63). Not finding Caddy, Benjy tries to talk to the girls walking by on their way home from school. Instead, he frightens them. One day the gate is unlocked when the girls pass by. "I opened the gate and they stopped, turning. I was trying to say, and I caught her, trying to say, and she screamed . . ." (p. 72; p. 64). Jason's response is that Benjy should be put in the state institution at Jackson, "*if Mrs Burgess dont shoot him first*" (p. 71; p. 63). Faulkner's readers have debated the implications of these three brief passages. Was Benjy merely trying to ask the girls about Caddy, or was he seeking to express his own sexual desires and really attacking the Burgess girl?

The last of the events that cluster about Caddy's wedding and its significance for Benjy takes place about the time of Quentin's suicide in June, 1910. In these two passages, Roskus, Versh, T. P., and Dilsey become almost a chorus commenting upon the Compson family. Roskus, who sees Benjy as a sign of bad luck, interprets Dan's howling and the cry of the squinch owl as signs of impending death. Dilsey's protest against these predictions of doom affirms again her Christian fortitude in the face of trouble. Whether Benjy, as some readers believe, actually has preternatural knowledge of coming events one cannot determine from the passage. The verdict of the Negroes, perhaps Dilsey included, remains that "*taint no luck on this place*" (p. 48; p. 34; compare p. 47; p. 33).

53

Mr. Compson dies on April 25, 1912, the anniversary of Caddy's wedding. The extensive passages covering this and related events indicate their recurrence—and thus importance—in Benjy's mind and suggest that, next to Caddy, Mr. Compson meant more to the idiot than anyone else. Placed in what seems to be the proper chronological order, the account of Mr. Compson's death begins when T. P. awakens Benjy to say that they are going down to his house. Benjy says, "I could smell it" (p. 53; p. 40). He is now seventeen, and his voice has changed ("You was bad enough before you got that bullfrog voice"—p. 54; p. 41). Outside Dan is howling; and as they walk towards the branch in the moonlight, Benjy can see "the bones where the buzzards ate Nancy, flapping black and slow and heavy out of the ditch" (p. 54; p. 42). At Dilsey's house, Luster and Quentin (Caddy's daughter) are fighting over some spools. When Benjy (now physically almost a grown man) takes the spools, Frony sends him to the barn where Roskus and T. P. are milking the cow.

Roskus continues to assert the absence of luck on the Compson place. "They aint no luck going be on no place where one of they own chillens' name aint never spoke" (p. 50; p. 37), he says in reference to Caddy, and he disapproves of "raising a child [Quentin] not to know its own mammy's name" (p. 50; p. 37). Again Roskus asserts that Benjy has preternatural knowledge. "He know lot more than folks thinks. . . . He knowed they time was coming, like that pointer done" (p. 51; pp. 37–38).

The final incident in this portion of Benjy's monologue relates to a visit the family makes to the cemetery. Somewhat afraid to ride in the carriage with T. P., now eighteen, driving, Mrs. Compson takes Benjy with her. Near the monument on the square, she stops to ask Jason to go with them. She would feel safer if he would. "Safe from what. . . . Father and Quentin cant hurt you" (p. 31; p. 12) replies Jason with his usual sardonic humor. The carriage moves along, and Benjy recognizes the proper order of its motion. "The shapes flowed on. The ones on the other side began again, bright and fast and smooth, like when Caddy says we are going to sleep" (p. 32; pp. 12–13).

Two brief passages record the death of Roskus, which takes place shortly after Mr. Compson's. Benjy says "*they moaned at Dilsey's house . . . and Blue howled under the kitchen steps*" (p. 52; p. 39). Told to take Benjy down to the barn, Luster refuses: "*I aint going down there. . . . I might meet pappy down there*" (p. 52; p. 40).

As one would expect, the longest portion, almost a third, of Benjy's monologue deals with the present, April 7, 1928, his thirty-third birthday. The sixteen years between the death of Roskus and *now* have left little impression upon his mental and emotional state; not even his castration in 1913 seems to have been traumatic enough to crowd out other experiences in his consciousness, though he is constantly aware of his mutilation. Faulkner seems to be saying that in the years intervening between the death of Mr. Compson and the flight of Caddy's daughter Quentin, no crucial events took place; rather the family continued its deterioration until the events of Easter, 1928, concluded its history.

As the novel opens, Benjy is looking "between the curling flower spaces" in the fence that separates the present Compson land from what once was Benjy's "pasture" but was sold to send Quentin to Harvard and now has become a golf course. Meanwhile, Luster searches in the grass for the quarter he has lost—the quarter that would admit him that night to the carnival show. Benjy watches the golfers take the flag in and out of the cup and then hit from the "table" or golf tee. Although these actions, and later the search for golf balls, have a literal level of meaning, they probably also have a sexual significance.

Luster reminds Benjy that today is his birthday. Later the reader learns that Luster's assertion that he bought Benjy the cake is a lie, though Luster's threat to eat all of the cake and even the candles is more credible. Luster takes Benjy along the pasture fence to the garden fence where Benjy, as he has on earlier occasions, snags on the nail. At this point, Luster's reference to snagging on the nail prompts Benjy to think of another time, in 1904, when he and Caddy delivered Uncle Maury's letter to Mrs. Patterson.

In the subsequent allusions to present time, Benjy continues to moan as he and Luster walk toward the branch. Luster gives him a "flower," actually a jimsonweed that is a variety of narcotic. Still crying, Benjy passes the carriage house, walks through the barn where Luster reminds the idiot that he *"aint got no spotted pony to ride now"* (p. 32; p. 13), and arrives at the branch (the same branch in which Caddy in 1898 had gotten her drawers muddy), where other little "children" are playing. Luster asks about his quarter, and there follows some good natured banter about the show, "white folks" and "niggers," and Luster's problems with Benjy. The humor continues when one of the golfers comes down the hill in search of a golf ball which Luster has already found. As the golfer calls his caddie, Benjy moans again. After threatening to whip him, Luster pushes Benjy into the branch. Luster tells the Negroes that Benjy still thinks the Compsons own the pasture, and they reply that *"folks dont like to look at a loony. Taint no luck in it"* (p. 39; p. 22). When Benjy attempts to take the golf ball, Luster refuses. His remark—*"What business you got with it. You cant play no ball."* (p. 51; p. 38)—prompts a sexual interpretation.

As they return to the house, Benjy wanders over to the swing where Quentin sits with the man in the red tie, who plays in the carnival show. It is the same swing where Caddy years earlier sat with Charlie, and Benjy tends to identify the daughter with the mother. After Quentin threatens to make Jason whip Luster for allowing Benjy to follow her, the man in the red tie tries to teach Benjy a match trick. Luster explains Benjy's handicap. Luster then finds a box of contraceptive condoms labeled "Agnes Mable Becky," and the man in the red tie remarks that someone has been here before and left a track.

Luster and Benjy go back to the fence to hunt for golf balls. Benjy moves along the fence to the gate "where the girls passed with their booksatchels" (p. 70; p. 62), and at once his mind turns to a time in 1910 when he waited at the gate for Caddy to come. When Benjy's mind returns to the present, he watches the golfers take the flag out, hit, and put the flag back. Luster tries to sell the ball he found, but the golfer merely puts it in his pocket. Luster, who cannot quiet Benjy even with the jimsonweed, tells Benjy that when Mrs. Compson dies Jason will send him to Jackson "where you can hold the bars all day long with the rest of the looneys and slobber. How you like that" (p. 73; p. 66). Luster knocks the flowers out of Benjy's hand. "'Beller.' Luster said. 'Beller. You want something to beller about. All right, then. Caddy.' he whispered. 'Caddy. Beller now. Caddy'" (p. 74; p. 66). But when he hears Dilsey coming, Luster tries to calm Benjy and explains: "Aint done nothing to him. . . . He just started bellering" (p. 74; p. 67). Dilsey is not deceived.

In the kitchen with Dilsey, Luster claims to be a model nurse for Benjy. Luster and Benjy eat the birthday cake that Dilsey has bought. Luster continues to tell lies to Dilsey and to torment Benjy. Finally Benjy burns his hand, and the ensuing commotion brings Mrs. Compson. "'What is it now. Cant I even be sick in peace. Do I have to get up out of

bed to come down to him, with two grown negroes to take care of him'"
(p. 78; p. 72). She continues to complain about Benjy's "bawling," and
Dilsey sensibly observes: "They aint nowhere else to take him. . . . We
aint got the room we use to have. He cant stay out in the yard, crying
where all the neighbors can see him" (p. 79; p. 73).

Luster takes Benjy to the library, but Jason orders Luster to take Benjy
back to the kitchen. Supper proves to be anything but a time of family
gathering in peace and tranquility. Jason and Quentin (Caddy's daughter) fight over her conduct with the man wearing the red tie. She complains about Benjy's slipper and declares her intention of running away.
As she tries to throw a glass of water at Jason, Dilsey catches her hand.

Finally, Quentin gives Luster the quarter for the show. He tries to get
Benjy to bed *"so I can get up there before it starts. . . . Just let them horns toot
the first toot and I done gone"* (p. 91; p. 89). Undressed, Benjy thinks about
his mutilation, and Luster says, *"Looking for them aint going to do no good.
They're gone"* (p. 92; p. 90). Together, they look out the window and
watch as *"the shaking went down the tree"* (p. 93; p. 91). Quentin has indeed run away to join the man with the red tie. The final comment in
Benjy's monologue belongs to Luster: *"Hear them horns. You get in that bed
while my foots behaves"* (p. 93; p. 91).

Despite Faulkner's own statements about the inadequacy of Benjy's
monologue to present the Compson story, the novelist has provided
through Benjy the essential information about the final deterioration of
this Southern family. At the end of the book, "Damuddy," Quentin, Mr.
Compson, Caddy, and Caddy's daughter have either died or departed.
The "family," if family it may now be called, consists only of Benjy, the
castrated idiot; Mrs. Compson, a complaining hypochondriac; and
Jason, a wholly selfish scoundrel.

Faulkner's interpreters have noted parallels between Benjy and Christ,
among them Benjy's thirty-third birthday on the Easter weekend, his
suffering, and innocence. He has also been associated with the suffering
servant in Isaiah and with Billy Budd as Adam before the fall.[17] But these
analogies may easily be strained too far. Benjy is not an allegory of
Christ. The Compson idiot stands at the end of the family deterioration;
he is not, like Christ, the salvation of the individual or family, much less
the hope of the world for a new order. Unlike Christ, he has no clearly
articulated message for others; he can only cry, moan, and bellow. At no

time does Faulkner lose sight of Benjy's humanity. His sensations, which constitute his life, focus upon his own needs for food, love, and physical satisfactions; and he makes no effort to fulfill the needs of others. Essentially, he is a passive observer of life and never an active participant except as a sufferer. The parallels to figures outside the novel, however, do enrich the portrait, particularly as they suggest that Benjy and Christ, as well as the suffering servant and Billy Budd, suffer innocently from evils they have not caused but that come to everyman as part of the human condition.

In Benjy's monologue there is much that he can neither know nor understand. Perhaps he is fortunate not to understand Luster's predictions of his future in the Jackson asylum. Benjy knows nothing of his father's pessimism, and he cannot understand the complexity of Quentin's love for Caddy, nor the extent of Jason's meanness. But that Benjy suffers and suffers intensely, there can be no doubt. Though he is perhaps necessarily almost wholly self-centered, Faulkner makes his suffering ultimately symbolic of the suffering of all men who cannot fully articulate their feelings. When Dilsey (later in the novel) tries to comfort him, Faulkner writes that Benjy "bellowed slowly, abjectly, without tears; the grave hopeless sound of all voiceless misery under the sun" (p. 332; p. 395). Benjy is beyond human help. Dilsey makes the point when she says "You's de Lawd's chile, anyway. En I be His'n too, fo long, praise Jesus" (p. 333; p. 396).

Although the firelight, the bright shapes of sleep, the jimsonweed, and the slipper or cushion may bring momentary surcease of his pain, only Caddy can provide effective comfort by supplying the love that Mrs. Compson never gave her son. The mere mention of Caddy's name is sufficient to summon to his consciousness the agony of loss that makes his suffering all but unbearable. Benjy's need for love outweighs all other yearnings. Since the past is ever accessible to him with all the immediacy of present reality, time can never diminish his heartache over the loss of his sister. Acutely, he feels, even if he does not understand, that a world without love is a world of individual loneliness without order or faith. To Benjy, hope is denied. He cannot, like Melville's Queequeg, the pagan harpooner lost in the vast Pacific, light a lantern and hopelessly hold up hope amidst that ocean of despair. Benjy's tragedy is that though he cannot hope, he yet knows the agony of hopeless yearning and despair. He belongs with those of the Lost Generation to whom Othello's phrase "but yet the pity of it" has application.

Although most readers consider Benjy's monologue the most difficult reading of the four sections of *The Sound and the Fury*, Quentin's section cannot be described as easy reading. Despite his mental limitations, for example, Benjy can be relied upon to present a fairly objective account of matters. To be sure, he cannot interpret or establish causal relationships among events; but he can record, camera-fashion, happenings as if they were immediately present to him. Quentin, on the other hand, though emotionally disturbed, is highly intelligent. He can interpret and he can make connections; in fact, he usually makes too many connections, so many that his thoughts often become chaotic and metaphorical. Benjy's monologue, moreover, contains references to a comparatively small number of events—about a dozen in all—whereas Quentin deals with more than fifty separate actions.

The two sections exhibit other notable differences. Although scene and time changes in both monologues are triggered by association of ideas, Faulkner employs conventional sentence structure for Benjy's narration; but in attempting to suggest Quentin's thoughts, which, of course, make no provision for punctuation, capital letters, or paragraphs, the novelist writes much of this "interior" monologue, though not all of it, without these editorial accessories. In both monologues the rapid and often abrupt shifts of the time frame can confuse the unwary reader. Quentin's section is the longest in the novel, actually one-third of the book. Benjy's section, as has been noted, concentrates on the events dealing with Damuddy's death in 1898, the changing of his name in 1900, and the present of 1928. Benjy also calls to mind Caddy's wedding in 1910 and Mr. Compson's death in 1912. In other words, three or four crucial events dominate the mind of Benjy. Quentin's suicide, to which Benjy vaguely alludes, is one of the last events in the idiot's monologue. The sixteen years between 1912 and 1928 are pretty much blank for Benjy. Although Quentin makes occasional references that document the entire Compson story to the time of his death, he devotes approximately sixty pages of his monologue to his present (June 2, 1910), thirty pages to the Dalton Ames affair in August, 1909, and twelve pages (the most chaotic portion of his monologue, set mostly in italic type except for the passages relating to Herbert Head) to Caddy's wedding on April 25,

1910, less than six weeks before his suicide. Though Benjy's world lies entirely within himself, his rendering is almost wholly objective. Quentin's account is highly subjective, so much so that the reader is never quite certain of its reliability. One must bear in mind, moreover, that although the majority of Quentin's references relate to comparatively recent events or to the actual present, his monologue takes place eighteen years prior to the Easter weekend in 1928, when the narratives of Benjy, Jason, and the omniscient author take place.

Predictably, critics have reached a variety of interpretations of Quentin's character.[18] Some readers have regarded Quentin as a "mentally deranged brother" who drowns himself because he cannot make his concept of life consonant with its realities. Others have emphasized his obsession with Caddy's virginity as actually more idiotic than Benjy's fanatic response to the sound of her name and the odor of her body. Scholars have pointed out parallels to Quentin in Don Quixote, in Hamlet, and in Byron's poetry. The connection with Hamlet is particularly strong because of Hamlet's concern with intellectual matters, incest, the nature of women, suicide, and his inability to take decisive action. Within the novel itself, Herbert Head calls Quentin "a half-baked Galahad." Faulkner's own verdict upon Quentin, included in the Appendix, which appears to cover all the important points raised in his monologue, must bear considerable weight with the reader.

> QUENTIN III. Who loved not his sister's body but some concept of Compson honor precariously and (he knew well) only temporarily supported by the minute fragile membrane of her maidenhead as a miniature replica of all the whole vast globy earth may be poised on the nose of a trained seal. Who loved not the idea of the incest which he would not commit, but some presbyterian concept of its eternal punishment: he, not God, could by that means cast himself and his sister both into hell, where he could guard her forever and keep her forevermore intact amid the eternal fires. But who loved death above all, who loved only death, loved and lived in a deliberate and almost perverted anticipation of death as a lover loves and deliberately refrains from the waiting willing friendly tender incredible body of his beloved, until he can no longer bear not the refraining but the restraint and so flings, hurls himself, relinquishing, drowning. (pp. 9–10; p. 411)

Virtually all of these views, particularly those of the author, have degrees of validity; whether any single one, however, or even a composite of all, adequately resolves Quentin's problems or interprets fully his character must remain a matter of individual persuasion.

Faulkner's phrase, "who loved death above all," makes the reader at once remember young Bayard Sartoris who returned from World War I with a death wish. The grandson of the courageous old Bayard of "An Odor of Verbena," young Bayard reached a point where purposeful activity was futile and death, therefore, a release if not a solution. When for him faith failed, Bayard sought his own death. In his case, the death wish was mingled with a guilt feeling toward his twin brother with whom he had a relationship that bordered upon the incestuous. To a degree, at least, Quentin seems to resemble young Bayard, the crucial relationship being for Quentin with his sister instead of his brother. One could go further and point out other similarities between the two young men (for example, neither could have said he had a mother). Anyone reading these two novels must feel a strong relationship between them; in fact, the similarity they share in theme and philosophical outlook prompts one to infer that they are both somehow related to Faulkner's own response to the intellectual problems of the Lost Generation and perhaps even to his own personal life. Yet Quentin was unquestionably more intensely personal to Faulkner than Bayard Sartoris and by far the more convincing as a person.

In the important opening scene of Quentin's monologue, the reader learns that Quentin has already determined to commit suicide by drowning himself; he even alludes to such details as the flatirons that will weigh down his body. Before these matters are revealed, however, the section opens with a significant paragraph. While sleeping, Quentin has forgotten time; but when he awakens, he is "in time" again, the shadow on the window sash reminding him that it is between seven and eight o'clock. (Shadows and time play dominant roles in Quentin's thoughts throughout his monologue, and readers compare Shakespeare's characterization of life as a walking shadow.) Quentin can also hear the ticking of his grandfather's watch marking the passage of time. His father had given him the watch (on his birthday) with the remark that in the machine that counts time may be found the burial place (mausoleum) of all hope and desire. Mr. Compson has given it to Quentin so that he may now and then forget about time and cease trying to conquer it, because the effort "only reveals to man his own folly and despair, and victory is an illusion of philosophers and fools" (p. 95; p. 93). Mr. Compson's words reveal his own attitude—he has lost faith in purposeful activity. Later the reader learns that Mr. Compson seeks death through alcohol.

Quentin, who at times seems much like his father, continues to remember Mr. Compson's statements. Mr. Compson said that Christ was really not crucified, has not died a sacrifice for humanity, but has instead been "worn away by the minute clicking of little wheels" (p. 96; p. 94)—the image suggests the nonhuman, mechanical, industrial order—and Quentin adds "that had no sister." From a remark Mr. Compson once made about idle habits, Quentin moves to the forthcoming boatrace between Harvard and Yale at New London that afternoon. The weather in June should be good. At the thought of the June weather, his mind moves to June as the "month of brides" and to Caddy. He recalls her wedding and the hymn "the voice that breathed" often sung as the wedding hymn in the Episcopal service. (John Keble's famous hymn: "The voice that breathed o'er Eden / That earliest wedding day / The primal marriage blessing— / It hath not passed away.") But to Quentin the voice that breathed o'er Caddy was not the voice of God but that of Benjy lying outside on the ground, drunk and bellowing at the loss of Caddy. Quentin's thoughts become a kind of synopsis of the entire event of Caddy's wedding—her running out to Benjy, the roses, the marriage announcement, her earlier loss of virginity, incest, and the family insistence that Quentin make good his year at Harvard purchased at the cost of Benjy's pasture. Even Jason's predicament is suggested in Quentin's thoughts.

After watching his roommate Shreve leave the room and refusing to go with his friend Spoade to meet some prostitutes—"to chase after the little dirty sluts, whose business" (p. 97; p. 96)—Quentin again thinks of his father's comment, "it was men invented virginity not women. . . . it's like death: only a state in which the others are left" (p. 97; p. 96). When Quentin replies, "But to believe it doesn't matter," Mr. Compson responds, "that's what's so sad about anything: not only virginity," and adds that "nothing is even worth the changing of it" (p. 97; p. 96). The passage suggests that Mr. Compson has already reached the state where he has lost faith in all purposeful activity.

As the scene continues, and Quentin has heard the last strokes of the Harvard bell, he thinks about an idea that often occurs to him: "If we

[Caddy and he] could just have done something so dreadful that they would have fled hell except us" (p. 98; p. 97). (In a subsequent passage that faintly recalls Dante, Quentin amplifies the idea: "*If it could just be a hell beyond that: the clean flame the two of us more than dead. Then you will have only me then only me then the two of us amid the pointing and the horror beyond the clean flame*" p. 135; p. 144.) The most "dreadful" act or sin Quentin can imagine would be incest. But Mr. Compson negates even that action: "That's sad too, people cannot do anything that dreadful they cannot do anything very dreadful at all" (p. 99; p. 98). Quentin responds that one can "shirk all things," but Mr. Compson answers, "Ah can you." This remark brings Quentin back to the present, and his shift to the present reveals the future. "And I will look down and see my murmuring bones and the deep water like wind, like a roof of wind, and after a long time they cannot distinguish even bones upon the lonely and inviolate sand. Until on the Day when He says Rise only the flatiron would come floating up." And then Quentin makes clear the point he has now reached: "It's not when you realise that nothing can help you—religion, pride, anything—it's when you realise that you dont need any aid" (p. 99; p. 98).

Going to the dresser and picking up the watch, Quentin breaks its crystal and sheds blood as he twists the hands off. The "little wheels clicking and clicking" behind its face remind him of "Jesus walking on Galilee and Washington not telling lies" (p. 99; p. 99). Meticulously Quentin lays out his clothes, packs his trunk, bathes, shaves, and writes two notes. At that moment he notices again the shadow that, like the watch, has continued to keep time. He stops "inside the door, watching the shadow move" (p. 100; p. 100), and the door, a traditional symbol of woman's sex, again reminds him of the same scene he had remembered only a few moments past: Caddy running through the door, "*running out of the mirror*" (p. 100; p. 100), the roses, "*the voice that breathed o'er Eden*," and Benjy's bellowing. The scene is etched deeply into Quentin's consciousness. Interrupted by Shreve's ironical question—"Is it a wedding or a wake?" (p. 101; p. 100)—Quentin returns to the present. (Benjy had fused Damuddy's funeral and Caddy's wedding in his mind, the wake and the wedding.) As he walks out of the dormitory, "the shadow on the stoop was gone" (p. 101; p. 101). When he steps into the sunlight, he finds his shadow again.

63

Although Quentin's movements throughout June 2, 1910, can be traced, his mental processes are generally more significant than his actions. After leaving the dormitory, he goes to the post office to mail his letter to Mr. Compson; fails to find Deacon, the Negro who meets Harvard boys at the train and marches in Decoration Day parades; and eats breakfast in Parker's restaurant. Afterwards, Quentin passes a jeweler's window "but I looked away in time" (p. 102; p. 102). The natural clock, "high up in the sun," however, will not let him forget time, and he returns to the shop. When the jeweler wishes to tell Quentin the right time, Quentin interrupts: "'Don't tell me,' I said. 'Just tell me if any of them are right'" (p. 103; p. 103). Finally, the jeweler replies: "'No. But they haven't been regulated . . .'" (p. 103; p. 104). Back of this conversation lies Quentin's distinction between "temporal" time and eternity. He wants to get outside time, to get into eternity, where nothing will change and the present continues forever. The jeweler's reply that the watches have not been "regulated" implies that man's time (and actions) has not been made or set to fit heaven's time (or order).

Leaving the jeweler, Quentin stops in a hardware store to purchase two six-pound flatirons to weight down his body in the water. He gets on a streetcar, sits beside a Negro, and thinks about the Negroes he knew at home. After the Negro gets off the car, Quentin sees a gull motionless in air, seemingly out of time. He gets off the car, walks across the bridge thinking about Gerald Bland and gazing at his own shadow in the water. Throughout much of this time, Quentin is also thinking about Caddy, Herbert Head, the wedding announcement, and Jason. Again and again, Quentin returns to Caddy's loss of virginity, what his father said, her marriage, and his own loss of belief in idealism. He gets on another car, going to Harvard; and, as he rides along, the scenes he sees alternate with his thoughts about Benjy's pasture and remembered conversations with his father. At Harvard, he meets the Deacon and later Shreve MacKenzie.

Shortly before noon, Quentin boards another car. The reader can sense the increased tension in Quentin's mind as he thinks about what his mother said about Caddy, Mrs. Compson's favoritism, and her differences with Mr. Compson (pp. 121–23; pp. 126–28). In rather quick succession, Quentin changes from one car to another, aware of what he is outwardly doing but inwardly preoccupied with thoughts of Caddy,

Head, and some of the events of his childhood. Leaving the car, he crosses another bridge on foot, looks down into the water, sees a large trout, and talks to three small boys who are arguing about swimming or fishing. In a small bakery, he finds a dirty little Italian girl whom he impulsively greets: "Hello, sister" (p. 144; p. 155). After he gives her some buns, he cannot lose her. While walking along with her, Quentin thinks about his own sister Caddy and his adolescent petting party with Natalie that ended with him jumping into a hog wallow to cleanse himself. Finally, the little girl's brother, Julio, charges Quentin with kidnapping if not "meditated criminal assault" (p. 159; p. 174). With the assistance of Shreve and the Blands, Quentin is released.

The Blands had invited Quentin to a party with some girls. When they cannot find him, they invite Shreve in his place. As they all ride back toward Harvard, Quentin thinks about Caddy, Dalton Ames, and his unsuccessful effort to fight Ames. When Bland makes a remark about a girl, Quentin strikes him; and when he returns to reality, Shreve is wiping blood off of him. Bland has given him a terrible beating. Again, Quentin sets out on another trolley car ride.

This time, Quentin returns to his dormitory room. It is twilight. "A quarter hour yet," he thinks, "And then I'll not be" (p. 192; p. 216). Thoughts about his mother and father, Benjy, Caddy, and his own body "in the caverns and grottoes of the sea tumbling peacefully to the wavering tides" (p. 193; p. 217) crowd into his mind. And as the last note of the Harvard bell sounds, Quentin finishes dressing, brushes his teeth, and remembers his hat. The reader is to infer that shortly afterwards, Quentin retrieved the flatirons he had hidden at the end of the bridge and went out of time.

Although these external events—his concern for his shadow, the significance of time, his encounter with the little Italian girl, his fight with Gerald Bland, for example—perform an important function in his monologue by relating the inner turmoil in Quentin's mind to outward reality, the actual revelation of Quentin's problems comes to the reader primarily through his thoughts about his family and the past—his childhood, his encounters with Dalton Ames and Herbert Head, and Caddy's wedding. Again and again, Quentin returns to these matters to brood over their implications. For this reason, the final estimate of his failure and to a degree that of the Compson family must depend upon an assessment of his relationships to his parents and Caddy. So far as this section of the novel is concerned, the data come from Quentin himself.

On repeated occasions Quentin documents the failure of his mother in every parental role in the home. His anguished cry near the end of his monologue *"if I'd just had a mother so I could say Mother Mother"* (p. 190; p. 213) summarizes her relationship to him. He is bitterly aware of the antagonism and bickering that divide her from her husband. Quentin remembers her saying to Mr. Compson: *"How can I control any of them* [the children] *when you have always taught them to have no respect for me and my wishes I know you look down on my people"* (p. 115; p. 118). The social position of the Compsons rankles in her mind. Her complaints against Mr. Compson influence her feelings toward the children. In his mind Quentin hears her saying: "I must go away you [Mr. Compson] keep the others I'll take Jason and go where nobody knows us so he'll have a chance to grow up and forget all this the others dont love me they have never loved anything with that streak of Compson selfishness and false pride Jason was the only one my heart went out to without dread" (p. 121; p. 126). Her favoritism towards Jason is matched only by her antagonism towards Benjy and Caddy. Quentin records her outburst: "what have I done to have been given children like these Benjamin was punishment enough and now for her [Caddy] to have no more regard for me her own mother" (p. 121; p. 126). The remainder of this lengthy, ironical diatribe, which in intensity and bitterness surpasses Hamlet's accusations against his mother, becomes a terrible indictment of Mrs. Compson's failure as wife, mother, and human being. The lack of traditional sentence structure makes the passage all the more credible as the tortured thoughts of a sensitive young man bitterly disillusioned by his realization of his mother's despicable character.

> I thought he [Benjamin] was my punishment for putting aside my pride and marrying a man who held himself above me . . . I see now that I must pay for your sins as well as mine what have you done what sins have your high and mighty people visited upon me but you'll take up for them you always have found excuses for your own blood only Jason can do wrong because he is more Bascomb than Compson while your own daughter my little daughter my baby girl she is she is no better than that when I was a girl I was unfortunate I was only a Bascomb I was taught that there is no halfway ground that a woman is either a lady or not but I never dreamed when I held her in my arms that any daughter of mine could let herself . . . I know things she's done that

I'd die before I'd have you know that's it go on criticise Jason accuse me of setting him to watch her as if it were a crime while your own daughter can I know you dont love him . . . I look at him every day dreading to see this Compson blood beginning to show in him at last with his sister slipping out to see . . . will you even let me try to find out who he is . . . you wont let me try we are to sit back with our hands folded while she not only drags your name in the dirt but corrupts the very air your children breathe Jason you must let me go away I cannot stand it let me have Jason and you keep the others they're not my flesh and blood like he is strangers nothing of mine and I am afraid of them I can take Jason and go where we are not known . . . try to forget that the others ever were[.] (pp. 122–23; pp. 127–28)

Quentin has already stated the conclusion to this passage before he begins to quote his mother. The conclusion, however, belongs before and after the passage: *"Done in Mother's mind though. Finished. Finished. Then we were all poisoned"* (p. 121; pp. 125–26).

The long passage just quoted occurs relatively early in Quentin's monologue. The fact that his mind returns to this matter at the end of his section, as he is trying desperately to resolve the issue of to be or not to be, emphasizes the significance he attaches to his mother. In a brief passage, he condenses the whole dismal story of the Compson household into a single image:

When I was little there was a picture in one of our books, a dark place into which a single weak ray of light came slanting upon two faces lifted out of the shadow. *You know what I'd do if I were King?* she never was a queen or a fairy she was always a king or a giant or a general *I'd break that place open and drag them out and I'd whip them good* It was torn out, jagged out. I was glad. I'd have to turn back to it until the dungeon was Mother herself she and Father upward into weak light holding hands and us lost somewhere below even them without even a ray of light. (p. 191; p. 215)

Nowhere does Quentin phrase so vividly as here the utter failure of his mother and, it must be said, his father as parents.

Quentin's passionate denials of his mother contrast sharply with his constant quotation of his father's remarks. That father and son had much in common appears almost self-evident. Repeatedly, Quentin remembers his father's remarks about the futility of action and the emptiness of idealism. Just as Quentin is getting ready to leave his room for the last time, he remembers that Mr. Compson taught his children that "all men are just accumulations dolls stuffed with sawdust swept up from the trash heaps where all previous dolls had been thrown away the sawdust flowing from what wound in what side that not for me died not" (p. 194; p. 218). Since Mr. Compson himself has lost faith in purposeful action, he can neither be expected to help his son to gain an acceptance of reality nor to react strongly to Quentin's talk of incest with Caddy. Quentin's last thoughts concentrate upon this issue. When he doubts that Mr. Compson is taking him seriously, the father answers "you wouldnt have felt driven to the expedient of telling me you have committed incest otherwise" (p. 195; p. 219). When Mr. Compson asks Quentin if he actually tried to make Caddy commit incest with him, Quentin replies: "i was afraid to" and adds "i was afraid she might and then it wouldnt have done any good but if i could tell you we did it would have been so . . . and then the world would roar away." His father answers: "you are still blind to what is in yourself to that part of general truth the sequence of natural events and their causes which shadows every mans brow. . . . you cannot bear to think that someday it will no longer hurt you like this now" (pp. 195–96; p. 220). Many readers believe that this fear that someday Caddy's actions will no longer matter to him is Quentin's basic motive for suicide. Mr. Compson, however, carries the matter a step further: he holds that a man commits suicide "only when he has realised that even the despair or remorse or bereavement is not particularly important to the dark diceman" (p. 196; p. 221). Quentin will not commit suicide until "you come to believe that even she was not quite worth despair." Although he asserts that he will never believe Caddy unworthy of his despair, and his suicide appears to prove Mr. Compson wrong at this point, not all readers have accepted Quentin's statement at face value. They point to the fact that in every encounter with Caddy, Quentin is hostile and assert that he finally comes to realize that Caddy is a bitch. Regardless of which conclusion one reaches, neither life nor time nor faith offers Quentin a motive for continued activity or existence.

Quentin's monologue imposes heavy demands upon the reader. Virtually everyone who reads it asks himself for the key to Quentin's failure. Was it Caddy who disillusioned him? Did he lose faith in honor and all other moral values that made life liveable for him? Was Mrs. Compson the ultimate cause of his suicide? Did Mr. Compson destroy his son's faith in purposeful activity? Was Quentin really mentally deranged? Was there not something larger and more fundamental than merely the loss of

Caddy's virginity at the core of his problem? Was Caddy right and did Quentin agree with her that "theres a curse on us its not our fault" (p. 176; p. 196)? After Quentin met Ames on the bridge (like the bridge from which Quentin later jumped to his death) and asked if he ever had a sister, did Quentin finally accept the answer: "no but theyre all bitches" (p. 179; p. 199) and thus anticipate Jason's premise? Did Faulkner wish the reader to view Quentin's monologue as a parable of the South's decline? Readers often long for some simple explanation that will place all of these matters into proper perspective and harmonize them into a single generalization. So far no one has succeeded in constructing such a generalization that will satisfy every reader, yet the effort is worthwhile, since it underscores the complexity of human life and Faulkner's art.

In one of his appearances at Nagano, Japan, Faulkner remarked that to him Jason "represented complete evil" and added that Jason was "the most vicious character in my opinion I ever thought of." [19] Jason provides abundant support for Faulkner's verdict. Readers have difficulty deciding upon his worst action. Surely among his most vicious deeds are his systematically defrauding young Quentin of the money sent by Caddy and his cheating of his own mother. Quentin's assertion contains a great measure of truth: "If I'm bad, it's because I had to be. You [Jason] made me" (p. 277; p. 324). Earlier she had said: "I'm bad and I'm going to hell, and I dont care. I'd rather be in hell than anywhere where you are" (p. 207; p. 235). Jason has made her life so miserable that she regrets ever having been born. His treatment of Caddy is equally despicable. After he had agreed to let her see her baby, only a person of consummate meanness would have thought of driving by and holding the baby up to the window of the hack. His final remark about this incident underscores the depth of his meanness: "I could see her running after us through the back window. 'Hit 'em again,' I says, 'Let's get on home.' When we turned the corner she was still running" (p. 223; p. 255). Although these acts have motivation, they cannot be excused. Just as despicable, perhaps, is Jason's gratuitous meanness when in front of Luster Jason burns the show tickets that have cost him nothing and for which he has no use. On two separate occasions, Dilsey speaks the blunt truth about Jason. As she tries to stand between him and Quentin, Dilsey exclaims, "I dont put no devilment beyond you" (p. 203; p. 230). Again, after Jason blames her for allowing Caddy to see her baby and Benjy, Dilsey declares: "You's a cold man, Jason, if man you is. . . . I thank de Lawd I got mo heart dan dat" (p. 225; p. 258). Her judgment seems accurate.

Although Jason's narrative often reminds readers more of a dramatic soliloquy than an "interior" monologue, it should be considered parallel to accounts of Benjy and Quentin. The three monologues offer several significant contrasts. As might be expected, each brother emphasizes the events in family history that have had the greatest impact upon his own life. As has been said, Benjy's sensations usually relate either to the past of 1898–1900 or to the present of 1928, and for the most part, Quentin's thoughts alternate between the events of his youth around 1899–1905 and the present of 1910 (including Caddy's wedding). The "sane" Jason lives intensely in the present, but those elements of his monologue that do relate to the past cluster around events that date from Caddy's marriage to Herbert Head to the present of 1928. His preoccupation with these matters, of course, stems from his sense of outrage over not having been given his "chance" in life, that is, his equivalent of Quentin's year at Harvard or Caddy's marriage. He is outraged because the family has done something for Caddy, Quentin, and even Benjy but, he believes, nothing for him.

The three brothers also have different concepts of time. Benjy has no real sense of time, since he cannot distinguish a cause and a resultant effect; and though he narrates with the past tense, the past is ever present to him. Quentin, whose sense of time is almost compulsive, longs to get out of time to a kind of frozen eternity of the "inviolate sands." But Jason, who values only the present, keeps reminding everyone that he has no time. "I haven't got any money," he says. "I've been too busy to make any" (p. 261; p. 303). On another occasion, he says, "They'll have time to tell you. I haven't" (p. 252; p. 293). Jason blames old Job for taking time off to go to the show, though at that very time Jason is taking time off to pursue Miss Quentin. At lunch, he blames Miss Quentin and Dilsey for wasting time, though he himself is late for the meal. To Jason, time is money. Unlike Quentin, Jason never asks if the clocks are right; he depends upon them because he believes that mechanical objects do not lie, only men lie.

Equally revealing is the attitude of the three men towards their sister Caddy. Benjy longs for Caddy's love and attention, the love that he has never received from his mother. He senses Caddy's sexual sins and reproves her for them, and he somehow dimly perceives that her marriage will forever remove her from him. Quentin rests his faith in living upon an ideal of honor dependent upon Caddy's virginity; and though on many occasions his encounters with her are marked by hostility over her sexual adventures, he loves his sister and, like Benjy, finds in her a measure of substitution for the love that his mother never provides him. Benjy and Quentin could both have exclaimed that they never had a mother but they did have a sister. Jason hates Caddy because her illicit pregnancy has deprived him of the chance offered him by Herbert Head, and Jason transfers his hate of Caddy to her daughter. Caddy's marriage is for each of the brothers a disastrous event.

Of perhaps less significance but certainly notable is the relationship of these three Compson children with their father. Mr. Compson is generally kind to all of his children, and whatever parental care and guidance Benjy receives he gets from his father. Quentin has been particularly close to Mr. Compson, whom he quotes from the beginning to the end of his monologue. Caddy pleads with Quentin to take care of Benjy and their father. Although the bond of love among these characters is not strong enough to save them, their affection provides whatever faint sunshine illuminates the generally dark, grim, and tormented atmosphere of the Compson home.

Jason and Mrs. Compson present a startling contrast to the others. Whereas Benjy and Quentin have never had a mother but have a sister, Jason has always had a mother who favors him over her other children and recognizes his fundamental kinship with her. Mrs. Compson declares repeatedly that Jason has "always been my pride and joy" (p. 243; p. 281). "Thank God you are not a Compson," she says (p. 218; p. 249). The division in the family between the Compsons—Mr. Compson, Quentin, Caddy, and Benjy—on the one side and the Bascombs—Mrs. Compson, Jason, and Uncle Maury—on the other appears clearly in Quentin's monologue but perhaps even more openly in Mrs. Compson's charges against Quentin and Caddy. "'They were both that way,' she says, 'They would make interest with your father against me when I tried to correct them. . . . They deliberately shut me out of their lives. . . . It was always her and Quentin. They were always conspiring against me. . . .

71

They always looked on you [Jason] and me as outsiders, like they did your Uncle Maury" (p. 278; pp. 325–26). Mrs. Compson's remarks must be taken in context with her other actions. What little respect readers may have left for her after reading Benjy's and Quentin's monologues evaporates when they learn that she forbade Caddy to come home and her name to be spoken in the family and said of Caddy's daughter: "If she could grow up never to know that she had a mother, I would thank God" (p. 217; p. 247). Her repudiation of Caddy reminds the reader of Mrs. Compson's earlier repudiation of her son when she changed his name from Maury (a name in her own family) to Benjamin.

Just as Mrs. Compson refuses to permit Caddy's name to be spoken in the house, Jason always thinks of his sister as a "bitch" and despises her for cheating him of his chance in Herbert Head's bank. His revenge upon Caddy takes the form of embezzling her money and ruining her daughter. Jason is equally contemptuous of his brother Quentin who had his chance, went to Harvard, and there learned only "how to go for a swim at night without knowing how to swim" (p. 213; p. 243). About Benjy, Jason is even more caustic because Benjy poses a threat to appearances. Jason offers a number of suggestions about what to do with Benjy. "You can send Ben to the Navy I says or to the cavalry anyway, they use geldings in the cavalry. . . . Rent him out to a sideshow; there must be folks somewhere that would pay a dime to see him" (p. 214; p. 243). On another occasion, Jason says: "Why not send him down to Jackson [site of the state insane asylum]. He'll be happier there, with people like him. I says God knows there's little enough room for pride in this family, but it dont take much pride to not like to see a thirty year old man playing around the yard with a nigger boy, running up and down the fence and lowing like a cow whenever they play golf over there. I says if they'd sent him to Jackson at first we'd all be better off today" (p. 239; p. 276). And as Jason concludes his monologue, he is still thinking about Benjy: "I could hear the Great American Gelding snoring away like a planing mill. I read somewhere they'd fix men that way to give them women's voices. But maybe he didn't know what they'd done to him. . . . And if they'd just sent him on to Jackson while he was under the ether, he'd never have known the difference" (p. 280; pp. 328–29).

For his father, Jason exhibits neither love nor respect. "I never had time to . . . drink myself into the ground like Father," remarks Jason

(p. 199; p. 224). On another occasion, Jason recalls: "Father wouldn't even come down town anymore but just sat there all day with the decanter I could see the bottom of his nightshirt and his bare legs and hear the decanter clinking until finally T. P. had to pour it for him" (p. 250; p. 290). Significantly, Jason does not drink. He has little sympathy even for his mother's alleged illnesses, and he systematically deceives her on money matters. In the end, the reader understands that Jason stands alone in the Compson household, a selfish, vindictive, embittered man, who has even less faith in his fellowmen than his father had but is totally lacking in any of his father's redeeming traits.

Jason's monologue has been called the "least Southern" of all the narratives in the novel.[20] He seems more a portrait of the small-town businessman typical of any region in the country than a specifically Southern figure, and he has many affinities with Sinclair Lewis' satirical exposure of the type in *Babbitt* (1922) and with Lewis' other exposé of the same kind of character in *The Man Who Knew Coolidge* (1928). Considered in this light, Jason becomes a sweeping indictment of the genus he represents. His opinions become an index to his character.

Although he works in a farmer's supply store, Jason has little respect for traditional rural values. He mentions the harshness and low pay of farm life, but he actually has nothing but contempt for the farmer. "It's a good thing the Lord did something for this country," he remarks; "the folks that live on it never have" (p. 256; p. 298). Jason despises the small rural businessmen illustrated by Earl, the owner of the store. "What the hell chance has a man got," argues Jason, "tied down in a town like this and to a business like this. Why I could take his business in one year and fix him so he'd never have to work again, only he'd give it all away to the church or something" (p. 246; pp. 284–85). Jason quotes in derision Earl's statement that "a man never gets anywhere if fact and his ledgers dont square" (p. 247; p. 286). The comment, of course, applies with particular force to Jason's own accounts of his use of his mother's money and Caddy's money sent him in trust for Quentin.

Against Jews and Negroes, Jason expresses the prejudices common throughout the country in the 1920s. He makes his attitude clear in a brief conversation he has with a drummer or traveling salesman. Jason has just expressed himself on farmers who grow cotton and make little or no money from their crops.

"Let him make a big crop and it wont be worth picking; let him make a small crop and he wont have enough to gin. And what for? so a bunch of damn eastern jews, I'm not talking about men of the jewish religion," I says, "I've known some jews that were fine citizens. You might be one yourself," I says.

"No," he says, "I'm an American."

"No offense," I says. "I give every man his due, regardless of religion or anything else. I have nothing against jews as an individual," I says. "It's just the race. You'll admit that they produce nothing. They follow the pioneers into a new country and sell them clothes."

"You're thinking of Armenians," he says, "aren't you. A pioneer wouldn't have any use for new clothes."

"No offense," I says. "I dont hold a man's religion against him."

"Sure," he says, "I'm an American. My folks have some French blood, why I have a nose like this. I'm an American, all right."

"So am I," I says. "Not many of us left. What I'm talking about is the fellows that sit up there in New York and trim the sucker gamblers." (p. 209; pp. 237–38)

Jason's comments about Negroes are consistently virulent. Repeatedly he refers to having to "feed a whole damn kitchen full of niggers" (p. 204; p. 231). "What this country needs is white labour," asserts Jason and adds: "Let these damn trifling niggers starve for a couple of years, then they'd see what a soft thing they have" (p. 208; p. 237). In his opinion "the only place for them [Negroes] is in the field, where they'd have to work from sunup to sundown. They cant stand prosperity or an easy job. Let one stay around white people for a while and he's not worth killing" (pp. 267–68; p. 312). At times he combines Yankees with Negroes: "And then a Yankee will talk your head off about niggers getting ahead. Get them ahead, what I say. Get them so far ahead you cant find one south of Louisville with a blood hound" (p. 248; p. 288).

Jason's comments on women are predictable:

"I never promise a woman anything nor let her know what I'm going to give her. That's the only way to manage them. Always keep them guessing. If you cant think of any other way to surprise them, give them a bust in the jaw." (p. 211; p. 240)
"I dont know why it is I cant seem to learn that a woman'll do anything." (p. 260; p. 303)
"Like I say you cant do anything with a woman like that, if she's got it in her. If it's in her blood, you cant do anything with her. The only thing you can do is to get rid of her, let her go on and live with her own sort." (p. 250; p. 290)

A wide gap exists between the concept of the sexual relationship between man and woman as the expression of human love and Jason's preference for whores who treat intercourse as a commodity for sale. He says bluntly: "I've got every respect for a good honest whore" (p. 251; p. 291). Certainly no one would ever accuse Jason of being even a "half-baked Galahad." The measure of difference between the two brothers is expressed by Quentin's idealistic concept of his sister's honor and Jason's admiration for the businesslike Lorraine. Jason is a thoroughgoing naturalist—for him such concepts as love, honor, duty, pity, and idealism have no practical values as guides for living.

Few readers attempt to defend Jason's brutal actions, his lack of human values, or his cold mercantile philosophy. Those who do attempt to palliate these traits point to the generally loveless atmosphere of the Compson home, his loss of opportunity, and the deterioration of the other members of the family. No one can deny that the youngest child in the family turns out to be an idiot, his sister bears an illegitimate baby whose paternity even she does not know, another brother commits suicide, his father drinks himself to death, his mother (as Jason himself knows) repudiates three of her children and feigns illness to cover her failure as a person and a parent, his uncle has always been a sponge and a drunkard, and his niece has become a promiscuous slut. These are matters that Jason, who could be called a family historian, knows only too well. Nevertheless, they neither excuse his meanness nor mitigate his evilness. He poisons all human relationships just as he would like to poison the pigeons, swallows, and sparrows that fly about the courthouse. In making a final estimate of his character, one remembers the prediction of Colonel John Sartoris in *The Unvanquished* that generations to come would see a time of "pettifogging and doubtless chicanery" as well as his instinctive fear of the Snopeses. In the Appendix, Faulkner writes that Jason "competed and held his own with the Snopeses who took over the town following the turn of the century" (p. 16; p. 420). Jason is not a Snopes; but one wonders if Mr. Compson, Benjy, Quentin, and Caddy would recognize him as a Compson. Mrs. Compson said to Jason: "You are a Bascomb, despite your name" (p. 200; p. 225), and she should have known.

What keeps Jason from being an incredible literary monster is his ironic humor. His eighty-page monologue of furious outrage against all comers succeeds because it is a merciless exposure of his own villainy phrased in an irony and wit that become comic. Often Jason seems to act as his own straight man and to remember humorous and heavily ironical conversations with a particular relish. When Uncle Maury writes to ask for money to "invest," Mrs. Compson defends him to Jason: "'He's my own brother,' Mother says. 'He's the last Bascomb. When we are gone there wont be any more of them.'" Jason replies: "That'll be hard on somebody, I guess" (p. 242; p. 279). Other examples crowd almost every page. Mrs. Compson's speeches, as remembered by Jason, are full of irony. Talking about the possibility of Jason's marrying, Mrs. Compson says: "But I'll be gone soon and then you can take a wife but you'll never find a woman who is worthy of you . . ." (p. 264; p. 307). Jason's answer to his mother proves a suitably ironic counterthrust. "I says yes I could. You'd get right up out of your grave you know you would. I says no thank you I have all the women I can take care of now if I married a wife she'd probably turn out to be a hophead or something. That's all we lack in this family, I says" (p. 264; pp. 307–308). Throughout Jason's sarcastic recital of his woes, real and imagined, the portrait of himself as both satirist and object of the satire stands out brilliantly against the comic background of his frustrations, the reality of his meanness, and the poverty of his spirit.

The swift change from the sustained sound and fury of Jason's monologue to the calm opening of the final section provides welcome relief. Easter Sunday morning "dawned bleak and chill. A moving wall of grey light out of the northeast which . . . seemed to disintegrate into minute and venomous particles" (p. 281; p. 330). In view of what happens on this Easter, the dawn seems a fitting harbinger of the day to come.

On the surface, matters have not changed greatly in the Compson household since the day before. Dressed at first in her Sunday garments, Dilsey stands in the door of her cabin "with her myriad and sunken face lifted to the weather, and one gaunt hand flac-soled as the belly of a fish. . . . The gown fell gauntly from her shoulders, across her fallen breasts, then tightened upon her paunch and fell again. . . . She had been a big woman once but now her skeleton rose, draped loosely in unpadded skin . . . until only the indomitable skeleton was left rising like a ruin or a landmark" (pp. 281–82; pp. 330–31). After changing her clothes, she enters the kitchen in her blue gingham dress and with a song begins the routine of the day's chores. The kitchen clock strikes five, but Dilsey says "eight oclock" (p. 290; p. 342), the true time.

What follows documents from the authoritative view of the omniscient author the circumstances of the Compson household that the reader has already learned from the monologues. Upstairs, first Mrs. Compson then Jason complain about the servants and Benjy. After dressing him, Luster brings the thirty-three-year-old idiot downstairs: "a big man who appeared to have been shaped of some substance whose particles would not or did not cohere to one another or to the frame which supported it. His skin was dead looking and hairless; dropsical too, he moved with a shambling gait like a trained bear. His hair was pale and fine. It had been brushed smoothly down upon his brow. . . . His eyes were clear, of the pale sweet blue of cornflowers, his thick mouth hung open, drooling a little" (p. 290; p. 342). Overall, this description suggests decay, disintegration, almost putrefaction, and seems to epitomize the state to which the Compson house has descended.

The scene in which Jason discovers that Quentin has robbed him and climbed down the pear tree ranks as one of the finest passages in the novel. The tree is the same that years before Caddy had climbed to look into the parlor at Damuddy's funeral while her brothers looked up at her muddy drawers. For the Compson children, surely it has been the tree of knowledge, the knowledge of life and death, of bitterness and agony, without any compensating ecstasy and joy. On Easter Sunday it is "in bloom and the branches scraped and rasped against the house[,] and the myriad air, driving in the window, brought into the room the forlorn scent of the blossoms" (p. 298; p. 352). Jason calls the sheriff and orders him to have a car ready for the pursuit of Quentin.

Thus concludes the opening scene of the final section of the novel. Actually, with it the action or plot line of the novel has been completed. Quentin has had her revenge, taken back her own money, and fled with the tent show pitchman. Jason has rushed out in vain pursuit of her. Mrs. Compson lies in bed and beside her is the Bible she has no intention of reading. Benjy, who sits in his chair, "his big soft hands dangling between his knees, moaning faintly" (p. 301; p. 356), begins to weep, "a slow bellowing sound, meaningless and sustained" (p. 301; p. 356).

Caddy and her brother Quentin have long since gone, one dead in life and the other lying in the cemetery. This scene could be the end; but Faulkner will not leave the novel at this point.

The three brief scenes that follow seem appropriate, even necessary. The first takes place at the church, the second relates Jason's frantic efforts to recover his money, and the third shows Benjy being driven to the cemetery. Each has an important part in the conclusion of the Compson story.

A master storyteller sets the first scene. After deciding to take Benjy to church with her, Dilsey emerges from her cabin again dressed in her maroon cape and purple gown. The rain has stopped. "The air now drove out of the southeast, broken overhead into blue patches. Upon the crest of a hill beyond the trees and roofs and spires of town sunlight lay like a pale scrap of cloth, was blotted away. Upon the air a bell came, then as if at a signal, other bells took up the sound and repeated it" (p. 303; p. 358). The occasion is Easter Sunday, and the bells ring out to the faithful the promise of the risen Christ. Yet nowhere does Faulkner make a sharper contrast than between the joy of the Easter story and the fall of the house of Compson. "Ben wailed again, hopeless and prolonged. It was nothing. Just sound. It might have been all time and injustice and sorrow become vocal for an instant by a conjunction of planets" (pp. 303–304; p. 359). The words summarize the Compson story. Benjy follows them "obediently, wailing, that slow hoarse sound that ships make, that seems to begin before the sound itself has started, seems to cease before the sound itself has stopped" (p. 304; p. 359).

Along the way to the service Dilsey rebukes Frony and others who are embarrassed by the presence of a "loony." Inside the simple country church, she listens to the Reverend Shegog preach upon the theme—"the recollection and the blood of the Lamb" (p. 310; p. 367). Faulkner's account of the sermon suggests a mystical experience: "With his body he [Shegog] seemed to feed the voice that, succubus like, had fleshed its teeth in him. And the congregation seemed to watch with its own eyes while the voice consumed him, until he was nothing and they were nothing and there was not even a voice but instead their hearts were speaking to one another in chanting measures beyond the need for words" (p. 310; p. 367). Almost, Shegog becomes momentarily Jesus and as his attitude becomes "that of a serene, tortured crucifix that transcended its shabbiness and insignificance and made it of no moment, a long moaning expulsion of breath rose from them, and a woman's single soprano: 'Yes, Jesus!'" (p. 310; p. 368).

The Reverend Shegog bears witness: "I got de ricklickshun en de blood of de Lamb!" (p. 311; p. 368). The sermon that follows fittingly refers to the great moments in the biblical history of an oppressed race. Part of what he says foreshadows the hymn that gives title to *Go Down, Moses*. "Dey passed away in Egypt. . . . Dey'll come a time. Po sinner saying Let me lay down wid de Lawd, lemme lay down my load" (p. 311; pp. 368–69). He offers an apocalyptic vision of angels in heaven, and his voice rises to a crescendo as he speaks of the crucifixion. "I sees hit, breddren! I sees hit! Sees de blastin, blindin sight! I sees Calvary, wid de sacred trees, sees de thief en de murderer en de least of dese. . . . I hears de wailin of women en de evenin lamentations . . . dey done kilt Jesus; dey done kilt my Son!" (p. 312; p. 370). As the congregation responds, Shegog turns to the life everlasting. "I sees de resurrection en de light. . . . I sees de doom crack en hears de golden horns shoutin down de glory, en de arisen dead whut got de blood en de ricklickshun of de Lamb!" (pp. 312–13; p. 370). As Shegog preaches and the faithful in the congregation make their fervent responses, Benjy sits quietly, "rapt in his sweet blue gaze" (p. 313; p. 370) of evident approval.

As he ranges over human history in the Easter sermon, the Reverend Shegog says relatively little about the resurrection; rather, he extols Jesus for his suffering and death on the cross. Shegog's message is a vision of eternity in which time or history will no longer be relevant and in which the faithful will exchange earthly burdens for golden glories of heaven. Beneath his rhetoric, however, beats a strong note of commitment to order, individual responsibility, and the unity of man's life in the Christian religion. There will be, affirms the Negro preacher, a final reckoning for man, a crack of doom, and a judgment day at which the wrongs of every people will be righted and the faithful vindicated. For Shegog, as for Dilsey, faith has never failed and heaven will never be lost.

Under the compelling influence of this apocalyptic vision, Dilsey sits "bolt upright beside [Benjy], crying rigidly and quietly in the annealment and the blood of the remembered Lamb" (p. 313; pp. 370–71). As she walks homeward, she continues to weep. She has indeed seen "de darkness en de death everlastin upon de generations" (p. 312; p. 370), but she also believes in "de resurrection en de light" (p. 312; p. 370). Her cryptic comment, twice repeated, "I seed de beginnin, en now I sees de endin" (p. 313; p. 371), may be taken to apply to the Compsons' last generation. The house of Compson has ended. As they approach the old house, Benjy, in action appropriate to the symbolic overtones of the story, begins "to whimper again, and for a while all of them looked up the drive at the square, paintless house with its rotting portico" (p. 313; p. 372).

While Dilsey and Benjy are sitting in church receiving spiritual comfort in the Easter promise of a better life hereafter, twenty miles away Jason is furiously and frantically pursuing Quentin in the vain hope he will recover some of the money he had already stolen from her. The sheriff, who knows Jason well and who has ideas about the real owner of the money, refuses to help him. Jason's mad dash to Mottson proves futile. For his trouble he receives only a blow on the head and advice to "keep going." As he sits in his car, trying to find someone to drive him back to Jefferson, he hears the clock strike the half hour and watches people walking along in their Easter clothes. The reader cannot forget that at this moment Dilsey and Benjy are sitting in church listening to the Reverend Shegog's sermon about the Easter resurrection.

This final scene of Jason's vain attempts to recover the money he has stolen from his sister, his niece, and his mother seems essential to the novel, if only for the sake of completeness. Until this point, Jason had convicted himself through his ironical diatribes against his family, his associates, and his circumstances. For once the reader sees him as others would see him. There is poetic justice in his loss of the money, his physical beating, and his futile gestures; the threads of his part in the novel are neatly tied by this final episode.

But Faulkner knew better than to conclude the novel with Jason. For symmetry of form as well as wholeness of theme, Faulkner returned to the timeless and symbolical Benjy. One cannot imagine how the novelist could have succeeded better than this splendid finale. Just as the novel opens with Benjy moving along the fence, hearing the golfers in his pasture shouting "Caddie," and responding with forlorn moans, so the novel draws to a conclusion as Benjy on Easter Sunday returns to the fence and hears a sound like Caddy's name once more. Luster, to whom

Easter means little and in whom there appears a streak of meanness that would do credit to Jason, makes matters worse by whispering: "Caddy! Beller now. Caddy! Caddy! Caddy!" (p. 331; p. 394). On this occasion, however, Faulkner makes clear the implications or symbology of Benjy's cries. As Dilsey tries to comfort Benjy, Faulkner writes a passage quoted earlier: "But he [Benjy] bellowed slowly, abjectly, without tears; the grave hopeless sound of all voiceless misery under the sun" (p. 332; p. 395).

In an effort to calm Benjy, Dilsey decides to send him to the cemetery. Although she has little confidence in Luster, she must rely upon him to drive the carriage. As they approach the square, "where the Confederate soldier gazed with empty eyes beneath his marble hand into wind and weather" (p. 335; p. 399), Luster sees Jason's car and a group of Negroes, determines to impress them, and turns left instead of right.[21] Accustomed to turning right at the monument, Benjy reacts instantaneously: "For an instant Ben sat in an utter hiatus. Then he bellowed. Bellow on bellow, his voice mounted, with scarce interval for breath. There was more than astonishment in it, it was horror; shock; agony eyeless, tongueless; just sound . . ." (p. 335; p. 400). Jason rushes to the carriage and turns Queenie's head around in the proper direction. As her feet begin "to clop-clop steadily again," Benjy becomes silent. "His eyes were empty and blue and serene again as cornice and façade flowed smoothly once more from left to right; post and tree, window and doorway, and signboard, each in its ordered place" (p. 336; p. 401). Although Faulkner offers no explanation, clearly Benjy, despite his handicaps, knows that without order, right and wrong, in the universe, life can only hold speechless horror and agony.

Great works of art must not simply be, they must mean. In many respects, Faulkner has chosen to offer his readers the "being" and left to them the meaning. One can hardly read this novel without continually stopping to ask himself the meaning, the why, the implication of this or that passage; and probably so long as this work retains its vitality, no final answers will be made. The "being"—one might say the life—revealed in *The Sound and the Fury* is as complicated as actual life, the human condition itself, that every man must interpret according to his perceptions. For this reason, the meanings tentatively suggested here are not proposed as the only or the absolute reading of Faulkner's work of art.

Essentially, what is this novel about? Some clue may be inferred from the familiar lines in *Macbeth*:

> To-morrow, and to-morrow, and to-morrow,
> Creeps in this petty pace from day to day
> To the last syllable of recorded time;
> And all our yesterdays have lighted fools
> The way to dusty death. Out, out, brief candle!
> Life's but a walking shadow, a poor player
> That struts and frets his hour upon the stage
> And then is heard no more. It is a tale
> Told by an idiot, full of sound and fury,
> Signifying nothing. (*Macbeth* V, v, 19–28)

The more one thinks about the book in terms of this passage, the closer the relationship between the two appears to be. Shakespeare's emphasis upon time (history) parallels the stress that Faulkner places upon it in every section of the work. "Out, out brief candle! / Life's but a walking shadow" could apply directly to Quentin, who is indeed a walking shadow and a poor player in life. Both stories are told at least in part by an idiot; and the entire novel, especially Jason's monologue, is full of sound and fury. Finally, if "signifying nothing" means futility, the phrase seems applicable to the activities of the Compson family.

But Faulkner's novel is more than merely an illustration of this passage from Shakespeare's play. On its most literal level, *The Sound and the Fury* is a book about the history of a remarkable family which had its origin in Scotland. Around the middle of the eighteenth century, one of its members emigrated to the Carolinas, and his descendants pushed westward to Mississippi. After several generations in which its members served as leaders, professional men, even governors, the Compsons began to experience failure. The downhill progress of the family became evident in Brigadier General Jason Lycurgus Compson II, but far more pronounced in his son Jason Compson III and his four children. The story Faulkner tells relates primarily to these last two generations.

No one would dispute the fact of the decline of the Compsons in these two generations. Mr. Compson, whose loss of faith in any purposeful human activity has negated even his desire to live, deliberately hastens his death through excessive drinking. Mrs. Compson seems always to have been a whining hypochondriac. Caring only for appearances, she disowns her daughter, insulates herself from her idiot son, refuses to be a mother to her eldest son, and acknowledges as "her own" only the son whose meanness, materialism, and greed have scarcely been equaled either in life or in art. Oblivious to the irony of her attitude, she would prefer to leave home with Jason and abandon Mr. Compson and her other children. Although Mr. Compson possesses some redeeming qualities, he must, because of his attitude toward life, bear much of the blame for the failure of his marriage and the failures of his children.

The children of this loveless marriage live lives of suffering, desperation, and failure. Maury (Benjamin) never develops mentally beyond the age of three. Despite her courage and efforts to help her idiot brother and her daughter, whom she conceived out of wedlock, Candace (Caddy) becomes a woman little better than a whore. After concluding that idealism cannot sustain purposeful activity, Quentin commits suicide; and Jason, the "sane" Compson, rages through a life so selfishly materialistic that he prefers a "good honest whore" to a wife. With this lost generation, the house of Compson disappears; there are no survivors to carry on the Compson name.

Few can read the record of these warped, twisted, unhappy lives and not seek the reasons for their plight. Why must these things be? Is it, as one character says, that there is a curse on the Compsons? Is "blood" the cause? Were the Compsons, like the Sartorises, unable to cope with the years of pettifogging and chicanery foreseen by old Colonel Sartoris? The questions crowd upon one another. To what extent did the Compsons dig their own graves? Caddy and her daughter say they are bad and cannot help it. Are they victims of forces beyond their control? What about Benjy? Is he a judgment upon the Compsons? Each of the Compson children seems to present a special case, yet one searches for a root or common cause that would explain their failures in living.

Henry Adams' postulate may provide the best clue to the meaning of the Compson experience. Like many of their contemporaries in modern life, the Compsons have lost faith in something outside of themselves that would provide them with a meaningful purpose for living. Without this faith, heaven is truly lost, and the Compsons have no need for a resurrection; no resurrection would help them. They already live the *now* in a timeless hell, and their history documents the tragedy of human life lived without the sustaining power of faith.

One may reach the same conclusion by noting that the Compsons live without love. Almost without exception, their lives turn inward upon the self. Sexual love has been reduced to physical lust. Love would bring faith and responsible action within the family and within the community; but the Compsons never reach this fundamental premise, and they recognize no external sanctions for moral action.

Benjy is almost as much a symbol as a person. His is a private world; adequate communication, difficult for anyone, he can never achieve. Purposeful activity is beyond him, yet he appears to love and that he suffers Faulkner leaves no doubt. Benjy symbolizes the tragic condition of man, the paradoxical fact that man must suffer, though suffering can only be deplored. The afflicted boy becomes the medium through which Faulkner suggests that there are moments in the life of everyone when he cannot articulate his own suffering, and the failure to communicate one's feelings makes his aloneness in the universe all the more painful. There is something of Benjy in the human condition itself.

Readers have always admired Dilsey. Particularly appealing have been her calm statement that "I does de bes I can" (p. 332; p. 396), her unselfish devotion to white and Negro alike, her courage in standing up for right, and her religious faith that gives direction to her life. These qualities provide a startling contrast to the sickness of character that pervades the Compson household. She offers the reader a good example of the wayfaring Christian who endures the vicissitudes of this life and looks for salvation in the next. That the resurrection is for her, Dilsey knows. She has no doubt that her name will be in the Book, "writ out" (p. 77; p. 71). Sustained by faith, she can act with purpose, and she can endure life, even with the Compsons. Whatever contrast she offers to the sick Compsons, Dilsey does not provide a way out of their plight. Although she may serve them and deplore their evil, she cannot bring them salvation. More sophisticated individuals like Mr. Compson and Quentin are not likely to adopt her simple faith. Faulkner's decision, however, to place Dilsey and Benjy side by side in the church scene at the conclusion of the novel invites speculation that the novelist attached considerable importance to such an unintellectual affirmation of faith, life, and order. Dilsey believes, not in man, but in God.

One cannot be so certain about Benjy. At least in this life, he cannot participate in the struggles of the believing, wayfaring Christians whom Dilsey represents. He has never had a properly functioning mind, and he is disqualified from life's primary activities. Benjy must ever be considered a special case. Nevertheless, Dilsey calls him "de Lawd's chile" (p. 333; p. 396), a judgment that confirms his uniqueness and underscores the appropriateness of his demand, in the final paragraph of the novel, for an ordered existence.

Neither admiration for Dilsey's Christian faith nor compassion for Benjy's plight, however, should obscure the central focus of the novel. The subject of *The Sound and the Fury*, succinctly stated, is the deterioration of the Compson family in its final two generations. Faulkner may imply that the causes of their decline are at least partially rooted in hereditary weaknesses and failures transmitted since Culloden from one generation to another, but he concentrates upon rendering the final dissolution of the family in the persons of Jason III, his wife Caroline Bascomb, and their four children. Although the degree of their individual responsibility for their plight may be debated, as a family they exhibit an almost total failure in personal relationships with each other, an unwillingness to engage in purposeful activity outside the family, and an appalling degree of self-centeredness that parallels their inability to conform to any standard of conduct external to themselves. In rendering their plight, Faulkner has made a strong negative statement, but he has also made a searching commentary upon modern times.

CHAPTER III

The Way of Naturalism

As I Lay Dying

IF ONE considers the first version of *Sanctuary*, which Faulkner began in January, 1929, and completed the following May, as substantially the novel published early in February, 1931, its immediate successor is *As I Lay Dying*, published four months earlier on October 6, 1930. Yet, in view of Faulkner's extensive rewriting of the galley proofs of *Sanctuary*, *As I Lay Dying* has a very real claim to a place in his canon immediately after *The Sound and the Fury*. Faulkner began *As I Lay Dying* on October 25, 1929, while he was employed on the nightshift at the powerhouse of the University of Mississippi, a supervisory job that mainly required him to be on the premises.[1] He finished the handwritten manuscript and dated it at the bottom of page 107, Oxford, Mississippi, December 11, 1929; and by January 12, 1930, he had, as was his custom, typed it in preparation for sending a finished copy to Hal Smith, to whom the work is dedicated.

Years later, while a writer-in-residence at the University of Virginia, Faulkner spoke repeatedly of the writing of *As I Lay Dying* as a tour de force. "I took this family," he said, "and subjected them to the two greatest catastrophes which man can suffer—flood and fire, that's all. That was simple *tour de force*. That was written in six weeks without changing a word because I knew from the first where that was going." At another session, he declared, "I knew when I put down the first word what the last word would be." Of all his novels, he thought it required the "least rewriting," in part, perhaps, because of its brevity; it is the shortest of his major works.[2] Faulkner's comments about the revisions, however, must be understood relatively, since the handwritten manuscript and the final typed copy reveal numerous deletions, changes, and minor revisions.

Among the most notable additions is the much-discussed sentence about the log that "surged up out of the water and stood for an instant upright upon that surging and heaving desolation like Christ."[3] Generally Faulkner's polishing of the *As I Lay Dying* manuscript rarely extended beyond the choice of individual words or the rewriting of phrases. Compared to the very extensive revisions that many of his novels underwent before publication—*Sartoris*, *Sanctuary*, *Absalom, Absalom!*, *The Unvanquished*, and *Go Down, Moses* are examples—*As I Lay Dying* seems to have been written in a single burst of creative energy.

In referring to the book as a tour de force, Faulkner may have had several matters in mind. He had written it very quickly—forty-seven days for the handwritten manuscript and an additional month for the typing. The plot, which deals with the adversities suffered by the Bundren family while taking the body of the mother from their home in the county to Jefferson for burial, moves for the most part in a straight line, like the action of the traditional blueprinted novel. That a writer of Faulkner's ability could narrate it in a few weeks' time is not surprising. What is remarkable is the form in which Faulkner cast the story; and when he called the work a tour de force, he may have had in mind the form more than the rapidity of composition.

As I Lay Dying consists of fifty-nine narrations or monologues, averaging about two pages in length, delivered by the seven members of the Bundren family and eight "outsiders." Although Faulkner never explained how he "invented" the form, many of its features have respectable literary antecedents. Its kinship with the Elizabethan stage soliloquy is readily apparent, since in both play and story the character's private speech reveals whatever portions of his experiences, thoughts, and motives the writer wishes to convey to the audience. The device is particularly useful, since the soliloquy or monologue may be straightforward, ironical, or satirical in tone. In the nineteenth century, such poets as Browning and Tennyson took the soliloquy out of the theatre and refined it into single poems designed to reveal the complexities of the speaker's character and at the same time to narrate an incident or story. Faulkner's monologues perform very much the same function in *As I Lay Dying*.

In 1915, however, Edgar Lee Masters, drawing upon the stage soliloquy, its refinements at the hands of the nineteenth-century writers, particularly Browning, and the Greek Anthology, published in *Spoon River*

Anthology more than two hundred short poems purporting to be epitaphs or speeches from characters possessing the immunities that only death can give. In these monologues, Masters stressed the psychological rather than the physical aspects of the speakers. Instead of attempting to write entire biographies, Masters usually concentrated upon a single but revealing situation. Many of the poems had been published earlier as separate entities, but when brought together in loosely arranged groupings, they seemed related. Often the monologue of one character provides the reader with important information about other characters, and the same incident is related from different points of view. Thus, the interconnections among the monologues allow the reader to make his own judgments of the relative validity of a specific individual's narrative. Despite the looseness of the form and its lack of a unifying, sustained plot line, the reader concludes the book possessing a comprehensive grasp of the Spoon River community. In the *Domesday Book*, published in 1920, Masters employed a similar technique to unravel the intricacies of Elenor Murray's character and the circumstances of her death. Near the beginning of the poem occurs a passage that seems almost to parallel Faulkner's intentions for Addie Bundren:

> Shall not I as a coroner in America,
> Inquiring of a woman's death, make record
> Of lives which have touched hers, what lives she touched;
> And how her death by surest logic touched
> This life or that, was cause of causes, proved
> The event that made events? [4]

In *The New Spoon River Anthology*, published in 1924, Masters continued to utilize the monologue-epitaph form that had been vastly successful in his earlier books. Although for American readers the immense fascination of the original *Spoon River Anthology* waned in the 1920s, Masters' work exerted a distinct influence upon Sherwood Anderson and probably William Faulkner. Anderson greatly admired *Spoon River Anthology*, which he read immediately after its publication, but he never conceded any influence from Masters. That influence, nevertheless, may be seen in the "new looseness of form" in *Winesburg, Ohio*, in Anderson's statements about "lives flowing past each other," [5] and in his use of earlier published individual stories to form a novel. Whether Masters' Spoon River monologue technique, as well as the ideas voiced by Anderson, passed directly from Masters to Faulkner or, as is more likely, from Masters and Anderson to Faulkner cannot be firmly established. Anderson's comment about "lives flowing past each other" can be applied to Faulkner's portrayal of the Bundren family, the lives of whose individual members touch but remain isolated—as was Addie Bundren's in life—throughout the journey to Jefferson. One might add that Anderson's insistence that *Winesburg, Ohio* was a novel written according to a "new looseness of form" has a parallel in Faulkner's belief that *The Unvanquished*, *The Hamlet*, and *Go Down, Moses* should be called novels rather than collections of stories.[6]

In *As I Lay Dying*, Faulkner retained many of the traditional features of the monologue as practiced by the dramatists and the poets, but he turned them to his own ends and did not hesitate to make innovations of his own. The "epitaph" or after-death setting of Masters' monologues survives in Addie Bundren's monologue positioned in the novel four or five days after she was put in her coffin and in the adjacent narratives of Cora and Whitfield that also seem reminiscent of Masters' work. Faulkner followed Masters' precedent in using multiple points of view to tell the story, and he kept the monologues brief. He continued Masters' emphasis upon the psychology of the characters, though Faulkner's work shows the effect of more sophisticated theories about thought processes and children's mentalities. Like Masters, Faulkner sought to remove himself from the narratives. In this respect, he was more successful than Masters, since Masters' critics maintained that the speech and opinions of the characters in *Spoon River Anthology* sounded very much like their creator. In *As I Lay Dying*, no author's voice or representative can be identified. The shift from poetry to prose seems hardly a significant alteration, since Masters' irregular, unrhymed free verse appears to many readers more like chopped-up prose than poetry, and Faulkner's prose often approaches the level of poetry.

Faulkner developed Masters' brief poetical monologues into a highly effective and very flexible device for telling a story, a very different instrument from the lengthy Joycean and Freudian monologues of *The Sound and the Fury*. Many of the monologues of *As I Lay Dying* are straightforward narratives, Faulkner making no effort to render the stream of consciousness. Even when Darl is recounting Addie's death—an event Darl can only imagine since he is miles away from the scene—the effect is not that of an interior monologue like Quentin Compson's but that of a narrator speaking in the first person, and the use of italics identifies clearly the change of scenes and the shift to Darl's thoughts. The same appearance of traditional first-person narrative often arises from the speeches of Anse, Cash, and such outsiders as Samson, Armstid, Moseley, MacGowan, Peabody, and Vernon Tull. The interior monologues Faulkner reserved primarily for the unstable members of the Bundren family, Darl, Vardaman, and Dewey Dell, though frequently their narratives contain little or no evidence of thought transcription. The result of Faulkner's careful and sparing use of the stream of consciousness in *As I Lay Dying* is a much more readable novel than *The Sound and the Fury*.

Faulkner's signal accomplishment in *As I Lay Dying* is to make the monologue include both narrative and commentary simultaneously without involvement from the author. Thus, the movement of the action from the making of the coffin, to Addie's death, and to the incidents of the journey to Jefferson is narrated through the consciousness of the speakers; and at the same time the private motives and characters of the Bundrens and their friends are firmly established. Faulkner can be highly selective in what information he supplies the reader. He can cut into the journey, for example, at any moment without having to account for a lapse in the narrative. In Addie's monologue, very dramatically but certainly abruptly, he gives the reader an account of her life severely limited yet sufficient to establish her attitude towards living and to define her relationships to those who counted in her life. By using the monologue form in this manner, Faulkner forces the reader to make his own judgments, since the author poses only as recorder.

Faulkner handled his form loosely, not bothering to resolve or correct discrepancies and inconsistencies that would have troubled craftsmen like Hawthorne or Henry James and that continue to irritate attentive readers. A notable example is the handling of time. Although Faulkner seemingly provides very precise notations of the days upon which the events of the story occur, they are actually inconsistent in several places. For example, Vernon Tull says that Addie *"laid there three days in that box"* and *"on the third day they . . . loaded her into the wagon and started"* (pp. 86–87). But at sundown on the first day of the Bundrens' journey, Samson says that Addie had been "dead in a box four days" (p. 110). Samson's statement would be consistent with the subsequent remark by

Moseley's clerk, Albert, on the fifth day of the journey, that the body had been "dead eight days" (p. 193) and with Darl's comment on the following day that she had "already waited nine days" to be buried (p. 224).

Very likely, Faulkner intended to keep the narrative basically in the present and as often as possible to make the monologues simultaneous with the developing action. The novel begins in this fashion: "Jewel and I come up from the field." Although many of the monologues retain this type of present-narration, inevitably the need to introduce past events to explain the present led Faulkner to shift the tense to the past and to resort to a form of flashback. (Earlier in *The Sound and the Fury*, he had solved this problem in Benjy's narrative by making all time equally present to Benjy's consciousness.) Darl's second section contains a good example: "'Where's Jewel?' pa says. When I was a boy I first learned . . ." (p. 10). In Dewey Dell's account of her dream, Faulkner uses the same technique but adds italics to help the reader: "I rose and took the knife from the streaming fish still hissing and I killed Darl. *When I used to sleep with Vardaman I had a nightmare once*" (p. 115).

The past seems essential to the full development of the story, but one wonders if the instances of events anticipated or mentioned out of order are not simply slips that should have been corrected. For example, at a point in the story when Addie still lies dying, Cora Tull complains that Addie was "not cold in the coffin before they were carting her forty miles away to bury her" (p. 21), yet more than forty pages later Cora announces Addie's death: "It's Addie Bundren. She's gone at last" (p. 65). Likewise, in a passage narrated in the present and mainly devoted to the preparations for the funeral and to Whitfield's sermon, Vernon Tull—the type shifts abruptly to italics—declares that Addie "*laid there three days in that box*" and repeats Cora's remark that the Bundrens will have to make a forty mile journey (pp. 86–87). Near the end of the novel, as the Bundrens are just arriving in Jefferson, Cash says that Anse "pulled up at Mrs Bundren's" (p. 225), yet Cash would have had no reason to know that Anse was contemplating marriage or that the second Mrs. Bundren was living in this house. Cash refers to her as Mrs. Bundren twice in this section.

Still other monologues take place at unspecified times yet contain necessary information about the on-going action. Tull's section, in which he describes the overturning of the wagon and loss of the mules in the river, occupies its proper chronological place in the plot, but the opening phrase, "When I told Cora how Darl jumped out of the wagon" (p. 145), indicates plainly that this monologue was spoken at some later date after Tull returned home. No specific time is assigned to Cora's section beginning "One day we were talking" (p. 158) or to Addie's monologue which follows Cora's immediately and is inserted in the story on the second day of the journey, five days after she died. And Whitfield's narrative, which completes the group, is also undated and out of place. Artistically, there seem to be no compelling reasons for these sudden shifts in the time sequence of the narrative, though they may reflect the speed with which Faulkner wrote the novel.[7]

Troublesome as Faulkner's difficulties in handling time may be, they are probably not so apparent to the reader as his mingling of highly sophisticated metaphors and vocabulary with the country speech of farmers. For the most part, the narratives of Anse, Cash, Dewey Dell, Vernon and Cora Tull, Samson, Armstid, and Whitfield are phrased in language and syntax appropriate to their status in life. The speeches of Anse, the Tulls, and Whitfield are laced with metaphors from the vocabulary of religious fundamentalism. Cash sounds always like a carpenter; Dewey Dell, with one or two exceptions,[8] talks like a country girl. Samson and Armstid reflect the speech of country folk. Addie's narrative shows that she has been better educated than the others. But the narratives of Vardaman and Darl, who between them narrate about half of the volume, often seem far different from what might reasonably be expected from persons of their background and experiences. Vardaman, for example, who has caught a fish "nigh long as he is" (p. 29), is still a very young child fascinated by the prospect of seeing a toy train in a store window. Adult experiences are beyond his comprehension. But in his monologues, Faulkner juxtaposes a child's vocabulary and pattern of sentences with those of a sophisticated adult. Speaking of his fish, Vardaman says: "Hit was a-layin right there on the ground. And now she's gittin ready to cook hit" (p. 55). This speech is followed immediately by a stream-of-consciousness passage that begins in a child's fashion but at once becomes something far beyond the simple thought processes of a child. "It is dark. I can hear wood, silence: I know them. But not living sounds, not even him. It is as though the dark were resolving him out of his integrity, into an unrelated scattering of components—snuffings and stampings;

smells of cooling flesh and ammoniac hair; an illusion of a co-ordinated whole of splotched hide and strong bones."

In Darl's monologues, the incongruity between the character and his speech is even more startling to the reader than in Vardaman's. Faulkner represents Darl as a rural farmer in his late twenties. To him, Faulkner assigns almost twice as many narratives as to anyone else. The absence of rural colloquialisms, mistakes in grammar, and oversimplified sentence structure lifts him above the level of the others, but no one can deny that he is intended to be a country boy without much education. Yet his vocabulary is astounding, and his speeches abound with phrases probably never spoken by any farmer nor ever heard on any farm in the South. In passages of straightforward narrative, he speaks of wood chips that look "like random smears of soft pale paint on a black canvas" (p. 71), the front of a barn as "the conical façade with the square orifice of doorway broken only by the square squat shape of the coffin on the sawhorses like a cubistic bug" (pp. 208–209), Jewel and Gillespie "like two figures in a Greek frieze" (p. 211), and "the dissolving proscenium of the doorway" to the barn (p. 211). Elsewhere, he records the progress of the Bundrens' journey: "We go on, with a motion so soporific, so dreamlike as to be uninferant of progress" (p. 101). Dewey Dell's dress, Darl says, "shapes for the dead eyes of three blind men those mammalian ludicrosities which are the horizons and the valleys of the earth" (p. 156). He is particularly responsive to the sights and sounds of nature. "The sun," he observes, "an hour above the horizon, is poised like a bloody egg upon a crest of thunderheads; the light has turned copper: in the eye portentous, in the nose sulphurous, smelling of lightning" (p. 39); and in another passage, he declares: "The air smells like sulphur. Upon the impalpable plane of it their shadows form as upon a wall, as though like sound they had not gone very far away in falling but had merely congealed for a moment, immediate and musing" (p. 72). The disparity between Darl's status as a poor-white farm boy and his highly artistic and sophisticated language takes away significantly from the realism of *As I Lay Dying*. Faulkner may have found himself trapped by the form he had adopted. An author who functions only as recorder of his characters' monologues must rely wholly upon their speeches for the narration and meaning of his work. Either he must limit his narrative to the language consistent with their education and experiences, or he must allow them the words and metaphors necessary to express the subtleties of feeling he wishes to ascribe to them. In the case of Darl, and to an extent Vardaman, Faulkner chose the latter alternative. As a result, the work gained in beauty and significance but lost in verisimilitude.

Useful as Darl is in the narration of the story, he is secondary to Anse, who is the motivating force in the plot. Faulkner probably never wrote a more thorough characterization, though in the end Anse remains something of an enigma that the reader must solve for himself. A tall, humped-over man, Anse's physical appearance is unattractive, even repulsive. Darl, whose harsh descriptions scarcely conceal his dislike of his father, repeatedly calls attention to Anse's shabby, unkempt exterior that seems to coincide with his inner character. His feet are badly splayed, and his shoes look "as though they had been hacked with a blunt axe out of pig-iron" (p. 11). He has lost his teeth. When he dips snuff "his mouth collapses in slow repetition," and the stubble on his unshaven face gives its lower part "that appearance that old dogs have" (p. 17). Later on, Darl again describes his father: "Pa lifts his face, slack-mouthed, the wet black rim of snuff plastered close along the base of his gums" (p. 72). A measure of Darl's contempt for Anse is apparent in the statement, which Dewey Dell later repeats (p. 25), that "He [Anse] was sick once from working in the sun when he was twenty-two years old, and he tells people that if he ever sweats, he will die. I suppose he believes it" (p. 17).

Darl's remark about his father's laziness receives support from Anse's conduct throughout the story and from the testimony of the neighbors. Although he is present in almost every scene in the novel, Anse does virtually nothing that requires physical exertion. For years he has given the appearance of helplessness so effectively that his children and his friends have done his work for him. Even when they know they are being taken, they continue. As Tull offers to help with Anse's corn, he says, "Like most folks around here, I done holp him so much already I cant quit now" (p. 32). Armstid expresses the common irritation of the neighbors: "Because be durn if there aint something about a durn fellow like Anse that seems to make a man have to help him, even when he knows he'll be wanting to kick himself next minute" (p. 183). Cora Tull also illustrates the neighbors' attitude. When the Tulls are about to leave Anse's home, Anse reaches for his shoes. Almost as if by reflex action,

Cora says at once, "Now Mr Bundren . . . dont you get up now" (p. 31); but when Vernon tells her about the wagon overturning in the river, Cora shrewdly remarks: "I notice Anse was too smart to be on it a-tall" (p. 145), and a moment later she declares: "If he had been a man, he would a been there instead of making his sons do what he dursn't."

Among the neighbors, Anse strikes a pose of a man who must be helped for reasons of fundamental, Christian, human kindness; but from his children, he harshly demands whatever they have or can produce for his own use. After Jewel had bought his horse by working at night throughout the summer, Anse blames him because he has "taken the work from your flesh and blood and bought a horse with it" (pp. 128–29). During the journey to Jefferson, Anse robs Cash of his money, barters away Jewel's horse in part payment for Flem Snopes's team of mules, and takes away Dewey Dell's abortion money to buy his teeth. She considers him a thief. Despite warnings from the town marshal and protests from Cash, Anse insists upon encasing Cash's leg in cement because "we done bought it now" (p. 197); and to protect himself from being sued for damages because of the fire in Gillespie's barn, Anse helps to capture Darl so that he can be committed to the insane asylum in Jackson.

Anse, however, is not without his defenses. In the beginning, rather comically, he blames his misfortunes upon the road in front of his house, "where every bad luck prowling can find it and come straight to my door, charging me taxes on top of it" (p. 35). Illogically but characteristically, he also blames the road for Darl's queerness and for Addie's sickness. He has heard men "cuss their luck, and right, for they were sinful men" (p. 37). But Anse has "done no wrong to be cussed by." He knows he is not religious, and he admits that he has done things "neither better nor worse than them that pretend otherlike," but he knows also that "Old Marster will care for me as for ere a sparrow that falls." His self-righteousness is equalled only by his self-pity. On several occasions, Anse laments that he is a "luckless man" (p. 81) or a "misfortunate man" (pp. 150, 155). In a speech heavy with irony he complains that "nowhere in this sinful world can a honest, hardworking man profit" (p. 104) and blames the townspeople for his misfortunes: "It takes them that runs the stores in the towns, doing no sweating, living off of them that sweats. It aint the hardworking man, the farmer" (p. 104). Anse's defenses sound hollow because they are contrary to fact. Basically he is a parasite living off his family and friends.

So far as the journey to Jefferson is concerned, the issue ultimately turns upon Anse's relationship to Addie. Anse justifies the journey on the basis of his "promise" to her that he would take her body back to Jefferson for burial with her family. But the question the reader must eventually decide for himself is whether Anse undertakes the journey out of a promise to Addie or out of his desire for a new set of teeth. Throughout the novel, Anse harps upon his "promise" to Addie. Often he refers to her as if she were directing the enterprise. "I give her my promise. Her mind is set on it" (p. 109; cf. p. 133), he says. At other times, he adds a religious tone: "I give her my promised word in the presence of the Lord" (p. 119). "I give her my word. . . . It is sacred on me . . . she will bless you in heaven" (p. 133). He keeps the children in line by such remarks as "It aint right. . . . It's a flouting of the dead" (p. 96); "it wouldn't look right, him [Jewel] prancing along on a durn circus animal and her wanting us all to be in the wagon with her that sprung from her flesh and blood" (p. 99); and *"She'll want it so. She was ever a particular woman"* (p. 87). In her monologue, Addie says, "when Darl was born I asked Anse to promise to take me back to Jefferson when I died" (pp. 164–65), but Anse peremptorily retorts: "Nonsense" (p. 165). The passage raises a serious doubt that Anse ever made such a promise. Doubts about Anse's commitment to Addie are further increased by the fact that in her last moments he violates his promise to keep "the team here [at home] and ready" (pp. 17, 18) in order to make three dollars for one more load. Nowhere in the novel does Anse appear to be a man of strict adherence to ethical principles.

Anse's neighbors and friends view the journey as anything but heroic. Rather, they see it as an outrage. Although Vernon Tull may misjudge the motive for taking Addie to Jefferson, he suspects that the actual reason for the journey is not the fulfillment of Anse's "promise" to Addie. Seeing Anse, "humped, mournful, looking at the empty road" (p. 133), Tull voices his opinion: "Just going to town. Bent on it. They would risk the fire and the earth and the water and all just to eat a sack of bananas." Cora believes that Anse is "flouting the will of God" (p. 21) and that a woman's place is with her husband and children "alive or dead" (p. 22). Samson speaks from the practical point of view: "you've got to respect the dead themselves, and a woman that's been dead in a box four days, the best way to respect her is to get her into the ground as quick as you can" (p. 110). His wife, Rachel, is vehement: "It's a outrage. . . . A outrage" (p. 111). Twice Lula Armstid makes the same comment: "It's a outrage. . . . He should be lawed for treating her so" (p. 178; cf. p. 179).

In evaluating Anse's relationship to Addie, the reader must take into account the testimony of those who describe his appearances at her deathbed and funeral. Most of the information comes from Darl, and he very much distrusts his father's sincerity. In the monologue in which he imagines Addie's death, Darl hints that Anse's deviousness stems really from a scheming, predatory intelligence. Darl envisions Anse as leaning above her bed in the twilight, "his humped silhouette partaking of that owl-like quality of awry-feathered, disgruntled outrage within which lurks a wisdom too profound or too inert for even thought" (p. 48). Later, as the coffin is being finished in the rain, Darl repeats his doubts. After describing the rain streaming slowly down Anse's face, Darl adds that "it is as though upon a face carved by a savage caricaturist a monstrous burlesque of all bereavement flowed" (pp. 73–74). In Darl's view, Anse's reaction to Addie's death is one of personal outrage: "he looks up at the sky with that expression of dumb and brooding outrage and yet of vindication, as though he had expected no less" (p. 73). But Darl's most damaging accusation against Anse occurs near the end of his monologue announcing Addie's death. For the full effect of the final sentence, which undercuts all that has gone before and leaves no doubt about what Darl thought of his father's motives, the passage must be read in its entirety.

> Pa stands over the bed, dangle-armed, humped, motionless. He raises his hand to his head, scouring his hair, listening to the saw. He comes nearer and rubs his hand, palm and back, on his thigh and lays it on her face and then on the hump of quilt where her hands are. He touches the quilt as he saw Dewey Dell do, trying to smoothe it up to the chin, but disarranging it instead. He tries to smoothe it again, clumsily, his hand awkward as a claw, smoothing at the wrinkles which he made and which continue to emerge beneath his hand with perverse ubiquity, so that at last he desists, his hand falling to his side and stroking itself again, palm and back, on his thigh. The sound of the saw snores steadily into the room. Pa breathes with a quiet, rasping sound, mouthing the snuff against his gums. "God's will be done," he says. "Now I can get them teeth." (p. 51)

Darl has probed the depths of Anse's character and exposed the inner drives that account for his eagerness to undertake a journey that seems decidedly at odds with his customary behavior.

On several occasions in the novel, Darl's emphasis upon Anse's desire for a new set of teeth receives support from Anse himself. While Addie lies dying, he vehemently denies having sent for Dr. Peabody because he will have to pay a fee for the visit, and Anse quotes Peabody as agreeing that he was not sent for. But earlier, in Darl's monologue, Darl quotes Anse as saying: "It's that durn doctor, liable to come at any time. I couldn't get word to him till so late" (p. 18). And in Peabody's monologue, the doctor says, "When Anse finally sent for me of his own accord . . ." (p. 40). At first the doctor does not wish to go, because he thinks that Addie's death would bring her release from Anse, but Peabody later realizes that "if it had finally occurred to Anse himself that he needed one [a doctor], it was already too late" (p. 41). Thus, if Darl and Peabody are believed, Anse has lied. But the motive behind Anse's lie appears clearly in his remarks: "And now I got to pay for it [Peabody's visit], me without a tooth in my head, hoping to get ahead enough so I could get my mouth fixed where I could eat God's own victuals as a man should, and her hale and well as ere a woman in the land until that day" (p. 36). At the end of the first day's journey the Bundrens, having found the bridge at Tull's gone, reach Samson's place, only to find his bridge out too. In his monologue, Anse seems to exult in the obstacles to the journey—an attitude noted later by Samson (p. 108) and Tull (p. 117). "There was old men," says Anse, "that hadn't never see nor hear of it [the river] being so in the memory of man. I am the chosen of the Lord, for who He loveth, so doeth He chastiseth" (p. 105), but almost immediately Anse makes a comment that reminds the reader of Darl's earlier assertion: "But now I can get them teeth" (p. 105). In this passage, Anse thinks about the glory of overcoming the river, but his conviction that he is the "chosen of the Lord" contrasts sharply with his usual self-pitying complaint about being a luckless man. The fact is that he has his heart set on his new teeth. He makes no mention of Addie. Later in the story, when Anse is trying to buy a team of mules from Flem Snopes, Anse tries to justify his offering Jewel's horse as part payment by saying: "God knows it. He knows in fifteen years I aint et the vituals He aimed for man to eat to keep his strength up, and me saving a nickel here and a nickel there so my family wouldn't suffer it, to buy them teeth so I could eat God's appointed food. I give that money. I thought that if I could do without eating, my sons could do without riding. God knows I did" (pp. 181–

82). How much credence is to be placed upon Anse's assertion that he "give that money," cannot be determined, but such an act would be inconsistent with Anse's character in the novel. His final act of taking Dewey Dell's money coincides with his character and parallels his robbery of Cash and sale of Jewel's horse.

Although some readers have seen Anse as a heroic man striving to perform an "ethical duty" or "a genuine act of traditional morality,"[9] the evidence against this interpretation seems almost overwhelming. Anse is not a man of principle. Rather, he is a man who breaks promises, lies, uses words with a cunning shiftiness, and robs his own children. The primary traits in his character are self-pity and selfishness. His absurd insistence upon his "promise"—if, indeed, he ever made one—serves as a cover-up for his obsession with his teeth. Faulkner could not have selected a more appropriate motivation for Anse's overwhelming desire to make the journey to Jefferson than his teeth. At once the means of man's survival and the gratification of his most basic appetite, the teeth underscore the powerful naturalistic forces that make him do what he does. To "get them teeth," that is, to survive, Anse will go to any lengths.

Although Anse is the only Bundren who gets anything from the journey to Jefferson, the children have their own reasons for going. None of them actually states that he is going out of love or respect for Addie. Only Anse actually tries to justify the journey in terms of Addie's wish; and Anse, whose word cannot be trusted, after they reach Jefferson, says to them: "You never pure loved her, none of you" (p. 218). Of the children, Dewey Dell has the most compelling motive, since she knows time is running out for her to get an abortion. Her pregnancy overrides all other concerns. "I heard that my mother is dead," she says; "I wish I had time to let her die. . . . It's not that I wouldn't [grieve] and will not it's that it is too soon too soon too soon" (p. 114). If Anse's resolution to continue the journey had ever flagged, Dewey Dell would have made him continue it; and on one occasion she reminds him of his promise (p. 109). But in the end, Dewey Dell knows that neither the pills nor the treatment administered by Skeet MacGowan will avail her. "It wont work. . . . I just know it wont" (p. 242).

Of all the children, Jewel appears to have the least selfish motive for going to Jefferson. Conceived in adultery, Jewel has always been an outsider, and for the most part he is seen by the reader through Darl, who continually taunts Jewel with veiled references to his birth. In his single monologue, he furiously rages at Cash for building the coffin where Addie can see and hear him, at the neighbors for sitting around in the house, and at Dewey Dell for fanning his mother. Jewel would like to be alone with Addie. Though the antagonism between Jewel and Darl increases in intensity throughout the novel, Darl's phrase, "the furious tide of Jewel's despair" (p. 92), is probably the best characterization of Jewel, since it implies his obsession with action and his despair over his mother's death. Jewel, more than anyone else, makes the journey possible. Unaware of his mother's words, he literally acts out her prophecy: "He is my cross and he will be my salvation. He will save me from the water and from the fire. Even though I have laid down my life, he will save me" (p. 160). But in saving his mother, he loses the horse that Darl repeatedly asserts is his mother (pp. 89, 95, 202). Thus, for Jewel the journey to Jefferson is doubly a disaster, while the future holds no prospect for happiness.

Darl is the only Bundren who disapproves of the journey and actively tries to prevent its completion. He is at least twenty-seven years old, two years younger than Cash.[10] The neighbors have long since known that Darl was "queer" and evidently threatened to take him away, because, Anse says, "he tends to his own business . . . [and] because he's got his eyes full of the land all the time" (p. 35). Although Anse does not really explain this remark, Dewey Dell's comment that "the land runs out of Darl's eyes; they swim to pinpoints" (p. 115) seems to suggest that Darl's eyes were often unusually wide-open. Vernon Tull also refers to Darl's eyes: "He dont say nothing; just looks at me with them queer eyes of hisn that makes folks talk. I always say it aint never been what he done so much or said or anything so much as how he looks at you. It's like he had got into the inside of you, someway" (p. 119). In ascribing special powers of insight to Darl, Faulkner was of course following a long line of writers reaching back at least to the Renaissance who imputed more than ordinary powers of perception to madmen and idiots. Relying upon this long-established concept of madness, Faulkner did not need to explain how Darl knew that Dewey Dell was pregnant, how he sensed something mysterious about Jewel's father, or how he could describe the death of Addie while he was miles away from the scene. Since the literary madman's laughter has also been a part of the tradition, Faulkner probably intended to make Anse's remark about Darl's laughter as one of the things that make "folks talk about him" (p. 99) help to alert the reader to Darl's madness and to prepare for Darl's hysterical laughter as he is thrown to the ground outside the cemetery and again as he is placed on the train to Jackson.

The paradox of literary madmen has always been that when they appear most mad, they may be most sane, and no one can say for sure when a man is mad or when he is sane. In *As I Lay Dying*, the question arises, is Darl mad or sane when he burns Gillespie's barn? Cash weighs the matter with excellent perception. He observes that Jewel has a right to blame Darl because Jewel had given up his horse to get his mother's corpse to town and "in a sense it was the value of his horse Darl tried to burn up" (p. 223). But Cash himself has also thought that it would be a blessing if God would "get shut of her in some clean way" and that when Jewel got her out of the river, he was going against God. Cash believes that Darl saw that one of them would have to do something. "I can almost believe," says Cash, "he done right in a way." But he agrees that most persons think only a crazy person would set fire to someone's barn and endanger his animals. Yet Cash still has reservations: "I aint so sho that ere a man has the right to say what is crazy and what aint" (p. 228).

Readers share Cash's sympathy for Darl because he is shabbily treated by the other Bundrens. The two older brothers have a close relationship, so close that they can communicate without words. As they begin to ford the river Darl thinks: "he [Cash] and I look at one another with long probing looks, looks that plunge unimpeded through one another's eyes and into the ultimate secret place where for an instant Cash and Darl crouch flagrant and unabashed in all the old terror and the old foreboding. . . . When we speak our voices are quiet, detached" (p. 135). In this same monologue, when Darl thinks about Jewel as a baby lying upon a pillow in his mother's lap, Cash—without any intimation of what Darl is thinking—remarks, "That pillow was longer than him" (p. 137). Throughout Darl's monologue, he is sympathetic to Cash. Near the end of the novel, after Darl has been thrown down by Anse, Jewel, and Dewey Dell, he looks up at Cash and says, "I thought you would have told me. . . . I never thought you wouldn't have" (p. 227). Darl feels that he has been betrayed; he can understand the others but not Cash. The scene takes on additional pathos from Cash's comment: "It was bad so. It was bad. A fellow cant get away from a shoddy job. He cant do it. I tried to tell him, but he just said, 'I thought you'd a told me.'" Asked if he wants Darl to go, Cash replies: "It'll be better for you. . . . Down there it'll be quiet, with none of the bothering and such." Cash cannot understand Darl's outburst of laughter that follows this remark. Faulkner leaves to the reader the decision whether life in the Jackson insane asylum would be better for Darl than life with Anse, the new duck-shaped Mrs. Bundren, and the children at home. Cash at least thought the asylum preferable for Darl; in his final speech in the novel, Cash repeats, "it is better so for him" and adds "this world is not his world; this life his life" (p. 250). As for Darl, he has no choice; but his final thought in the novel suggests that he still believes he has been betrayed: "Darl is our brother, our brother Darl. Our brother Darl in a cage in Jackson where . . . looking out he foams" (p. 244).

By almost any standard, Cash is the best of the Bundrens and perhaps as finely drawn a character as Darl. Early in the novel, Faulkner makes Cash a somewhat comic figure, especially when he lists thirteen reasons for making the coffin on the bevel (pp. 77–78) and when he gives an overly exact measurement of his fall from the church (p. 85). But as the novel progresses, Cash becomes more and more an admirable figure. Even from the beginning, Faulkner presents him as a good, careful workman and the only Bundren to have any steady employment. As might be expected, Anse objects to Cash's working for others and complains that his broken leg has deprived the family of his services (p. 35). Cash is admired by the neighbors and respected by the other members of the family. Darl's judgment seems almost an understatement: "A good carpenter. Addie Bundren could not want a better one, a better box to lie in" (pp. 4–5). He has high standards; he knows it is "better to build a tight chicken coop than a shoddy courthouse" (p. 224). Throughout the novel, Darl and others see Cash as a calm, composed, uncomplaining, even-tempered man. He is solicitous about Anse's welfare, he keeps Jewel's confidence and secretly does Jewel's work around the house to help him buy the horse, and he warns Darl to jump while he tries to keep the wagon from overturning and the coffin from being thrown into the river. On the journey, Cash endures without complaining six days of torment from his broken leg and suffers additional agony from the cement. In his quiet, unassuming way, he sees as much as Darl. Cash understands the family, especially Anse, Darl, Jewel, and Dewey Dell.

Cash is never outspoken. Nowhere in the novel does he explicitly voice his love or grief for his mother, yet he may have had more affection for her than had any of the other Bundrens. Both his grief and his love for Addie are concentrated in his brief statement about the coffin: "I am going to bevel it" (p. 74). In this remark Faulkner has combined Cash's pride in his work with his feeling for Addie. The thirteen reasons Cash gives for the beveling only conceal his real reason. Basically he is an advocate of decency and order. Since he has made the coffin to "balance with her" (p. 85), he disapproves of the women laying Addie in it out of order, that is, reversed, so that the flare-out bottom of her wedding dress may be spread out (pp. 82–83); and his repeated warnings about its lack of balance (pp. 92, 102, 138, 157) may be understood as protests against the journey itself. If Cash has a defect, it is probably that he is too passive. As has been seen, he recognizes the justness of Darl's effort to stop Anse from carting Addie's decaying and smelling corpse on what has become a senseless odyssey, but Cash takes no action. He understands Jewel's animus against Darl and infers that Dewey Dell has informed Gillespie of Darl's arson, but he remains silent. He knows better than to allow Anse to put the cement on his leg, but he submits instead of making an effective protest. In both his strengths and his weaknesses, Cash is unlike the other Bundrens. Near the end of the novel, Cash, always patient, forbearing, and slow to make judgments, wonders if he really has anything in common with Jewel, Dewey Dell, and Vardaman. "I feel kin to them, all right," he says, "but I dont know" (p. 224).

Appropriately, Faulkner assigns the final monologue, a kind of summing up of the story, to Cash. He describes the appearance of Anse and the new Mrs. Bundren walking along with him. The new teeth, Cash says, have made Anse "look a foot taller, kind of holding his head up, hangdog and proud too" (p. 249). The duck-shaped woman "with them kind of hard-looking pop eyes" carries one of those "little graphophones," perhaps similar to the one Cash had earlier hoped to buy for himself. Had Faulkner written an "appendix" or aftermath to *As I Lay Dying*, the reader would probably learn that Anse never ceased to brag about the obstacles he overcame during the journey, that he continued to live off the work of his family and friends, and that he eventually wore out his second wife. Jewel, having neither mother nor horse, kept on raging furiously through life. Dewey Dell bore her illegitimate child, worked, and had other children. Until the duck-shaped woman made her presence felt in his life, Vardaman believed his mother was a fish and speculated about his own existence. Only Cash learned from the experience. A sadder and wiser man with one leg shorter than the other, he will limp at an even more deliberate pace through the remainder of his life.

Although *As I Lay Dying* is largely the story of the Bundrens' journey, it is also, as the title implies, the story of Addie Bundren, who lies dying throughout the first third of the book. Except for her single, brief monologue, placed somewhat beyond the middle of the book, after her coffin has fallen into the river, she does not directly appear; and only if the reader believes that Anse and his children undertake their journey out of respect, duty, or affection for her, a concept to which very serious objections exist, does she influence the journey plot. The reader receives fragmentary and highly prejudiced glimpses of her through her family, the Tulls, Whitfield, and Peabody. Yet in a fashion at once very real but macabre and grotesque, she is an intensely present person throughout the novel, first as a dying woman and later as a putrefying corpse. The Bundren journey is only part of *As I Lay Dying*; the other part is Addie's story; and the two parts ultimately deal with the same theme.

Faulkner offers the reader very little biographical information about Addie. Though she came from Jefferson, he learns nothing about her mother or siblings, if any, and about her father only the remark that he "used to say that the reason for living was to get ready to stay dead a long time" (p. 161), a very significant observation for the novel and one that reminds Faulkner's readers of the kind of statements Mr. Compson made in *The Sound and the Fury*. Since Addie taught in the country school, she must have had an education, which, on the basis of the language in her monologue, lifts her considerably above the level of Anse and others. Her request to be taken back to Jefferson to be buried with her father and her "people" is really an admission of her kinship with the townspeople as well as an endorsement of her father's attitude towards living. The long-standing conflict between town and country appears in Addie and elsewhere in the novel[11] and may partly account for her antagonism towards the rural people among whom she lives.

On her deathbed, Addie reminds the reader of Tull's mother, who, he says, worked every day for seventy years before one day lying down on the bed, shutting her eyes, and remarking: "You all will have to look out for pa the best you can. . . . I'm tired" (p. 29). Addie, however, shows the signs of the hard wear Tull thought the lot of all country women. Cora notices that Addie's "face is wasted away so that the bones draw just under the skin in white lines. Her eyes are like two candles when you watch them gutter down into the sockets of iron candle-sticks" (p. 8). Darl remarks upon the "curled, gnarled inertness" of her hands "from which weariness, exhaustion, travail" have not yet departed (p. 50). Addie, as she says, has cleaned her house and is ready to die, but she looks not ahead to her reward but backwards over her life as she prepares to stay dead a long time. In her mind she is still thinking about the purpose of living. Her monologue makes difficult reading because she often moves from one subject to another without clear transitions, uses vague or indefinite pronouns that confuse her meaning, and makes statements capable of multiple interpretations. In her monologue, as well as in her life, she has difficulty in communicating through words.

While thinking back over her life, Addie remembers that as a young woman teaching school she would look at the children and think that having children seemed to be the only way she could get ready to stay dead. Then she would hate her father for ever having "planted" her (p. 162). Only when she switched the children until the blood ran did she feel that she had really entered their lives, her blood and theirs mingling forever. Without any further explanation, she says, "And so I took Anse." The implication is that she saw that to enter fully into the lives of others, she must transmit her blood to them in motherhood. Later on, she will speak of "the terrible blood, the red bitter flood boiling through the land," by which she probably means her own sexuality, which also lies behind her cryptic remark "And so I took Anse." But when she becomes pregnant with Cash, she knows that living is "terrible" and that "words are no good" (p. 163). She knows that motherhood, fear, and pride are only words, invented by those who have never experienced the reality of the acts themselves. And she knows that Anse has never really communicated with her and that her aloneness has never been violated until Cash came. To the other words that have no meaning, she adds Anse's word *love*. She understands that "when the right time came, you wouldn't need a word for that [love] anymore than for pride or fear. Cash did not need to say it to me nor I to him" (p. 164). (The right time does come as Cash makes Addie's coffin. Just before she dies, she raises herself and shouts out of the window, "You, Cash . . . . You, Cash!" [p. 47]. No other child gets this mark of recognition from the dying woman.)

Then she learns she is pregnant with Darl. She first thinks Anse has tricked her, but later realizes that she and Anse both have been tricked "by words older than Anse or love" (p. 164). Addie does not explain the phrase but she may mean that they have both been tricked by marriage or their human sexuality. With the birth of Darl, Addie knows that her father had been right, "even when he couldn't have known he was right anymore than I could have known I was wrong" (p. 165), that is, wrong to have believed the words of Anse. Henceforth Anse was dead to her, though he does not know it, and probably never knows. Just before Addie is finally buried in Jefferson, he gives his version of their relationship. "The somebody you was young with," he says, "and you growed old in her and she growed old in you, seeing the old coming on and it was the one somebody you could hear say it dont matter and know it was the truth outen the hard world and all a man's grief and trials" (p. 224). Although she permits him to continue to lie with her and bears him two more children, she has shut him out of her inner life.

Having abandoned Anse, Addie concludes that the reason for living is "the duty to the alive [that is, the life force or principle], to the terrible blood, the red bitter flood boiling through the land" (p. 166). For ten years, she bears no more children. Then, in her affair with Whitfield, she again seeks to realize her "aliveness" and sexuality through acts of sin that bring Jewel, whose name suggests his preciousness to her. [12] When it is over, she still feels, as she says, that "my children were of me alone, of the wild blood boiling along the earth, of me and of all that lived; of none and of all" (p. 167). To clean her house in preparation for dying, she gives Dewey Dell to Anse "to negative Jewel. Then I gave him Vardaman to replace the child I had robbed him of [Cash]. And now he has three children [Darl, Dewey Dell, and Vardaman] that are his and not mine" (p. 168).

In understanding Addie's position, the reader receives some assistance from Cora Tull. Although Cora's judgments are more often wrong than right, she occasionally makes a telling point that sheds light upon Addie. Such misjudgments as her assertion that Darl was the only member of the family who had "any natural affection" (p. 20), that Jewel is "a Bundren through and through" (p. 21), that Addie has been a "faithful wife" (p. 159), and that Whitfield is "a godly man if ever one breathed God's breath" (p. 159) make the reader smile and seriously damage Cora's credibility. Yet Cora is probably right when she remarks that Addie "lived, a lonely woman, lonely with her pride" (p. 21) and that Addie has had a "hard life" (p. 159). And when Addie says that Jewel has been her cross and will be her salvation, Cora, according to her belief, is correct when she says Addie has "spoken sacrilege" (p. 160). Addie defends herself by repeating her distinction between words and deeds. She implies that Cora is one of those persons "to whom sin is just a matter of words, to them salvation is just words too" (p. 168).

Addie's condemnation of words may be somewhat misdirected. Actually, her rejection of Anse is not that he spoke words of love but that he did not match his words with actions. He uses words to hide his shallowness, just as Whitfield uses words to expiate his sin. In both instances, the essence of the matter is not a person's words but his insincerity in using them. Action, moreover, without words can be just as purposeless as words without action. Jewel illustrates the point. While Cash tries to determine the best way to cross the river, Jewel interrupts: "I dont give a damn. Just so we do something" (p. 139). What Addie sought and did not find was the combination of words and action.

Faulkner has weighted the case against Cora. Her errors in judgment, propensity for gossip, smugness, and self-righteousness make her an unattractive person and cast doubt upon whatever she says; yet the position she represents must be respected. With all her faults, she has more human warmth than the dominating and inwardly turned Addie. The difference between the two women is startlingly evident at Addie's funeral. Addie's experience in life has led her to conclude that living is terrible and that she will stay dead a long time. She looks forward only to staying dead. As Cora Tull moves along in the wagon towards her home, she joyously sings: "I am bounding toward my God and my reward" (p. 86). However dimly it may illuminate her actions and her talk, Cora's life is shaped by a religious vision. Her moral sanctions are those precepts that she believes were given man by the same deity who created the universe. That deity governs both man and nature. When her husband asserts that the log overturned the wagon in the river, Cora retorts: "Log, fiddlesticks. . . . It was the hand of God" (p. 145).

Cora is a religious person; Addie is not. Addie has no use for such words as love, motherhood, sin, and salvation, for she has found out about living not through precepts but through experience. She recognizes only the law of nature. What counts for her is not God's law but "the wild blood boiling along the earth" (p. 167), that is, the natural force of human sexuality. By the time "the wild blood boiled away and the sound of it ceased" (p. 168), she has given life to the next generation and can prepare to stay dead a long time, in fact, forever. In Darl's words, Addie's aliveness has been merely a "clotting" (p. 156) in the cycle of nature. Appropriately, she does not stop at New Hope.

Dissimilar as Addie and Anse appear to be throughout *As I Lay Dying*, they have similar motivations and reach similar conclusions about the nature of living. Just as the powerful natural force of self-preservation drives Anse to Jefferson for his teeth, so the "wild blood boiling along the earth"—the urge to reproduce the species—motivates Addie's life. Anse holds that living is an outrage; Addie thinks it is terrible. In a sense, Anse can be viewed as an illustration of Addie's belief that life consists only of the natural cycle of birth, reproduction, and death. Anse moves only when he is prodded by the natural forces that impel him to eat and to reproduce and that will ultimately kill him. At the end of the novel, with his new teeth he can eat, and with the new Mrs. Bundren he can beget another brood of children. Addie's and Anse's lives together confirm Darl's naturalistic observation: "How do our lives ravel out into the no-wind, no-sound, the weary gestures wearily recapitulant: echoes of old compulsions with no-hand on no-strings: in sunset we fall into furious attitudes, dead gestures of dolls" (pp. 196–97). The remark recalls Mr. Compson's assertion that "all men are just accumulations dolls stuffed with sawdust swept up from the trash heaps where all previous dolls had been thrown away" (*The Sound and the Fury*, p. 194; p. 218).

Despite its occasional spots of humor, *As I Lay Dying* is a gloomy book. In large measure, it is the story of a decaying, smelling corpse on a journey that is an outrage to the dead and to the living. Above the coffin, wheel the ever-present, black scavengers in tireless circles, while around it cluster the Bundrens. Those in the family who insist that the journey be undertaken conceal their private, selfish ends under the pretense of honor to the dead. Except perhaps for Cash, these people lack the warmth of human kindness; toward each other, they are suspicious, resentful, and vengeful. In the words of Dewey Dell, each is "a tub of guts" (p. 56). Unlike the Sartorises and the Compsons, the Bundrens have never been other than they are now; they have no history and no need of any, because nature prods them along towards a future that will inevitably repeat the present. Perhaps even more than *The Sound and the Fury*, *As I Lay Dying* is a tale told in part by a madman, full of sound and fury, signifying the human futility that results from the absence of love or brotherhood. With *Sartoris*, *The Sound and the Fury*, and *Sanctuary*, *As I Lay Dying* belongs to the fiction written in the wastelands of the Lost Generation.

CHAPTER IV

Spring's Futility

Sanctuary

FAULKNER's remarks about the composition of *Sanctuary* may have been a great disservice to the book. About a year after the novel was published on February 9, 1931, he wrote in the introduction for the Modern Library edition that "this book was written three years ago" and that "to me it is a cheap idea, because it was deliberately conceived to make money." He explained how the novel came to be written. After *Sartoris* was accepted by a publisher, Faulkner recalled, "I began to think of books in terms of possible money." He continued: "I took a little time out, and speculated what a person in Mississippi would believe to be current trends, chose what I thought was the right answer and invented the most horrific tale I could imagine and wrote it in about three weeks and sent it to [Harrison] Smith, who had done *The Sound and the Fury* and who wrote me immediately, 'Good God, I can't publish this. We'd both be in jail.'"

Faulkner's remark that the book was a "cheap idea" written to make money and his later comment that it was "basely conceived" [1] tainted the work for years as a piece of sensationalism and commercialism. Despite the efforts of scholars, the ghost of these charges has been difficult to lay. A brief account of the composition of the novel may help to refute these aspersions and perhaps explain what Faulkner meant by his comments. The heart of the matter, as will be seen, lies in the fact that Faulkner wrote this novel twice and during the second writing transformed a poor work into an artistic achievement.

In January, 1929, a short time before *Sartoris* was to be published on the last day of that month, Faulkner began what was to be the first version of *Sanctuary*. He already had the title. As the work progressed, he constantly shifted material from this place to that, added new incidents, tried several opening scenes, cut and pasted where he decided upon changes, and frequently revised. After finishing the manuscript, he made additional changes while typing it out with "two fingers." On page 358, the final sheet of the typed manuscript, he placed the date May 25, 1929. This was the manuscript he sent to Harrison Smith.

The publisher immediately turned it over to three women who read and recommended manuscripts for publication. By early June, 1929, their verdict had been rendered—"very shocking," cannot publish.[2] If Faulkner had hoped, as he apparently did, that the novel would become a popular success, make considerable money for him, and permit him to marry Mrs. Estelle Oldham Franklin, Smith's decison not to publish it represented a severe disappointment. (Despite the refusal, Faulkner was married on June 20.) By the end of October, he had begun another novel, *As I Lay Dying*, and had dismissed *Sanctuary* from his mind.

Harrison Smith, however, kept the manuscript. In May, 1930, he decided to publish the novel and ordered his typesetters to begin to set the galleys. They were interrupted by the copy for *As I Lay Dying*, but in mid-November they began again and Faulkner received galley proof. On several occasions, he described his reactions. "I read it and it was so badly written," he noted, "it was cheaply approached. The very impulse that caused me to write the book was so apparent, every word; and then I said I cannot let this go."[3] The remainder of the textual history of *Sanctuary* appears in the introduction to the Modern Library edition: "Then I saw that it was so terrible that there were but two things to do: tear it up or rewrite it. I thought again, 'It might sell; maybe 10,000 of them will buy it.' So I tore the galleys down and rewrote the book. It had been already set up once, so I had to pay [$270, or half the typesetting cost] for the privilege of rewriting it, trying to make out of it something which would not shame *The Sound and the Fury* and *As I Lay Dying* too much and I made a fair job." Almost a quarter of a century later, speaking at Nagano, Faulkner recalled the circumstances of the composition of *Sanctuary* and insisted that in the second version "I did everything possible to make it as honest and as moving and to have as much significance as I could put into it."[4]

In other words, Faulkner decided that no less than a complete overhauling of the original manuscript would suffice. A detailed examination of the two manuscripts would show the countless changes in small matters as well as several more fundamental alterations in artistic focus and philosophical content. Perhaps the most important revision concerned Temple Drake. In the early draft, Faulkner seems to have concentrated upon the expansion of the Horace Benbow material that had been stricken from *Flags in the Dust*. Horace's mildly incestuous feelings toward his sister Narcissa and his relations with other women had been prominent elements in the story. In the revision, Faulkner notably reduced the emphasis upon these aspects of Horace's role and at the same time moved Temple Drake nearer the center of his fictional stage. In addition, he tied Narcissa and Horace's stepdaughter Little Belle into the Temple Drake story. To a degree, however, the novel retains the bifurcation that marks a number of Faulkner's novels (especially, the Anse—Addie plots of *As I Lay Dying* and the Lena Grove—Joe Christmas plots of *Light in August*), since Horace's story and its significance exist independently of Temple's life and its meaning. Surprisingly, Faulkner did not tone down the violence of the novel; rather, if anything, he increased it by adding the unjust conviction of Lee Goodwin and his lynching by the mob. He also added the final account of Popeye's life story and the irony of his execution for a crime he did not commit.

Whether Faulkner had made, as he claimed, "a fair job" of the novel remains the individual reader's decision. Contemporary readers bought *Sanctuary*; whether from admiration or from curiosity stimulated by reviewers' accounts of its violence and subject matter is hard to say. Issued early in February, 1931, the work had sold 3,519 copies by March 4 and more than 7,000 by early April, probably more than the total sales of all the author's other work combined.[5] Its contents, including nine killings and a corncob rape, were certain to produce shock and widespread distaste among certain reviewers. Although many expressed strong disapproval, others admired the power of the book. Some said that it had placed Faulkner in the first rank among young American novelists;[6] others, for example, Henry Seidel Canby in *The Saturday Review of Literature*, cited Faulkner as a prime example of "American sadism."[7] Some of the most derogatory comments about the novel and its author came from Southern reviewers. Although the New Orleans *Times-Picayune* reviewer, a woman, admired the work in close to extravagant terms,[8] the writer for the Memphis *Evening Appeal* thought *Sanctuary* repulsive, putrid, stark hideousness and called it a "devastating, inhuman monstrosity of a book that leaves one with the impression of having been vomited bodily from the sensual cruelty of its pages."[9]

The reception of *Sanctuary* in the novelist's hometown was somewhat like the outrage expressed in Asheville, North Carolina, over the publication less than two years earlier of *Look Homeward, Angel*. Asheville citizens were enraged at Thomas Wolfe's thinly disguised portraits of themselves. In Oxford, however, the reaction was primarily shock at the subject matter, though Baptists deeply resented Faulkner's blunt remarks about religious bigotry in their congregation. A strongly conservative town of fewer than fifteen hundred potential adult readers, the Oxford community was wholly unprepared for Popeye, Temple Drake, and Red. The scenes in Miss Reba's brothel were viewed as scandalous and unfit for fiction. Oxford residents, however, read the book, even if they felt obliged to send their servants to purchase it for them at one of the local drugstores, the only place in town where the work was offered for sale. As the primary topic of conversation, *Sanctuary* rapidly displaced local talk about the ever-worsening depression and Governor Theodore Bilbo's unjust firings of many respected and admired professors at the University of Mississippi. Although the book had supporters, especially among younger readers, few openly expressed approval. Faulkner's father, it is said, deplored the work and thought about trying to have it removed from public sale. Unquestionably, the book placed Faulkner in an unfavorable light in Oxford and throughout the state. Many years would pass before the feeling would be reversed.

Faulkner scholarship continues to be somewhat divided about the merit of *Sanctuary*. The shock and horror it once produced have long since ebbed away, replaced by more considered judgments. Serious readers give scant attention to the notion of it being a "cheap idea." Some critics, notably Albert Camus, have thought the novel as good as and perhaps better than anything else Faulkner ever wrote.[10] Considerably less enthusiastic than Camus, Melvin Backman has called it the "bitter dregs of Faulkner's creativity" during the period in which he wrote *The Sound and the Fury*.[11] Perhaps the judgment of Cleanth Brooks represents the most balanced appraisal of contemporary criticism: "If *Sanctuary* is in some respects Faulkner's most pessimistic novel, it is certainly one of his most brilliant."[12] Although it may not be the greatest of his works, no one would question its importance to those who wish to know and understand Faulkner's essential contribution to American literature.

Although citizens of Oxford, Mississippi, doubtless recognized considerable local material in *Sanctuary*, they probably knew little if anything about the initial germ of the story. Sometime in the mid-1920s, presumably in a French Quarter bar in New Orleans, or perhaps in Memphis, a young girl told Faulkner about being abducted and raped by a Memphis gangster who used for the assault an incredibly unnatural instrument. The gangster was impotent and in sexual relations accustomed to using substitutions for his impotence. The famous corncob may have actually been a far more humane and "natural" instrument than that recounted in the original story.[13] In the novel, Faulkner replaced the girl with an "Old Miss" coed and a student at the University of Virginia, whose identities at least one "Ole Miss" professor as early as 1932 claimed to have known. The novelist used the impotent Memphis gangster but based the fictional character upon an actual Memphis criminal whose name and career closely paralleled those of Popeye.

Strong evidence exists that Faulkner modeled Popeye after Neil Karens (or Kerens) Pumphrey (1904–1931).[14] From childhood Pumphrey was nicknamed Popeye because of his habit of opening his eyes very wide when he became excited. By the time he became the most famous Memphis underworld figure of the 1920s—his notoriety rivaled that of Scarface Al Capone, or Dutch Schultz, or Legs Diamond—newspaper stories generally referred to him simply as Popeye. The son of a wealthy cotton man who dealt in real estate and the daughter of the attorney general of Arkansas, Popeye Pumphrey began his criminal record about 1924 when he was charged with bootlegging. For the next seven years, he was arrested time and again on charges of bootlegging, robbery, gambling, assault to murder, swindling, in fact, just about every criminal activity imaginable except sexual crimes. Only once did the charges ever result in a conviction. His career in crime reached a climax on June 22, 1929, shortly after Faulkner sent the first version of *Sanctuary* to Harrison Smith. On that night, Popeye Pumphrey was standing in front of the La Salle Hotel in downtown Kansas City with four other gunmen, two of whom were wanted for murder and two of whom were never identified. Suddenly guns blazed, and the two men wanted for murder were killed. As Popeye broke and ran from the others, he was shot in the back but survived. The unidentified men escaped. The case received national coverage in the press. Shortly afterwards, Popeye was arrested in Hot Springs, then in Birmingham, and again in Saratoga Springs. Set free, he returned to Hot Springs, where on October 28, 1931, he was found shot through the head. Two notes and a pistol found near the body indicated that he had committed suicide. Faulkner's *Sanctuary* had been published eight months earlier.

One can never be certain about the extent of Faulkner's indebtedness to Popeye Pumphrey for the Popeye of *Sanctuary*. Various possibilities always exist. The novelist may have taken only the name and general outlines of his career in bootlegging, gambling, and shooting. Faulkner may have known and used aspects of Pumphrey's career that are not now known. In addition, Faulkner may well have borrowed some of the details of the fictional character from the lives and personalities of other gangsters. Most likely, whatever factual material he took, he embellished it with details from his own imagination to meet the requirements of his plot.

Nevertheless, contemporary readers should remember that the gangster activities of the 1920s that provide the underworld backdrop of *Sanctuary* formed a prominent part of the national scene. Although America had known some form of organized crime throughout its history, the 1920s witnessed an extraordinary growth of criminal gangs. They owed their formation to the Volstead Act of October 28, 1919, passed by Congress to enforce the Eighteenth Amendment to the Constitution by prohibiting the manufacture, sale, and transportation of intoxicating liquors. Scarcely had the act been passed when criminals in the large cities established gangs to secure monopoly control over the trade in illegal liquor. Gangs fought gangs in deadly "gang warfare" to secure their claims to given territories. Such phrases as "bump off," "take for a ride," and "gangster rule" entered the language through newspaper and magazine stories of criminal activities. Although the strength of the prohibition movement always lay in the rural areas, much of the illegal supplies of whiskey entered the urban gangster market from country stills. Almost from the very beginning, enforcement of the act in the cities faltered because of widespread violations and local political corruption. In a comparatively short period after the federal government took over the task of enforcing the law, its courts were jammed with more than 600,000 cases of violation.

Meanwhile, gangsters moved from liquor into prostitution, gambling, and the "numbers" racket. Some invaded the restaurant business and evening entertainment, while others occasionally ventured into such sports as baseball. In the 1920s, organized crime became a big business. At the base of its operation was physical force—the pistol and the submachine gun; and its setting became the nightclub, the speakeasy, the roadhouse, and the brothel. Jazz was its music. To some observers, it seemed as if the gangster had become a primary American institution. In 1925, the mid-year of the decade, F. Scott Fitzgerald wrote *The Great Gatsby*. Its hero, whose name suggested a "gat," slang for pistol, enacted a new version of the American dream in which the exercise of the old Benjamin Franklin virtues created the gangster instead of the honest hero.

Although the most notorious centers of gangsterism were in the big cities of the North—New York, Boston, Philadelphia, and Chicago—in the South, Memphis and New Orleans competed with them in the dubious rivalry. Faulkner knew both places, but he knew Memphis better. Memphis had long suffered from a reputation as a leading center for urban crime. In the early years of the twentieth century, particularly, its name had been associated with lawlessness. [15] Had it existed with the biblical Sodom and Gomorrah, it was said, God would have had to destroy Memphis first. A traveler returning to St. Louis once wrote that the "only difference between Memphis and hell is that Memphis has a river running along side of it" whereas hell's river ran through it. As early as 1903, Memphis had 504 saloons, and the number steadily increased year by year; the prohibition amendment merely forced them into the hands of the gangsters.

In the years before World War I and afterward, prostitution flourished in Memphis. The famous tenderloin area on Main Street south of Linden and along Third, Fourth, and Mulberry streets contained scores of "houses." By far the most elegant brothels, however, were found on Gayoso Street. They were often conservatively described as "red hot and low down." The names of the madams and their most beautiful girls were well known throughout the city. Dora Smith operated a "quality" house of Creole girls, while Mary Smith and Dora Craddock specialized in Negro prostitutes. Mae Goodwin, the queen of the Memphis underworld, managed a notorious house across from the Union Station until the night of October 9, 1916, when she was shot and killed by John

Revinsky, probably in a dispute over stolen diamonds.[16] Revinsky was sentenced to a long prison term but made several escapes before being caught for the last time in 1928. His career may have contributed a few details to Faulkner's Popeye. Probably the most celebrated of the Memphis madams, however, was Grace Stanley, a wrinkled, obese brown woman, mistress of Stanley Hall or the Stanley Club. Among her girls was Birdie Butler, the midnight queen of Gayoso Street, said to have been the most beautiful prostitute in Memphis. Like Miss Reba Rivers of *Sanctuary*, Birdie Butler and the other ladies of negotiable virtue in Stanley Hall catered to many of the rich and often the prominent citizens of the city. Birdie met men of her own race in call houses safely hidden from view, the most famous of which was run by Lizzie Hood or "Dark Lizzie," reputed to have been also a conjure woman.

However elegant the downstairs rooms of Stanley Hall and the houses of Dora Craddock, Mae Goodwin, and others may have been, the upstairs work rooms were neither so garish nor so splendidly furnished. Faulkner's description of Temple Drake's room in Miss Reba's house strikes close to reality. "The light hung from the center of the ceiling, beneath a fluted shade of rose-colored paper browned where the bulb bulged it. The floor was covered by a figured maroon-tinted carpet tacked down in strips; the olive-tinted walls bore two framed lithographs. From the two windows curtains of machine lace hung, dust-colored, like strips of lightly congealed dust set on end. The whole room had an air of musty stoginess, decorum; in the wavy mirror of a cheap varnished dresser, as in a stagnant pool, there seemed to linger spent ghosts of voluptuous gestures and dead lusts. In the corner, upon a faded scarred strip of oilcloth tacked over the carpet, sat a washstand bearing a flowered bowl and pitcher and a row of towels; in the corner behind it sat a slop jar dressed also in fluted rose-colored paper."[17]

Illegal liquor, prostitution, gambling, and racketeering, flourishing as they did in the nightlife of the city, helped to make Memphis in the 1920s the "Murder Capital of the U.S.A." Statistics document this dismal distinction. In 1916, for example, Memphis had almost three times as many homicides per hundred thousand population (89.8) as its nearest competitor (Atlanta). Two years later, according to a pamphlet published by the Prudential Insurance Company, Memphis led all other cities in the country in the per capita rate of murder and received the title "murder town." At the same time, the city also led in the suicide rate. If

William Faulkner needed a source book for any of the many killings that occur in *Sanctuary*, he could readily have found material firsthand in Memphis or secondhand in the Memphis newspapers.

Although readers of *Sanctuary* today must place the work against the general background of gangsterism in the 1920s, they must also remember that Faulkner had learned a good deal about crime and criminal trials from day-to-day living in Lafayette County. In a period when the electronic communication industry had not yet begun to dominate leisure time activity, citizens of rural communities like Oxford exhibited intense interest in local politics, local crime, and all kinds of court trials. The Oxford courthouse was the scene of many a dramatic trial, and citizens at home and in the square often debated the testimony of each witness and the legal maneuvers of the lawyers. Down at the jail only a scant block from the courthouse, mobs could gather quickly, and more than one lynching began in the street outside. About the time Faulkner was working on *Sanctuary*, he was also writing a short story, first entitled "Drouth" and later "Dry September," that dealt with the senseless fury of mob violence, which Faulkner may have witnessed more than once in his youth. In writing *Sanctuary* and *Light in August*, he almost certainly recalled the lynching of Nelse Patton. On September 9, 1908, Patton, a Negro trusty at the jail, was sent to deliver a message to a white woman who lived north of town. While in her house, Patton attacked her, cut her throat with his razor, and attempted to assault her daughter. The brother of one of Faulkner's schoolmates, aged fifteen, shot Patton as he attempted to flee the sheriff's posse. That night, a huge mob, inflamed by a former United States senator, broke through the outside wall of the jail—an action that required almost six hours of strenuous effort— shot and killed Patton, castrated the body, and hung it from a tree on the square.[18] Although this incident took place in 1908, the place where the hole was made in the outside wall of the Oxford jail and later repaired with new brick remained visible until the jail was torn down in 1960. Faulkner never forgot this affair, which probably suggested details of the killings of Joanna Burden and Joe Christmas in *Light in August*. He used similar material in other works, including "Pantaloon in Black" (in *Go Down, Moses*) and *Intruder in the Dust*. Without doubt, the trial and lynching of Lee Goodwin owe a great deal to Faulkner's firsthand knowledge of such matters.

In a discussion of the realities behind *Sanctuary*, an important matter for readers to remember is that as melodramatic and sensational as the novel may seem, the core of the story had a basis or foundation in the life of Memphis and Oxford. In the novel, Faulkner fused exceptionally well a number of seemingly diverse elements: the account of the bizarre abduction and rape of the girl from Memphis; the abortive journey of an Ole Miss coed to a baseball game in Starkville; the Memphis underworld of the tenderloin brothels and roadhouses; and the trial and lynching of an Oxford Negro. In addition, the singing murderer and the barber's college students, who in their rural innocence mistake Miss Reba's brothel for a boardinghouse, probably had their prototypes in real life.[19] To an extraordinary degree, Faulkner's skill in shaping these diverse but related elements into an artistic whole and into a commentary upon good and evil in modern life reveals the depth of his genius as a storyteller and a critic of society.

Although divergent in subject matter and focus, *Sartoris*, *The Sound and the Fury*, *As I Lay Dying*, and *Sanctuary* were written from very similar philosophical positions and reflect Faulkner's reaction to the spiritual struggles that plagued many writers in the 1920s. All four novels deal with the character or quality of modern life and reach similar conclusions. In *Sartoris* and *The Sound and the Fury*, Faulkner chronicled the decline of the Sartorises and the Compsons from families of leaders to families of persons so ineffectual in meeting life's problems that life itself became meaningless or intolerable. In *As I Lay Dying* and *Sanctuary*, he continued his assessment of modern times. In *As I Lay Dying*, the Bundrens live and act in circumstances far different from those of the Sartorises and Compsons; but the rural folk are no better equipped for purposeful living than the aristocrats and much less intellectually aware of their plight. In *Sanctuary*, of course, such characters as Popeye, Lee Goodwin, Ruby Lamar, Tommy, and Miss Reba inhabit a world vastly distant from that of the Sartorises, Compsons, and Bundrens; but in Horace Benbow, his sister Narcissa, Temple Drake, and Gowan Stevens, Faulkner returned to the Compson "class," and they more than the inhabitants of the underworld form the philosophical center of *Sanctuary*.

By using *The Sound and the Fury* as representative of the three earlier novels, the reader can distinguish the progression of Faulkner's thought and art in *Sanctuary*. The great difference, aside from artistic achievement, lies in the shift of emphasis from the internal world to the external. The monologues of the Compson brothers turn inward, and, in general, the world they explore is the inner, private, isolated world of the mind itself. For the most part, the Compsons, especially Benjy and Quentin, but even Jason too, do not interact with society. But in *Sanctuary*, the internal perplexities of the Compsons have been replaced by the external forces of the community, specifically, the Baptist Church, the ladies of society, the courts of justice, and the network of crime embracing bootlegging, murder, and prostitution but stretching its tentacles from Memphis, Tennessee, down to the isolation of Frenchman's Bend in Yoknapatawpha County, and beyond, even to Jackson, Mississippi. There is evil in *The Sound and the Fury*; but it is seen largely as an aberration of the individual character; a weakness, perhaps even an inherited weakness, a loss of faith, a failure of ideals, or at least the wrong choice of ideals. In *Sanctuary*, evil becomes an active force that the individual carries within him; and the community, which represents a much larger integer of evil, functions, in fact, as a coconspirator. The stage of *Sanctuary* is a wider world than that of *The Sound and the Fury*, and within that world there is no refuge or sanctuary from the evil that pervades it.

The difference between the implicit meanings of the two novels may be measured in terms of Quentin and Horace. Quentin Compson, a very young man, has unrealistically placed his faith in existence upon the continuance of his sister's virginity. The question for him is not so much the loss of Caddy's honor as it is the loss of his belief in an absolute, without which he finds no purpose to existence. Horace Benbow, in middle age, seems initially better off than Quentin; at least Horace seems better prepared for the business of living. A lawyer of some experience, he remains an idealist. He takes action to bring about the reality of his ideal by endeavoring to establish the innocence of Lee Goodwin—the name suggests the Confederate general and an ironic thrust by combining Lee with Good-win, who loses—and thereby to vindicate the justice of the community. But Horace is defeated by the gangster underworld, by the ruthless amorality of his own sister, by the apparent motiveless malignity of Temple Drake, and by the active evil in the community, symbolized by the Baptist Church and the lynch mob. At the end of the novel, Horace realizes that he actually had little chance of making justice prevail. As Narcissa drives him "home," Faulkner observes that "there was still a little snow of locust blooms on the mounting drive." Looking at it, Horace remarks, "It does last. . . . Spring does. You'd almost think there was some purpose to it" (p. 350). If disillusionment could be measured, Horace's would be greater than that of Bayard, Mr. Compson, Quentin, or Addie.

In some respects, Horace and Quentin reach the same conclusion by different routes. Yet there is a difference. Quentin's idealism stands or falls upon a private test that has no real justification for success; in fact, one might even argue that since lasting virginity is a denial of life, Quentin's test is itself immoral. Horace is defeated, primarily, by external forces. In part, he is ineffectual, unenergetic, perhaps even blind to realities; but the odds against him are enormous, almost overwhelming. If he cannot make justice prevail, at least he gains what Quentin never achieves, a clear sight of evil outside of himself and an awareness of the potential evil within himself. Horace achieves a degree of self-knowledge that, for all his introspection, Quentin never attains. Quentin is one of the sad young men, whereas in his maturity Horace (like Cash Bundren) becomes a sadder but wiser man who conceivably could return again to the fight. Thus, to a degree at least, in moving from *The Sound and the Fury* to *Sanctuary*, Faulkner turned from an examination of the individual's contemplation of the ideal to a study of the individual's role in bringing justice to the community. Henceforth in Faulkner's fiction the interaction of the individual with the community would become a major theme.

To a considerable extent, *Sanctuary* is a novel about women. Without its female characters, there would be no plot, but, even more significantly, without them the problem of evil would be only partially stated. In fact, so heavily weighted is the relationship between evil and women that some readers have held that Faulkner bore a grudge against women. Although the issue cannot be fully resolved, it is not likely to be forgotten. At the center of the discussion is the character of Temple Drake.

Almost over the shoulders of the town boys who stand outside the university gymnasium looking in at the coeds on the dance floor, the reader first sees Temple "with her high delicate head and her bold painted mouth and soft chin, her eyes blankly right and left looking, cool, predatory and discreet" (p. 32) passing from one partner to another, "her waist shaped slender and urgent in the interval." One of the boys imitates "in a bitter, lilting falsetto" what must have been one of Temple's characteristic remarks, "My father's a judge" (p. 33). Later on, Faulkner describes her as "long legged, thin armed, with high small buttocks—a small childish figure no longer quite a child, not yet quite a woman" (p. 106). She is "on probation" for "slipping out at night" (p. 65). The information given in these brief comments contains a hint of her character. Although she has led a sheltered life, she will take some risks for the delights of misbehavior, knowing that basically she is secure in her present situation. She knows she can handle matters; her father is a judge. She could be characterized as a typical campus flirt or coquette, the kind of girl who "promises much but delivers little," a tease. In all of her actions one senses a precarious innocence and a very delicate balance preventing her from falling to a grimmer reality.

Later, out at the old Frenchman's place, as she becomes frightened by the sinister atmosphere of the place and its occupants, she recalls this carefree, irresponsible world of dancing, frivolity, and games. On one occasion, she thinks "of the school, the lighted windows, the slow couples strolling toward the sound of the supper bell, and of her father sitting on the porch at home, his feet on the rail, watching a negro mow the lawn" (p. 59). She thinks of the baseball game at Starkville, "the pennant-draped train . . . ; of the colorful stands; the band, the yawning glitter of the bass horn; the green diamond dotted with players" (p. 43). She imagines her father "sitting on the veranda, in a linen suit, a palm leaf fan in his hand, watching the negro mow the lawn" (p. 62). Even at Miss Reba's in Memphis, Temple cannot forget the world she has left. "The hour for dressing for a dance, if you were popular enough not to have to be on time. The air would be steamy with recent baths, and perhaps powder in the light like chaff in barn-lofts, and they [the girls at school] looking at one another, comparing, talking whether you could do more damage if you could just walk out on the floor like you were now" (p. 181).

The degree of Temple's unawareness of her playing with life becomes evident from her conversation with Ruby Lamar. As the sinister atmosphere of Lee Goodwin's ménage begins to produce a vague sense of alarm in Temple, she remarks to Ruby: "I'm not afraid. . . . Things like that dont happen. Do they? They're just like other people. You're just like other people. With a little baby. And besides, my father's a ju-judge" (p. 64). After Temple has explained that she was going to the baseball game at Starkville, that Gowan had stopped for some whiskey, and that she is on probation for slipping out at school, Ruby retorts: "Oh, I know your sort. . . . Honest women. Too good to have anything to do with common people. You'll slip out at night with the kids, but just let a man come along. . . . Take all you can get, and give nothing. 'I'm a pure girl; I dont do that'" (p. 66).

What Temple later discovers is that "things like that" do happen and those circumstances that have hitherto shielded her from evil in its basest reality do not exist at Frenchman's Bend. Although separated by merely a few miles from the campus, she is in another world. Her constant running around in front of these men proves to be the worst defense she could possibly have made, though ironically it is the only defense she knows. Readers dispute whether Temple actually invites her rape. The point has been made that when she flees down the road from the house and then returns to it, she is acting from her ambivalent feelings toward sexual experiences. Unquestionably, Temple's intrusion into Frenchman's Bend and her subsequent actions there prompt Popeye to kill Tommy and to rape her with the corncob. Despite the absence of a plain statement from the novelist himself, one infers that the evil within Temple has something to do with the evil response she evokes from Popeye. And by the time she recounts the nightmare experience at Frenchman's Bend to Horace in Miss Reba's house, Temple seems to think little about the actual rape. "It just happened," she says. "I dont know. I had been scared so long that I guess I had just gotten used to being." She continues in a bright, chatty monologue until "suddenly Horace realized that she was recounting the experience with actual pride, a sort of naive and impersonal vanity, as though she were making it up" (pp. 258–59).

Earlier, as Popeye was taking her to Memphis, Temple has opportunities to escape. Although she screams while they are driving in unpopulated areas, she becomes silent when they pass through towns; and when Popeye stops at a filling station, she has a first-rate chance to flee. She does leave the car, but she is apparently concerned only that some boy would see her. Unquestionably there are greater depths to Temple's evil than mere concern for appearances. The fact is that she readily takes to the perversions she encounters in Miss Reba's brothel, and she finds Red an agreeable lover. She escapes—a relatively easy task—from Miss Reba's house only to arrange to meet Red—a meeting that will end in his death. She has become, in an almost unbelievably short time, a thoroughly vicious, immoral woman.

Nothing in Temple's brief but rapid progress down to the depths of human degradation and wickedness equals the deliberate perjury with which she sends Lee Goodwin to his death for a crime he did not commit. Critics have defended her on the ground that she may have been afraid of Popeye—and Faulkner twenty years afterward, writing in *Requiem for a Nun*, said it was fear of Popeye that caused her to testify against Goodwin—but within *Sanctuary* the novelist is silent on the point. If she fears Popeye, she seems also to have had some affection for him; on at least two occasions she calls him "daddy," a term that in the 1920s could also mean lover. She may have decided that Popeye meant more to her than Goodwin, or that she simply did not care what happened. Admittedly these theories are difficult to reconcile with the fact that Popeye has killed the only man for whom Temple seems to have had real feeling, even if the feeling was more lust than love. The reader's final glimpse of Temple in Paris as "sullen and discontented and sad" does not resolve the issue.

Physically, Narcissa Benbow has little in common with Temple Drake. Narcissa, ten years a widow, is "a big woman, with dark hair, a broad, stupid, serene face" (p. 27). Although "she had never been given to talking, living a life of serene vegetation like perpetual corn or wheat in a sheltered garden instead of a field" (p. 127), she can be shrewd, devious, and ruthlessly energetic when "appearances" are involved.

Because of her concern with appearances, Narcissa thoroughly disapproves of Horace's actions on behalf of Ruby and Lee Goodwin. She tells Horace that she thought it "dreadful" when he "took another man's wife and child away from him," "dreadful" when he "just walked out of the house like a nigger and left her," and equally reprehensible when he cleaned the house in Jefferson with "all the town looking on . . . refusing to stay here [at Narcissa's house] where everybody would expect you to stay" (p. 138). Much worse, in her opinion, was Horace's "meddling" in the affairs of a woman he himself had said was "a street-walker, a murderer's woman" (pp. 138–39). Narcissa becomes even more angry when she learns that Horace has taken Ruby to their house. Her character and attitude are precisely defined in her remark after Horace has explained the plight of Ruby and her child: "I dont want to think about her. I wish

I had never heard of the whole thing. To think that my brother. . . . But to bring a street-walker, a murderess, into the house where I was born" (p. 140). Asked why he must "do such things," Horace answers: "I cannot stand idly by and see injustice" (p. 141).

Horace can scarcely believe the inflexibility and inhumanity of her attitude. When he learns that the ladies of the Baptist Church have forced the hotel proprietor to turn Ruby and her baby out of the hotel ("I got a certain position to keep up myself," p. 216), Horace cannot imagine who told them about Ruby. Suddenly, it dawns upon him that Narcissa has betrayed him. She will listen to no argument about the justice or humanity of the case. As for Lee Goodwin's being an innocent man, Narcissa answers: "I dont see that it makes any difference who did it. The question is, are you going to stay mixed up with it?" (p. 221), and Faulkner adds, "her cold, unbending voice shaped the words in the darkness" (p. 221).

Although the details of the district attorney's subsequent actions are not entirely clear, Narcissa's intention in telling him about Clarence Snopes's Memphis connections with the Goodwin case is plain. In conveying this information which eventually leads to the testimony of Temple and the conviction of Lee Goodwin, Narcissa asks: "'So the quicker he [Horace] loses, the better it would be, wouldn't it? . . . If they hung the man and got it over with.' His [the district attorney] hands became perfectly still. He did not look up. She said, her tone cold and level: 'I have reasons for wanting Horace out of this case. The sooner the better. . . . I just want Horace out of this business as soon as possible'" (pp. 317–18). In view of Narcissa's lack of moral principles, her cold, inhuman disregard of an innocent man's life, and her betrayal of her own brother, one would have difficulty choosing between Narcissa Benbow and Temple Drake.

Miss Jenny's attitude towards Horace, Narcissa, and the Goodwin case often puzzles readers of *Sanctuary*. At the age of ninety she should have had, one thinks, more concern for principle and less for expediency. Though she scoffs at Narcissa's talk about Horace's bringing "a street-walker, a murderess," into the house where she was born, Miss Jenny does point out that as a lawyer Horace was having too much personal involvement with the case. "Folks might begin to think you know more than you've told," she says (p. 140). Miss Jenny also scoffs at the suggestion that Narcissa would betray Horace's confidence. "Do you think Narcissa'd want anybody to know that any of her folks could know people that would do anything as natural as make love or rob or steal?" (p. 141). Nevertheless, Miss Jenny's advice for Horace to take Ruby to the hotel can be understood as the suggestion of a practical realist. Likewise, her remark to Narcissa stems from a kind of realism that Faulkner attributed to women: "You dont wonder. You just do things and then stop until the next time to do something comes around" (p. 223). In perception and principle, Miss Jenny falls short of one's expectations.

Temple Drake, Narcissa Benbow, and, even to a degree, Miss Jenny are a sorry lot. Temple and Narcissa are cruel, despicable women sadly lacking in moral principles and moral courage but amply endowed with sexuality. Faulkner intimates that the evil that is fully apparent in these women is but an outward manifestation of the evil that exists by nature in all women. Perhaps that part of Horace Benbow's disillusionment that affects him far more intimately than the evil he has faced in the courtroom and the community arises from his recognition of the signs of this innate "woman-evil" in his own stepdaughter who serves as a device to link Temple and Narcissa. Doc Hines, in *Light in August*, calls it "bitchery."

Little Belle Mitchell makes four brief appearances in the novel, three of which are confined to Horace's thoughts and the fourth to a telephone conversation. At the opening of the novel, Horace, on his way from Kinston to Jefferson, encounters Popeye at the spring. Intimidated by the gangster, Horace eats supper at Frenchman's Bend, drinks too much, and begins to talk in incoherent sentences. Clearly, however, he is thinking about Little Belle and remembering that she has picked up a drunk on the train. He recalls that "from my window I could see the grape arbor, and in the winter I could see the hammock too" (p. 13). The blooming of the wild grape he associates with spring; the hammock, visible in the winter but hidden by the ferment in the spring, he links to sexuality. Both symbols he links to Little Belle: "What blossoms grapes have, this is. It's not much: a wild and waxlike bleeding less of bloom than leaf, hiding and hiding the hammock, until along in late May, in the twilight, her—Little Belle's—voice would be like the murmur of the wild grape itself" (p. 14). He speaks to Little Belle about picking up the boy, and she retorts that he picks up "Shrimp!" Her reference is to

Horace's practice of bringing home a package of shrimp to his wife every Friday since his marriage. In the reconciliation that follows, as Little Belle embraces him, Horace sees her face in the mirror. "There was a mirror behind her," he says, "and another behind me, and she was watching herself in the one behind me, forgetting about the other one in which I could . . . see her watching the back of my head with pure dissimulation" (pp. 15–16). Horace concludes from this incident that "nature made the grape arbor, but Progress invented the mirror" (p. 16). "Progress" has also invented the rouge or paint she uses to enhance her attractiveness to men. (In his description of Temple, Faulkner emphasizes her "bold painted mouth," p. 32.)

About midway in the novel, Little Belle appears for the second time. On this occasion, Horace associates the man she picked up on the train with Gowan Stevens, a student at the University of Virginia. Gowan proposes marriage to Narcissa, and upon being refused he takes Temple to Frenchman's Bend, gets drunk, and abandons her. After Horace returns to town, he looks at the photograph of Little Belle. Again, his mind returns to the grape arbor at Kinston, to summer twilight, and to "the murmur of voices darkening into silence . . . into the pale whisper of her white dress, of the delicate and urgent mammalian whisper of that curious small flesh . . . in which appeared to be vatted delicately some seething sympathy with the blossoming grape" (p. 200). Suddenly, he looks at her face in horror and despair as he realizes that the face is "older in sin than he would ever be."

On the occasion of Little Belle's third appearance, Horace contemplates her photograph in his room. As he looks, the small face seems "to swoon in a voluptuous languor . . . leaving upon his eye a soft and fading aftermath of invitation and voluptuous promise and secret affirmation like a scent itself" (pp. 267–68). Then in a passage difficult to explicate on a literal level, Horace's mind moves from Little Belle to Temple Drake in images that seem to come into focus, blur, and then merge into each other. Faulkner's use of the pronoun *she* could refer to either woman. Horace seems to see Temple lying in the shucks being raped and Little Belle riding on a train "bound naked on her back on a flat car moving at speed through a black tunnel" in a long upward slant (p. 268), while "far beneath her [Little Belle or Temple?] she could hear the faint, furious uproar of the shucks." As these images crowd into his mind, Horace retches over the lavatory.

Horace's fears about his stepdaughter are underscored in his final telephone conversation with her at the house party. Almost before he can greet her, he hears a scuffling sound and a masculine voice breaks in to say: "Hello, Horace; I want you to meet a—" (p. 360). The sentence is never finished, but Horace hears Little Belle explain: "It's Horace! I live with him!" In a voice "breathless, controlled, cool, discreet, detached," she concludes the conversation by promising to write tomorrow. The voice could just as well have been that of either Temple or Narcissa. Thus, in Little Belle's four short appearances, Faulkner has brilliantly used her to provide a commentary upon Temple and Narcissa. Together they have confirmed Horace's worst imaginings about the innate bitchery of women and probably contributed as much to his disillusionment as the Baptists, the injustices of the law, and the lynch mob.

Of all the female characters, only Ruby Lamar, who is several times called a streetwalker, seems to have any virtue. Her name is formed from a compound of a precious gem and either the name of a Confederate hero or that of a street in Oxford. Without the advantages of Narcissa or Temple or Miss Jenny, Ruby has qualities about which they know nothing: love, loyalty, and toughness. For her courageous, but violent, unfaithful, and at times criminal lover, Ruby has prostituted herself to get him out of prison; and despite his ingratitude and cruelty to her, she continues to sacrifice herself for him. One of the most poignant scenes in the novel occurs when she recounts the story of her life with Lee Goodwin and declares that she expects to pay Horace as she paid Goodwin's lawyers before (pp. 330–34). Although she cannot prevail, this uneducated common-law wife and former streetwalker acts on the side of justice and goodness and lives up to her name.

In its larger context, *Sanctuary* must be seen as marking a definite point in Faulkner's career. In *Sartoris*, *The Sound and the Fury*, and *As I Lay Dying*, he had concentrated upon the private sufferings, desires, and disillusionment of individuals. In *Sanctuary*, he began to open out his canvas and to shift his emphasis to the community at large. Faulkner's attack upon organized religion (here represented by the Baptist Church and its "ladies"), the Christian hypocrites in the town, and the pharisee-like unconcern of the hotel proprietor indicts the aggregate of an entire community. Even worse is the suggestion of a connection between the Memphis underworld and its brothels and the political capital of Mississippi in Jackson, as Clarence Snopes moves back and forth between the

two cities with stops at Jefferson. On an even deeper level stands the figure of Popeye, symbolical, Faulkner later said, of evil, but also a version
of the mechanical, unfeeling man in modern life.

Easily one of the most impressive scenes in all of Faulkner's fiction is
the opening of *Sanctuary*. Horace Benbow, who has stopped by a spring
to drink from its naturally clean, pure water, suddenly looks up: "He
saw, facing him across the spring, a man of under size, his hands in his
coat pockets, a cigarette slanted from his chin. His suit was black, with a
tight, high-waisted coat. His trousers were rolled once and caked with
mud above mud-caked shoes. His face had a queer, bloodless color, as
though seen by electric light; against the sunny silence, in his slanted
straw hat and his slightly akimbo arms, he had that vicious depthless
quality of stamped tin" (p. 2). Horace knows at once that Popeye carries
a pistol. His eyes are "two knobs of soft black rubber." He spits into the
spring, an act violating the purity of nature that foreshadows his later
actions in the novel. "His skin had a dead, dark pallor," continues
Faulkner. "His nose was faintly aquiline, and he had no chin at all. His
face just went away, like the face of a wax doll set too near a hot fire and
forgotten. Across his vest ran a platinum chain like a spider web" (p. 4).
The words, taken by themselves, make one recoil from this unnatural
man: bloodless color, electric light, vicious, stamped tin, knobs of rubber, dead skin, no chin, and so on.

Throughout the novel, Faulkner continues to heap additional repulsive details upon this already repulsive character. At various times, he
describes Popeye as a short man resembling a "modernistic lampstand"
(p. 5), a thug, a gorilla, afraid of an owl but capable of cruelly shooting a
friendly dog or murdering an associate. He is impotent and sickly. His
unnatural rape of Temple and subsequent perversion in Miss Reba's
brothel, like his spitting in the spring, are crimes against nature itself.
Almost to the end of the novel, his actions are thoroughly consistent
with the description and character provided him by his literary creator.

In the final chapter of the novel, however, Faulkner writes a somewhat
puzzling account of the life of Popeye as a kind of appendix to the main
story, an appendix that reminds the reader of the Appendix to *The Sound
and the Fury*. According to this account, Popeye was born on Christmas
Day, probably a victim of congenital syphilis. His grandmother was a
pyromaniac who died in the fire she herself set. At three years, he looked
like a one-year-old. He could neither walk nor talk until he was four. By

the time he was five, he had no hair, and the doctor knew that he would always be impotent and would "never be any older than he is now" (p. 369). As a young boy, he cut up while alive two lovebirds and in similar fashion cut up a half-grown kitten. He grew up in a home for incorrigible children. Later, he went each year to visit his mother in Pensacola. After the trial of Lee Goodwin, Popeye sets out on his annual journey. On the way, he is arrested in Birmingham for the murder of a policeman and taken to a small Alabama town. Although innocent of the charge, Popeye will allow no lawyer to represent him, and he makes no defense. He is convicted, the jury being out "eight minutes," the same length of time it took the jury to convict Lee Goodwin. Popeye still makes no move to appeal the verdict, and he is hanged for a murder he did not commit. Faulkner seems to provide no satisfactory reason for Popeye's unwillingness to defend himself or appeal the verdict.

This sketch of Popeye's life, in fact, raises certain questions that strongly influence the reader's assessment of his character, questions that Faulkner never wholly solves. Are readers to assume, for example, that in transcendental fashion Popeye's outward appearance reflects the inward state of his mind and body? If the cause of his evil lies in the syphilitic condition he contracted at birth from his syphilitic parents, can he be held accountable for his later actions? In other words, given his background, his bodily sickness, and his resultant mental retardation, is Popeye, like Benjy, a special case? Does Faulkner's final account of Popeye lessen our condemnation of him though not the evil he represents? Like the Compson children, is Popeye another illustration of the visitation of the sins of the parents upon the children of succeeding generations? The answers to most, if not all, of these questions would appear to be in the affirmative. Popeye, in a large measure, does appear to be a character in whom outward marks of disease become manifestations of an inner spiritual disease or evil that desecrates the natural order of health and goodness. In a larger sense, this same inner disease corrupts the community and by extension modern life itself.

Despite its power, almost everyone who evaluates *Sanctuary* in terms of the entire body of Faulkner's work ranks it below his best fiction. Readers complain of obscure passages that seem needlessly difficult reading, the stacking of the cards against Horace and Ruby, and the novelist's failure to provide vital information at crucial moments in the story. Too many questions about the plot and the characters remain unanswered.

Why did Temple, for example, perjure herself at the trial? Why did Clarence Snopes turn up in Jefferson with a black eye just before the trial? How did the district attorney get his information? What was the significance of Judge Drake's role in the trial? Answers to these questions have generally proved to be no more than theories, conjectures, or guesses. At his best Faulkner would have provided the information needed for the resolution of such problems as these.

Perhaps an even more cogent criticism of *Sanctuary*, however, relates to the novelist's failure to provide an overall philosophical framework to which the reader can relate the events of the story. From this point of view, *Sanctuary* seems a piece of impressionism that reminds one of an imagist poem turned into prose. In a measure, *The Sound and the Fury* also suffers from the absence of a philosophical premise; but in the instances of Quentin, Jason, and their parents, one can discern a cause and effect relationship and behind it a moral universe. In *Sanctuary*, however, Faulkner seems to be saying that "the way things are" only evil prevails. Lee Goodwin scorns Horace Benbow's assumption that "the law, justice, civilization" (p. 156) will protect the individual, and the remainder of the novel proves Lee Goodwin correct. The law operates to defeat justice; justice prevails only from the chance operation of forces evil in themselves (Popeye's trial is a case in point), and civilization produces whole communities full of Narcissas, Baptists, and Snopeses. If *Sanctuary* presents an accurate picture, a representative account, of the modern world, the reader can only affirm that it is sick beyond recovery and agree with Horace Benbow that the promise of spring is merely an annual event of no significance. Viewed in this light, the novel ranks with *As I Lay Dying* as Faulkner's bitterest account of the wasteland of the Lost Generation.

Faulkner may have overstated his case, not only against women and the community but also against the intellectuals. The Temple-Popeye plot, unfolding the bizarre circumstances of their sexual experiences, may be the source of the novel's popular appeal, but neither Temple nor Popeye brings much depth or meaning to the work. Popeye, of course, acts without the full possession of human faculties, and his evil deeds may be viewed as a kind of transcendental reflection or correspondence between his grotesque, distorted, and abnormal physiology and his outward acts. He may not be morally responsible; but in the light of her family background and educational level, Temple should have had a greater awareness of the issues. Instead, she begins and ends a shallow figure. Nowhere in the novel does she exhibit a consciousness of her wrongdoing; and lacking that awareness, she cannot be expected to show any repentance. She is not a tragic figure. Unlike Caddy Compson, who loved Quentin, Benjy, and her daughter, Temple acts only from her sexual urges which are the same—though in Temple's case wholly unrestrained—natural forces that moved Addie Bundren and that, Horace sees, will move Little Belle. Yet, unlike Addie Bundren, Temple has no sense of obligation or duty to anyone and carelessly contributes to the killing of the innocent and the guilty alike. As a study of evil, Temple remains a one-dimensional character. She cannot "carry" the meaning of the novel.

On the other hand, Horace Benbow, a much more complicated figure than Temple, stands at the center of the work. If the story is to have meaning, it must be found in Horace's experiences and perceptions. By the end of the book, he has looked into the heart of darkness and seen the ancient evil of woman's bitchery lurking in Temple, Narcissa, and Little Belle. At the same time, he has probed the depths of evil in the community and learned by bitter experience the wrongs it can generate. Horace's concern for moral principle, justice, and civilization exalts him above everyone else in the novel, and his defeat becomes symbolic of the defeat of civilization, law, and justice in the modern world. One cannot imagine a society of Goodwins, Baptists (as Faulkner depicts them), Popeyes, and "bitches" as fit for decent, purposeful living. Yet Horace, despite his defeat, has something of Milton's virtue; he can "see and know and yet abstain."

As in many of Faulkner's novels, the title does not appear in the work itself, and the appropriateness of it—as well as its application to the content—must be determined by the reader. Cleanth Brooks has suggested that Faulkner had in mind a passage from Joseph Conrad's *Chance*: "A young girl . . . is something like a temple. You pass by and wonder what mysterious rites are going on in there, what prayers, what visions? The privileged man, the lover, the husband, who are given the key of the sanctuary do not always know how to use it. . . . Simply by chance . . . I had seen the saddest possible desecration, the withered brightness of youth, a spirit neither made cringing nor yet dulled but as if bewildered in quivering hopelessness by gratuitous cruelty; self-confidence destroyed and, instead, a resigned recklessness, a mournful callousness."[20] The connection between this passage and Faulkner's attitude towards women in *Sanctuary*, particularly Temple, as she sits in the Luxembourg gardens at the conclusion of the novel, is tempting to pursue. Few readers can forget the picture of Temple listening to the music of Massenet, Scriabine, and Berlioz in the rain. "Rich and resonant the brasses crashed and died in the thick green twilight, rolling over them in rich sad waves. Temple yawned behind her hand, then she took out a compact and opened it upon a face in miniature sullen and discontented and sad. . . . She closed the compact and from beneath her smart new hat she seemed to follow with her eyes the waves of music, to dissolve into the dying brasses, across the pool and the opposite semicircle of trees where at sombre intervals the dead tranquil queens in stained marble mused, and on into the sky lying prone and vanquished in the embrace of the season of rain and death" (pp. 379–80). Temple, like Caddy, seems to have vanished into the Paris of the expatriate exiles.

Other interpretations, with varying degrees of validity, have been suggested. The title has been taken to apply to Miss Reba's brothel, as the place where Temple finds sanctuary. More plausible is the inference that there is a connection between the name Temple and the title *Sanctuary*. The body of Temple Drake, or temple, has been broken into; and the sanctuary, the intimate recess of her body and spirit, has been violated. Perhaps the final irony of this interpretation is that though the temple has been raped and the innermost sanctuary plundered, there was little within worth robbing. No one can be certain what Faulkner meant when he chose the title, but speculation will probably continue and add interest and depth to the novel.

Although there may be no critical consensus regarding its meaning, *Sanctuary* continues Faulkner's examination of the 1920s which he began in *Sartoris* and amplified in *The Sound and the Fury* and *As I Lay Dying*. If, on balance, the manuscript of *Sanctuary* would have profited from more thought and further revision, the discerning reader will find in it a powerful indictment of a society that seemingly has lost sight of the fundamental moral values that have enabled man to rise from the level of primitive anarchy to purposeful living. It is the last of Faulkner's works to reflect the pessimism that was widespread among the artists of the postwar decade.

CHAPTER V

Life as a Journey

Light in August

NOTWITHSTANDING the presence in *Sanctuary* and *Light in August* of passages of Faulkner's most brilliant work, many readers have found these two novels the least attractive of his fiction. They plunge the reader down into the gloomy depths of human degradation and uncover the hearts of those who neither "fit in" nor "relate" affirmatively to society yet as human beings desperately need its compassion and understanding. Like Popeye, Lee Goodwin, and the singing murderer in *Sanctuary*, Joe Christmas, Doc Hines, Simon McEachern, and others in *Light in August* are "bad" men who commit evil deeds. Unattractive as they are, Faulkner seems to be asking, what yet can be said for them? One cannot doubt that they undergo suffering, torment, and anguish as they rush down the wretched streets of their lives and along the way inflict pain, even death, upon others. What makes them act as they do? Faulkner's most ambitious effort to answer these questions may be found in these two works but especially in *Light in August*.

Besides dealing with characters who are at odds with the "normal" patterns of behavior established by society, the two novels contain scenes that are generally reminiscent of each other. The atmosphere of Miss Reba's brothel in Memphis Faulkner seems to have thought appropriate for parts of *Light in August*. The description of Miss Atkins, the dietitian at the orphanage, lying naked in bed with the shades drawn recalls the account of Temple Drake lying in the twilight at Miss Reba's, while both Hines and the dietitian call the matron of the orphanage "the madam." Joe Christmas and Joe Brown, moreover, engage in bootlegging, the occupation of Popeye and Lee Goodwin in *Sanctuary*. Temple's phrase, "something is going to happen to me," is repeated by Joe Christmas.[1]

Other similarities exist between the trial and death scenes of Lee Goodwin and Joe Christmas, some of the details being based upon the same event in Oxford history.

As has been noted earlier in the discussion of *Sanctuary*, for the account of the trial and lynching of Lee Goodwin, Faulkner had already used elements of the Nelse Patton story. In *Light in August*, he again used this event for some aspects of the killing of Joanna Burden, and for the murder of Joe Christmas he very likely combined elements of the Patton affair with details from another Oxford case. Faulkner's biographer observes that in 1920, Leonard Burt, a Negro, was being tried for the murder of his wife, and as he was being taken to the courthouse, according to the account in the Oxford *Eagle*, "he made a desperate attempt to escape by snatching Whitehead [the deputy] to his knees and dashing off up the alley, running between the jail and the row of store buildings on the north side of the public square."[2] One of the police officers shot the man as he fled, and on the next day the man died of his wounds. Thus, for Joe Christmas' escape, Faulkner had an actual escape upon which to base his fiction; and in combining details from these two crimes to construct his account of the murder of Joanna and the trial and death of Joe Christmas, the novelist was following his custom of using, where possible, actual events to underscore the reality of his work.

Interesting as these similarities between *Sanctuary* and *Light in August* are to the reader, the most important link between the two novels lies in Faulkner's treatment of the religious elements of the Jefferson community. In the earlier novel, Faulkner sharply castigated organized religion, specifically the Baptists, for a lack of moral courage and responsibility in the community and even suggested that religion had been allied upon the side of evil. Protestantism, or Calvinism, in its dogmatic, punitive, emotional, fundamentalist aspects becomes a central fact in the unhappy life of Joe Christmas and a corrosive influence in the twisted lives of Eupheus Hines, Simon McEachern, Gail Hightower, and Joanna Burden. By associating it with racism and sex, Faulkner greatly expanded the criticism he had begun in *Sanctuary*. Not since Sinclair Lewis' *Elmer Gantry*, published in 1927, had an American novelist mounted so explosive an attack upon religious fundamentalism as Faulkner made in *Light in August*.

On August 17, 1931, six months after *Sanctuary* was published, Faulkner began to write *Light in August*. At the top of the first page of his manuscript, he wrote the words *Dark House*. No one knows whether he intended this title to apply to the house in which Gail Hightower sat each day at twilight waiting for evening to come, or whether he meant it to apply to Joanna Burden's gloomy old colonial plantation house, which Faulkner on several occasions in the novel describes as a "dark house" (see pp. 215, 243, 245, 266). But one afternoon while the novelist and his wife were sitting on the side porch of Rowan Oak, Mrs. Faulkner commented that the light in August seemed somehow different from other times in the year. Faulkner agreed and walked into the house, and when he returned, the title had been changed to *Light in August*.

The precise meaning or application of the title has remained somewhat general if not actually vague. It has been explained as a reference to a rural expression to the effect that a cow or mare becomes "light" after she has been delivered of her calf or foal. On one occasion at the University of Virginia, Faulkner explicitly denied this interpretation, saying: "No, I used it because in my country in August there's a peculiar quality to light and that's what that title means. It has in a sense nothing to do with the book at all, the story at all."[3] Subsequently, in his interviews at the University of Virginia, Faulkner elaborated upon the meaning of the title:

In August in Mississippi there's a few days somewhere about the middle of the month when suddenly there's a foretaste of fall, it's cool, there's a lambence, a luminous quality to the light, as though it came not from just today but from back in the old classic times. It might have fauns and satyrs and the gods and—from Greece, from Olympus in it somewhere. It lasts just for a day or two, then it's gone, but every year in August that occurs in my country, and that's all that title meant, it was just to me a pleasant evocative title because it reminded me of that time, of a luminosity older than our Christian civilization. Maybe the connection was with Lena Grove, who had something of that pagan quality of being able to assume everything, that's—the desire for that child, she was never ashamed of that child whether it had any father or not, she was simply going to follow the conventional laws of the time in which she was and find its father. But as far as she was concerned, she didn't especially need any father for it, any more than the women that—on whom Jupiter begot children were anxious for a home and a father. It was enough to have had the child. And that was all that meant, just that luminous lambent quality of an older light than ours.[4]

Faulkner's comments strengthen the inference made by some readers that he somehow wished the title to relate to Lena Grove. Her name and character remind one somewhat of the older Greek pagan religion that celebrated nature in contrast to the later harshness of Western Protestantism. Her first name is a diminutive of the Greek *Helena*, meaning torch or light, while her last name may imply a reference to the sacred groves of Diana whom Faulkner may have associated with Joanna Burden. Lena's stay in Joe Christmas' cabin while her baby is being born provides a symbolic link between her and Joanna. These suggestions, however, do not rest upon conclusive evidence.

Within the novel, there are several references to particular qualities of light. For example, at the beginning of Chapter 20, Faulkner mentions "the final copper light of afternoon," and a few sentences later Hightower remembers "how that fading copper light would seem almost audible, like a dying yellow fall of trumpets" (p. 441), a phrase that echoes the passage in *Sartoris*—"a dying fall of horns along the road to Roncevaux." Perhaps the most important passage relating to the title occurs near the end of the novel. As Hightower sits beside the window, the wheel of his imagination begins to turn, and Faulkner writes: "In the lambent suspension of August into which night is about to fully come, it seems to engender and surround itself with a faint glow like a halo. The halo is full of faces" (p. 465). To bring all of these scattered passages into a sharp exposition of the title seems an almost impossible task. In a not too precise manner, they do imply the revelation that the novel will make within its brief time span in August.

After that August afternoon when he changed the title from *Dark House* to *Light in August*, Faulkner continued to work at the manuscript. During the fall he made good progress, and by February, 1932, he was working on Chapter 19, in which Percy Grimm murders Joe Christmas. On February 19, 1932, he finished the manuscript and signed his name and the date at the end. As was his custom, he began to type out the final copy, revising as he went. One of the changes he made seems particularly interesting. In the autograph manuscript, Joe Christmas arrived in Jefferson at the age of thirty; thus, his death would have occurred when he was age thirty-three. Very likely because Faulkner did not wish to make an analogy between Christmas and Christ (their initials are the same) too exact, he changed the date so that Christmas would die at age thirty-six. The alteration weakens the case of those who understand Joe Christmas as a Christ-symbol. Faulkner made other changes as he typed

the copy for the printer, but they seem less significant for the interpretation of the novel. By March the typescript had been completed, and by
July he was reading galley proof. In October he received his author's copies, and the reviews began to appear in the newspapers and magazines.

The reviews suggested no clear pattern of critical reaction. Most conceded Faulkner's power and skill as a rising young novelist and acknowledged *Light in August* as a better novel, "less violent and more understanding," than *Sanctuary*. J. Donald Adams, writing in the *New York
Times Book Review*, found Faulkner's "somewhat crude and altogether
brutal power which thrust itself through his previous work disciplined
to a greater effectiveness than one would have believed possible in so
short a time," while Henry Seidel Canby, writing in the *Saturday Review
of Literature*, thought Faulkner needed more "self-discipline." Herschel
Brickell, a sympathetic Mississippian, wrote in the *North American Review* that Faulkner's new novel proved him "capable of a great deal of self-
discipline" and offered additional proof of his genius. Less favorable reviewers complained, as they had done in the past, of "compounded,
unhyphenated words which . . . smell like James Joyce" and characters
whose activities take place "almost entirely in the viscera."[5]

Almost from the first, readers have remarked upon the lack of unity in
the novel. The story of Lena Grove exists almost wholly independently of
the account of Joe Christmas. So separate are these plots that Lena never
even sees Joe, and Joe is never even aware of Lena's existence. Furthermore, Joe Brown, Byron Bunch, and, to a lesser degree, Gail Hightower, who form whatever connection there is between the two characters, seem unessential to the Joe Christmas story, which is viewed as the
main plot line of work. In support of this assessment, one could note that
Faulkner himself said that he began the novel "knowing no more about it
than a young woman, pregnant, walking along a strange country road."[6]
In other words, except for Lena Grove, Faulkner began to write before he
had in mind any of the characters or incidents that would constitute the
largest portion of the finished work. At the very beginning, the Joe
Christmas story was in no sense integral to the plot of the novel. That
Hightower's story touches only lightly upon those of Lena and Joe
Christmas tends to strengthen the case against a unified conception.
Those who raise these issues conclude that Faulkner never successfully
joined these episodes, and his inability to fuse them prevents a satisfac-

tory overall interpretation of the work. Subsequent criticism, however, has endeavored to show that the various actions, though very much separate, do come together to contribute to the meaning of *Light in August*. That is, the novel does possess a wholeness. The following discussion of the Lena Grove motif supports this interpretation.

Perhaps the most important contribution of the Lena Grove story to the artistic wholeness of *Light in August* is that of contrast, often called counterpoint, to that of Joe Christmas. In most respects, she and her experiences are almost exact opposites to the personality of Christmas and the events in his life. These contrasts are reinforced even by the qualities they have in common. As the novel opens, Lena Grove, who like Christmas is an orphan, journeys along the road that leads from Doane's Mill in Alabama, where her unborn child was conceived, towards Jefferson, Mississippi. Like Joe Christmas three years earlier, she enters the Jefferson community a stranger. Her journey, symbolizing her life-experience, which envelopes the novel and bears comparison with Joe Christmas' fifteen-year odyssey—he calls the life-road a street—stops only for a short time in Jefferson, where Joe Christmas' street ends, and keeps on going at the conclusion of the novel. Unlike Joe Christmas, who views the idea of marriage or children as a betrayal, Lena is seeking to marry her seducer. "I reckon a family ought to all be together," she says, "when a chap comes. . . . I reckon the Lord will see to that" (p. 18; cf. p. 285); but her idea of God is vastly different from that of Christmas. Lena moves with a calm faith that the Lord will provide—to her, God is good. Joe Christmas' experiences have been the antithesis of such a faith. If God exists at all for Christmas, He closely resembles the Calvinistic God of justice and punishment. Thus, the contrasts or counterpoint between Joe and Lena are established early in the book, though the reader will not become aware of them until after he has learned the life history of Joe Christmas.

Faulkner repeatedly underscores the sharp division between the two leading characters. For four weeks Lena travels "a peaceful corridor paved with unflagging and tranquil faith and peopled with kind and nameless faces and voices" (p. 4) as she advances towards Jefferson "in identical and anonymous and deliberate wagons as though through a succession of creakwheeled and limpeared avatars, like something moving forever and without progress across an urn" (p. 5; the urn reference recalls Faulkner's fondness for Keats's great ode). Folks have been kind, she says to Armstid; "they have been right kind" (p. 10). Armstid takes her to his house for the night; and Mrs. Armstid, despite her disapproval of unwed pregnant women and her doubts about Lucas Burch's intentions, breaks her china bank to give her egg money to help Lena. In Jefferson, Lena continues to receive the same kindly treatment from the community despite her assertions that "I wouldn't be beholden. . . . I wouldn't trouble" (p. 12). First Byron Bunch, then Mrs. Beard receive Lena kindly, and Mrs. Beard feeds her and gives her a place to sleep. The keynote to the community's reception of the betrayed and deserted girl is kindness.

Joe Christmas' life-experiences have been the opposite of Lena's. After a wretched childhood, Christmas reaches manhood as he strikes his foster father and leaves him apparently dead on a dance floor to begin a journey down "the street which was to run for fifteen years" (p. 210). "From that night," writes Faulkner, "the thousand streets ran as one street, with imperceptible corners and changes of scene, broken by intervals of begged and stolen rides, on trains and trucks, and on country wagons with he at twenty and twentyfive and thirty sitting on the seat with his still, hard face and the clothes . . . of a city man and the driver of the wagon not knowing who or what the passenger was and not daring to ask. The street ran into Oklahoma and Missouri and as far south as Mexico and then back north to Chicago and Detroit and then back south again and at last to Mississippi" (pp. 210–11). The minuteness of detail here underlines the importance of this passage to Christmas' story. "He thought that it was loneliness which he was trying to escape and not himself. But the street ran on: catlike, one place was the same as another to him. But in none of them could he be quiet. But the street ran on in its moods and phases, always empty: he might have seen himself as in numberless avatars, in silence, doomed with motion, driven by the courage of flagged and spurred despair" (p. 213). Finally, "one afternoon the street had become a Mississippi country road," and Joe Christmas approached the Burden house near Jefferson.

Out of work and hungry, Christmas gets a job at the planing mill. After he has worked several days, Byron Bunch, realizing that Joe has had no food, offers to share his dinner pail. Joe Christmas' instant reply is harsh and hostile: "I aint hungry. Keep your muck" (p. 31). Six months later, Joe still has nothing to say to anyone, and no one knows anything about him. He wants no kindnesses; he helps no one and trusts no one. What he wants, he takes. The community and Lena Grove have a close rapport based upon mutual kindness and humanity. The community rejects Joe Christmas, and he rejects it.

Antithetical as Faulkner makes Lena Grove and Joe Christmas, at certain points in the novel their lives have something in common. As Lena reaches the outskirts of Jefferson, she sees the smoke from the fire that is destroying the Burden House. Christmas has fled, leaving behind his empty cabin, which he has shared with his partner Joe Brown (Lucas Burch). Byron Bunch takes Lena to this cabin, which Lena views as a kind of home, since Lucas Burch, her seducer, lived there. (If Faulkner had made the cabin a stable or manger, one wonders if Lena would have been interpreted as a Mary figure instead of the more usual earth mother.) In Joe Christmas' cabin, attended by Gail Hightower and Mrs. Hines, with Doc Hines present but asleep, Lena gives birth to her baby.

The scene in which Lena's baby is born contributes significantly to the novel's unity of theme and action as well as to the overall meaning. The resemblances to the earlier scene at the birth of Joe Christmas are too close to be mistaken or to have been unintended by the novelist. As Lena's child is born, Mrs. Hines, "with the face of a tiger," glares at the sleeping old man, her husband, on the cot. She snatches "the still unbreathing child and held it aloft. . . . Then the child breathed and cried, and the woman seemed to answer it, also in no known tongue, savage and triumphant" (p. 381). Hightower tries to reassure and calm her by saying, "He's [Hines] quiet. He's not going to take it away this time" (p. 381). In her mind, of course, Mrs. Hines has gone back to the birth of Joe Christmas, and she thinks Lena is Milly and the baby Milly's. Later, when Hightower returns, Lena tells him that Mrs. Hines keeps on calling the baby Joey "when his name aint Joey" (p. 387). Lena says: "She [Mrs. Hines] keeps on talking about—She is mixed up someway. And sometimes I get mixed up too, listening. . . . She keeps on talking about him like his pa was that . . . the one in jail, that Mr Christmas. She keeps on, and then I get mixed up and it's like sometimes I cant— like I am mixed up too and I think that his pa is that Mr—Mr Christmas too" (pp. 387–88).

The inference that the birth of Lena's baby is a symbolic reenactment of the birth of Joe Christmas gains credence from the reader's realization

142

that had Joe Christmas actually been the father of Lena's baby, the same ambiguity over the baby's race would have also been repeated, since the question of Joe Christmas' race remained as uncertain as the racial identity of Milly's "Mexican" seducer. The great difference between the earlier scene and this scene is that the birth of Lena's baby is viewed as a blessed event rather than a proof of bitchery and "the Lord God's abomination" (p. 360).

Very likely Faulkner intended readers to understand the birth of Lena's baby as an event optimistic for the future. Although a bastard, her son is not a pariah, an Ishmael, or an outcast. He begins life in an atmosphere of blessedness and love; he represents the promise of the future. Joe Christmas' journey through life ran along a street that became a sewer and twisted itself into a closed circle so that he ended where he began. Lena's journey is not complete; for her, Jefferson is only a stopover and her journey open-ended. Hightower's prediction for her may be understood as that of Faulkner: "*She will have to have others, more* remembering the young strong body from out whose travail even there shone something tranquil and unafraid. *More of them. Many more. That will be her life, her destiny. The good stock peopling in tranquil obedience to it the good earth; from these hearty loins without hurry or haste descending mother and daughter*" (p. 384). Like Ántonia Cuzak of Willa Cather's *My Ántonia*, Lena Grove is a "rich mine of life, like the founders of early races." [7]

In another sense, Lena's baby seems almost to take the place of the child that Joanna wanted. Hightower makes the connection. "'Poor woman' [Joanna], he thinks. 'Poor, barren woman. To have not lived only a week longer, until luck returned to this place. Until luck and life returned to these barren and ruined acres.' It seems to him that he can see, feel, about him the ghosts of rich fields, and of the rich fecund black life of the quarters, the mellow shouts, the presence of fecund women, the prolific naked children in the dust before the doors; and the big house again, noisy, loud with the treble shouts of the generations" (p. 385). To Hightower, the birth of Lena's baby is a healing event, a promise of renewed life. He is confident of her destiny.

This same note of cautious optimism continues to pervade the final chapter through which Lena's story envelopes that of Joe Christmas. The tone is now comic. Like Armstid at the beginning of the novel, the furniture dealer sounds the authentic note of the community. As a kind of nature goddess, Lena is strong enough to reject Byron Bunch when she wishes but unwilling to dispense with him entirely. Probably the reader is to believe that into some future truck, or wagon, or cabin, wherever they are, she will admit him. Meanwhile, Byron's life has been radically changed for the better by his love for her. Together they continue the open-ended journey. After the hate and violence of the square in Jefferson, this scene brings peace and tranquility once more and exemplifies the rural traditions of which Faulkner approved. Because of her trust in God, her simplicity, and her sincerity, Lena easily wins the affection of the Jefferson community and Faulkner's readers. Like Eula Varner in *The Hamlet*, though a much more lovable character, Lena Grove is a kind of earth goddess to whom it is fitting that Byron Bunch should offer obeisance.

Between the opening and closing of Lena Grove's progress through Jefferson, Faulkner narrates the awesome story of Joe Christmas. As a study in man's alienation and isolation, Christmas' history approaches the intensity of Melville's Ahab. Morally speaking, Joe Christmas is a bad man. Without love, honor, compassion, and honesty, he willfully alienates himself from his fellowmen by a long succession of evil, often criminal deeds. Any list of his actions would include stealing from his foster mother, criminally attacking his foster father and leaving him for dead, living with various Negro and white women (usually prostitutes), bootlegging, running berserk in a church service and fracturing the skull of one of the worshipers, murdering Joanna Burden, and escaping from custody. Throughout his journey down the street of life, he breaks the laws of both man and God. Because few, if any, of Faulkner's readers have much in common with a man who has this kind of record or have ever had any doubt about their racial identity, the novelist faces a particularly difficult task in persuading readers to sympathize with the plight of Joe Christmas. If *Light in August* is to be successful, Faulkner must supply a convincing explanation of the causes and motives that lie behind Joe Christmas' hostility and alienation.

Within the novel itself, Faulkner offers an explanation which he was to elaborate years later at the University of Virginia. As a child in the orphanage, Joe follows a Negro around the yard and once asks him, "How come you are a nigger?" The man responds: "Who told you I am a nigger, you little white trash bastard?" Joe answers, "I aint a nigger."

There follows the crucial assertion: "You are worse than that. You dont know what you are. And more than that, you wont never know . . . dont nobody but God know what you is" (p. 363). Despite the arguments of those who believe that Christmas was a mulatto or at least part Negro, the fact is that the issue of Joe's racial origins remains in doubt—and must remain in doubt—throughout the novel.

At the University of Virginia, Faulkner repeated and elaborated this explanation of Joe Christmas' plight. Asked if Joe Christmas was supposed to be part Negro, Faulkner replied: "I think that was his tragedy—he didn't know what he was, and so he was nothing. He deliberately evicted himself from the human race because he didn't know which he was. That was his tragedy, that to me was the tragic, central idea of the story—that he didn't know what he was, and there was no way possible in life for him to find out. Which to me is the most tragic condition a man could find himself in—not to know what he is and to know that he will never know." In another interview, Faulkner returned to the same point: "The only person in that book [*Light in August*] that accepted a tragic view of life was Christmas because he didn't know what he was and so he deliberately repudiated man. He didn't belong to man any longer, he deliberately repudiated man."[8]

Certainly the novel offers a great deal of evidence to support this interpretation of Joe Christmas' character. From his earliest experiences in the orphanage to his death, Christmas suffers the mental anguish and doubt of not knowing his identity. Again and again, he alternates between the Negro community and the white community, living first with one and then with the other. He is particularly angered by those who seem not to care one way or the other about his race. Able to pass for white or Negro, free to choose, he refuses to make the choice. Perhaps one of the strongest motives he has for killing Joanna Burden is his realization that she is pushing him towards a final choice, since her plans for him depend upon his proclaiming himself a Negro. Near the end of his life, however, he does come close to allying himself with the Negro community.

Fleeing from the sheriff's posse, Joe Christmas meets a Negro woman wearing her husband's shoes. He swaps his for those she is wearing. On one level, the change of shoes helps him to confuse the sheriff's dogs, but the act may have additional significance. As he pauses to lace the brogans, "the black shoes, the black shoes smelling of negro," it seems to him that "he could see himself being hunted by white men at last into the black abyss which had been waiting, trying, for thirty years to drown him and into which now and at last he had actually entered, bearing now upon his ankles the definite and ineradicable gauge of its upward moving" (p. 313).

Thus, the wearing of the Negro shoes appears to parallel and perhaps symbolize Joe's increasing commitment to the Negro race. Interestingly, here he seems to recognize the pressures of the whites forcing him toward this commitment (though it was Joanna Burden more than anyone else), yet the choice of the shoes was an act of free will. As Christmas enters Mottstown, where he will in effect surrender himself, he is sitting on the seat of a wagon, "with planted on the dashboard before him the shoes, the black shoes smelling of negro: that mark on his ankles the gauge definite and ineradicable of the black tide creeping up his legs, moving from his feet upward as death moves" (p. 321). One must be careful, however, about the inferences to be made from this scene. There is very little in the passage to warrant the assertion that at the close of his life Christmas irrevocably joined the Negro community; and there is no additional evidence in the novel to support such a conclusion, unless it is Gavin Stevens' theory that Faulkner at Virginia labeled "an assumption, a rationalization."[9] The matter of Joe Christmas' identity remains ambiguous as Faulkner apparently intended that it remain; and the tensions of Christmas' life remain unsolved until the moment of his death.

Although Christmas' ambiguous racial identity accounts for much of his hostility towards society, other factors, particularly religion and women, contribute to what Faulkner calls Joe's tragic view of life. Joe's remark just before he leaves his cabin to murder Joanna Burden, "it's because she started praying over me" (p. 98), has its origin in the actions of his Grandfather Hines and foster father, Simon McEachern. One can scarcely imagine two more vicious and intolerant examples of Protestant or Calvinistic religious fanatics than these two men. Hines, whose characteristic exclamation is "bitchery and abomination" (p. 350), murders Joe's father and bears the responsibility for Joe's mother's death, preaches white supremacy to Negroes, and blasphemously considers himself advisor to God. Hines, the reader must conclude, has gone beyond religion to become pathologically grotesque. Faulkner's portrayal of him reaches a climax near the end of Chapter 16, in the passage where Hines reports a conversation he has had with God.

And they come and took him [Christmas] away. Old Doc Hines saw him go away in the buggy and he went back to wait for God and God come and He said to old Doc Hines, "You can go too now. You have done My work. There is no more evil here now but womanevil, not worthy for My chosen instrument to watch." And old Doc Hines went when God told him to go. But he kept in touch with God and at night he said, "That bastard, Lord," and God said, "He is still walking My earth," and old Doc Hines kept in touch with God and at night he said, "That bastard, Lord," and God said, "He is still walking My earth," and old Doc Hines kept in touch with God and one night he wrestled and he strove and he cried aloud, "That bastard, Lord! I feel! I feel the teeth and the fangs of evil!" and God said, "It's that bastard. Your work is not done yet. He's a pollution and a abomination on My earth." (p. 365)

Mrs. Hines, whose life he has ruined, understands clearly the nature of her husband. She says that he took "God's name in vain and in pride to justify and excuse the devil that was in him" (p. 352). That Doc Hines is unsuccessful in raising a mob to lynch Joe Christmas after he has been captured comes as a relief to most readers.

Perhaps even more influential in forming the character of Joe Christmas is Simon McEachern. For him the "two abominations are sloth and idle thinking, the two virtues are work and the fear of God" (p. 135). McEachern represents the type of religious bigot who worships a God of wrath and justice, and like his God, McEachern is totally without compassion or love. Typical of his belief is the prayer of this "ruthless man who had never known either pity or doubt" and who can neither love nor forgive: "He asked that the child's stubborn heart be softened and that the sin of disobedience be forgiven him also, through the advocacy of the man whom he had flouted and disobeyed, requesting that Almighty be as magnanimous as himself, and by and through and because of conscious grace" (p. 143).

Oddly enough, Joe Christmas finds in McEachern's implacable authoritarianism a measure of security. Joe knows "where he stands" and what to expect. He can see law and justice in McEachern. What Joe does not learn from his foster father is love, or mercy, or pity. What has shocked the boy in the affair with the orphanage dietitian is that instead of the punishment he expects, she offers him an apparent reward. She is unpredictable. The situation with McEachern, however, seems "perfectly logical and reasonable and inescapable." Moreover, Joe learns that "he and the man could always count upon one another, depend upon one another" (p. 149). McEachern remains constant, and Joe understands

that he must endure until he can physically oppose his foster father's inflexibility with his own intractableness. Twelve years after his adoption,
Joe becomes a man when he faces McEachern and says, "Dont you hit me
again" (p. 154). Resistance has made Joe a man but in so doing it has also
established for him a way of life. Meanwhile, the circumstances of his
youth with McEachern have prompted Joe to lie, to steal, and, finally, to
murder. From the role of passive acceptance of his suffering, Christmas
becomes an aggressor. Not surprisingly, in many respects Christmas the
man resembles Simon McEachern (and at times Doc Hines). They share
that same rigidity, that same unbending intolerance and arrogance, and
that same implacability that Faulkner attributes to Protestant fundamentalism. The great difference between them lies in the fact that Joe
Christmas hates religion and the code of behavior that McEachern would
impose upon all society. Unlike McEachern, Joe also suffers inwardly
from his extreme self-centeredness, from the uncertainty of his racial
identity, and from his relationships with women.

Joe Christmas' troubles with women may be explained in large measure by their unpredictability, though one should not exclude such other
matters as his ambiguous racial allegiance, religious attitudes, and deep-
seated sexual antagonisms. From the very first, women seem not to have
been hostile to him. In the orphanage, the young girl named Alice found
him appealing. The dietitian, it is true, plotted against him with Hines
but the novel contains no suggestion that Christmas ever knew of her
plans. What disturbed Joe was the fact that when he expected punishment from her, he received rewards. She did not fit into his concept of
justice or predictable action. When Mrs. McEachern offered food, she
again reversed the pattern of conduct that Joe expected. He scorns her
efforts to mitigate the punishments of her husband, hurls her food
against the wall (he would repeat the action in Joanna's house), and later
steals her money (as he would later murder Joanna).

Almost instinctively, Joe rebels against the biological functions of
women. When he kicks and strikes the young Negro girl, he could not
have told why he fought; yet he experiences a physical revulsion that
reminds him of the toothpaste incident in the orphanage. The feel of
her flesh and the smell of her body overwhelm him. When he first
learns about menstruation, he experiences a similar revulsion which he
conquers after he kills a sheep and puts (washes?) his hands "in the yet

warm blood of the dying beast, trembling, drymouthed, backglaring"
(p. 174). He learns to accept it as fact, but he must learn it all over again
from Bobbie. After her explanation, he strikes her, escapes to the woods,
and imagines he sees a row of urns in the moonlight. "Each one was
cracked and from each crack there issued something liquid, death-
colored, and foul. . . . He vomited" (p. 178). He cannot become recon-
ciled to nature until he has taken Bobbie to the scene. Thereafter, Joe
sleeps with many women, white and Negro, but he never loves them: he
uses them.

During the fifteen years of Joe's wanderings, he often "bedded with
the women and paid them when he had the money, and when he did not
have it he bedded anyway and then told them that he was a negro"
(p. 211). One night, however, the woman looked at him with no surprise and answered: "'What about it? . . . You ought to seen the shine I
turned out just before your turn came.' . . . It took two policemen to
subdue him. At first they thought that the woman was dead" (p. 212).
After that, Christmas was sick for two years; the identity problem had
merged with the sex problem.

Christmas' experiences and hostilities converge and often repeat
themselves in his relationship with Joanna Burden. Hunger drives him
to enter her kitchen where she greets him with food and a lighted candle.
Soon they live double lives: by day he works as a white man, but by night
he is a Negro in Joanna's bed; by day she is a wise counselor for Negro
women, but by night she is a woman possessed with inordinate sexual
desires. In their isolation from the community, they are strangely alike.
For a time their sexual appetites coincide; but with Joanna's desire for a
child and the approach of her menopause, Christmas begins to feel
threatened. He uses her, but he recognizes that she sees him as an object,
a Negro, who needs help. As she pushes him towards a racial commitment, his hostility increases.

The relationship with Joanna becomes intolerable to him when her
religious feelings, which had been quiescent during the early days of
their affair, begin to reassert themselves. During the period of their passion, she had thrust aside her religious feelings, and towards the end she
had wanted to prolong the sexual relationship. "I'm not ready to pray
yet," she says. "Dont make me have to pray yet. Dear God, let me be
damned a little longer, a little while" (p. 250). But in the end, she yields

149

to her religious scruples and demands that Joe kneel to pray with her. Her insistence upon Joe's kneeling and praying recalls the scenes of his childhood with the McEacherns, and Christmas realizes that to consent to her demands would be to negate an entire lifetime of resistance. Acquiescence would, in fact, end his alienation but it would also force a commitment. Ever since leaving the orphanage, Joe has rejected female help, refused to make any final or binding racial commitment, and denied the commands of religion. All of these forces come together in Joanna. Faulkner writes that before Christmas goes to her bedroom on the final night "he believed with calm paradox that he was the volitionless servant of the fatality in which he believed that he did not believe. He was saying to himself *I had to do it* already in the past tense; *I had to do it. She said so herself*" (p. 264). After Joanna has prayed for herself and Joe (the scene reminds the reader of McEachern praying for himself and Joe), she says: "Then there's just one other thing to do," and he repeats "There's just one other thing to do" (p. 265). The fact that she has two bullets in the chambers of the pistol strengthens the inference that she had decided to kill Christmas and herself.

No simple explanation or interpretation of Joe Christmas' unhappy life seems adequate. Like most human beings, he sinned greatly himself and yet was greatly sinned against. On the one hand, the forces of religious bigotry and racial intolerance did much to blight his life from its beginning. The odds were against him. On the other hand, if the individual does have some control over his emotions and actions, Joe's failure in life may be viewed as the result of his rejection of love, his unwillingness to give of himself, and his refusal to recognize the common humanity of others. Perhaps his greatest enemy was himself. Wronged himself, he yet wronged others. He is most to be pitied, however, for his human weaknesses, though the reader may also become indignant over the evil done to him. That Christmas somehow attained a kind of peace through his final agony, Faulkner seems trying to make clear in the final description of Christmas lying on the floor "with his eyes open and empty of everything save consciousness, and with something, a shadow, about his mouth. For a long moment he looked up at them with peaceful and unfathomable and unbearable eyes" (p. 439). The peace that Joe Christmas attains is the release that death brings from the torments of living. It cannot be taken as the peace that comes through the resolution of life's problems, or the recognition of self, or the fulfillment of a great moral vision. From Christmas' death, one receives neither the redemption of a Lear, nor the ripeness of a Hamlet, nor the waste of an Othello. Joe Christmas dies as he lived, an alien in life, a man without a commitment save to himself. While Lena Grove's journey moves onward, the street of Joe Christmas' life ends abruptly and bequeaths nothing to the future.

Thoughtful readers of *Light in August* have frequently raised certain questions about Joe Christmas that seem to remain unanswered at his death. Why, for example, after successfully eluding the sheriff's posse for about a week, did Christmas suddenly enter Mottstown and walk around the streets until someone recognized him? What made him decide virtually to seek his own death? Another seemingly incongruous action relates to his attempted escape. After apparently deciding to plead guilty in order to escape the death sentence, why, as he is being brought to the courthouse, did he make a sudden break for freedom? And having once decided to break, why did he run to Hightower's house? Some critics have argued that Mrs. Hines persuaded him to escape and told him he would find sanctuary or help from Hightower. But if this explanation is accepted, why did Joe strike down Hightower inside the house? Symbolically, of course, for Christmas to find death in Hightower's house is appropriate, since they are both outcasts and guilty of sins against society. But Joe would have known that Hightower's house would be a dead end. Finally, once Christmas knew that all was lost, why did he not use the pistol in his hand? Despite the ingenious theories that can be offered to answer these questions, most of them will probably remain unsolved enigmas.

One other critical problem should be mentioned in connection with the life and death of Joe Christmas. To what degree was his life determined by forces over which he had no control? Was he morally responsible? Was he free to choose what kind of life he would live? Probably no firm answer can be given to these questions. Certain evidence in the novel suggests that Joe Christmas believed he was free to choose. In a passage already cited, Faulkner declares that Joe "believed with calm paradox that he was the volitionless servant of the fatality in which he believed that he did not believe." On another occasion, as he stands in Joanna's kitchen door, he would look out and see, "perhaps with foreboding and premonition, the savage and lonely street which he had chosen of his own [free] will, waiting for him" (pp. 243–44). Again, when Joanna mentions marriage, Joe feels tempted by the thought that marriage *"would mean ease, security, for the rest of your life. You would never have to move again"* (p. 250). But almost simultaneously, Joe thinks that if he fits into the pattern of society, "I will deny all the thirty years that I have lived to make me what I chose to be." The inference is that Christmas did believe that he himself chose the street down which his life ran; but did Faulkner believe that Joe made a choice? One cannot be entirely certain.

In other passages, Faulkner appears to refer to some all-powerful supernatural person who moves men around on a kind of chessboard. Joe Brown, for instance, thinks about men being "without reason moved here and there by an Opponent who could read his moves before he made them and who created spontaneous rules which he and not the Opponent, must follow" (p. 414). Describing Percy Grimm's pursuit of Joe Christmas, Faulkner writes: "He [Grimm] was moving again almost before he had stopped, with that lean, swift, blind obedience to whatever Player moved him on the Board" (p. 437). The Player moves Grimm as a "pawn" and even enables him to breathe. The car of men stops "just where the Player had desired it to be" (p. 438). After Grimm reaches Hightower's house, "it was as though he had been merely waiting for the Player to move him again, because with that unfailing certitude he ran straight to the kitchen" (p. 439). Finally, Grimm's last brutal act is introduced with the phrase, "but the Player was not done yet" (p. 439). Faulkner had spoken of the Player and the Pawn at the end of *Sartoris*. How far the author intended this concept of an external power controlling the destiny of men to explain the conduct of Joe Christmas remains another unanswered question. Although Christmas may have had a feeling of inevitability in the killing of Joanna Burden, one would hesitate to argue that he is not a free agent. To deny him responsibility for his actions would strengthen Faulkner's case against the pernicious influence of religious fundamentalism in men's lives, but at the same time such a denial would lessen Joe's stature as a human being. Likewise, the deity in control of men's lives would appear to support religious bigotry just as the "Player" who controls the actions of Percy Grimm moves him towards the savage murder of Joe Christmas. Faulkner most likely did not intend to absolve either Christmas, or Grimm, or any other character of moral responsibility for his actions. Although the novelist's theological beliefs were probably not those of most Protestant sects, his consistently humanistic outlook upon man's moral responsibility, his assertion of the value of human love and brotherhood, and his recognition of man's potential for virtue make wholly unacceptable such a reading of an all-controlling deity forcing man to evil acts. Faulkner may have accepted the paradox that some acts of men seem almost fated or even predestined yet they result from man's own agency.

Although the novelist devoted almost three times as much space to Joe Christmas as he did to any other character in *Light in August*, Faulkner chose to put Hightower and Lena Grove on his fictional stage at the conclusion of the novel. Lena's story has already been cited as providing a contrast to that of Christmas and as enveloping the novel with an optimistic note approaching comedy. The account of Gail Hightower, presented in the greatest detail after the death of Joe Christmas, performs a similar function of contrast on a much more sophisticated level. Of all the characters in the novel, Hightower is probably the one with whose experiences and personality Faulkner's readers can most easily identify and sympathize. To a degree, Hightower represents a middle ground between Christmas and Lena Grove, and within the novel he connects her story with that of both Christmas and Joanna Burden.

To Joe and Joanna, Hightower offers both contrasts and parallels. Whereas Joe has no past and no sense of history, Hightower lives in the past of his grandfather even more intensely than Joanna is affected by her ancestors. All three characters are highly introspective individuals, the men perhaps more so than Joanna, and each seeks in his or her own way to find peace and tranquility. All of them live "outside" of the community. Joe seeks to find himself through headlong resistance to society's patterns; Joanna reverts to religion; and Hightower, as his name implies, completely withdraws. He feels he has bought "immunity." All of them are extremely self-centered, the men conspicuously lacking in love and real generosity. Joanna sinks into unrestrained sensuality as a kind of substitute for the absence of love in her life. Outcasts from society as these three characters are, they make the novel seem top-heavy with alienation. In many respects, *Light in August* is a compelling examination of those "who don't fit in."

Hightower's way of life, particularly, touches the experiences and feelings of those who have wanted to escape the sordidness and petty meanness of everyday living, those who hate to compromise principles with realities, and those who prefer the past to the present. An educated man, an intellectual, and an idealist, Hightower has remarkably clear perceptions. As a young man, he enters the seminary with the idealistic faith that "if ever truth could walk naked and without shame or fear, it would be in the seminary" (p. 453). In the church he feels he can see his entire life "sheltered from the harsh gale of living and die so, peacefully" (p. 453). The seminary means "quiet and safe walls within which the hampered and garmentworried spirit could learn anew serenity to contemplate without horror or alarm its own nakedness" (p. 453). His longing for security first within the walls of the seminary and later within the church becomes Hightower's most serious mistake. Under the influence of the daughter of one of his teachers, who herself longs to escape the seminary's walls, Hightower schemes to get a place in Jefferson. In the "demagoguery, the abasement, the small lying" (p. 456) required to obtain that place, Hightower could have learned a great deal about the practical workings of the church that he does not learn until almost too late.

As minister and husband, Hightower fails because of his desire to withdraw from the disputes, issues, and troubles of humanity into a romantic past. After he resigns as minister, he often sits by his window at nightfall and listens to the music coming from his former church: "listening, he seems to hear within it the apotheosis of his own history, his own land, his own environed blood: that people from which he sprang and among whom he lives who can never take either pleasure or catastrophe or escape from either, without brawling over it. Pleasure, ecstasy, they cannot seem to bear: their escape from it is in violence, in drinking and fighting and praying" (p. 347). They cannot pity, for "to pity . . . would be to admit selfdoubt and to hope for and need pity themselves" (p. 348). Finally, Hightower understands that what is "destroying the Church is not the outward groping of those within it nor the inward groping of those without, but the professionals who control it and who have removed the bells from its steeples" (p. 461). The churches of the world have indeed become a barricade or rampart planted "against truth and against that peace in which to sin and be forgiven which is the life of man" (p. 461). By the time Hightower has obtained this insight, he has also recognized his own sins and his own need for forgiveness.

What separates Hightower from Christmas more than anything else is Hightower's ability, near the end of his life, to recognize the nature of his failure. Hightower receives help from Byron Bunch who begins as Hightower's disciple but ends as his tutor. Bunch, like Hightower, withdraws from society, but when Bunch falls in love, his perspective changes. Bunch begins to help others (eventually he even tries to get Hightower to provide an alibi for Joe Christmas). Joe Brown or Lucas Burch stand somewhat in the same relationship with Joe Christmas that Byron Bunch does to Hightower, but Brown is either incapable of helping or unwilling to help anyone. Lena Grove does not have the same influence upon Lucas Burch that she exerts upon Byron Bunch. Joe Christmas may have found peace in death, but he never grasps the cause of his failure. He may be released, but he is not redeemed. He is not a tragic hero because he never sees himself clearly enough to recognize his own fatal flaws.

Hightower is a much more tragic figure than Joe Christmas, since the minister finally sees himself as he is, recognizes his mistakes, and ends a better man than he began. By gaining a self-knowledge that Christmas never attains and by finally making a commitment to others, Hightower resolves his alienation. He understands that he has "acquiesced" and even "served" the corruption of the church (p. 461). He has used it for his own ends, as a way to obtain a self-centered peace. In his marriage he has betrayed his trust. As he thinks to himself, "perhaps in the moment when I revealed to her not only the depth of my hunger but the fact that never and never would she have any part in the assuaging of it; perhaps at that moment I became her seducer and her murderer, author and instrument of her shame and death" (p. 462). As the wheel of thinking turns, he sees himself in his pulpit as "a figure antic as a showman, a little wild: a charlatan preaching worse than heresy, in utter disregard of that whose very stage he preempted, offering instead of the crucified shape of pity and love, a swaggering and unchastened bravo killed with a shotgun in a peaceful henhouse, in a temporary hiatus of his own avocation of killing" (p. 462). Here Hightower realizes that by living in the dead past he has denied his responsibilities towards the living. He now also realizes that in appearing as a martyr, "making it appear that he was being driven" (p. 463) into the very peace and quiet he had always wanted, he was also serving his own ends. For the first time in his life, Hightower sees himself for what he is. Self-recognition is always the first step towards redemption. His alibi for Joe Christmas, though it comes too late to save him, is a complete reversal from Hightower's earlier unwillingness to help. No other character in *Light in August*, and only a very few others in Faulkner's novels, reaches this level of humanity.

Although more than one critic has called *Light in August* Faulkner's finest work, many readers leave it with a vague feeling of dissatisfaction hard to define precisely. Despite its flashes of brilliant writing, the parts of the novel seem somehow not to come together as one piece. To some readers, Faulkner appears to be telling four, five, perhaps six separate stories that can be forcibly merged but do not seem to flow together organically. Even the narrative form has problems. Although at the beginning Faulkner follows a traditional pattern of narration, soon the sharp breaks between episodes and character histories, the interruption of forward action to insert background material, and the introduction of new characters near the end (for example, Percy Grimm and the furniture dealer) puzzle many readers. To others, perhaps the greatest weakness of the work is Faulkner's failure to tie the reader's sympathy firmly to Joe Christmas. Often Christmas is not a much-to-be-pitied, suffering victim; at times he is a vicious criminal loose in society. Something of the same problem confronted Melville in writing *Moby-Dick*: does the reader view Ahab as a tragic figure to be pitied because he stands for the suffering of all mankind? Or, is Ahab simply an evil, blasphemous, "ungodly god-like man" who brings himself and the society of which he is a part to ultimate destruction? Because of Joe Christmas' failures in love, his selfishness, beatings, murders, and other evil deeds, does he forfeit the reader's sympathy? Or, despite his weaknesses, hostilities, and lack of self knowledge, may he be understood as a prototype of suffering mankind? Of course, there are no ready-made answers to these questions. The thoughtful reader will consider carefully all of the evidence before he renders his own verdict.

CHAPTER VI

The Stubbornness
of Historical Truth

Absalom, Absalom!

PERHAPS the earliest mention of *Absalom, Absalom!* occurs in a letter
from Faulkner to Harrison Smith in February, 1934. In it, Faulkner said
that he had put aside *Requiem for a Nun* and a work about the Snopeses to
write another novel which he intended to call *Dark House* or "something
of that nature." Clearly, from what follows, the novel is *Absalom, Absalom!* Wrote Faulkner: "It is the more or less violent breakup of a household or family from 1860 to about 1910. . . . The story is an anecdote
which occurred during and right after the civil war; the climax is another
anecdote which happened about 1910 and which explains the story.
Roughly, the theme is a man who outraged the land, and the land then
turned and destroyed the man's family." One can grasp how far Faulkner
had gone in his conception of the major outlines of the novel by his next
remark. "Quentin Compson, of the Sound & Fury, tells it, or ties it together; he is the protagonist so that it is not complete apocrypha. I use
him because it is just before he is to commit suicide because of his sister,
and I use his bitterness which he has projected on the South in the form of
hatred of it and its people to get more out of the story itself than a historical novel would be. To keep the hoop skirts and plug hats out, you
might say." [1] Faulkner promised to complete it by fall.

Six months later, the book was still "not quite ripe," though Faulkner
did have the final title, *Absalom, Absalom!* (afterwards at the University
of Virginia, he said that the title occurred to him simultaneously with
the idea of writing about a man who wanted sons and the sons destroyed
him). [2] In August, 1934, he wrote Harrison Smith: "I have a title for it
which I like, by the way: *Absalom, Absalom*; the story is of a man who
wanted a son through pride, and got too many of them and they de-

stroyed him."[3] As will be seen, these early remarks about the title and the subject or theme of the novel become important in arguments over the interpretation of the work. Because of the complexity of his artistic design, the writing proved exceptionally difficult.

So troublesome, in fact, was the composition that Faulkner turned aside to write *Pylon* and several short stories; but on March 30, 1935, he made a fresh start, having at hand what he had written the year before and other material from various short stories, published and unpublished, relating to the life and character of Thomas Sutpen. In composing, he cut up and pasted together fragments of this earlier work, revising, adding where necessary, and at times even recutting and repasting. One can well understand his remark at the University of Virginia that when he resumed work on *Absalom, Absalom!* in the spring of 1935, he "almost rewrote the whole thing."[4] Before it was finished, he would be interrupted by the tragic death of his brother, Dean Faulkner, in an airplane accident and the necessity of a trip to Hollywood to make some ready money as a screenwriter. By the end of 1935 or early 1936, most of the writing had been completed. The last page was dated "31 Jany 1936" and signed "William Faulkner." Even so, in April, 1936, he wrote a new version of the important first chapter; and as the novel was put into galley type, he made additional changes.

Probably in May, 1936, Faulkner decided that to help the "average" reader follow the plotline, he would supply several appendices at the end of the volume. Accordingly, he prepared a chronology of events, a genealogy of seventeen of the characters, and a map of Yoknapatawpha County. The difficulty readers of the novel would experience in correctly keeping in mind the chronological relationships of the story was foreshadowed by Faulkner's own errors, both in the text and in the chronology. For example, in the chronology Faulkner dated Rosa and Quentin's September visit to Sutpen's house and Rosa's subsequent December visit as "1910" instead of "1909." (Quentin committed suicide in June, 1910, and his death is mentioned in the genealogy as 1910.) Curiously, neither in the chronology nor in the genealogy did he mention Goodhue Coldfield's wife, who died at the birth of Rosa, but who was obviously alive in 1838 when Ellen married Thomas Sutpen. Furthermore, no mention is made of Mrs. Coldfield while the aunt arranges for Ellen's marriage; neither is Mrs. Coldfield present at the wedding. There are other discrepancies between the chronology and the text. For example, on Charles Bon's tombstone, his age is given as *"33 years and 5 months"* and his death as occurring in 1865,[5] but in the chronology Bon is said to have been born in 1829. Moreover, the tombstone indicates that Bon was born in New Orleans, while the chronology indicates Haiti. In all these instances the text must be assumed correct and the end data erroneous. If the discrepancies and errors disturb the modern reader, he may take some comfort in the realization that even after forty years the task of preparing such chronological addenda remains a formidable undertaking. Modern editions of the novel retain the original entries in both chronology and genealogy.

To accompany the chronology and the genealogy, Faulkner devised a map of the fictional Yoknapatawpha County. Mississippi readers at once recognized its remarkable resemblance to Lafayette County, the fictional county being bounded on the north by the Tallahatchie River and on the south by the Yoknapatawpha River and Frenchman's Bend and bisected by the railroad running north and south. Four main roads intersect near the center of the county. By identifying the scenes of his earlier novels, Faulkner called attention to the interrelationships among his fictional works. Among the places identified are old Bayard's bank, the Sartoris Plantation, the Compson land, Mottstown, the bridge where Anse Bundren and his children tried to cross the river with Addie's body, Joanna Burden's house, the courthouse where Temple Drake testified, the jail, and the Holston House. In all, Faulkner located twenty-seven places, and at the bottom he printed the caption: "Jefferson, Yoknapatawpha Co., Mississippi / Area, 2400 Square Miles—Population, Whites, 6298; Negroes, 9313 / William Faulkner, Sole Owner & Proprietor."[6] Soon, though not immediately, it would become the most famous county in America and the object of worldwide attention. When the volume was published, the map, printed in red and black, was folded in among the endpapers.

In September, 1936, Faulkner read galley proof of *Absalom, Absalom!*, and on October 26, Random House published the work. Although many now believe it Faulkner's finest achievement, contemporary reviewers failed notably to estimate the novel's significance. Writing in the *New Yorker*, Clifton Fadiman candidly admitted that he did not understand why the novel had been written or even what it was about, but he found it "the most consistently boring novel by a reputable writer to come my way during the last decade." Fadiman concluded that the novel pointed "to the final blowup of what was once a remarkable, if minor, talent." Having a much clearer idea than Fadiman about the content of the work, the reviewer for *Time* warned readers to make "allowances for Quentin's false or true hypotheses . . . and for the bias and confusion of his informants," while at the same time he characterized the book as "the strangest, longest, least readable, most infuriating and yet in some respects the most impressive novel that William Faulkner has written." In the *Forum*, Mary Colum pronounced it "too incoherent" and "unsuccessful" and lamented that Faulkner could not have had the advantage of "threshing out his technical ideas around a café table" with other writers. There were some favorable reviews. Herschel Brickell thought it would "rank as one of its author's major works," and Malcolm Cowley considered it Faulkner's "strongest" and "most unified" novel. Cowley wrote that the "note of incest suggests Byron, but elsewhere it is Poe whose spirit seems closest to the story—especially at the end, where Sutpen's Hundred collapses like the House of Usher." After calling Faulkner a modernized "Poe in Mississippi," Cowley devoted a substantial portion of his review to his theory that the "hidden subject" of the novel is "the decline of the South after the Civil War." According to Cowley, "Sutpen's Hundred, the mansion that rotted and finally burned, is obviously a symbol of Southern culture" and "Sutpen's curse is the result of his relations with Negroes." Cowley, whose literary criticism exhibited a social and even political edge, spoke for the liberal, often anti-Southern *New Republic* and for Northern readers who applauded Faulkner as a Southerner committed to exposing Southern racial intolerance. The reviews, whether good or bad, gave the novel considerable publicity. A second printing of 2,500 copies was required shortly after publication, and a third printing of 1,400 copies was run on November 19.[7] The record was not spectacular, but it was respectable.

For the most part, reviewers, apparently puzzled by the title, made little effort to draw a parallel between Sutpen and the Old Testament account of David and Absalom. Within the novel, no reference is made to the biblical story; the plot relates wholly to Mississippi. In view of the centrality of Sutpen's mansion to the work, the earlier title, *Dark House*, may quite possibly reflect another source of inspiration. Certainly, many old antebellum plantation houses and mansions in the Oxford area, some well kept and others deserted and rotting, could have supplied the prototype of Sutpen's ill-fated mansion. Of the well-preserved houses, Faulkner's own, upon which he was laboring to meet the payments at the very time he was writing *Absalom, Absalom!*, represented a good example. Rowan Oak, acquired by the novelist in 1930, had been built about 1844 by Colonel Robert B. Shegog. An Irishman, Shegog had settled in Lafayette County and commissioned William Turner, an English architect, to build for him a house replete with columns and portico and landscaped in front with a cedar-lined drive, brick-bordered flowerbeds, and magnolia trees. Faulkner had already borrowed Shegog's name to use for the Negro preacher in *The Sound and the Fury*.

Other houses, however, may have contributed more than Rowan Oak to *Absalom, Absalom!* In the northeastern section of the county, Alexander Hamilton Pegues before the Civil War owned 5,000 acres, and though he had not fought in the war, his home had been destroyed. His brother, Colonel Thomas Pegues, had also possessed vast tracts of land, and his house had been planned by an English architect with a French-sounding name. Closer to Oxford, though twelve miles out, was the old Shipp place, built by Dr. Felix Grundy Shipp, who came to the county in 1833 with sixty-five relatives and slaves. In Faulkner's day, the house was abandoned. Another landowner was Wash Jones, and in the family burying ground of an old house southwest of Oxford, Faulkner could have found the names of Jones and Bond. The truth is that more than one home in the neighborhood could have prompted Shreve's remark about Sutpen's mansion: "*You have seen the rotting shell of the house with its sagging portico and scaling walls, its sagging blinds and plank-shuttered windows, set in the middle of the domain which had reverted to the state and had been bought and sold and bought and sold again and again and again*" (p. 213). Other passages in *Absalom, Absalom!* have the same tone. As Quentin approached Sutpen's mansion on a hunting trip, "he looked up the slope . . . where the wet yellow sedge died upward into the rain like melting gold and saw the grove, the clump of cedars on the crest of the hill dissolving into the rain as if the trees had been drawn in ink on a wet blotter—the cedars beyond which, beyond the ruined fields beyond which, would be the oak grove and the gray huge rotting deserted house half a mile away" (p. 187). Even more remarkable is Miss Rosa Coldfield's description:

Rotting portico and scaling walls, it stood, not ravaged, not invaded, marked by no bullet nor soldier's iron heel but rather as though reserved for something more: some desolation more profound than ruin, as if it had stood in iron juxtaposition to iron flame, to a holocaust which had found itself less fierce and less implacable, not hurled but rather fallen back before the impervious and indomitable skeleton which the flames durst not, at the instant's final crisis, assail. . . . and I running out of the bright afternoon, into the thunderous silence of that brooding house where I could see nothing at first: then gradually the face . . . already there, rocklike and firm and antedating time and house and doom. (p. 136)

To appreciate the centrality of the Sutpen mansion in the novel, one has only to recall the emphasis Faulkner places upon it as the setting for the major actions of the Sutpen story, for example, its planning and construction by the French architect and the half-wild slaves, the visits of Henry and Bon, Ellen's death, the burial of Charles Bon, Sutpen's return from the war, Rosa's affront and outrage, the murder of Sutpen, the deaths of Judith and Charles Etienne Saint-Valery Bon, and the final scenes with Quentin and Rosa that conclude in the conflagration that destroys it in December, 1909. From beginning to end, the mansion is the center of the story. It seems never to have known joy; again and again the reader views it through the narrator's eyes as a grim, rotting, desolate, haunted house. Sutpen's mansion is to *Absalom, Absalom!* what the scaffold is to Hawthorne's *The Scarlet Letter* and the *Pequod* is to Melville's *Moby-Dick*.

In addition to the material at hand for the Sutpen mansion, Faulkner had a number of "rag-tag and bob-ends of old tales and talking" (p. 303) which he used to develop the complete novel. Until 1979 several of these old tales existed only in manuscript and have not been generally known; but to those interested in the material with which the novelist built his fiction or in the craft of writing novels, these preliminary sketches have prime value.[8] Not the least of their significance is the inference to be drawn from them that Faulkner early in his career had in mind many of the stories that he would later incorporate into his novels. In 1925, for example, Faulkner went to Europe with William Spratling, and probably either during the trip or shortly afterwards wrote four stories: "Evangeline," "Mistral," "Snow," and "The Big Shot." One of the remarkable features of these stories is that each employs a "frame" consisting of a young man named Don and his unnamed friend merely identified as "I."

Don and "I" in each story learn the basic facts of a biographical event, much as Quentin and Shreve learn the facts of Sutpen's biography, and then collaborate in an endeavor to fill out the bare facts with plausible motives. In other words, possessing only a minimum of historical fact, they seek to fabricate the whole of the story through conjectures. In no case, however, does Faulkner state that their theories or conjectures represent the truth of the matter, and there is no "authorized" or author-sanctioned voice to tell the reader what is actually the truth of the matter. This aspect of the Don and "I" stories is important, because Faulkner utilized precisely the same technique in writing *Absalom, Absalom!*

Of the four stories, "Evangeline" is the most important "source" for *Absalom, Absalom!* It bears directly upon the second half of the novel when Quentin Compson and Shreve McCannon, in a Harvard dormitory, take over the telling of the story and improvise or imagine or conjecture many of the moot questions raised by the accounts offered earlier by Miss Rosa, Mr. Compson, and General Compson. Quentin and Shreve concentrate their attention upon the relationships among Judith, Henry Sutpen, and Charles Bon. Much of the scenario of this portion of *Absalom, Absalom!* has been anticipated by events and conjectures contained in "Evangeline."

In "Evangeline," Don asks his friend, who narrates the story in the first person, to investigate a ghost in the old Sutpen house, supposedly vacant for the past forty years. Don has already learned much of the background of the Judith-Bon-Henry triangle, and the two men conjecture that the ghost in the house may be Judith. As the story progresses, the identity of the ghost becomes not so important as the efforts of the two young men to discover the truths of the past (history) that explain or account for the ghost. In this endeavor, they are not entirely successful. Still assuming that the ghost is Judith, the narrator, like Rosa Coldfield and Quentin Compson in *Absalom, Absalom!*, visits the house now guarded by an old Negro named Raby Sutpen, who plays the role taken by Clytie in *Absalom, Absalom!* She shows the narrator Henry Sutpen, who has been living in the house ever since the death of Judith and is now dying in a foul room upstairs. On the table beside him lies Charles Bon's picture case that Judith pounded shut with a poker to keep it from ever being opened. Later that night, Raby sets the house on fire and dies with Henry in the flames. The next day, after rain has cooled the remains of the house, Bon's picture case is found. The narrator manages to open it. He recognizes the face of a Negro woman and reads the French inscription to her husband, dated August 12, 1860.

As a short story, "Evangeline" suffers from too many unresolved complications of plot, character, and motive; but as a point from which to observe the development of *Absalom, Absalom!* in Faulkner's mind over a period of years, the piece has considerable significance, because many of its features passed into *Absalom, Absalom!*, while others underwent considerable change; and as Faulkner thought about the story, he added a great deal to enrich its character and humanity. The crucial question in both short story and novel concerns Henry Sutpen's reasons for opposing the marriage of his sister to Charles Bon.

In "Evangeline," certain facts of the Bon-Judith affair can be established. During the academic year 1856–1857, at the University of Mississippi, Henry Sutpen meets Charles Bon, an attractive orphan from New Orleans. The two men become friends, and Henry brings Bon home with him. During the visit, Bon meets Henry's sister and begins to court her. Later, arrangements are made for Henry to spend the summer of 1858 in New Orleans with Bon. Instead of staying three months, however, Henry returns in three weeks and immediately begins to oppose Judith's romance with Bon. Henry will give no reasons for his attitude. In the fall the two men return to the university but do not speak to each other. At Thanksgiving, Henry and his father exchange angry words about Bon's forthcoming visit at Christmas. On Christmas Eve, Colonel Sutpen announces Judith's engagement to Bon and the next morning prevents a duel between Henry and Bon. Henry leaves home for three years. Bon is graduated in 1860, and the wedding is announced for the following year. In the spring of 1861, Henry returns home in uniform, receives a letter from Bon, who is staying in a hotel in the village, and responds by meeting Bon. Without Henry's opposition, the marriage takes place, and immediately the two young men leave amicably for the war. In 1865 Judith receives a letter from Bon saying he has survived the war, but Henry returns with Bon's body. He has been killed by the last shot of the war. As Bon is being buried, a young Negro girl in the house sees a face in the air, the head upside down. The face seems somehow related to the ghost that Don asks his friend to investigate. At this point, Don no longer takes an active part in the story.

During the narrator's visit to the Sutpen house, he fails to learn the answers to some of the key questions that trouble him. Raby Sutpen will not say precisely what Henry Sutpen learned during that visit to New Orleans, nor will she explain how Bon lied to Henry. In a passage that foreshadows Mr. Compson's remark in *Absalom, Absalom!* that "it's just incredible. It just does not explain" (p. 100), the narrator conjectures that Henry's opposition must have been based upon something more than the relationship between Bon and the woman. Among the matters never resolved or explained are the precise information Henry learned in New Orleans, the nature of Bon's lie, the exact date of Bon's first marriage, and the time when Henry first learns about that marriage. Actually, no real evidence exists to show that Henry killed Bon. That conjecture, as well as the brother-sister relationship between Henry and Raby, comes from the narrator's imagined, dreamlike conversation with Bon, Henry, and Raby.

What the narrator does learn, however, is that Henry Sutpen, not Judith, is the "ghost" in the Sutpen house and that Charles Bon had with him when his body was brought to the house the picture case containing not the picture that Judith had given him but the portrait of a Negro woman inscribed to her husband and dated August 12, 1860. This last information leads the narrator to infer that he knows what Henry Sutpen would have thought worse than the marriage and what had compounded the bigamy to the point where the pistol was necessary. (This is the same information that Judith obtained when she looked at the case just before Bon's burial.) Although in *Absalom, Absalom!* Faulkner radically altered the story by replacing Don and "I" with Shreve and Quentin, by connecting the conjectures they make with Quentin's life and character, and by substituting miscegenation and incest in place of bigamy, many of the unanswered questions in "Evangeline" survive into the novel, the most important being the general theme of the stubbornness of history to relinquish its truths. "Evangeline" would be sufficient in itself to show that rather early in his career Faulkner had already sketched out portions of the basic material he would later use in *Absalom, Absalom!*, but there are other stories that also contributed to the final rendering of the Sutpen legend.

The motif of the murdered bridegroom implied in "Evangeline" lies at the center of the Judith-Henry-Bon triangle in *Absalom, Absalom!*, and in one sense Thomas Sutpen himself provides another example, though he refuses to be a bridegroom by marrying Milly. Faulkner, moreover, had suggested the motif in *The Sound and the Fury* in the effort of Quentin first to murder Dalton Ames and later in his wish to shoot Herbert Head. Sometime during this period in his career, Faulkner wrote several other stories that relate to this general theme. In "Selvage," which Faulkner expanded into "Elly" and published in 1934,[9] Elly, a young virgin, becomes engaged to a dull but respectable assistant cashier in the bank. Shortly before the wedding is to take place, Elly gives herself to Paul de Montigny, who, according to her grandmother, is a Negro from New Orleans. When Paul refuses to marry her, Elly causes the car in which she, the grandmother, and Paul are riding to careen over a precipice. Elly is the only survivor, and Paul becomes in effect the unwilling bridegroom who is murdered. The murdered bridegroom also appears in "Mistral."[10] As Don and "I" approach a small Italian town, they learn that a funeral will take place that afternoon. The dead man has been engaged to marry the young ward of the priest; the banns have been read, and the wedding is to take place after the harvest. Suddenly and mysteriously, the wealthy prospective bridegroom dies, poisoned, perhaps, either by the girl or the priest. As in *Absalom, Absalom!*, the bridegroom is murdered and the bride has become a widow before she is a bride. Another bridegroom dies (murdered?) in "Snow." After descending from a ledge high in the Swiss Alps, Don and "I" attend the funeral of a guide who months earlier has plunged to his death when he cuts the rope that binds him to his three companions so that his bride and his client, always referred to as the Big Shot, might be pulled to safety by a partner. The body could not be recovered until the snow has melted in the spring. Don and "I" learn that the accident took place on the day after the guide's wedding and that immediately afterward the bride, who was a widow as soon as she became a bride, went away with the Big Shot. "Snow" leaves many unanswered questions in the reader's mind, one of them being whether the Big Shot tried to kill the guide.[11] Neither "Elly" nor "Mistral" nor "Snow" exhibits the close relationship with *Absalom, Absalom!* that "Evangeline" does, but they reinforce the evidence that Faulkner was interested in narrators who make their own conjectures about incomplete or fragmentary historical fact and in variations upon the theme of the murdered bridegroom.

The last of the so-called Don and "I" stories, "The Big Shot," contains no reference to a murdered bridegroom. The element of conjecture and speculation on the part of the narrator and his friend is much less than in the other pieces, but the story offers a direct parallel to the incident that prompts Thomas Sutpen's "design" in *Absalom, Absalom!* In "The Big Shot," Dal Martin, when only a small boy, is turned away from a rich man's door in almost exactly the same fashion that Sutpen is turned away from the plantation owner's door in the novel. As a result of this act, Martin formulates a design to acquire the money and things that enable the rich man to scorn those less endowed with wealth and material possessions. Martin, whose actions at times also suggest incidents in the career of Flem Snopes, succeeds in his design until he lacks only respectability to complete it. His goal will be achieved when his daughter, who resembles Temple Drake in *Sanctuary*, receives an invitation to the socially elite ball of the Chickasaw Guards. Among Martin's employees is Popeye, whose appearance, character, and behavior foreshadow the Popeye of *Sanctuary*. At the end of the story, Martin's ambitions collapse when Popeye runs over the daughter and she dies in a charity hospital.

These stories, as well as other fragments in the "Rowan Oak Papers," [12] demonstrate convincingly that the final composition of *Absalom, Absalom!* was the result of experimentation and the interweaving of ideas that Faulkner had tried out for a number of years. They constitute the lumber out of which he constructed a great work of literature. A more detailed comparison between the stories and the novel than that given here would accentuate the artistic rightness of Faulkner's judgment in deciding what parts to use and what matters to discard in composing the novel. *Absalom, Absalom!* was not written in a blinding flash of inspiration; rather, like most great novels, it resulted from patient, laborious thinking, experimenting, and revising of the kind that transformed these ordinary stories, for the most part rejected even by the editors of the slick magazines, into a masterpiece.

Implicit in what has already been said about the "rag-tag and bobends of old tales and talking" about the Sutpen legends, the lumber with which Faulkner constructed his novel, are several of the problems that beset the reader of *Absalom, Absalom!*, and others will become apparent to him as soon as he begins to turn the pages of the book. He soon realizes, for example, that in the 1980s he is reading a book written in the mid-1930s; that when Faulkner wrote it in the mid-1930s he was establishing the *now* or present time of the novel in 1910; and that although the *now* time of the novel is 1910, the crucial events of the story took place in the years before and after the Civil War. In other words, for to-day's reader the truth about Thomas Sutpen must be reached through layers and layers of history.

The task of plunging down through the layers of history to the truth below becomes even more difficult when the reader begins to understand that the various narrators of the novel cannot be relied upon for the truth. Rosa Coldfield's portion of the story, for example, is obviously strongly colored, swayed, or biased by her hatred for Sutpen. Mr. Compson's account not only reaches back to community gossip but also to General Compson's report of a conversation he once had with Sutpen. Likewise, it contains a good deal of Mr. Compson's own skepticism of all human action and veracity. And as for Shreve and Quentin, who narrate the last half of the book, the omniscient author tells us that they were "creating between them, out of the rag-tag and bob-ends of old tales and talking, people who perhaps had never existed at all anywhere, who, shadows, were shadows not of flesh and blood which had lived and died but shadows in turn of what were . . . shades too, quiet as the visible murmur of their vaporizing breath" (p. 303). Both Quentin and Shreve, for different reasons, are far from unbiased observers, and what they provide is admittedly a tangle of conjectures, surmises, and theories.

And, finally, after the reader has studied the data presented by the narrators who did have some connection, however tenuous or biased, with Sutpen himself and taken into consideration the conjectures and imaginings of Quentin and Shreve, he still must make up his own mind about the truth of Sutpen. At the University of Virginia, one of the students asked Faulkner if any of the persons who talks about Sutpen had the right view, or, said the student, "is it more or less a case of thirteen ways of looking at a blackbird with none of them right?" Faulkner's reply goes to the central problem of *Absalom, Absalom!*

> That's it exactly. I think that no one individual can look at truth. It blinds you. You look at it and you see one phase of it. Someone else looks at it and sees a slightly awry phase of it. But taken all together, the truth is in what they saw though nobody saw the truth intact. So these are true as far as Miss Rosa and as Quentin saw it. Quentin's father saw what he believed was truth,

that was all he saw. But the old man was himself a little too big for people no greater in stature than Quentin and Miss Rosa and Mr. Compson to see all at once. It would have taken perhaps a wiser or more tolerant or more sensitive or more thoughtful person to see him as he was. It was, as you say, thirteen ways of looking at a blackbird. But the truth, I would like to think, comes out, that when the reader has read all these thirteen different ways of looking at the blackbird, the reader has his own fourteenth image of that blackbird which I would like to think is the truth.[13]

To the disappointment of some readers of *Absalom, Absalom!*, Faulkner provides no officially sanctioned or authorized voice or omniscient narrator who will render the verdict or establish the truth of the matter. Despite what he said about the fourteenth image of the blackbird being the truth, readers will probably never reach a consensus about the Sutpen affair, but the burden of understanding and interpretation has been placed squarely upon the reader.

The result has been a great variety of interpretations of *Absalom, Absalom!* At the University of Virginia, Faulkner was asked if the novel were Quentin's story. He replied, "No it's Sutpen's story"[14] and characterized Quentin's approach to Sutpen as "one of the most erroneous." A recent critic, nevertheless, has written that "Sutpen's is not unquestionably the primary story. It is at least as easy—for me much easier—to see the story of Quentin Compson in the foreground of *Absalom, Absalom!* and to hear in the book's title Jason Richmond Compson's grief for his son Quentin."[15] Others have seen the novel as a parable of the South, an exposition of the American dream, a modern treatment of the biblical account of David and Absalom, a ghost story in a Gothic setting, or the exposition of a theory of history.

If there is any general agreement upon even the broadest implications of this novel, it is that Faulkner has written a study of the process of arriving at historical truth and, perhaps, the meaning of history itself. Faulkner realized that if life is to have any profound meaning for the individual, that meaning must be reached through history. He understood that the essence of history is the individual and his humanity; and Faulkner may have known intuitively that when all the documents and the visible data have been examined, there yet remains a gap between them and the individual, a gap that perhaps may best be closed by the novelist or the biographer. One of the central passages in *Absalom, Ab-*

salom! relates to this matter. Shreve has just observed that Quentin talks like his father:

> *Yes. Maybe we are both Father. Maybe nothing ever happens once and is finished. Maybe happen is never once but like ripples maybe on water after the pebble sinks, the ripples moving on, spreading, the pool attached by a narrow umbilical water-cord to the next pool which the first pool feeds, has fed, did feed, let this second pool contain a different temperature of water, a different molecularity of having seen, felt, remembered, reflect in a different tone the infinite unchanging sky, it doesn't matter: that pebble's watery echo whose fall it did not even see moves across its surface too at the original ripple-space, to the old ineradicable rhythm . . . Yes, we are both Father. Or maybe Father and I are both Shreve, maybe it took Father and me both to make Shreve or Shreve and me both to make Father or maybe Thomas Sutpen to make all of us.*
> (pp. 261–62)

What Faulkner seems to be saying is that the present flows out of the ripples of the past and that each act or event in history may subsequently take on an importance or significance unknown or undreamed when it took place.

The passage calls to mind Edgar Lee Masters' *Domesday Book*, mentioned earlier in connection with *As I Lay Dying*. In the initial verses of his volume, Masters declares that in any life "Fate drops a stone, and to the utmost shores / The circles spread." The ripples of Elenor Murray's life spread in endless circles and profoundly influence the lives of persons she has never even known or met. Both Masters and Faulkner narrate their stories from multiple points of view; although each narrator is biased, he adds to the information given the reader. Like Thomas Sutpen, Elenor Murray may be viewed as a symbol of a culture—she as an allegory of America and he as an allegory of the South. Finally, although the coroner in Masters' volume renders a verdict about her death, Masters leaves the final estimate of her life and its meaning to the reader who has, in Faulkner's words, the "fourteenth image" of the blackbird.

Faulkner, however, writes from a vivid awareness that the past may shape the present and that, as Henry Adams recognized, the individual imposes upon history an ordering of his own. This way of thinking accounts for the constant retracing of events in *Absalom, Absalom!*, since the individual who perceives the event likewise enters into the event as he orders it in his own consciousness and it becomes a part of his experience. For this reason, each reader, Faulkner believed, must discover his own Sutpen; and the Sutpen known by Rosa Coldfield or conceived by Mr. Compson, or Shreve, or Quentin, different as their concepts are, cannot be the reader's Sutpen. Likewise, Quentin becomes not the subject of the novel but only one of the media through which the reader obtains his data for an act of the imagination. Faulkner seems to have wanted the reader to participate in this historical exercise. Much of the difficulty that the reader all too often experiences in discovering his Sutpen and the implications of the novel arises from the need to separate fact from conjecture and to understand the individual bias of each narrator.

As any reader of *Absalom, Absalom!* knows, its plot is not developed chronologically or in a straight line. Information reaches the reader through the narrators who often provide different versions of the same event, sometimes with additional details. In most instances, however, Faulkner carefully separates material that the reader can accept as fact from what is mere opinion or conjecture. The most reliable narrator in the novel is General Compson (Quentin calls him "Grandfather"), a contemporary and friend of Thomas Sutpen. On one occasion, in conversation with General Compson, Sutpen relates the story of his life. Much of the knowledge about Sutpen's life, especially his early life, derives from this conversation.

Thomas Sutpen's birth takes place in the mountains of western Virginia in 1808. He spends his childhood in log cabins in a land where there are no Negroes—the inhabitants look down only at Indians over their rifle sights. "Where he lived," Quentin quotes General Compson as saying, "the land belonged to anybody and everybody and so the man who would go to the trouble and work to fence off a piece of it and say 'This is mine' was crazy; and as for objects, nobody had any more of them than you did because everybody had just what he was strong enough or energetic enough to take and keep" (p. 221). Although this primitive society into which Sutpen is born has been called a kind of Eden, the rifles pointed at Indians and the premise that one holds land only by physical force hardly suggest a high level of morality or a Utopian setting. The notion that the land belongs to everybody, however, is an idea that Faulkner seems to have cherished, since it appears in several other novels, notably *Go Down, Moses*. The point that Faulkner wishes to establish is that Sutpen as a child has no knowledge of a society in which there is an order of master and servant, racial prejudice, and a notably unequal distribution of material goods. Of all these matters, Sutpen is ignorant, one could say *innocent*. When Sutpen is ten and still innocent, the family moves down from the mountains into the Tidewater region, and there Sutpen experiences the shock that changes his entire life.

Just how ignorant or innocent Sutpen is, he himself does not fully realize until at either thirteen or fourteen he is sent with a message for a wealthy plantation owner. Expecting to be invited into the house, Sutpen approaches the front door, only to be told by a servant to go around to the back. As a result of this experience, Sutpen formulates a design to acquire, take, seize, by whatever means possible, the possessions that will prevent him from ever being humiliated again and give him the same or greater place in society than that held by the wealthy plantation owner.

To accomplish his design, Sutpen recognizes at once that he will need "first of all and above all things money in considerable quantities" (p. 243). He is later quoted as saying that he would "require money, a house, a plantation, slaves, a family—incidentally of course, a wife" (p. 263). In school, Sutpen learns that there is "a place called the West Indies to which poor men went in ships and became rich, it didn't matter how, so long as that man was clever and courageous: the latter of which I believed that I possessed, the former of which I believed that . . . I should learn" (p. 242). Accordingly, Sutpen goes to the West Indies, where in a slave rebellion he sides with the plantation owner, receives serious wounds, and marries the owner's daughter. About this wife, at first Sutpen says merely that he put her aside because "I found that she was not and could never be, through no fault of her own, adjunctive or incremental to the design which I had in mind, so I provided for her and put her aside" (p. 240). Later, in another passage, Sutpen tells General Compson that "they [presumably the plantation owner and his Spanish wife] deliberately withheld from me the one fact which I have reason to know they were aware would have caused me to decline the entire matter, otherwise they would not have withheld it from me—a fact which I did not learn until after my son was born" (p. 264). Sutpen does not provide additional information. In the light of Quentin's remarks and the assumptions of many readers of the novel, one should note here that neither Sutpen nor any other person in the novel who is in a position to

172

have known ever asserts that Sutpen put his first wife aside because she had Negro blood, or that Charles Bon was Sutpen's son, or even that Sutpen ever thought Charles Bon was his son.

Citizens in Jefferson knew nothing about Sutpen's past on "that Sunday morning in June in 1833 when he first rode into town" (p. 11). Although the source of his money remains a mystery to the townspeople—and to the readers of the novel as well—Sutpen buys with Spanish coin "a hundred square miles of some of the best virgin bottom land in the country" (p. 34), leaves Jefferson after the deed is recorded, and returns two months later with a French architect and a wagon load of "wild negroes" who can speak no English (p. 36). In the next two years, the French architect and the "wild negroes" build him a mansion. "Unpainted and unfurnished, without a pane of glass or a doorknob or hinge in it, twelve miles from town and almost that far from any neighbor, it stood for three years more surrounded by its formal gardens and promenades, its slave quarters and stables and smokehouses" (p. 39). Even while the mansion stands empty, Sutpen begins to put on what Rosa Coldfield called "spectacles" (p. 40) in which Sutpen fights with his wild slaves and which later will make his son Henry sick at his stomach while his sister Judith watches unmoved. Meanwhile, helped by the seed cotton that General Compson lends him, Sutpen plants his fields and makes his land produce.

Townspeople are amazed to see Sutpen appear in the Methodist church with Goodhue Coldfield, a merchant, a Methodist steward, and a man "with a name for absolute and undeviating and even Puritan uprightness . . . who neither drank nor gambled nor even hunted" (p. 43). No one in Jefferson—nor, for that matter, the reader of the novel—ever knows exactly how Sutpen gains a hold upon Coldfield, but the suggestion is that Sutpen persuades Coldfield to engage in a business enterprise from which Sutpen profits greatly and which Coldfield apparently comes to regard as less than honorable. Perhaps because of this "deal," Coldfield consents to his daughter Ellen's marriage to Sutpen. The wedding, arranged by Ellen's aunt, takes place in 1838. Since Rosa Coldfield was not born until 1845, Mrs. Coldfield must have been alive at the time of the wedding; but no mention is made of her at the wedding and none of the narrators ever mentions her absence. Soon two children, Henry and Judith, are born, and with Clytemnestra or Clytie, Sutpen's daughter by a slave

woman, Sutpen now has a family of five. Seemingly, his "design" is nearing completion.

By 1859 Henry Sutpen has become a student at the University of Mississippi. There he meets Charles Bon, a somewhat fastidious, wordly-
wise law student from New Orleans. The two young men become
friends, and at Christmas Henry invites Bon to visit at Sutpen's Hundred. During Bon's visit, Ellen Coldfield regards him as a potential and
acceptable suitor for Judith. In June, Henry brings Bon home again for a
brief visit before he returns to New Orleans. In that same summer
Thomas Sutpen also visits New Orleans (the reader never learns for certain the object or result of that visit, though the narrators speculate that
Sutpen went there to find out about Bon). In the fall of 1860 both boys
return to Oxford, and at Christmas Henry again brings Bon home. "And
then something happened. Nobody knew what. . . . But anyway, when
Christmas day came, Henry and Bon were gone" (p. 79). Later, Quentin
and Shreve conjecture that Sutpen learned in New Orleans that Bon was
his son and that Sutpen told Henry on Christmas Eve that there could be
no marriage between Bon and Judith because of Bon's Negro blood (not
mentioning the sibling relationship). But, however plausible this supposition seems, no evidence exists in the novel for its being fact. Moreover, as will be shown, no evidence exists to support the conjecture that
Bon knew Sutpen was his father and, of course, that Henry was a half
brother. These are matters unknown to Rosa Coldfield, to Mr. Compson,
and to General Compson; they have their origins in the imaginations of
Quentin Compson and, to a lesser degree, Shreve McCannon.

Early on that Christmas morning, Henry and Bon depart for New Orleans where Henry learns about Bon's octoroon mistress or wife and his
child. Without returning to Sutpen's Hundred, Henry and Bon enlist in
the University Grays and leave for war. Sutpen also departs for the war.
He becomes an officer in Colonel John Sartoris' regiment and replaces
Sartoris at the next annual election of officers. In 1862, disappointed
over the broken marriage plans and Henry's disappearance, Ellen Coldfield dies. Once during the war, in 1864, Sutpen makes a journey home
to bring the tombstones for Ellen's grave and later his own. Throughout
the war, Judith and Clytie, with some help from Wash Jones, run the
plantation. At the close of the war, Henry and Bon return, but at the
gates of the Sutpen mansion Henry kills Bon with "the last shot of the

war." Wash Jones rides to Rosa Coldfield's house and brings her out to
Sutpen's Hundred, and she is there when Thomas Sutpen returns from
the war. With the help of Wash Jones, Sutpen at once begins to rebuild
his design and refuses to take part in any of the planters' attempts to
establish law and order in the society. Sutpen maintains that "*if every man
in the South would do as he himself was doing, would see to the restoration of his
own land, the general land and South would save itself*" (p. 161). Still endeavoring to establish a dynasty, he becomes engaged to Rosa Coldfield; but
at his suggestion that they delay marriage until a male child is born, she
leaves in outrage that prompts her hatred of him for the remainder of her
life. In a final effort to obtain a male heir, Sutpen seduces the granddaughter of Wash Jones. When the child is born female, Sutpen angers
Wash Jones, who kills his employer with a scythe and a few hours later
his granddaughter and her baby before the sheriff kills him.

Although Thomas Sutpen's story ends with his death in 1869,
Faulkner accounts for his survivors. One afternoon in the summer of
1870, Bon's octoroon mistress and Charles Etienne Saint-Valery Bon
(the son of the octoroon and Charles Bon), then age eleven, visit Sutpen's
Hundred and remain a week with Judith and Clytie. In December,
1871, when the octoroon is dying, Judith sends Clytie to New Orleans
to bring back the boy. After living at Sutpen's Hundred for a decade,
Charles Etienne is arrested in a fight at a Negro ball. General Compson
pays Charles Etienne's fine, tells him to leave the vicinity, and in words
that recall Joe Christmas, adds: "Whatever you are, once you are among
strangers, people who dont know you, you can be whatever you will"
(p. 204). A year later, Charles Etienne returns "with a coal black and
ape-like woman and an authentic wedding license" (p. 205), and in 1882
their son Jim Bond is born in one of the dilapidated slave cabins that
Charles Etienne has rebuilt at Sutpen's Hundred. Charles Etienne remains on the Sutpen place and farms part of the plantation on shares. In
1884 he contracts yellow fever (in the "Chronology" the disease is small-
pox). During his illness, Judith, who nurses him, also contracts the disease; she dies and a short time afterwards Charles Etienne. Rosa orders
her gravestone and the inscription for it. Jim Bond lives on with Clytie;
and once when Quentin and four other boys venture out to Sutpen's
Hundred, he sees Clytie and the idiot Jim Bond, a "*hulking slack-mouthed
saddle-colored boy*" (p. 214), who could not have told anyone who he was.

Presumably, Jim Bond lives on at Sutpen's Hundred with Clytie until 1909. In September, 1909, Rosa Coldfield and Quentin Compson journey out to Sutpen's Hundred and find in the rotting mansion Jim Bond, Clytie, and Henry Sutpen. Now an old man, Henry has returned home to die. Afraid that Rosa will have Henry arrested for the murder of Charles Bon more than forty years ago, Clytie begs Quentin: "Make her go away from here. Whatever he done, me and Judith and him have paid it out" (p. 370). After what could have been only a moment's conversation with Henry, Quentin hurriedly leaves the mansion with Rosa.[16] In December, Rosa returns to Sutpen's Hundred with an ambulance to get Henry and give him medical care. Thinking that Rosa has come to arrest Henry for the old murder, Clytie sets the mansion on fire. She and Henry Sutpen die in the flames, and Jim Bond, "the scion, the last of his race, seeing it too now and howling with human reason now since now even he could have known what he was howling about" (p. 376), continues to howl about the place. No one can catch him. In January, 1910, Rosa Coldfield dies.

The foregoing account represents the principal facts about Sutpen that can be established from reliable information. Considered by themselves, the facts raise more questions than they answer because of the absence of data at crucial points. Mr. Compson's exclamation rings true: "It's just incredible. It just does not explain. Or perhaps that's it: they dont explain and we are not supposed to know" (p. 100). The reader would like to know the authentic origins of Charles Bon, particularly his racial origins. The reader would like to know if Bon was in fact the son of Thomas Sutpen and the half brother of Judith and Henry. He would also like to know the real reason why Henry shot Bon at the gates to Sutpen's Hundred. Just before the war ended, did Sutpen actually reveal to Henry something previously unknown to him?

About Thomas Sutpen there are other questions the reader would like to have answered. What was it, for example, that was withheld from Sutpen in Haiti that made him put away his first wife? Most readers wonder about the precise nature of his dealings with Goodhue Coldfield that enabled Sutpen to marry the merchant's daughter. Again, the question of the relationship between Judith and Charles Bon is never actually settled. Why did Sutpen forbid the marriage, and did he know that Bon was his son? Upon these questions hinges almost half of the novel, particularly the portion devoted to Quentin's and Shreve's agonized speculations about the possible incestuous marriage. Finally, the reader would like to have a definitive answer to Thomas Sutpen's own question: "Where did I make the mistake" (p. 263) in the design?

The questions raised in the novel are not matters of idle curiosity. Only when the reader begins to examine these issues does he realize that probably more than half of *Absalom, Absalom!* consists of the conjectures and speculations of the various narrators about motives and events that cannot be established by the known facts. At that point, one begins to suspect that for Faulkner, historical facts tend not to explain anything. Understanding of history can only come through the imaginative reconstruction of the past, and for history to make sense to the present the historian must perform an act of the imagination. Within *Absalom, Absalom!* the narrators perform this imaginative reconstruction; but the reader, outside the novel, must reconstruct in his imagination not only the conjectures of the narrators but the narrators themselves before he can arrive at his own Sutpen, Henry, Bon, Judith, Rosa, and others. Even more, he must make that final construct of the overall meaning of the Sutpen story.

The meaning of *Absalom, Absalom!* must be approached not only through an examination of the established facts of historical data but also through an understanding of the particular biases and distortions of the narrators. Rosa Coldfield, for example, exhibits a very strong animus against Thomas Sutpen. Throughout her part of the novel, she calls him a demon or an ogre. She hates the fact that he came from nowhere, had no antecedents and no family tradition, and was not a gentleman. She recoils in horror from the "spectacle" of Sutpen inviting his neighbors to come to watch him fight in the stable with his slaves in combats without rules to prevent eye-gouging and other foul play. These are matters that she has long considered, facts she has searched for a clue to the enigma of Sutpen that always has escaped her. But they are ancillary to the main event, the crisis of her life, that takes place when Sutpen invites her to produce him a bastard to insure him a male heir. Repeatedly she says she holds no brief for herself (pp. 18, 159, 163, 164, 165); but after forty-three years of outrage at this proposition, she has made up her mind. She can see "*the accelerating circle's fatal curving course of his ruthless pride, his lust for vain magnificence, though I did not then*" (p. 162). Often she thinks of

177

Sutpen as a madman, but she realizes that "*it was only his compelling dream which was insane and not his methods*" (p. 166). She gives him credit for getting manual labor out of Wash Jones, for keeping out of the night-riders, and for getting "*at the lowest possible price the sole woman available to wive him, and by the one device which could have gained his point*" (p. 166). In the end, Rosa, like the other narrators, searches the past for some logic to history and admits her failure to find a satisfactory answer. She says to Quentin:

> *I will tell you what he [Sutpen] did and let you be the judge. (Or try to tell you, because there are some things for which three words are three too many, and three thousand words that many words too less, and this is one of them. It can be told; I could take that many sentences, repeat the bold blank naked and outrageous words just as he spoke them, and bequeath you only that same aghast and outraged unbelief I knew when I comprehended what he meant; or take three thousand sentences and leave you only that Why? Why? and Why? that I have asked and listened to for almost fifty years.)* pp. 166–67

Despite her prejudice, Rosa's judgment must be considered in any evaluation of Thomas Sutpen. Rosa recognizes his energy; she can see reason in his methods, however much she hates them; and she knows his pride and passion for "vain magnificence." Through her realization of Sutpen's besetting materialism, rationality, and self-centeredness, she reaches close to the center of Sutpen's enigma when she denounces the insanity of his dream. Although Rosa Coldfield's outrage over his blunt, rationalistic "proposition" may arise in part from her own wounded vanity, even more it expresses the fundamental human truths of Western culture that enduring sexual relationships must be based upon giving, the abnegation of self, the outward reach of one individual to another and that marriage must be more than a mechanism for human breeding. Sutpen's greatest defect is that he recognized no obligation or responsibility to others, knew nothing of a love that effaces one's selfish desires, and presumed that everyone else acted upon similar motives. The ripples of his actions badly blighted Rosa's life.

Initially, Mr. Compson seems better qualified than Rosa Coldfield to explain Sutpen. Mr. Compson, to be sure, lacks her direct contact with Sutpen, but Mr. Compson has obtained much of his information from General Compson, whose factual information the reader usually accepts as accurate. Mr. Compson appears to be a mature, scholarly, rational, skeptical, detached but interested observer who is working out a challenging problem. Nevertheless, he is given to speculation; and when confronted with the absence of fact or motive, he endeavors to make plausible conjectures. For example, to explain Mr. Coldfield's rather surprising objection to the war, Mr. Compson assigns it to a merchant's hatred of waste. He recognizes Sutpen's desire for respectability and the necessity of his securing the right wife, and he agrees with Rosa that Sutpen acted from vanity and pride. He even speculates on the reasons no one came to Ellen's wedding. Mr. Compson also provides an extensive account of Rosa Coldfield herself and her relationships with her father, mother, aunt, sister, and, to a degree, Sutpen. Most important of all Mr. Compson's conjectures, however, are those that relate to the crucial elements of the Sutpen story. Mr. Compson invents the theory that Sutpen opposed the marriage of Judith and Charles Bon because of Bon's octoroon mistress. (The theory that Bon was Judith's half brother is Quentin's idea.) Yet Mr. Compson is forced to concede that he is baffled. He knows that something is missing. The best explanation he can offer is that Sutpen was "underbred." In explanation, Mr. Compson says: "He [Sutpen] was like John L. Sullivan having taught himself painfully and tediously to do the schottische, having drilled himself and drilled himself in secret until he now believed it no longer necessary to count the music's beat, say. He may have believed that your grandfather or Judge Benbow might have done it a little more effortlessly than he, but he would not have believed that anyone could have beat him in knowing when to do it and how" (p. 46). Mr. Compson's meaning is that Sutpen, lacking the civilization or moral awareness of a General Compson or a Judge Benbow, acts mechanically. His movements do not come "naturally." General Compson, as quoted by Quentin, makes a similar point when he says that Sutpen in his innocence "believed that the ingredients of morality were like the ingredients of pie or cake and once you had measured them and balanced them and mixed them and put them into the oven it was all finished and nothing but pie or cake could come out" (p. 263). Implicitly, General Compson and Mr. Compson, as well as Miss Rosa, are saying that Sutpen all too easily brushed aside questions of value. Speaking of Sutpen's "design," General Compson quotes him as saying "whether it was a good or a bad design is beside the point" (p. 263), but the rightness or wrongness of the design is precisely the point at issue.

The design was bad because it did not arise from or even include the ingredient of human affection, love, or even "the milk of human kindness." Interestingly, none of the narrators speculates upon whether Sutpen, even if he had had moral instruction, would have been able to change his nature. The question recalls Tom Jones and Blifil in Henry Fielding's novel *Tom Jones*. Could Blifil, by an act of will, have acquired the *bona natura* that motivated Tom (and later Mark Twain's Huckleberry Finn)? Or is the propensity for love and self-giving a trait that comes innately to the individual and descends through the generations? Sutpen's character poses the issue but Faulkner does not resolve it.

The accounts of Sutpen by Miss Rosa Coldfield and Mr. Compson (including the information from General Compson) occupy the first half of the novel and concentrate upon Sutpen and his design. At Chapter Six, the setting of the work moves from Jefferson, Mississippi, to Cambridge, Massachusetts, that is, to Quentin's room in the Harvard dormitory. Quentin tells the Sutpen story to his roommate, Shreve, an outsider, who is interested but puzzled by the South. At the University of Virginia, Faulkner said that "Shreve was the commentator that held the thing to something of reality. If Quentin had been let alone to tell it, it would have become completely unreal. It had to have a solvent to keep it real, keep it believable, creditable, otherwise it would have vanished into smoke and fury." [17] Shreve does often interrupt to steady Quentin who has a marked tendency to become highly emotional; but as the unraveling of the causes and motives of the principals in the novel proceeds, both boys become so aroused that they lose some perspective. The final pages of the novel illustrate this increasing tension upon both of them. They become too involved to render an authoritative verdict for the reader.

The change in the scene from Mississippi to Massachusetts also coincides with a shift in the emphasis in the interpretation of the Sutpen affair. Although concerned with Sutpen, Quentin is passionately interested in the Henry-Judith-Bon relationship. In this matter he tends to identify with Henry, and Shreve with Bon. At one point in Chapter Eight, the omniscient narrator comments:

> Shreve ceased. That is, for all the two of them, Shreve and Quentin, knew he had stopped, since for all the two of them knew he had never begun, since it did not matter . . . which one had been doing the talking. So that now it

was not two but four of them riding the two horses . . . : four of them and then just two—Charles-Shreve and Quentin-Henry, the two of them both believing that Henry was thinking. . . . So it was four of them who rode the two horses through that night. (pp. 333–34)

First, two of them, then four; now two again. (p. 345)

Shreve ceased again. It was just as well, since he had no listener. Perhaps he was aware of it. Then suddenly he had no talker either. . . . Because now neither of them were there. They were both in Carolina and the time was forty-six years ago, and it was not even four now but compounded still further, since now both of them were Henry Sutpen and both of them were Bon, compounded each of both yet either neither. (p. 351)

In these passages, both young men become so intensely involved in their imaginative search for meaning in the Sutpen legend that they lose their individual identities. The observant reader, however, cannot escape the inference that although Quentin talks about Sutpen, he is far more interested in reconstructing the chain of cause and effect that leads to the murder of Charles Bon. In seeking a reason for Quentin's concern with Henry and Bon, the reader may bring his own knowledge of events outside the novel to account for this preference.

Although *Absalom, Absalom!* was not offered to the reading public as a sequel to *The Sound and the Fury*, Faulkner's selection of Quentin Compson and his father and grandfather as narrators and the dating of the *now* of the novel shortly before Quentin's suicide invite a comparison, particularly a comparison with the earlier Quentin. Asked at the University of Virginia if a reader could feel that the Quentin of *Absalom, Absalom!* is the same Quentin who appeared in *The Sound and the Fury*, "that is, a man thinking about his own Compson family, his own sister," Faulkner replied: "To me he's consistent. . . . Quentin was still trying to get God to tell him why, in *Absalom, Absalom!* as he was in *The Sound and the Fury*." [18]

Of the parallels that have been noted between the two novels, the most important relate to Quentin's relationship with Caddy and Dalton Ames in *The Sound and the Fury* and to Henry Sutpen's relationship with Judith and Charles Bon in *Absalom, Absalom!* Had Quentin taken Dalton Ames's pistol and killed him on the bridge, Caddy would have become a widow before she was a bride—just as Judith was—and Quentin would have "saved" his sister as Henry "saved" Judith. That this matter was very much on Quentin's mind is evident from a passage near the end of Rosa Coldfield's narration in Chapter Five. Early in her account, Rosa describes what she imagines happened: "*a shot, then an interval of aghast surmise above the cloth and needles which engaged them, then feet, in the hall and then on the stairs, running, hurrying, the feet of a man: and Judith with just time to snatch up the unfinished dress and hold it before her as the door burst open upon her brother . . . and then the two of them, the two accursed children . . . looking at one another across the up-raised and unfinished wedding dress*" (p. 135). Many, many pages later, Rosa ceases her diatribe against Sutpen, and Faulkner completes the chapter with a rendering of Quentin's thoughts and conjectures:

> But Quentin was not listening, because there was also something which he too could not pass—that door, the running feet on the stairs beyond it almost a continuation of the faint shot, the two women, the negress and the white girl in her underthings (made of flour sacking when there had been flour, of window curtains when not) pausing, looking at the door, the yellowed creamy mass of old intricate satin and lace spread carefully on the bed and then caught swiftly up by the white girl and held before her as the door crashed in and the brother stood there, hatless, with his shaggy bayonet-trimmed hair, his gaunt worn unshaven face, his patched and faded gray tunic, the pistol still hanging against his flank: the two of them, brother and sister, curiously alike as if the difference in sex had merely sharpened the common blood to a terrific, an almost unbearable, similarity, speaking to one another in short brief staccato sentences like slaps, as if they stood breast to breast striking one another in turn neither making any attempt to guard against the blows.
>
> > *Now you cant marry him.*
> > *Why cant I marry him?*
> > *Because he's dead.*
> > *Dead?*
> > *Yes. I killed him.* (p. 172)

Quentin's memory of Caddy "standing in the door"[19] and his abortive encounter with Ames may lie behind this entire passage. One can read *Absalom, Absalom!* without a knowledge of Quentin's effort to kill Dalton Ames in *The Sound and the Fury*, but that knowledge helps greatly to explain why Quentin "was not listening" to Rosa Coldfield.

Quentin's brooding over Caddy in the earlier novel helps also to explain his readiness in *Absalom, Absalom!* to advance the theory that the impediment to Bon's union with Judith lay in the incestuous nature of the marriage. One remembers Quentin's remark about "Saint Francis talking about his sister" and adding: "Because if it were just to hell; if that were all of it. Finished. If things just finished themselves. Nobody else there but her and me. If we could just have done something so dreadful that they would have fled hell except us. *I have committed incest I said Father it was I it was not Dalton Ames. . . .* When he put the pistol in my hand I didn't. That's why I didn't. He would be there and she would and I would." [20] Quentin returns to the idea again and again. In another passage, he says, *"if youll just wait I'll tell you how it was it was a crime we did a terrible crime it cannot be hid . . . I'll tell Father then itll have to be because you love Father then we'll have to go away amid the pointing and the horror the clean flame."* [21] The two passages just quoted combine Quentin's desire to kill Dalton Ames with his notion that the most "dreadful" crime that could be committed would be incest. In *Absalom, Absalom!*, Quentin's conjecture that the threat of incest was an impediment to Bon's marriage to Judith is very consistent with his attitude in *The Sound and the Fury*.

Equally consonant with Quentin's belief in *The Sound and the Fury* that incest would send a person to hell is Quentin's imagining in *Absalom, Absalom!* of Henry's attitude toward the Bon-Judith marriage. According to Quentin's theory, Henry Sutpen debated the matter with himself and cited Duke John of Lorraine, who married his sister, as if Henry "hoped possibly to evoke that condemned and excommunicated shade to tell him in person that it was all right" (p. 346). Incest, Quentin imagines Henry thinking, would bring *"eternal damnation"* in hell for the *"four of us"* (p. 347). Still, Henry will not give outright permission for the marriage; but since the war is drawing to a close, Henry knows he must make a decision. One night the Colonel sends for Henry. In the imagined conversation that follows, Thomas Sutpen acknowledges Henry (*"Henry, Sutpen says—My Son,"* p. 353) but continues to forbid the marriage. At this point, Henry makes his decision:

> —He must not marry her, Henry.
> —Yes. I said Yes at first, but I was not decided then. I didn't let him. But now I have had four years to decide in. I will. I am going to. (p. 354)

At this point, Quentin imagines that Sutpen told Henry that Bon's *"mother was part negro"* (p. 355). Immediately following this scene, Quentin imagines another exchange between Henry and Bon, in which Bon says:

183

—So, it's the miscegenation, not the incest, which you cant bear.
Henry doesn't answer.
. . . He [Sutpen] *didn't need to tell you I am a nigger to stop me. . . .*
—You said, could have stopped you. What do you mean by that? . . . But now?
You mean you—
—Yes. . . .
—Think of her. Not of me: of her.
—I have. . . . Now I am thinking of myself. . . .
—No, Henry says.—No. No. No.
. . . His [Bon's] *hand vanishes beneath the blanket and reappears, holding his*
pistol by the barrel, the butt extended toward Henry. (pp. 356–57)

Henry's failure to accept the pistol which Bon offers him and inability to
kill Bon at this moment remind the reader again of Quentin Compson's
encounter with Dalton Ames in which under almost the same circumstances Quentin fails to protect Caddy's honor. In considering the use
Faulkner makes of incest and miscegenation in *Absalom, Absalom!*, one is
surprised that Faulkner chose to make miscegenation more "horrible" to
Henry (i.e., to Quentin) than incest, although Faulkner may have felt
that the incident would be "in character" because of the Southern fear of
miscegenation. On the other hand, one could argue that in 1865 and in
1910 and in 1936 either incest or miscegenation would have been a serious impediment to marriage in any planter's family in the South or any
industrialist's family in the North, particularly if the marriage were
being pressed by one party who was thinking only of himself. Yet one
cannot deny Faulkner's interest in both problems, since he would later
make incest and miscegenation prominent factors in the great bear story
of *Go Down, Moses.*

In any event, not only have Shreve and Quentin, particularly Quentin, shifted the emphasis in the novel away from the design of Henry
Sutpen to the tangle of brother-sister-bride-groom relationships, but
also by imagining these highly charged scenes of confrontation and revelation between Thomas and Henry Sutpen and between Henry and
Charles Bon, they have forcibly presented a number of assumptions or
conjectures to provide a "plausible" motive for Henry's murder of Bon, a
murder that, if Quentin's theory is correct, amounts to fratricide. Quentin has in fact used the Sutpen story to establish a historical parallel or
justification for his own attitudes and circumstances relating to his sister
and her lover. He has broadened his sexual difficulties by superimposing

miscegenation upon incest and made his personal problems symbolic of his fears for the South. Characteristically, he virtually ignores the miscegenation he imagines has already been accomplished in the Sutpen story (between Sutpen and Bon's supposed part-Negro mother). Shreve, however, unaware of Quentin's personal affinities with the Sutpen affair, carries the miscegenation theme to its ultimate conclusion by asserting that the world will eventually be filled with the progenies of the idiot Jim Bonds who result from incest and miscegenation. Quentin's response to this imagined eventuality is to deny vehemently that he hates the South and shortly after to commit suicide. Neither he nor Shreve can be considered reliable narrators; Quentin, indeed, is the most biased of all.

Since almost any great work of art may be shown to have multiple meanings, the final interpretation of *Absalom, Absalom!* will depend greatly upon the reader's approach to the material. At least three very different interpretations have been suggested: the biblical parable or allegory; the history of the South; and the complexities of the human condition. Each of these evaluations should be considered before one makes up his mind.

The biblical analogy, of course, is suggested by the title itself, but it is reinforced by Faulkner's known admiration for the Old Testament stories. At Nagano, he remarked that "I read the Old Testament for the pleasure of watching what these amazing people did, and they behaved so exactly like people in the 19th century behaved."[22] The Sutpen story, moreover, does resemble generally the biblical account of David. In the Book of Samuel, David, like Sutpen, was sent on an errand that changed his whole life; but when David killed Goliath, Saul, who had promised David one daughter, gave him instead another woman. David put her away and fled the country, as Sutpen fled Haiti. Then David used questionable means to obtain Bathsheba, as Sutpen did to obtain Ellen Coldfield. Afterwards, the prophet Nathan said: "Thus saith the Lord, Behold, I will raise up evil against thee out of thine own house and . . . the child also *that is* born unto thee shall surely die" (II Samuel 12:11–14). Even closer to the Sutpen story is the account of David's son Amnon who forced incestuous relations with his half sister Tamar and then was killed by his brother Absalom. Then Absalom rebelled against his father and brought about the ruin of David's house. When David heard about the death of Absalom, he spoke his grief: "O my son Absalom, my son, my son Absalom! would God I had died for thee, O Absalom, my son, my son!" (II Samuel 18:33). Sutpen never uttered such a lament.

The biblical analogy, regardless of the number of parallels that can be identified, scarcely holds the key to the novel. David's recognition of his guilt and responsibility for his separation from his sons makes him much more of a tragic figure than Sutpen. Much more valid is the suggestion that Sutpen's story documents in a general way the thesis that people in the nineteenth century did behave in a fashion similar to those recorded in the Old Testament and that Sutpen's story shows the recurrence of historical patterns.

Probably more cogent than the biblical analogy is the theory that in *Absalom, Absalom!* Faulkner was writing a parable of Southern history. Those who take this view assert that Sutpen is the South and his story duplicates the history of the South, morally, politically, and socially. The South, especially Mississippi, is seen as a region developed by back-countrymen (Sutpen came from the mountains of western Virginia) who turned planter in a frontier society and made fortunes overnight in cotton and slaves. After these men were defeated in the Civil War, the South covered their defeat by romanticizing them into "gentlemen" and building elaborate myths around them. The fact is, the South had no true aristocracy, because just below the veneer of the Southern "aristocrat" was a frontiersman. If any difference exists between the Sartoris family and the Sutpen family, it is simply that Faulkner romanticizes Sartoris into the Southern legend while presenting Sutpen as the reality which exposes the myth. Based upon such premises, these readers emphasize the similarities between Sutpen and their reading of Southern history. Often the tendency is to derive Sutpen from this concept of Southern history rather than to find Southern history in Sutpen.

Although the advocates of the Southern history interpretation offer persuasive arguments, there are objections to the theory. The Jefferson community discerned a difference between Sutpen and other planters in the neighborhood, regarded him as a kind of interloper, and disapproved many of his actions. The relationships between Sutpen and those around him, characterized as they were by ruthlessness and inhumanity towards both whites and Negroes, were not typical of the South. Other critics call attention to the similarity between Sutpen and the Northern noveau riche capitalists of roughly the same era. Sutpen reminds one of the robber barons, and his "innocence" or ignorance or disregard of moral values stands comparison with the robber barons' bribery of public officials, cutthroat business tactics, and inhumanity towards the working classes. The difference is that the South lost the Civil War, but materialism was a besetting sin in the nineteenth century, North and South. Without a belief in a deity but with a passionate addiction to the possession of things, Sutpen represents a forerunner of the type of modern American who operates by plan in a rationalist, scientific manner. Like Jay Gatsby, Thomas Sutpen illustrates, in part at least, the perversion of the American dream because he is materially successful for the wrong reasons. Finally, the Southern history or Southern-myth interpretation of the novel severely limits its value to readers everywhere by confining its significance to political rather than human values. After all, Faulkner was writing about men and not movements. (The same objection, of course, may be made to the limitation of the entire Yoknapatawpha fiction to a small area in north Mississippi.)

Although either the biblical or political interpretation of *Absalom, Absalom!*, or both, may be satisfactory to certain readers, they represent only a partial view of the work. To a degree at least, they become—like the several accounts of Sutpen—only one version; that is, they are biased or severely narrowed in focus. Perhaps the most convincing approach to the novel is to consider it as an effort to discover truth, an effort which must engage not only the narrators of the story but also the reader himself. It is also a powerful illustration of the difficulties faced by those in modern times who would seek the truth either of the present or of the historical past. The timeless truth of history that emerges from the novel, however, is that when man permits materialism and greed to dominate his life he will fail as a human being. In this respect, *Absalom, Absalom!* is a companion piece to *The Sound and the Fury*, for the consequences of human greed, loveless human relationships, and individual self-centeredness appear in both works. Both the Compsons and the Sutpens fail in the very qualities that can make human life a rich and rewarding experience. That the Compson family deteriorates into the idiot Benjy moaning and slobbering on the bars of the Jackson asylum and that the Sutpens deteriorate into the idiot Jim Bond howling pathetically outside the embers of Sutpen's mansion cannot be attributed to coincidence.

Probably no single view of *Absalom, Absalom!* contains all the truth. Yet, if one must choose, General Compson's judgment that Sutpen was innocent, that is, he did not know, may offer the best premise with which to begin to find the truth. Sutpen's life story—and even the conjectures of the various narrators—documents his failure to exercise what Milton called right reason, that is, the proper perception of moral values. Though Sutpen was self-centered, he had no self-knowledge. He recognized no obligation or responsibility to others, and he knew nothing of love or compassion. The purpose of human action, he thought, was to acquire material possessions, and those possessions included wives and sons as well as slaves. Human experience, had he known it, had already proved him wrong. His not knowing was his mistake, but it is the truth that must be discovered in *Absalom, Absalom!*

Chapter VII

The Civil War
and Reconstruction

The Unvanquished

AT ONE of his sessions with students at the University of Virginia, Faulkner was asked: "What book would you advise a person to read first of yours?" The novelist replied, "If you are asking me to give an objective answer I would say maybe *The Unvanquished*. . . . Because it's easy to read. Compared to the others, I mean." [1] For a reader uninitiated into the complexities of Faulkner's novels, the remark has merit. The novel is "easier" reading because the syntax is simpler and the handlng of time less complicated than in most of Faulkner's novels. Moreover, *The Unvanquished*, dealing, as it does, with the Civil War and Reconstruction, represents one of the poles of history from which Faulkner measured motion to his own time; and in it, the reader beginning his study of Faulkner's work will find clearly stated many of the issues and themes that the novelist treats elsewhere in his fiction. In addition, *The Unvanquished* contributes significantly to the reader's understanding of Faulkner's attitude towards history.

Several of Faulkner's critics, however, have objected strenuously to the use of *The Unvanquished* as an introduction to his fiction. Michael Millgate, for example, writes that "the discriminating reader who begins with *The Unvanquished* is likely to find within its covers little incentive to read further in Faulkner's work and few indications of those qualities which make him a major writer." [2] Others have complained that the book is not typically "Faulknerian," that the stories are romantic and sentimental versions of the "Southern myth," and that the work scarcely deserves to be called a novel. Perhaps the primary difference between Faulkner's judgment and that of his critics is that in recommending the book to the reader unfamiliar with his fiction Faulkner was thinking of reading difficulties, while his critics were emphasizing their dissatisfaction with the content of the book. Readers generally agree that *The Unvanquished* does impose fewer demands upon them than most of Faulkner's novels, but not all agree with the objections to its form and content.

The circumstances surrounding the original composition of the stories in *The Unvanquished* lend support to its critics. Evidence from Faulkner's correspondence suggests that he wrote the first six stories to make some ready cash, tailored them for the *Saturday Evening Post*, and may have regarded them contemptuously. In the spring of 1934 he pushed aside *Absalom, Absalom!*, which he was then writing, to compose several stories for quick sale to the *Saturday Evening Post*. Among them was "Ambuscade," finished possibly in April or May. A short time later, he sent "Retreat" and predicted to his agent that the "third story" ("Raid") would be "the most novel (damn the word) of all." By this time, Faulkner had in mind a series of six stories, but the last three stories proved difficult to write. Early in the summer, he complained to his agent: "I have been stewing for about three weeks now on the Post stories. I have been trying to cook up three more with a single thread of continuity, like the other three, with the scene during Reconstruction time. I cannot get started."[3] Faulkner never entirely solved the difficulty. When the complete series of stories was assembled in *The Unvanquished*, the disparities in tone, atmosphere, and content between the first three stories and those which followed became very much apparent. For the present, Faulkner decided that he needed one or two stories to come between Granny Millard's mule trading exploits and the Reconstruction period.

The editors of the *Saturday Evening Post*, however, would not pay Faulkner's price for the series; and Faulkner, still having difficulty with the continuity of the episodes and needing immediate money, accepted an offer to work in Hollywood during July. Upon his return to Oxford at the end of the month, he was undecided about whether to continue the stories for the *Post* or resume work on *Absalom, Absalom!* He hoped that the editors would keep the matter open for a few months longer. In September he sent them the fourth and fifth stories ("The Unvanquished" and "Vendée"), and by mid-October he had made the changes in "Vendée" that the editors had requested. He had also finished the sixth story, "Drusilla" (later to be called "Skirmish at Sartoris"), though in December he planned to rewrite it. Meanwhile, the *Post* had published the first three stories ("Ambuscade" on September 29, "Retreat" on October 13, and "Raid" on November 3); but for some reason they held the fourth and fifth stories ("The Unvanquished" and "Vendée") for more than two years. Meanwhile, "Drusilla" had been published by *Scribner's Magazine* in April, 1935.

Faulkner worked hard on these six stories, planned them to exhibit a kind of progression (though not necessarily the kind of progression required for a novel), and tailored them to please the editors and readers of the *Saturday Evening Post*. Yet, in a letter to Morton Goldman, his literary agent, Faulkner wrote disparagingly of them. He declared that so long as he was forced to write "trash," he did not care who bought it so long as the price was high. When he sacrificed a high price to a lower one, it would be "to write something better than a pulp series like this."[4] The comment is tantalizingly brief. Exactly what features of the stories he considered trash and pulp, he did not specify. Unfortunately, the remark has followed the stories from the *Saturday Evening Post* and *Scribner's Magazine* into *The Unvanquished* and lent support to the belief that the Hollywood experience exerted an unfortunate influence upon Faulkner's artistic standards.

At this point, the literary history of *The Unvanquished* becomes a complicated tangle of events and motives, though certain facts can be readily established. Faulkner spent a large part of 1935 working on *Absalom, Absalom!* and writing short stories designed for such periodicals as the *Post* and *Scribner's*. In January, 1936, he finished the novel; and, except for brief intervals, he worked in Hollywood throughout the remainder of the year on such motion pictures as *Banjo on My Knee*, *Gunga Din*, *The Last Slaver* (released as *Slave Ship*), and *Splinter Fleet*. *Absalom, Absalom!* was published on October 26, 1936. At that time, Faulkner had no immediate plans for writing another novel. The fourth and fifth stories in his Civil War series, "The Unvanquished" and "Vendée," appeared in the *Post* (November 14 and December 5, respectively). On December 28, 1936, the novelist wrote Bennett Cerf at Random House to ask what he thought about publishing them as a "book." Without obtaining a commitment from Cerf, Faulkner returned to Hollywood; and, throughout the first half of 1937 he contributed substantially to the film version of *Drums along the Mohawk*. Apparently, Cerf delayed for months a final decision about publishing the stories as a volume.

For Faulkner, reprinting these stories had certain advantages. Without a new novel in mind and needing money, he may have turned to the publication of them in book form as an easy, quick means of getting another book into print and adding to his income; and he may, as his biographer suggests, have wished to make the series into a volume that would have permanent artistic value.[5] For his part, Cerf, after the departure of Faulkner's friend and former editor-publisher Hal Smith from the firm, may have wished to strengthen Random House's connection with the novelist by agreeing to publish his next book, especially one that would be easy for readers to understand. Undoubtedly, both men believed that a book containing Civil War material would have sales appeal to a wide audience. Solid evidence supported this expectation.

In July, 1934, while Faulkner was "stewing" over the final three stories in his Civil War series, Charles Scribner's Sons published *So Red the Rose*, by Faulkner's friend, Stark Young, a native Mississippian and former Oxford resident, then drama critic for the *New Republic*. Young's novel, which has never since been out of print, almost at once appeared on the best-seller lists and soon had sold more copies than all of Faulkner's work combined. To publishers and authors alike, Young's amazing success convincingly demonstrated that in a depression-troubled nation, thousands of readers would grasp eagerly a story of Southern idealism in an age beset by even greater problems than those currently confronting Americans. In November, 1935, the success of the novel was matched by the enthusiasm of the public for Paramount's motion picture version, based upon the adaptation by Maxwell Anderson and Laurence Stallings, directed by King Vidor, and starring Margaret Sullavan and Randolph Scott. In June, 1936, the Macmillan Company scored an even greater success with Margaret Mitchell's *Gone With the Wind*, which, by the time Faulkner mentioned to Bennett Cerf the possibility of issuing the six Civil War stories, had sold a million copies. The Civil War was plainly a saleable item in the marketplace, a fact that would not have escaped either William Faulkner or Bennett Cerf.

Whatever his reasons, Cerf eventually decided, probably before the middle of June, 1937, to publish Faulkner's Civil War book. Still in Hollywood, Faulkner made revisions and additions to the six stories. On July 24 he announced to his agent that Random House was going to collect the pieces into a "book." In the same letter, he wrote that because Random House needed an additional story to fill out the volume he had just finished "An Odor of Verbena." Faulkner had sent it to the *Saturday Evening Post*, and he hoped that the editors would buy and publish it immediately so that the book could appear. (They did not accept the story.) In closing, Faulkner remarked that he would leave Hollywood about the middle of August for Oxford but expected to be in New York early in October. By the time Faulkner reached New York, *The Unvanquished* was well along on its way to publication, and not a great deal of time remained for any final revisions. The illustrations were being drawn by Edward Shenton; and, about the time of publication, *Time* magazine was expected to publish a cover story about Faulkner and the book. Cerf and his associates at Random House were optimistic about the success of the volume. *The Unvanquished* was published on February 15, 1938[6] (without the benefit of the *Time* cover story). On the following day, the motion picture rights were sold to Metro-Goldwyn-Mayer for $25,000.

The textual history of *The Unvanquished* reminds one of Faulkner's revision of the first manuscript version of *Sanctuary*. In revising that novel, Faulkner said he transformed a "basely conceived" manuscript ("a cheap idea," he wrote, "because it was deliberately conceived to make money") into a work of art which he felt would not "shame" his finer novels. As has been seen, his Civil War stories had also been designed to make money, and upon at least one occasion Faulkner had referred to them as "trash" and "pulp." He had the opportunity to reshape or rewrite them into a work of art; and very probably he began his revisions with that intention. As the work progressed, his interest in revising the stories may have flagged. This slackening of his enthusiasm, if true, would help to account for the fact that the changes in the first three stories, "Ambuscade," "Retreat," and "Raid," are far more extensive than in the other three published pieces. Exactly why Faulkner did not bother to correct the numerous time discrepancies—if he were actually aware of them—in the second group of stories cannot be determined. He may have felt, of course, that they needed little additional polishing, especially since the role of Bayard as narrator was much better established in them than in the first group, and he may have ignored the time problems because he assumed that most readers would not be troubled by them.[7] They were not evident when the stories were published as individual pieces in the magazine; yet it seems strange that the copy readers or editors at Random House did not insist that the most glaring inconsistencies be corrected before the book was published. Even a brief analysis of the alterations that Faulkner made in the original stories as he prepared them for publication in *The Unvanquished*, however, provides a rare glimpse of the author in his workshop.

Faulkner consistently made changes that would significantly enhance the pictorial quality of a word or phrase. Often, he added short passages to make each action or appearance of a character more concrete or vivid. Repeatedly, he pruned away the general word to replace it with a specific word or phrase. In "Ambuscade," for example, "with a hoe" becomes "with the point of a hoe"(p. 3); "I stooped and caught up the dust" becomes "So I stooped and caught both hands full of dust and rose" (p. 7); and "But it [soap] was gone now—even the taste of it" becomes "But it was gone now—the suds, the glassy weightless iridescent bubbles; even the taste of it" (p. 40). He made the same type of changes in "Retreat." Granny's "Sunday dress" becomes her "Sunday black silk" (p. 41); the soldier's "pair of Yankee pants" becomes a "pair of blue Yankee pants with a yellow cavalry stripe like Father wore home last summer" (p. 52); and Uncle Buck's "beard" becomes his "tobacco-stained beard" (p. 60). In "Raid," "that summer" becomes "that Christmas" (p. 91); "When I looked back, the woman was still standing there by the road" becomes "When I looked back she was still standing there, holding the baby and the bread and meat Granny had given her" (p. 96); and "Drusilla leaning forward a little and holding Bobolink" becomes "Drusilla leaning forward a little and taut as a pistol hammer holding Boblink" (p. 118). In general, these are the changes an experienced writer would make in his rough draft to add color, definiteness, and interest to his manuscript. That Faulkner needed to make them suggests that he wrote the magazine stories hastily, even carelessly. Considered individually, these revisions neither alter the meaning of the work nor add substantially to its quality; but taken as a whole they markedly improve each story and the finished book.

At various places, but especially in the first three stories, Faulkner added incidents or lengthened descriptions to add substance to the plot. In "Ambuscade," he expanded the account of Bayard and Ringo's "living map" of the Vicksburg battlefield to make their play and Loosh's response to it symbolic of the war itself; he elaborated the descriptions of the stock pen and the trunk to make these scenes more impressive; and he extended a single reference to "cokynut cake" into an incident revealing Ringo's character. In "Retreat," he again lengthened the trunk episode; and in "Raid," he added significantly to the account of the railroad. In "Skirmish at Sartoris," however, he deleted a passage in which he had summarized earlier events to make the story understandable to readers of *Scribner's Magazine*.

Of all the changes Faulkner made, those relating to the development of individual characters are the most significant, since in these revisions he endeavored to give emphasis, direction, and meaning to the work. In "Ambuscade," for example, Faulkner added considerably to the role of Colonel Sartoris. In the published short story, the Colonel seems almost a "walk-on" stereotype; whereas in the book he emerges as a larger than life character, a war hero, almost a living legend, exemplifying both the strengths and weaknesses of the Confederate leaders. Faulkner added extensive details about the Colonel's uniform, his horse, his office, his desk, and his library (the contents of one bookcase are listed by specific titles). Bayard sees him as a child would revere his father. These passages impressively expand the part of the Colonel and help to make him the major figure he must become if his actions and Bayard's changing attitude towards him in the later "Skirmish at Sartoris" and "An Odor of Verbena" are to have their proper effect. Other revisions in "Ambuscade" underscore the character of Loosh as the disaffected slave who will betray the family to the Yankees. Faulkner repeatedly brings Loosh before the reader, provides an account of his parentage, and emphasizes his uncanny knowledge of the progress of the war. In addition, the novelist has added passages to develop and underscore the relationship between Bayard and Ringo, which may remind readers of the relationship between Henry Sutpen and Charles Bon. Faulkner places great stress upon the lack of racial antagonism between Bayard and Ringo, their similar childhood ("born in the same month" and "fed at the same breast," p. 7), and their role as symbols of the South. The insertion of the sentence beginning "we stood there above our ruined Vicksburg" (p. 6) adds significance to their roles and suggests the meaning of the war to the whites and Negroes alike. The expansion of the Bayard-Ringo passages likewise deepens the theme of white-Negro relations that will be developed in the stories to follow.

In addition to brief passages that help to define the roles of Louvinia and Joby in "Retreat," Faulkner added the lengthy discussion of Uncle Buck and Uncle Buddy and their views regarding slavery and land-ownership. This material not only prepares the reader for Uncle Buck's role in the pursuit of Grumby (in "Vendée") but also foreshadows his part in *Go Down, Moses.* Interestingly, in revising the sentences about Uncle Buck (pp. 58–59), Faulkner systematically replaced the word *holler* with *shout*, reserving *holler* as more appropriate for Ringo (pp. 76–77). In "Raid," Faulkner notably enriched the character of Bayard through the addition of a splendid passage (pp. 106–13) in which he interprets the ruined railroad as symbolic of the war itself and its meaning. Additions to the roles of characters in other stories occur not so extensively but on occasion help to define roles. In "Riposte in Tertio," for example, Faulkner added a passage about Ringo's artistic abilities ("he was smarter than me," p. 142), and throughout this story and in "Vendée" Faulkner added brief phrases or sentences to keep the sinister figure of Ab Snopes before the reader.

The most important revisions that Faulkner made in the magazine stories, however, relate to the character of Bayard Sartoris and to the first three stories in the book. Apparently, very early in the revision process, Faulkner saw that to give the book thematic unity he had to enhance greatly the role of the narrator. In writing the first three magazine stories, Faulkner had used the narrator device, but for the most part the narrator seemed almost a Huckleberry Finn type of character. In writing "The Unvanquished," "Vendée," and "Skirmish at Sartoris," however, Faulkner made his narrator a much older man who both narrates and interprets the events of his childhood and youth. The magazine versions of "Ambuscade," "Raid," and "Retreat" contain very few instances of the type of comment often found in the later stories: "I know now that I didn't. . . . I don't know . . . I don't know" (p. 174); "I don't remember touching the door . . ." (p. 175); "I know what did happen, but even now I don't know how, in what order" (p. 208); "When I think of that day . . ." (p. 215); "It was not until years later that he told me . . ." (p. 244). In revising "Ambuscade," "Raid," and "Retreat," Faulkner inserted passages, several of them lengthy additions, to make Bayard's role as older narrator and commentator consistent with the later stories. Among the plentiful instances of this kind of revision, one could cite for illustration such passages as those beginning "But we were just twelve . . ." (p. 17); "But I don't know whether I saw it or not . . ." (p. 21);

"He and Granny were like that . . ." (p. 50); "There is a limit to what a child can accept. . . . And I was still a child . . ." (p. 75); "possibly it was more the need to keep even with Ringo . . . than a boy's affinity for smoke . . ." (p. 106); and "We never did overtake them, just as you do not overtake a tide" (p. 116). These additions help to define Bayard's role in the book. As a man looking back upon his childhood and youth, he can select and recount those experiences he considers significant—events that made an impression upon him at the time and have continued to be vivid to him—and, when he wishes, he can reflect upon the meaning of what he narrates. The *then* and *now* furnish points of comparison that neither Faulkner nor his readers can ignore. The novelist's evident recognition of the need to add these passages, as well as their considerable length, helps to account for the fact that the revisions are much more extensive in the first three stories than elsewhere in the volume. Although *The Unvanquished* gains thematically from the increased emphasis upon the role of Bayard as an adult evaluating his boyhood experiences, Faulkner failed to remove entirely the boy-narrator quality of some of the scenes. A certain confusion or blurring of point of view results in places, most notably in the first three stories.[8] Typical of the incidents that seem to be narrated by a boy instead of a man is the account of the Union officer's refusal to notice Bayard and Ringo hiding beneath Granny Millard's skirts in "Ambuscade" (pp. 35–36).

Few writers have ever reworked so extensively their previously published work. An unsympathetic critic might conclude that Faulkner had published six short stories in rough drafts, patched them together with a few connectives and additions, and republished them as a book. Certainly, he had never before reworked published material on such a scale; yet despite his improvements he did not fundamentally change or radically alter the original stories. Except for the addition of "An Odor of Verbena," which Faulkner hoped also to sell and publish before the book appeared, the work remained essentially the same as it appeared in the *Saturday Evening Post* and *Scribner's Magazine*. The pattern of publication, revision, and republication in book form, however, evidently appealed to Faulkner, because he would later develop the manuscripts for *The Hamlet* and *Go Down, Moses* in a similar fashion. In each instance, the procedure would prompt critical uncertainties about the nature and form of these volumes.

No one has ever decided absolutely whether *The Unvanquished* is a novel or merely a collection of stories. In the novelist's surviving letters written during the composition of the stories and in the months prior to Random House's decision to publish the material in book form, Faulkner gives no intimation that he is writing a novel. Yet, loosely considered, after the fashion of Sherwood Anderson's *Winesburg, Ohio* and perhaps Ernest Hemingway's *In Our Time*, Faulkner's *The Unvanquished* possesses sufficient unity to be called a novel, and many of Faulkner's critics commonly refer to it with this term. In support of their position, they argue that in *The Unvanquished* Faulkner presents a view of Southern society during the Civil War and Reconstruction, that the development of Bayard Sartoris is the central theme in all the stories, that the effects of slavery and the beginnings of "Snopesism" are pervasive themes, and that the final story brings all or most of these motifs into final perspective.

The usual tests applied to a fictional work to establish it as a novel include the criteria of a unified theme, the presence and development of the same characters throughout the work, a definite time and place for the action, and a suspensive plot. *The Unvanquished* meets several of these standards. Unquestionably, the device of using Bayard Sartoris as the narrator who is reliving through memory his childhood and youth contributes a measure of unity to the book. The technique reminds one somewhat of Willa Cather's use of Jim Burden as the narrator of *My Ántonia*, though in her novel the time span is much greater than in Faulkner's work. At least three major characters—Bayard, Colonel Sartoris, and Ringo—appear throughout the work, and two of them, Bayard and the Colonel, undergo significant development. The time scheme may be precisely identified: with the exception of the final episode, the action takes place against the background of the Civil War and its immediate aftermath and spans Bayard's life between the ages of twelve and fifteen. The final story, in which Bayard is twenty-four, may be viewed as a kind of coda to the earlier events. What *The Unvanquished* lacks is a suspensive plot in the traditional sense. Generally, the familiar "blueprinted" novel begins with a statement of a conflict of character or situation, proceeds to a further complication of these elements, and concludes with their resolution. It exhibits a definite beginning, middle, and ending. Only by considerable wrenching can *The Unvanquished* be forced into such a mold. Instead, each individual story has suspensive action, but that action is resolved within the story and does not carry over to the succeeding narrative. Very likely the lack of suspensive action is due to Faulkner's original conception of the work not as a novel but as a group of related yet separate short stories. To have given them the kind of internal suspense characteristic of most novels would have been an impossible task. In most other respects, the work belongs to the novel genre.

When *The Unvanquished* is considered as a novel, the central character becomes the narrator, Bayard Sartoris, and its primary theme the maturing of this impressionable young boy during the years of his adolescence in the Civil War and Reconstruction. To be fair to Faulkner, today's reader must approach the work aware of his own biases and attitudes towards these events. The contemporary Civil Rights movement, only in its infancy when Faulkner was writing these stories, has profoundly affected current attitudes toward history and literature. Among historians it has produced a continuing and vehement debate about the significance of the war in American history, the nature of the slave society in the South, the quality of the individual slave's life, and the interpretation of Reconstruction. Very likely, until the issues involved in the rise of minorities in American life have been settled to the satisfaction of a future generation, historians will continue to advance partisan views of Southern history. The Civil Rights movement has also proved unsettling to literary critics and even to nonprofessional readers. Literary historians of the future may raise the question whether Faulkner's early admirers—and detractors—did not praise or blame him according to the degree to which his work affirmed their own social thinking. These same literary historians may also argue that his reputation shortly before he received the Nobel Prize, and afterward, owed something to those who saw in his fiction support for their social goals and took advantage of the opportunity to make use of him. At any rate, the thrust of American minorities for both a better self-image and a more favorable interpretation of their contribution to American life has made many of the incidents that Faulkner includes in both *The Unvanquished* and *Go Down, Moses* very sensitive topics; and the reader's attitude toward the complex of issues represented by the minority movement may exert considerable influence upon his evaluation of these and other works by Faulkner. If the artistic value of his fiction is to be fairly assessed, however, the reader must make a conscious effort to divorce his political views from his literary judgments. Otherwise, Faulkner's work may be ensnared in the net of partisan propaganda—oddly enough—either as a liberal or conservative apologist. One must remember that Faulkner's view of history is not necessarily the view of contemporary readers and that Faulkner possibly may never have fully made up his mind about the mid-nineteenth-century pole of his historical measurement. The ambivalence of his attitude may be reflected in Quentin Compson's agonized cry over the South at the end of *Absalom, Absalom!* "*I dont hate it! I dont hate it!*"; but it may also be seen in Bayard Sartoris' final comment upon his father at the end of "An Odor of Verbena."

That Faulkner intended white–Negro relations to be a significant though subordinate theme in *The Unvanquished* appears from the content of the original stories but much more from the increased emphasis he placed upon these matters in his revisions. In Loosh, Faulkner depicted a young, discontented slave, angry at the injustices of slavery, and ready at the first opportunity to betray his master's wealth to the Yankees. His anger finds expression in his passionate cry to Granny Millard. When she asks him "who are you to give it [the family silver] away," he exclaims: "Let God ax John Sartoris who the man name that give me to him. Let the man that buried me in the black dark ax that of the man what dug me free" (p. 85). A moment earlier, Loosh's outburst, "I going. I done been freed; God's own angel proclamated me free and gonter general me to Jordan," connects him with the mass of Negroes moving along the road to their "homemade Jordan" (p. 115) near Hawkhurst.

Except for Loosh, the Sartorises have good rapport with their slaves. Joby, Louvinia, Ringo, and even Philadelphy evidence no sign of discontent with the system that makes the Sartorises responsible for their welfare. That the slaveholders recognized their responsibility may be inferred from Granny's wartime welfare projects, her compassion for Negroes met on the road, and Drusilla's rebuke of her mother. When Aunt Louise says that the Yankees should be responsible for the Negroes at the river since "they brought it on themselves," Drusilla quickly reminds her: "Those Negroes are not Yankees, Mother" (p. 105). The theme of white responsibility for the welfare of Negroes looks ahead to Faulkner's treatment of race relations in *Go Down, Moses.*

At the other extreme from Loosh, Ringo seems more like Bayard's brother than a slave. Granny and the Colonel treat him as a member of the family. As has been noted earlier, Faulkner added passages to emphasize the closeness of the relationship between the two boys and Ringo's intelligence. Bayard's twice repeated comment, "Father was right; he [Ringo] was smarter than me" (pp. 91, 142), underscores Faulkner's intention. The reader must accept Bayard's statement, however, on faith, because except for Ringo's drawing accomplishments and perhaps his quick-witted action in helping Granny to escape from the Yankees, Bayard offers almost no evidence of Ringo's intellectual attainments. Bayard says plainly that unless prompted by an immediate necessity Ringo had little interest in learning. In the early stories Ringo does seem more mature for his age than Bayard; but after Granny's death, Ringo's role in the book diminishes considerably, and in the last three stories he functions more as a source for humor than for action. While Bayard is developing morally and intellectually, Ringo remains a static figure much in the background. In "An Odor of Verbena," he wants to follow the same course of action Bayard and he had taken to avenge Granny's death. Bayard remarks that Ringo was "twenty-four too, but in a way he had changed even less than I had since that day when we nailed Grumby's body to the door of the old compress" (p. 248). Ringo's lack of importance in the last part of the book leads the reader to believe that Faulkner did not intend to make race a central issue in *The Unvanquished*.

Faulkner's decision to place the narrator between the author and the reader makes Bayard central to an understanding of *The Unvanquished*. Although as narrator Bayard at times reflects upon the significance of his experiences, the reader must not only judge from Bayard's comments but also draw inferences from matters about which he offers no commentary. From such information, the reader must obtain his concept of the growing maturity of Bayard, the suffering of Southerners at home behind the lines, the uncertain position of slaves after the Emancipation Proclamation, and the actions of such persons as Colonel Sartoris, Rosa Millard, Drusilla Hawk, Ab Snopes, Ringo, and Loosh. Gradually, Bayard and all other characters become subordinate to the essential subject of the book: the influence of the Civil War upon the people of the South.

Although Bayard is too young for active participation in the fighting, the war, as seen through his memories, is an ever-present, determining factor in his boyhood. The families of the South's fighting men who lived in the fringe areas of the conflict never knew when a sudden visit from their soldiers would bring a welcome pleasure or a surprise appearance of Federal troops sweeping through the area would bring disaster. In "Ambuscade," Bayard remembers little about the military campaigns, but he never forgets his father's unexpected visit home after the fall of Vicksburg, the sinister actions of the slave Loosh, and the encounter with the Federal soldiers two days later. The implications, however, of Loosh's exclamation that "Gin'ral Sherman gonter sweep the earth and the race gonter all be free!" (pp. 25–26) and the Yankee officer's remark that "I have three boys myself" (p. 38), the young boy seems not to have understood, and Bayard as narrator makes no comment. The problem many readers encounter in evaluating the developing character of Bayard is the credibility of these incidents, especially the account of the two boys hiding beneath Granny Millard's skirts. In "Retreat," the action continues to take place in areas not firmly held by either Confederates or Yankees. Bayard remembers vividly the digging up of the family silver, the ride to Jefferson in the wagon, Uncle Buck's speech about Colonel Sartoris' demotion and return home to organize an irregular company to harass the Federals, and their eventful but abortive journey toward Memphis. Although Bayard's vivid recollections of the pursuit of the stolen mules, the swiftness and grace of Jupiter, and the Colonel's capture with the help of Ringo and Bayard of an entire Yankee company are matters that any "child" would have long remembered, the reader again has difficulty believing that such events could have taken place. Much more credible are the final episodes of this story—the escape of the Colonel, the burning of the house, and the defection of Loosh and other slaves.

In the first three stories of *The Unvanquished*, Bayard's narrative focuses upon the events of the war that immediately affected him. Often he accepts the deprivations of the war without any sign of emotional involvement on his part. For example, "Raid" opens with the terse statement, "Granny wrote the note with pokeberry juice" (p. 87); and in similar fashion, Bayard makes the low-keyed, unemotional statement: "We lived in Joby's cabin then, with a red quilt nailed by one edge to a rafter and hanging down to make two rooms" (p. 88). He seems more interested in the "insides" of the big clock that he and Ringo found in the ashes of their home. Without visible emotion, he remarks that on their way to deliver the note to Colonel Dick, they saw "a burned house like ours, three chimneys standing above a mound of ashes, and then we saw a white woman and a child looking at us from a cabin behind them" (p. 93). But as they get nearer to Hawkhurst, Bayard's memories of the desolation become more emotional. "And then the sun rose and we went on, too, along that big broad empty road between the burned houses and gins and fences. Before, it had been like passing through a country where nobody had ever lived; now it was like passing through one where everybody had died at the same moment" (pp. 94–95). Where the Hawks's house should have been, he is not surprised to find "the same mound of ashes, the same four chimneys standing gaunt and blackened in the sun like the chimneys at home" (p. 98). The desolation of his cousin's house, however, Bayard could accept, as he had accepted the burning of his own home; but the railroad, which he had only seen once before in his life, was an entirely different matter.

More than anything else, the railroad symbolizes the war for Bayard. Earlier, during a visit to his Cousin Denny, Bayard has seen it when the tracks ran "straight and empty and quiet through a long empty gash cut through the trees" and the light shone on the rails "like on two spider threads" (p. 99). He has even watched a locomotive speed past "all full of smoke and noise and sparks and jumping brass" (p. 100). Now, in place of the railroad are only a "few piles of charred ties . . . a few threads of steel knotted and twisted about the trunks of trees and already annealing into the living bark" (p. 109). He and Ringo have heard about battles, and they know a war existed, though, as Bayard says, "we had no proof of it" (p. 107). The sight of the twisted rails supplies that proof. For Bayard, "this, to us, was it." In the physical evidence of the railroad's destruction and under the spell of Drusilla's account of the race between the Confederate and Yankee locomotives along that section of track, the entire war congeals into a single instant. Even years later, as Bayard remembers this scene, he cannot conceal his vicarious, highly emotional participation in the flight of that Confederate locomotive. "She told it (and now Ringo and I began to see it; we were there too)" (p. 110). In his imagination, the instant vision of that locomotive, racing down the track on its mad flight from Atlanta, becomes "the momentary flash and glare of indomitable spirit starved by three years free of the impeding flesh" (p. 110). To Bayard, it was as if "the gray generals themselves had sent the word, had told them, 'You have suffered for three years; now we

203

will give to you and your children a glimpse of that for which you have suffered and been denied.'" And Bayard adds: "Because that's all it was. I know that now" (p. 111). The locomotive requires only an instant to rush by and vanish. "Only," says Bayard, "not gone or vanished either, so long as there should be defeated or the descendants of defeated to tell it or listen to the telling."

Almost as impressive to Bayard as the burned houses and the ruined railroad is the plight of the slaves who have suddenly attained freedom. As Granny, Bayard, and Ringo journey toward Hawkhurst, they hear groups of Negroes hurrying along the road at night. Once at dawn they find a woman in the road holding her baby and sobbing. Unable to keep up, she has been abandoned by the others, including her husband. In her refusal to return home, she explains the reason for their flight: "Hit's Jordan we coming to. . . . Jesus gonter see me that far" (p. 96), a remark that seems almost to prompt the question asked by Isaac McCaslin in *Go Down, Moses*: "What corner of Canaan is this?" (p. 279). At Hawkhurst, Drusilla tells them about hearing the Negroes passing through the night. "We sat up listening to them, and the next morning every few yards along the road would be the old ones who couldn't keep up any more, sitting or lying down and even crawling along, calling to the others to help them; and the others—the young strong ones—not stopping, not even looking at them" (pp. 103–104). Caught up in a mass religious hysteria, the Negroes believe they are about to pass over Jordan and enter a heaven of freedom. Never having been responsible for food, clothing, and shelter, they have no thought of these matters and no concept of the burdens of freedom. Granny, Drusilla, and even the Federal troops are powerless to turn them back. Although Bayard narrates the incident without comment, the scene presents in compelling fashion the plight of the freed Negroes, homeless, helpless, and deluded by religious emotionalism. The incident becomes a striking prelude to Faulkner's discussion of freedom in *Go Down, Moses*. In that novel, the naïve concept of freedom held by Fonsiba's intellectual husband suggests that in Faulkner's measurement of history even in the closing years of the century—and perhaps beyond—the Negro race will not have progressed very far towards a recognition of the practical restrictions that responsible living in society places upon the individual's freedom.

In the remainder of "Raid" and the stories that follow, the war itself recedes farther into the background of Bayard's boyhood. "Riposte in Tertio" is a continuation of the yarn begun in the last portion of "Raid" when the Federal orderly confuses the names of Granny's mules (Old Hundred and Tinney) with the number she has lost. Although Bayard accounts for the prominence of Ringo in "Riposte in Tertio" by reiterating that Ringo was "smarter than me" (p. 142), the mule trading affair provides little additional insight into Bayard's character. The primary theme relates to Granny's efforts to provide for the families and former slaves in the community. Her resourcefulness and success are indirectly conceded by the Yankee lieutenant who finally shuts down her operation: "I'd rather engage Forrest's whole brigade every morning for six months than spend that same length of time trying to protect United States property from defenseless Southern women and niggers and children. . . . God help the North if Davis and Lee had ever thought of the idea of forming a brigade of grandmothers and nigger orphans, and invading us with it" (pp. 163–64). Granny's effort to secure capital to enable Colonel Sartoris to rebuild his plantation after the war results in her brutal murder and motivates Bayard's actions in the following story, "Vendée." Her death at the hands of Grumby, a man who claimed to have been a Confederate soldier under Forrest, probably should be interpreted as the consequence of the shift in her motive from the community's welfare to personal gain, in other words, her vulnerability to the temptations posed by Ab Snopes. Equally valid, however, would be the assertion that her death results from a series of assumptions she makes: that Grumby was a former Confederate soldier, that "what side of a war a man fought on made him what he is" (p. 170), and that "Southern men would not harm a woman" (p. 171). Depending upon Grumby's true identity, one or more of these assumptions proves fatally incorrect. Had Faulkner established beyond question Grumby's identity as a former Confederate, Granny's statement that "even Yankees do not harm old women" (p. 174)—and, in fact, the entire incident—would have a deeply ironical aspect.

The death of Granny marks the halfway point in the book and a definite change in its atmosphere. The tone of the first three stories, in which she is the central character, has been light and humorous. The action has underscored the resourcefulness of Southerners in their struggle for survival on the periphery of the fighting. Now, as Granny's place is taken by

Drusilla and Ringo's by Bayard, the stories become grim, realistic accounts of violence that suggest that the aftermath of the war was worse than the war itself. Ringo comes close to the truth when he declares, "This war ain't over. Hit just started good" (p. 229). Only occasionally is the grimness relieved by a flash of humor, usually from Ringo, whose cheerful banter often masks a serious reality. In the passage quoted above, for example, Ringo continues: "Used to be when you seed a Yankee you knowed him because he never had nothing but a gun or a mule halter or a handful of hen feathers. Now you don't even know him and stid of the gun he got a clutch of this stuff [new script dollars] in one hand and a clutch of nigger voting tickets in the yuther."

"Vendée" strains the credulity of the reader. The story is melodramatic in the true sense of the term, since the action stems not from character but from events. The earlier stories contain no hint or suggestion that these two fifteen-year-old boys, seeking to revenge the murder of Granny, could or would track and kill a man of Grumby's ruthlessness, nail his body to a compress door, cut off his hand, and fasten it to a board above her grave so that she would "lay good and quiet" (p. 211). In the preceding episode, Bayard has largely been ignored by Granny and Ringo in their mule trading schemes; but in "Vendée" Bayard emerges as an avenger out of the Old Testament. Overnight, he has not only accepted the frontier notion of personal justice but also carried it to the extreme of mutilation. The description of Bayard placing Grumby's severed hand above Granny's grave does much to lessen the reader's sympathy for the young boy. That Bayard, as an older man remembering this event in his life, makes no explanation or comment upon it contributes to the basic weakness of the story. Although "Vendée" may serve as a rendering of the depths to which ordinarily law-abiding persons may sink in a society that has fallen apart and, later, as a contrast or "counterpoint" to Bayard's actions after the death of his father, this story seems the least attractive incident in *The Unvanquished*.

The title of the last of the original six stories published in the *Saturday Evening Post* and *Scribner's Magazine*, "Skirmish at Sartoris," applies both to the "skirmish" between Drusilla and the Jefferson ladies who have never surrendered and to the more serious affair between the ex-Confederates and the carpetbaggers in control of the Negro votes. In the feminine skirmish, Drusilla suffers defeat. The women of the age of Mrs.

Habersham, Aunt Louisa, and Mrs. Compson demand Drusilla's obedience to the code of behavior expected from a Southern girl of a good
family. She must wear dresses, refrain from working with men in the
field, and marry the man who in the eyes of her mother had compromised
her. Although Faulkner's handling of the zeal of the Jefferson ladies to
make Drusilla "an honest woman"—and even Bayard's comments upon
the thoughts of women about the follies of men—makes the incident
somewhat of a "tempest in a teapot," other interpretations are possible.
To those who view her marriage as a private affair, these outraged women
could reply that after the war or, for that matter, any time, the enforcement of moral standards in the community should not take second place
to the election of a town official. On the other hand, the readiness of these
women to throw away the ballot box to hasten a marriage ceremony may
be seen as Faulkner's criticism of the lack of interest of Southern women
in the political problems of the community. Faulkner may also have intended to use Drusilla as an illustration of the growing inflexibility of
Southern society and to state this truth in a lighter vein. Perhaps, the
entire incident should be read as more humorous than symbolic or
critical.

In the other "skirmish," Bayard recounts, with little commentary, the
struggle of his father and other former Confederate soldiers to restore
civil government that had broken down in Jefferson during the war.
They are opposed by two members of the Burden family (and other carpetbaggers) who have come from Missouri with a commission from
Washington to help the freed Negroes. According to Ringo, the Burdens
are purchasing Negro votes to elect as town marshal Cassius Q. Benbow,
an illiterate ex-slave who formerly drove the Benbow carriage. Although
their motives are never precisely stated, presumably Colonel Sartoris and
the white community seek to prevent Uncle Cash's election because they
believe him wholly unqualified to serve as marshal and resent the efforts
of the Burdens to elevate the recently freed slaves to political power. In
Bayard's account of the confrontation that follows, when Sartoris enters
the voting place in the hotel, the Burdens shoot at him. The Colonel
then kills both Burdens with his derringer.

This version of the "skirmish" has particular interest for Faulkner's
readers because it is the third time Faulkner told the story. In *Sartoris* old
man Falls told it to Bayard in 1919. In old man Falls's account, the Colo-

nel on that day in "'72" confronts the Negroes and the two (unnamed) Missouri carpetbaggers, who have herded the Negroes up the road toward the store. When the carpetbaggers see the Colonel, they back away with their hands in their pockets and curse him. With the ballot box between his feet, the Colonel dares the Negroes to approach to vote. They scatter, and he shoots several times over their heads. After reloading his derringer, the Colonel follows the carpetbaggers to Mrs. Winterbottom's boardinghouse, walks up to their room, where they face him with their pistols on the table in front of them. Outside old man Falls and others hear three shots. Afterwards, the Colonel comes downstairs and apologizes to Mrs. Winterbottom for messing up her room. Probably this account of the incident is meant to be the least reliable. At ninety-four, old man Falls has been telling this story for the past fifty years. In the telling and retelling, the single confrontation has been doubled, the hotel has become a store, the Colonel has placed the ballot box between his feet, and he hastens the flight of the Negroes with shots from his derringer. Above all, either old man Falls has forgotten that Bayard, to whom he is telling the story, was present when the "skirmish" occurred, or Faulkner decided later to make Bayard witness to the affair.

In 1931, four years after he finished *Sartoris*, Faulkner wrote another version of the affair in *Light in August*. In that novel, Faulkner identifies the two Burdens whom the Colonel shot as Joanna Burden's grandfather and half brother, both named Calvin, and provides a lengthy account of the Burden family. Descended from a New England minister, the Burdens have lived mainly in Missouri. The men in the family have a long pedigree of religious bigotry, violence, and killing. Above everything else, they hate and curse slaveholders. Joanna explains that the former Confederates in Jefferson hated her family as Yankees, foreigners, and carpetbaggers, who stirred up the Negroes to murder and rape. She feels that the war was too recent for the whites to be sensible, and she supposes that Colonel Sartoris became the town hero because he killed an old onearmed man and a boy. Joanna says nothing about the Burdens' fanatic hatred of slaveholders, the buying of Negro votes, or Uncle Cash's qualifications for office. She makes no mention of the Burdens being armed, much less of their firing the first shot or cursing the Colonel.

What is remarkable about the three versions is that Faulkner has presented three different approaches—even three different sets of "facts"—

to the same event, but left the "truth" for the reader to establish for himself. Despite old man Falls's embroidery upon the story, he has pictured the Colonel as a courageous, if arrogant, leader of men, whose deeds have almost become a legend. So great is old man Falls's admiration for his hero that he concludes his account by declaring that he "sort of envied them Nawthuners."[9] In telling her side, Joanna admits that she does not know who was right, and she explains her father's failure to kill Sartoris on the ground that perhaps her father was French enough to understand that a man must act as the society in which he was born had taught him to act.[10] On the other hand, Bayard's account makes no mention of the carpetbaggers "stirring up the Negroes to murder and rape."[11] Bayard makes no judgment upon the rightness or wrongness of his father's action, but he quotes the Colonel as saying that he is going to the sheriff to make bond, because "we are working for peace through law and order" (p. 239). But whether the reader interprets this statement as ironical or factual may depend somewhat upon his view of the early days of Reconstruction. Insofar as "Skirmish at Sartoris" is concerned, this rather ambiguous remark leaves the verdict open. For the present at least, Sartoris has won the skirmish, but in his victory the separation of the Negroes from the whites has advanced one step farther. Paradoxically, had Sartoris lost and Cassius Q. Benbow been elected, the same development would probably have taken place.

Unquestionably, "An Odor of Verbena" is the most important story in *The Unvanquished*. The seriousness of its theme and its relationship to the issues raised in the earlier stories suggest that Faulkner may have written it to give depth and significance to the entire work by advancing the narrative to the end of Bayard's youth. At twenty-four and near the completion of his law studies, Bayard has readied himself for the trial that he knows he will one day face. In the twenty-four hours that comprise the time span of this story, Bayard confirms his manhood and finishes his "education" for life. He becomes "The Sartoris."

Since "An Odor of Verbena" relates primarily to Bayard's character as delineated by his thoughts and actions, the crucial point is his perception of values. In understanding Bayard and in placing him in the context of the Sartoris family—and, perhaps, by extension, in context with the Southern tradition—one must not forget that Bayard is just as much a product of that tradition or value system as is John Sartoris. If Bayard alters the tradition—often it is called "the code"—one must observe that the potential for alteration must have been inherent in the Sartorises' values. (Interestingly, one of the differences between Ringo and Bayard that emerges in this final story is that during the years when Bayard is reaching his moral maturity Ringo's character remains unchanged.) Likewise, one must not forget the parallels between Bayard and his father. If Colonel Sartoris, after years of fighting and violence, determines that he must accomplish some "moral housecleaning" (p. 266) by refusing to kill or engage in further violence, Bayard, a young man but one who has already engaged in a barbarous act of revenge, follows in his father's footsteps and accomplishes his own version of a "moral housecleaning" by refusing to avenge his father's murder.

Since the actions of both Colonel Sartoris and Bayard are often evaluated in terms of the "Southern code," the term, which is frequently loosely employed and seldom defined, requires some explanation. In its most favorable light, the Southern code or tradition was actually a complex of values by which a man could govern his conduct in the pursuit of worthwhile activities. It placed a high value upon personal responsibility and action in accordance with principle (honor), truth, and courage. It recognized the individual's responsibilities to those dependent upon him and to the community at large. At the same time, it strongly identified a man's character with the reputation of his family over several generations. To say, for example, that a man was "an Armstrong from Bolivar County," or "a Breckinridge from Marshall County," or "a McGehee from Panola County" was to imply a certain standard of living and personal conduct. Although violence was not an integral part of the code, the self-consciousness of the individual and his need to protect his personality could lead to violence, particularly in matters of personal honor and in areas where the legal machinery of justice was not strongly entrenched in the community. When a man felt that he or a member of his family had been injured, he felt justified in demanding satisfaction from the guilty party. As a practical matter, juries could not be depended upon to punish the guilty. (The records of Faulkner's own family contain numerous instances where juries acquitted men under such circumstances.) The sensational nature of these conflicts have often overshadowed the other elements of the code.

In dealing with the Southern code or tradition, one must not forget that individual differences exerted a great deal of influence upon the actions of persons who tried to mold their lives by its principles. Granny Millard, for example, lived by the Southern code. While she conducted her personal war with the Yankees and assumed responsibility for the old, women, and children, both whites and Negroes, in the community, she acted within the code. When she sought her selfish gain, she violated its principles. In "Raid," Drusilla speaks for the tradition when she rebukes Aunt Louise for denying their responsibility for the welfare of the Negroes, and in "An Odor of Verbena," Drusilla shows a feeling of responsibility for the creation of a better society when she argues the superiority of John Sartoris' dream over that of Thomas Sutpen. But Drusilla cannot adapt her values to the different circumstances that arise after the war, though she concedes that Bayard has the courage she admires above everything else. Among the members of John Sartoris' generation, Aunt Jenny lives by the Southern code but adapts to new conditions: she will still believe in Bayard's courage even if he spends the day in the stable loft. Despite his dreams, Colonel Sartoris throughout much of his later life fails to square his conduct with the ideals of the Southern code. Granny, Drusilla, and the Colonel thus try to pattern their lives by the tradition, but they do not always act according to its values. Their examples suggest that to say that Faulkner rejected the Southern code or tradition in *The Unvanquished* is to oversimplify the complexities of human character. The Sartorises are not automated personifications of ideas, and only after the reader has understood them as fallible human beings should he consider them as symbols, if at all.

More than any other of the stories that form *The Unvanquished*, "An Odor of Verbena" belongs to Bayard. The events in it—events that years later remain fresh as yesterday in his memory—are shaped by the inner turmoil of his mind and emotions. Perhaps no better example can be found of what Faulkner meant by the human heart in conflict with itself as the only subject for great writing. Now twenty-four, Bayard has, appropriately, been studying law; and now as he reflects upon his father's life in relation to his own, he must reconcile the moral law with his own emotions and the mores of the community. His reaction to his father's murder will provide the crucial test of his development from youth to manhood. All of his earlier life bears directly upon the decision that he must make within a few hours. For these reasons, whatever judgment the reader makes of the entire book must be framed to a considerable extent upon this final episode.

When Professor Wilkins flings open the door to Bayard's room, the clock of events begins to run in "An Odor of Verbena." Bayard knows what is coming. Already he has determined that to kill is a moral evil and that if there is to be hope and peace, the killing must stop. Bayard does not know, however, whether he has the courage to translate these beliefs into action; and he cannot cease to revolve the issues in his mind as the pressures mount to force him to conduct himself within the pattern of the traditional, expected, and even approved course of action. Almost at once Bayard becomes aware of these pressures. He notices, for example, that Wilkins and his wife fully expect him to attempt to avenge the Colonel's murder. Although as a lawyer Wilkins would affirm the principle "thou shalt not kill," Bayard does not expect him to act contrary to his "blood and raising and background" (p. 249). The remark reminds the reader of Joanna Burden's assertion that a man must act as the society in which he was reared has trained him to act. As Bayard rides towards Jefferson with Ringo, he knows too what Ringo expects of him. (Ringo's single remark, "We could bushwhack him. . . . Like we done Grumby that day," seems a curious error in fact, but his reference to Grumby underscores the contrast between Bayard's earlier act and his present intention.) Bayard can also imagine the scene at his home: his father lying in the parlor with his sabre beside him and Drusilla waiting there with the sprig of verbena in her hair and the two loaded pistols in her hands. [12] Thus, even before he gets to Jefferson, Bayard has felt pressure from Professor and Mrs. Wilkins, Ringo, and Drusilla moving him within the pattern of the tradition he has already determined to deny.

The second section of the story provides a certain amount of exposition chiefly designed to help the reader understand Bayard's emotional tension over his father's life and character, though the narrative may raise almost as many questions as it answers. Although the setting of this part consists largely of flashbacks to conversations Bayard had with Drusilla when he was twenty and another in August, 1874, only two months prior to the killing of his father, Bayard's reflections range over many of the earlier incidents in the book, notably the events in "Riposte in Tertio," "Vendée," and "Skirmish at Sartoris." They also include comments about the rebuilding of the Sartoris home, the beginning of Colonel Sartoris' partnership with Redmond in the railroad venture, and reference to the hill man whom the Colonel may have shot needlessly.

The real subject of the second section, however, is Bayard's judgment of his father's life and character. As advocate for the Colonel, Drusilla speaks of his dream of trying to rebuild the community; and against Bayard's immediate comparison of it to Sutpen's dream, she argues that Sutpen was selfishly ambitious only for himself, whereas the Colonel was trying to aid the entire country. (Drusilla's remarks remind one of Granny Millard.) She defends the killing of the two carpetbaggers on the grounds that in the realization of any worthwhile dream, inevitably someone will get hurt. Drusilla's comments, however, do not silence Bayard's growing doubts about his father's character and acts. Four years later, after the railroad has been finished and Colonel Sartoris has defeated Redmond for the legislature, Bayard realizes that much of the trouble between the two men stems from his father's "violent and ruthless dictatorialness and will to dominate" (p. 258). The Colonel was wrong to taunt Redmond for not fighting in the war. Even such friends as George Wyatt begin to see that he has killed too many men; but when Bayard voices this thought to Drusilla, she reminds him of his own killing of Grumby and says there are worse things than killing.

The talk about killing and dreams prompts Drusilla to say that she thinks the finest role a man can play is to love a woman and then die young because he "believed what he could not help but believe and was what he could not (could not? would not) help but be" (p. 261). The remark applies to her relationship with Gavin Breckbridge and could be made to fit Drusilla's own role in the war but it also could apply to Bayard if Bayard were to discover he loved Drusilla. In the passionate kissing scene that follows, Bayard is fully aware of the sexual nature of Drusilla's desire; but when he tells his father, the Colonel ignores the incident. Faulkner does not provide sufficient material for a reader to be certain of the implications of the remark and the incident that follows. Did her remark relate to Gavin or did it relate to Bayard as a man who could love her and then die in an act demanded by the tradition? Was Drusilla in love with Bayard? Did the Colonel ignore the incident because he had no great sexual love for his wife or because he felt he had more important matters on his mind? At the University of Virginia, Faulkner said that he doubted that there was any romantic attraction between Drusilla and Bayard,[13] but the passage itself hardly supports this interpretation.

Certainly Bayard considered his embrace with Drusilla serious enough to require his telling (admitting to?) his father; but the Colonel seems too much engrossed in defending his violence to be bothered. Bayard now sees his father as a man who has killed so often that he can never have inner peace, while the Colonel defends his action by saying that he has "acted as the land and the time demanded" (p. 266). He could have added that in 1874, the *now* of "An Odor of Verbena," the troubled days of Reconstruction were almost at an end and law and order were returning to the state. The Colonel tells Bayard that circumstances are changing, that the future will be a time of "consolidation, of pettifogging and doubtless chicanery," that he has accomplished his aim, and that he is tired of killing no matter what the reason. The reader infers that to deal with the times to come, the Colonel has educated Bayard in the law. As this scene, very important to the meaning of the story, concludes, the Colonel declares his intention of going the next day unarmed to meet Redmond.[14] Much of the interpretation of Colonel Sartoris' character and of Bayard's later actions depends upon the significance attached to these passages. Did the times and the land demand the Colonel's acts of violence? As the Reconstruction period neared its end, did the times require different measures, even different types of men? Was the Colonel's prediction of pettifogging and chicanery in the years ahead valid? What did Faulkner think about the rightness or wrongness of the Colonel's defense?

At the conclusion of the second section, the issues that generate the conflict in Bayard's heart have been fully stated for the reader. Although the Colonel's guilt or innocence has not been established (except perhaps in the case of the hill man), at the end of his life he acknowledges his need for a "moral housecleaning" and in meeting Redmond he renounces violence as a way of settling personal disputes. In somewhat similar fashion, Bayard has also determined that he will not continue the pattern of action he followed in killing Grumby. Bayard must face Wyatt and his men; he must face Drusilla; and he must keep his resolution as he stands beside the coffin of his father. Finally, the next morning he must meet Redmond. That Bayard successfully proves his courage and thereby alters the tradition of violence vindicates not only his morality but also by implication his father's act as well, since together they have shown that even the refusal of one party to engage in deadly personal conflict will

214

ultimately stop the practice. With the sprig of verbena she leaves upon his pillow, Drusilla tacitly acknowledges his victory.

Bayard's action, thus, should be seen not as a denial of his father but as a completion of the family housecleaning begun by the Colonel. Bayard himself makes the point as he enters the house after his meeting with Redmond: "I didn't need to see him again because he was there, he would always be there; maybe what Drusilla meant by his dream was not something which he possessed but something which he had bequeathed us which we could never forget, which would even assume the corporeal shape of him whenever any of us, black or white, closed our eyes" (p. 291). The tantalizing vagueness of this remark may be due to Faulkner's own ambivalent or uncertain attitude toward his great-grandfather and Southern history during the period of Reconstruction. Faulkner disapproved the violence of the time, but he was unwilling wholly to condemn those who, like his great-grandfather, participated in these events. On the other hand, if by the Colonel's dream Bayard meant the recovery of the community from the war, the restoration of law and order, and an end to the vendetta type of violence, his final comment about his father becomes an affirmation of the good qualities in the Southern tradition and includes both races.

Chapter VIII

Materialism in the Country

The Hamlet

WHILE Faulkner was shaping the material for *The Unvanquished*, he had in mind the general content of *The Hamlet*, which appeared in 1940.[1] Between these two works such a close relationship exists that any-one seeking to understand Faulkner's thought should take account of the connections and the contrasts they exhibit. For the two volumes, Faulkner brought together, with revisions, stories that he had already published and manuscripts written earlier but still unpublished. The utilization of such material undoubtedly strongly influenced the plots of both and has prompted readers to question whether either book should be called a novel.

Another connection between *The Unvanquished* and *The Hamlet* lies in the fact that they are studies of contrasting families. *The Unvanquished* deals with the Sartoris family, consisting primarily of Granny Rosa Mill-ard, Colonel John Sartoris, Drusilla Sartoris, and Bayard, as they react to the events of the Civil War and Reconstruction. *The Hamlet* likewise em-phasizes the lives and characters of the Snopes family, but the time is advanced to the first decade of the twentieth century. At its best, the Sartoris family exhibits courage, leadership, and a realization of its re-sponsibility for the welfare of the community. So long as Granny Mill-ard, for example, conducts her mule-trading business in an unselfish manner, she and the community prosper; but when her motive becomes personal gain, she falls victim to the unscrupulous Ab Snopes. In *The Hamlet*, Ratliff likewise falls victim to the Snopeses when he allows greed to become his motive, and Flem Snopes proves a far more corrosive force than his father, Ab Snopes. Faulkner's general attitude towards the change from the dominance of the Sartorises to that of the Snopeses may be inferred from his remark at the University of Virginia about the Compsons (one could substitute the Sartorises): "I feel sorry for the Compsons. That was blood which was good and brave once, but has thinned and faded all the way out. Of the Snopes, I'm terrified."[2] Although in *The Unvanquished* the later years of Colonel John Sartoris' life are marred by violence, he finally renounces killing as a solution; but before he dies, he forecasts an era to come in which "pettifogging and doubtless chicanery" would dominate. In *The Hamlet*, those modern times of pettifogging and chicanery arrive with the Snopes family. Thus, *The Hamlet* may be viewed as a kind of historical development of the social and moral changes that Faulkner saw beginning to take place after the Civil War.

Other interesting, though perhaps less significant, links exist between *The Hamlet* and Faulkner's earlier work. In addition to the use of characters whom the reader has already met in other volumes, *The Hamlet* contains outstanding examples of Faulkner's fondness for the humorous sketch or tall tale of the kind he had employed effectively in earlier fiction. Labove's ineffectual pursuit of Eula Varner may recall to some readers Jason Compson's hopeless chase of his niece Quentin. The famous spotted horses yarn is the kind of outrageous tale that reminds one of Granny's adventures with the Union officers and even Colonel John Sartoris' single-handed capture of a Yankee company. The revenge of Mink Snopes upon Jack Houston has something of the same tone as Ringo and Bayard's revenge upon Grumby. The story of the buried family silver and money on the old Frenchman's place offers a parallel to the burying of the Sartoris family's silver. The account of the wild stallion that kills Lucy Pate in *The Hamlet* may bring to the reader's mind the wild stallion that almost killed Bayard. The innocence and hunger for love displayed by the idiot Ike Snopes reminds one of Benjy; and Jody Varner's concern for his sister's honor has precedent in Quentin Compson's obsession with Caddy's virginity. Flem Snopes exhibits qualities very much like those of Jason Compson and even Thomas Sutpen. Although other connections could be cited, these examples show the infinite variety of Faulkner's handling of similar elements of fiction and offer evidence of his long preoccupation with the kind of material that he used in *The Hamlet*.

Faulkner's readers have often observed that the tone of *The Hamlet* is realistic, whereas that of *The Unvanquished* is markedly romantic. *The*

Hamlet, to be sure, does contain some very romantic writing, for example, the pastoral lyric or prose-poem that forms the primary content of the Ike Snopes incident, or Ratliff's dream of Flem in hell, or even the main incident of the spotted horses story. Beneath the comic veneer of many of the episodes in *The Hamlet*, however, an underlying grimness often finds expression in the prose and sets the predominant "tone" of the volume. A good example is the ending of the spotted horses incident, where the men of the community, sitting on the porch, turn their heads away while Flem tells Mrs. Armstid that the Texas man has taken her money. They, as well as Flem, know the implications of this lie in terms of the suffering she and her children will endure. Other episodes, for example, Mink's bitterness, meanness, and brutality, serve as an effective check upon the comic and romantic parts of the work. In addition, the critical edge to the satire that informs many of the episodes of *The Hamlet* emphasizes its atmosphere of realism. Probably for most readers, *The Hamlet*, because of its greater variety of incident and character, its predominantly realistic character, and the depth of Faulkner's insight into the society of the modern twentieth-century community, will always seem a greater work than *The Unvanquished*.

The long gestation period of *The Hamlet* may account for much of its superiority to *The Unvanquished*. The continuing study of Faulkner's early manuscripts has clearly demonstrated that from the beginning of his literary career he intended to write a novel about the Snopes family. Very likely so early as the summer of 1926, he began a story he called "Father Abraham"; but after writing about 14,000 words, he put it aside late in 1926 or early in 1927 to write "Flags in the Dust," the manuscript that ultimately became *Sartoris*. The title, "Father Abraham," may have been appropriated from the proposed title of Sherwood Anderson's biography of Abraham Lincoln, but in Faulkner's work the title may refer ironically to the biblical Abraham who led his people into the Land of Canaan, the promised land full of milk and honey.

As "Father Abraham" opens, Flem Snopes is at the peak of his career, the president of the bank in Jefferson. At once, however, Faulkner turns the reader's attention to Flem's beginnings "in the hill cradled cane and cypress jungles of Yocona River" near Frenchman's Bend. Examination of the manuscript reveals not only details of plot but also even phrases that appear in *The Hamlet*. Examples include the description of Flem's eyes as the color of stagnant water, the ruined appearance of the old Frenchman's mansion, Eula as a girl with "eyes like cloudy hothouse grapes," the spotted horses, Flem's treatment of Henry Armstid and his wife, and even Ratliff, who is called V. K. Suratt and described as a patent medicine drummer instead of a sewing-machine agent. The story of "Father Abraham" thus encompasses the beginnings of Flem in Frenchman's Bend', his rise in Varner's store, marriage to Eula Varner, and return from Texas with the spotted horses. Flem's career would then have reminded readers of the rednecks and poor whites who supported such political figures in Mississippi as James K. Vardaman, Theodore G. Bilbo, and Lee M. Russell. About the middle of page twenty-five of the manuscript, Faulkner stopped writing, though at times afterwards he added to the story.

By the end of September, 1927, Faulkner had finished (except for some revision and the cutting of the manuscript by Ben Wasson) "Flags in the Dust," though it was not to be published (as *Sartoris*) until January, 1929. Between the time that Faulkner stopped work on "Father Abraham" and the completion of the manuscript of "Flags in the Dust," he probably thought more about the Snopes family, because he included in it a kind of capsule history of Flem's activities after leaving Frenchman's Bend. (This portion of Flem's story, however, would not be told until almost thirty years later when *The Town* was published.) Because of the comment about the family and its pertinence to the development of the Snopes saga in Faulkner's mind, the passage is important to his readers:

> This Snopes was a young man, member of a seemingly inexhaustible family which for the last ten years had been moving to town in driblets from a small settlement known as Frenchman's Bend. Flem, the first Snopes, had appeared unheralded one day behind the counter of a small restaurant on a side street, patronized by country folk. With this foothold and like Abraham of old, he brought his blood and legal kin household by household, individual by individual, into town, and established them where they could gain money. Flem himself was presently manager of the city light and water plant, and for the following few years he was a sort of handy man to the municipal government; and three years ago . . . he became vice president of the Sartoris bank. . . .
>
> He still retained the restaurant, and the canvas tent in the rear of it . . . ; and it served as an alighting-place for incoming Snopeses, from which they spread to small third-rate businesses of various kinds . . . where they multiplied and flourished.[3]

In addition to Flem's career in Jefferson, Faulkner includes a thumbnail sketch of Montgomery Ward Snopes. This Snopes had feigned a health disability to avoid the draft but had gone to France with Horace Benbow in the Y.M.C.A. service. Although tailored to fit other characters (notably Byron Snopes and Gavin Stevens), basically this same story is told in *The Town*. In *Sartoris*, Horace makes the point that he is "very much disappointed" in Montgomery Ward Snopes and asserts that the Snopeses are "parasites";[4] but to learn what Montgomery Ward did to merit this disapproval, the reader must wait until he reads *The Town*. The evidence from *Sartoris*, however, shows that by 1927, Faulkner had thought through the Snopes saga far beyond the point where he stopped writing the manuscript of "Father Abraham."

Other evidence confirms the strength and persistence of Faulkner's interest in the Snopes material. In *Sanctuary*, the first version of which was written between January and June, 1929, Faulkner introduced the shady politician Clarence Snopes and the naïve Virgil Snopes. In 1931 and 1932 Faulkner wrote several short stories that he would incorporate—with more or less reworking—directly into *The Hamlet*. "Spotted Horses," the account of the horse auction, was published by *Scribner's Magazine* in June, 1931; "The Hound," the story of the Houston murder, came out in *Harper's* in August, 1931; while "Lizards in Jamyshyd's Courtyard," the tale about the treasure hunt, appeared in the *Saturday Evening Post*, February 27, 1932. Faulkner was, as he told a friend, "whittling away" at the Snopes novel, though he knew that publication was at least two years away.[5] Sometime in 1932 he tentatively chose for it the title "The Peasants," probably from the novel of that name by Balzac. In May, 1934, while he was working on the stories for the *Post* that would eventually be published as *The Unvanquished*, Phil Stone, Faulkner's close friend and literary advisor, began a partial biography of the novelist in the Oxford *Eagle*. Writing of the rise of the "redneck" in Mississippi politics, Stone noted that Faulkner's grandfather and uncle had supported Vardaman. Asserted Stone: "It is this social and political upheaval that is the dominant theme of Faulkner's saga of the Snopes family . . . which work, if ever completed, may become his greatest book and possibly the grandest book of humor America has yet seen."[6] In September, 1934, Faulkner finished and sent to the *Saturday Evening Post* "The Unvanquished" (later called "Riposte in Tertio") and "Vendée." These are the two stories that contain the account of Ab Snopes's collaboration with Granny Millard, his betrayal of her to Grumby, and his encounter with Ringo and Bayard as they pursue Grumby. The events in them take place at an earlier period than the action of "Father Abraham." Thus, Faulkner extended the Snopes material backwards as well as forwards in time. "The Unvanquished" and "Vendée" are important for *The Hamlet* because they provide clues to Ab's character at a time before he—as Ratliff says—"soured."

For the time being, Faulkner worked only spasmodically on the Snopes material, preferring instead to write *Absalom, Absalom!* Early in November, 1938, he finished the short story "Barn Burning," much of which he would incorporate into *The Hamlet*. In December, however, he wrote a letter to Robert Haas at Random House, saying, "I am working at the Snopes book. It will be in three books, whether big enough to be three separate volumes I dont know yet, though I think it will. The first one I think will run about 80,000 words. I am half through with it."[7] In the remainder of this lengthy letter, Faulkner included a summary of the three novels he planned to write, calling them in order, "The Peasants" (now *The Hamlet*); "Rus in Urbe" (later *The Town*); and "Ilium Falling" (or *The Mansion*).

At this point, Faulkner was writing the Snopes volume in earnest. Years of thinking and writing were about to come to fruition as new material and old coalesced in his mind. In January, 1939, he wrote to Bennett Cerf at Random House that he hoped to finish it in April. Throughout the spring and summer, he wrote and rewrote, revised, cut, and expanded the short stories he had written earlier. He added a considerable amount of entirely new material. By October he was virtually finished, and he wrote Saxe Commins, his editor, suggesting that the volumes bear the titles they presently have. In January, 1940, Faulkner was correcting the galleys. Random House published *The Hamlet* in March. It represented Faulkner's twelfth published novel; and, although many reviewers praised his achievement, few recognized its centrality in Faulkner's fiction.[8]

Looking back upon what has been said about the long foreground of *The Hamlet*, one cannot ignore the fact that before writing his novel Faulkner spent years of his maturity thinking about the character of the people and the conditions of life in his own area. The Snopes stories slowly evolved in his mind until he finally concluded that the time was ripe for him to bring at least some of them into focus within a single book while leaving others to be included in the later volumes of the trilogy. Very likely, Faulkner thought that this novel would be his greatest single achievement, and there are critics who do believe that in the Snopes saga he reached the pinnacle of his artistic success. Doubtless Faulkner was aware that in his other work he had dealt as adequately as he could with the past of his own region and considered himself now ready to become his own Shreve or Quentin as he analyzed the human condition in the twentieth century. In *The Hamlet*, he became a severe critic of modern times, but Faulkner did not leave his readers without to a degree affirming the continued human potential for a better life. Thus, those who wish to understand Faulkner should seek in *The Hamlet* to grasp both the essence of his criticism and the measure of his faith.

Because Faulkner habitually paid meticulous attention to matters of time and provided an abundance of time-indicators throughout the Snopes trilogy, the reader may be certain that the Snopeses are his own, twentieth-century contemporaries. Although no specific dates are given in *The Hamlet*, by using as a point of reference the dates on Eula Varner's tombstone in *The Mansion*, one can quickly determine precisely when a number of events in *The Hamlet* took place. With the knowledge that Eula was born in 1889 and died in 1927, one can establish that Flem Snopes made his appearance in Frenchman's Bend in 1902, when Eula was thirteen. They were married in 1907, and early in the following year their daughter Linda was born. Likewise, in 1908, Mink Snopes murdered Jack Houston, and Flem moved his family to Jefferson. Thus, the action of *The Hamlet* covers the years 1902–1908.

No reader can forget the straightforward, richly suggestive, opening sentences that Faulkner wrote to define the hamlet or rural community of Frenchman's Bend: "Frenchman's Bend was a section of rich river-bottom country lying twenty miles southeast of Jefferson. Hill-cradled and remote, definite yet without boundaries, straddling into two counties and owning allegiance to neither, it had been the original grant and site of a tremendous pre–Civil War plantation, the ruins of which . . . were still known as the old Frenchman's place" (p. 3). Faulkner located his mythical community, as this passage indicates, "twenty miles southeast of Jefferson," that is, near the border of Lafayette and Calhoun counties, south of Tula, in the region of the old Dallas settlement, now absent from most maps of the area, but still remembered by the older citizens of Oxford as the birthlace of Lee M. Russell, a Mississippi governor and associate of Bilbo, who may have contributed to Faulkner's profile of Flem Snopes. Today very little is left of the Dallas settlement except the cemetery where one can still read on tombstones the names and dates of persons who might be encountered in Faulkner's books. For those who seek the hard-core historical fact behind Faulkner's fiction, almost nothing remains of Frenchman's Bend—except the cemetery.

At the beginning of *The Hamlet*, Frenchman's Bend has already experienced several migrations. The old Frenchman himself brought slaves and built the kind of mansion customary among wealthy Southern antebellum planters. All that is now left of his tenure is the decaying mansion and the legend of "the money he buried somewhere about the place when Grant overran the country on his way to Vicksburg" (p. 4). After the Frenchman came new settlers originally from "England and the Scottish and Welsh Marches." These men brought no slaves and no fine furniture. Their descendants in the region still plant cotton, distill whiskey, and live to themselves. Of these people, Will Varner is the chief man, "a farmer, a usurer, a veterinarian" (p. 5).

Varner now owns a good deal of the original grant including the site of the ruined mansion, where he likes to sit in a homemade chair "trying," as he says, "to find out what it must have felt like to be the fool that would need all this" (p. 6). He virtually rules the settlement. His power base is economic: he owns the best land, the cotton gin, the blacksmith's shop, the store. He lends money, takes—and often forecloses—mortgages, advances "furnishings" on next year's crops, keeps the sharecroppers' books, functions as veterinarian, and, when he wishes, stuffs ballot boxes. His son, Jody, lacking the father's initiative and intelligence, clerks in the store and otherwise helps in the business of usury.

The present social and economic arrangements in Frenchman's Bend, however, are about to be challenged by the invasion of the Snopes family. Ab, the father, seeks to farm on shares a plot of ground managed by Jody Varner. Ab is known to V. K. Ratliff, an itinerant sewing-machine agent and close friend of Will Varner, as an arsonist and troublemaker. According to Ratliff, Ab "aint naturally mean. He's just soured" (p. 27). In explaining his comment, Ratliff provides a brief but far more favorable account of Ab's activities with Granny Millard and Colonel John Sartoris than the facts given in *The Unvanquished* would warrant; and as the final and most important reason for Ab's conduct, Ratliff tells the story of the Ab Snopes–Pat Stamper horse trade. "Pat eliminated him from horse-trading," explains the sewing-machine agent; "And so he just went plumb curdled" (p. 29). For most readers, neither Ratliff's account of Ab's Civil War actions nor the long, comic story of the Pat Stamper affair really accounts for Ab's character. Although some critics have been sympathetic to Ab—and later to Mink Snopes—because of their poverty and sharecropper status, one should remember that from the very earliest mention of him in *The Unvanquished*, Ab has been a dishonest, shifty, treacherous individual.

The main subject of *The Hamlet*, however, is neither the life of Will Varner nor the character of Ab Snopes; rather it is the career of Ab's son, Flem Snopes. His unvoiced but no less clearly articulated threat of barn-burning, backed by his father's known if "unproved" record of arson, obtains for Flem a job in the Varner store, a post from which he rapidly rises in a series of froglike leaps that become the focus of the "Flem" section of the novel. Faulkner's description of Flem establishes him at once as a grotesque character with predatory characteristics. (Flem fulfills almost every element of Sherwood Anderson's definition of grotesqueness in the opening chapter, "The Book of the Grotesque," in *Winesburg, Ohio*.) Of Flem, Faulkner writes:

> . . . a thick squat soft man of no establishable age between twenty and thirty, with a broad still face containing a tight seam of mouth stained slightly at the corners with tobacco, and eyes the color of stagnant water, and projecting from among the other features in startling and sudden paradox, a tiny predatory nose like the beak of a small hawk. It was as though the original nose had been left off by the original designer or craftsman and the unfinished job taken over by someone of a radically different school or perhaps by some viciously maniacal humorist or perhaps by one who had had only time to clap into the center of the face a frantic and desperate warning. (pp. 51–52)

Elsewhere Faulkner adds other details. When Flem first comes to the Bend, his face is "as blank as a pan of uncooked dough" (p. 22); he chews tobacco steadily (p. 22) and spits not merely from necessity but often to emphasize a gesture or to underscore a point. He wears a gray cloth cap (p. 19) and cheap gray trousers (p. 22). When he begins to work in the store, he has a new white shirt that bears the creases and streaks where "the cloth had lain bolted on a shelf" (p. 51) and "a new pair of rubber-soled tennis shoes" (p. 54). But perhaps the most distinctive feature—it becomes his trademark—is his necktie, "a tiny machine-made black bow which snapped together at the back with a metal fastener. It was not two inches long . . . a tiny viciously depthless cryptically balanced splash like an enigmatic punctuation symbol against the expanse of white shirt" (pp. 57–58). Throughout the three novels of the Snopes trilogy, Flem retains this appearance, and an alteration in his clothing—for example, the exchange of the cap for a black hat—always marks a significant change in his status.

Flem's rise in Frenchman's Bend recalls Benjamin Franklin's precepts for acquiring wealth or at times the career of a Horatio Alger hero. Beginning with nothing, Flem works hard, takes no vacations, keeps his own counsel, and saves his money. He replaces the old Varner system of casual, haphazard bookkeeping with a calculating efficiency—an early version of cost accounting or perhaps computerized billings—that never makes a mistake. He buys cheap and sells dear. He gives no credit. He counts the pennies and he takes advantage wherever he can. One of the few Negroes in the hamlet explains Flem's operations. "He lent me five dollars over two years ago and all I does, every Saturday night I goes to the store and pays him a dime" (p. 70). The farmers are pretty sure that Flem cheats them, but they will not unite to deal with him. As Vernon Tull remarks to Ratliff, "It aint right. But it aint none of our business" (p. 71).

Flem's progress is steady. He moves from the farm to the village. He replaces Jody at the scales of the gin. He sits at Will Varner's knee with the ledgers when Will makes the yearly settlement with the farmers. He is responsible for the new herd of cattle that appears on one of Varner's farms. And soon Flem brings other Snopeses to the Bend and establishes them in jobs. In place of the Negro blacksmith, Flem installs I. O. Snopes who in turn brings his cousin Eck to learn the business. Before long, Ratliff notices Ike Snopes, then Mink Snopes, then Launcelot or Lump Snopes, until finally he can imagine Jody Varner standing over Flem in the store and shouting: "I want to make one pure and simple demand of you: . . . How many more is there? . . . Just what is it going to cost me to protect one goddamn barn full of hay?" (p. 67).

Flem has meanwhile moved into the Varner house and begun to ride in a new buggy over the old plantation with Varner. After learning at first hand how Flem has cheated the idiot Ike and dealt with his kinsman Mink, Ratliff can understand the direction of Flem's froglike leaps to power and wealth, but only when the sewing-machine agent glimpses Flem sitting in the flour-barrel seat from which Will Varner has been accustomed to survey the old Frenchman's property does Ratliff begin to comprehend the significance of Flem's activities in the community.

Throughout the "Flem" section of *The Hamlet*, Faulkner emphasizes the rural community's relish for "trading" or barter. Stories of "trades," often amounting to tall tales, are a familiar aspect of rural life in the literature of the Old Southwest humorists, particularly among such writers as A. B. Longstreet and Joseph Glover Baldwin. In their hands the sharp trade is exploited as a source of comedy. In narrating the Ab Snopes–Pat Stamper trade, Faulkner follows their practice, and Ratliff speaks within the tradition when he mentions "the entire honor and pride of the science and pastime of horse-trading in Yoknapatawpha County" (p. 34). (The remark also helps to make plausible the horse trading in the spotted horses episode.) Ratliff is a trader; when not engaged in selling sewing machines, he spends "the rest of the time trading in land and livestock and second-hand farming tools and musical instruments or anything else" (p. 13). Although he knows that perhaps only Will Varner has any business "fooling" with the Snopeses, Ratliff cannot resist trying his hand.

From his very first encounter, Ratliff learns that instead of being a mere pastime, trading with the Snopeses is a deadly serious affair. Ratliff shrewdly plans a two-part trade, hoping to defeat Flem each time. Although one cannot be certain, the implication is that Ratliff approached Mink Snopes believing that Mink would make Flem pay for the sewing machine. The plan succeeds admirably. Mink gives Ratliff two notes and a message to Flem: "Say 'From one cousin that's still scratching dirt to keep alive, to another cousin that's risen from scratching dirt to owning a herd of cattle and a hay barn. *To owning cattle and a hay barn*'" (p. 76, italics added). Mink, of course, is threatening to burn Flem's barn. The second part of the trade involves the goats. By intentionally "talking too much" about his wish to buy goats, Ratliff leads Flem to purchase all the goats in sight. When Flem demands a high price for them, Ratliff offers the two notes and the message. Flem does not really need to hear Mink's message. Ratliff's victory would be complete but for one detail. In the trade he discovers that the Isaac Snopes on the note is the idiot boy and that Flem is his guardian. Rather than allow Flem to make capital out of the idiot's inheritance, Ratliff burns the note. All he gets is the satisfaction of knowing that Flem cannot use it again. Ratliff's comment on the trade becomes one of the key passages in the novel: "I just never went far enough. . . . I quit too soon. I went as far as one Snopes will set fire to another Snopes's barn and both Snopeses know it, and that was all right. But I stopped there. I never went on to where that first Snopes will turn around and stomp the fire out so he can sue that second Snopes for the reward and both Snopeses know that too" (p. 88). In other words, Ratliff had underestimated the moral depravity of Flem and his tribe. The sewing-machine agent's message to Will Varner, "it aint been proved yet neither"—*it* referring to the other man that could risk fooling with the Snopeses (cf. p. 28)—has taken on additional significance. The contest between the two men would resume later.

Probably as a foil to Flem, Faulkner created Eula Varner. She is one of his finest artistic achievements. In Flem, Faulkner embodied modern man's greed for material possessions. In Eula, he fashioned the symbol of man's sexual desires. In both, he included an element of the comic. Sexually precocious, at the age of thirteen, Eula is "a soft ample girl with definite breasts . . . and eyes like cloudy hothouse grapes and a full damp mouth always slightly open" (p. 10). She was then "already bigger than most grown women and even her breasts were no longer the little, hard, fiercely-pointed cones of puberty or even maidenhood" (p. 95). Having apparently "reached and passed puberty in the foetus" (p. 114), Eula now "seemed to listen in sullen bemusement, with a weary wisdom heired of all mammalian maturity, to the enlarging of her own organs" (p. 95). In this young girl who is yet unaware of her sexual attractiveness, Frenchman's Bend has produced an extraordinary female, worthy of comparison with the fabled women of Greek mythology. "Her entire appearance," wrote Faulkner, "suggested some symbology out of the old Dionysic times—honey in sunlight and bursting grapes, the writhen bleeding of the crushed fecundated vine beneath the hard rapacious trampling goat-hoof" (p. 95). She was, as he said, "a moist blast of spring's liquorish corruption, a pagan triumphal prostration before the supreme primal uterus" (pp. 113–14). Indeed, she was quite capable of transforming even the very wooden desks and benches in the crude schoolroom of Frenchman's Bend into "a grove of Venus" (p. 114), and while sitting at recess on the schoolhouse steps, she "postulated that un-girdled quality of the very goddesses in . . . Homer and Thucydides" (p. 113).

At the same time that Faulkner imputes to her the quintessence of feminine sexual appeal, he adds a note of grotesque humor. This modern goddess is "incorrigibly lazy. . . . She simply did not move at all of her own volition. . . . It was not that she insisted upon being carried when she went anywhere. It was rather as though, even in infancy, she already knew there was nowhere she wanted to go" (p. 95). Her father cares little about her education. "All we want anyway," he says, "is to keep her out of trouble until she gets old enough to sleep with a man without getting me and him both arrested" (p. 98). Her brother, Jody, who is determined that she would go to school, is forced to provide transportation. On one occasion Jody asks her to walk from the schoolhouse to the store; but when she agrees, he is outraged by the result. " 'No wonder she agreed so easy and quick to walk to the store and meet me!' he cried. 'If you could arrange to have a man standing every hundred feet along the road, she would walk all the way home! She's just like a dog! Soon as she passes anything in long pants she begins to give off something. You can smell it! You can smell it ten feet away' " (p. 99). The corset Jody insists that she wear does not seem to help matters. When the reader learns that "spring's liquorish corruption" eats a cold sweet potato wherever she goes, he cannot help but laugh at the comedy. Like Flem, but defined in a vastly different set of terms, Eula is a grotesque figure.

The long description of Eula's charms leads inevitably to an account of her sexual experiences. The schoolmaster, Labove, seems a natural first victim. Watching day after day this rural Venus, Labove reaches a point where he cannot resist attempting to possess her. Faulkner explains: "He [Labove] did not want her as a wife, he just wanted her one time as a man with a gangrened hand or foot thirsts after the axe-stroke which will leave him comparatively whole again" (p. 118). His attempted rape fails utterly. Eula, who is not yet ready for sexual adventures, easily casts him off with the blunt remark: "stop pawing me. . . . You old headless horseman Ichabod Crane" (p. 122); and she pays such little attention that she forgets the incident. The next day she appears at school, "tranquil, untroubled . . . carrying the cold potato which at recess she would sit on the sunny steps and eat like one of the unchaste and perhaps even anonymously pregnant immortals eating bread of Paradise on the sunwise slope of Olympus" (p. 123). Although Eula utterly defeats Labove, he accurately forecasts her future: "He could almost see the husband which she would someday have. He would be a dwarf, a gnome, without glands or desire, who would be no more a physical factor in her life than the owner's name on the fly-leaf of a book. . . . the crippled Vulcan to that Venus, who would not possess her but merely own her by the single strength which power gave, the dead power of money. . . . He saw it: the fine land rich and fecund and foul and eternal and impervious to him who claimed title to it" (p. 118–19).

The time does come, however, when Eula is ready to surrender. After helping Hoake McCarron to fight off the ambush of other potential suitors, Eula assists in her seduction by supporting "with her own braced arm from underneath," Hoake's injured side (p. 139). Three months later, the community knows that Eula is pregnant; but her father is the last to learn. Varner's action is comic. As Jody frantically hunts for a pistol to protect the family's honor, Varner exclaims: "Hell and damnation, all this hullabaloo and uproar because one confounded running bitch finally foxed herself. What did you expect—that she would spend the rest of her life just running water through it?" (pp. 143–44).

Varner, however, does take action to preserve the family honor. Flem's price includes an undisclosed sum of cash, a deed to the old Frenchman's place, and the wedding license. Eula, the sex goddess, "the supreme primal uterus," "spring's liquorish corruption," has been yoked to the "crippled Vulcan," the impotent Flem Snopes, whom she calls "that man," or "the man," or "Mr Snopes, saying it exactly as she would have said Mr Dog" (p. 146). A dismal future awaits her. As Ratliff watches the final events of this human catastrophe and the departure of Flem and Eula for Texas, he has a vision of Flem in hell. In the nether regions, Flem is just as successful as he had been on earth. Though his soul on earth has not been very large, in hell it begins merely as a "*dried-up smear under one edge*" of a matchbox (p. 150); but soon Flem is sitting on the Devil's throne.

Book Three, "The Long Summer," presents serious problems for those who believe that a novel should possess unity of action and assert that the main plot of *The Hamlet* relates to the career of Flem Snopes. Throughout this "long hot summer" Flem is absent in Texas. Consequently, the episodes of this section are digressive in terms of Flem's progress in the community of Frenchman's Bend. For the most part, the two events of this book—Ike's romance with the cow and the Mink–Houston affair— have nothing to do with Flem. It is true, of course, that in the Mink– Houston conflict, Faulkner lays the foundation for Mink's hatred of Flem, a hatred that in *The Mansion* will lead to Flem's death. Those who read *The Hamlet* between its publication in 1940 and the appearance of *The Mansion* in 1959, however, would have had no reason to suspect this eventuality.

Critics have called attention to the various aspects of "love" in the novel, though the view of this concept as the central theme of *The Hamlet* seems unacceptable. Although Eula's encounter with Labove, her seduction by Hoake McCarron, and her marriage to Flem in Book Two may represent varieties of sexual relationships, the word *love* is hardly appropriate for any of them. Furthermore, in "The Long Summer," the idiot's romance with the cow, Jack Houston's common-law relationship followed by his marriage to Lucy Pate, and Mink Snopes's marriage to a former prostitute may be viewed as types of "love"; but love or the sexual motif hardly warrants recognition as the major theme of the work.

A balanced interpretation of Book Three would probably concede that it is digressive to the Flem Snopes material that is the center of the novel. On the other hand, the incidents in this section are loosely related to the life of the Frenchman's Bend community. Moreover, they represent particularly fine and compelling writing whose exclusion from the work would be a great loss to its richness and variety. Merely for the sake of unity, one would not willingly part with them; and though they may occupy a disproportionate amount of space in the book, some justification may be made for them.

Ike Snopes belongs to a long line of idiots that Faulkner uses for various purposes in his fiction. Ike reminds one of Benjy: "the figure of a grown man but barefoot and in scant faded overalls. . . . As he passed the gallery he looked up and Ratliff saw the face too—the pale eyes which seemed to have no vision in them at all, the open drooling mouth encircled by a light fuzz of golden virgin beard" (p. 81). A few pages later, Faulkner writes that Ratliff saw again "the mowing and bobbing

231

head, the eyes which at some instant, some second once, had opened upon, been vouchsafed a glimpse of, the Gorgon-face of that primal injustice which man was not intended to look at face to face and had been blasted empty and clean forever of any thought, the slobbering mouth in its mist of soft gold hair" (p. 85). Like Benjy Compson, Ike is an innocent; and he has feelings, he suffers, and he loves. The object of his devotion is a cow. Any examination of this episode should begin with the plain statement that the novelist in treating Ike's bestiality or sodomy does not approve of the perversion.

The Ike–cow episode has been called a pastoral idyll, a poetical fantasy, an idealized tribute to love, which in Frenchman's Bend (and by extension, in modern times) can exist only in an innocent's world. His love for the cow contrasts sharply with the loveless relationship between Eula and Flem. (It also contrasts with Benjy's largely self-centered world.) Ike's selflessness lies at the opposite pole from Flem's Snopesism. Indeed, if Ike is a Snopes—one notices that he calls himself "Ike H-mope" (p. 85), apparently unable or unwilling to say Snopes—he is a contradiction, because his idealism has nothing in common with Snopes realism.

The problem Ike presents to many readers lies in the form his love takes. In *The Sound and the Fury*, Benjy Compson's love for Caddy represents an acceptable human relationship. In *The Hamlet*, Ike's romance with the cow follows an age-old tradition of human sexual perversion— sodomy or bestiality. The inhabitants of Frenchman's Bend recognize it for what it is. Faulkner, however, endeavors to lift the entire affair out of its real implications to a level where he can use it to show devotion and love in their spiritual purity, a situation that otherwise does not exist in Frenchman's Bend or perhaps even in modern times. To a degree, Ike's story becomes a fable or myth. Unfortunately, Faulkner's treatment of the incident sometimes alternates between descriptions of great poetical beauty and realistic passages that border on comic burlesque. Many readers, for example, interpret the passage where Ike receives "the violent relaxing of her [the cow's] fear-constricted bowels" (p. 173) and afterwards tries "to tell her how this violent violation of her maiden's delicacy is no shame, since such is the very iron imperishable warp of the fabric of love" (p. 174) as a jarring intrusion into the general atmosphere of pastoral lyricism. Such passages seem to mock or even parody the prevailing attitude toward the subject and to render the tone of the entire passage uncertain, even inconsistent. For the most part, however, the incident is narrated without prurience. It serves as a sharply contrasting counterpoint to the sterility of the Eula–Flem relationship and the fierce, lustful passion of Mink and his wife.

At the end of section two (p. 186), Faulkner abandons the pastoral and poetic mode and returns to the everyday life of the community. The Snopes faction, particularly Lump, is preparing to exploit the idiot's ignorant perversion for economic gain. Lump has pulled the plank off the wall of Mrs. Littlejohn's barn at just the right height for spectators to watch. The men of the community sneak around to witness Ike's degradation. Mrs. Littlejohn demands of Ratliff: "What do you think I think when I look out that window and watch them sneaking up along that fence?" (p. 197). Ratliff rebukes her: "Only all you done was think." But when he denounces Lump, Mrs. Littlejohn answers in righteous indignation: "It aint that it is, that itches you. It's that . . . that particular Snopes is making something out of it. . . . Or is it because folks come and watch? It's all right for it to be, but folks mustn't know it, see it" (p. 198). Ratliff, who has already nailed the plank back into place, answers that it is finished. She need not tell him that Ike has nothing else, or that at the least Ratliff could leave Ike the cow, or that it is none of Ratliff's business. He admits he is not sure of his motives, but he implies that his conscience is clear and that he can sleep at night. Actually, Ratliff stops the "performance" because he knows that under any circumstances sodomy is a perversion of the order of God and nature and that the presence of it in Frenchman's Bend exerts a corrosive influence upon the morality of the community. The action he takes is a frontal assault upon Snopesism, and in this instance he unquestionably makes decency prevail.

In the Jack Houston–Mink Snopes episode, which begins abruptly and bears little connection with the immediately preceding romance of Ike and the cow, Houston is clearly the better man. Faulkner provides a lengthy biographical sketch of his early life and marriage to his childhood lover Lucy Pate. Faulkner's characterization of her as a woman "with an infinite capacity for constancy and devotion" (p. 205) places her among the relatively few good women of marriageable age in his fiction. Their marriage is a good one until suddenly she is killed by the stallion

Houston has bought her as a wedding present. Afterwards, Houston grieves for her "in black, savage, indomitable fidelity" (p. 205). One of the most moving passages in all of Faulkner's fiction describes Houston's feelings in the April moonlight of their bedroom. Although Houston is a proud man, at times arrogant, he can be generous. He is kind to Ike, cleaning the idiot's overalls, giving him some money, and offering to give him the cow. In the dispute with Mink over the yearling, the law appears to be on Houston's side. There is little in Houston's conduct or character to justify murder.

Attempts of Faulkner's readers to connect the Houston murder with the Ike–cow romance and even the Eula–Flem marriage seem strained because the focus of the Houston–Mink affair is not sex but murder. Actually, Faulkner fashioned the account of the murder of Houston from a short story, "The Hound," published about seven years earlier. In the original story, which had nothing to do with the Snopeses, the murderer is named Ernest Cotton. In rewriting it for *The Hamlet*, Faulkner expanded it greatly by providing the long account of Houston's early life that reminds one of Joe Christmas' wanderings and by suggesting that Houston's first wife and mistress was much like Mink's wife. In the revision, the emphasis the novelist places upon Mink as a proud but vindictive tenant farmer who, angered by his bad luck and exasperated by his hatred of the establishment, seeks to relieve his feelings through violent action makes him reminiscent more of Ab Snopes than of Flem.

Critics who write from a liberal point of view have interpreted Mink Snopes as an admirable character and suggested that Faulkner wished readers to sympathize with Mink as a victim of the tenant farming system. Although he may receive the reader's compassion, the novelist has not made Mink an attractive person. His name suggests his character. Naturalists describe the mink as a solitary, active, restless little animal who kills not only for food but also for the mere pleasure of killing. He travels from stream to stream and has a home only during the breeding season. Mississippi farmers know that the mink is a wanton killer who, once in the chicken yard, will not leave until the last chicken lies dead. In *The Hamlet*, Ratliff looks "at the fierce intractable face [of Mink] with its single eyebrow, thinking *Fox? cat? oh yes, mink*" (p. 89). Afterwards, Ratliff remarks to one of the farmers lounging on the gallery of Varner's store: "So Flem's got some more cousins still. Only this here seems to be a different kind of Snopes like a cotton-mouth is a different kind of snake" (p. 91). Elsewhere, the reader learns that "no man in that country, white or black, would work for him at any price" (p. 193). Even his wife remarks upon his venomous character: "I've had a hunded men, but I never had a wasp before. That stuff comes out of you is rank poison" (p. 238). His character remains consistent throughout the novel; even at the trial, Faulkner calls attention to Mink's "small, neatly-combed, vicious and ironlike incorrigible head" (p. 333). The standards of comparison or metaphors thus used to characterize Mink are uniformly repugnant: mink, fox, cat, cottonmouth moccasin, wasp, poison. (The portrait suggests low burlesque and grotesqueness.) Perhaps Mink's only admirable trait is courage, though without the guidance of morality it is misdirected. Mink is a different kind of Snopes, for one doubts if either Ab or Flem would murder from ambush. The fact that Mink is poor, has encountered bad luck, and works within a hard economic system does not justify his murder of Jack Houston.

Faulkner concludes Book Three with the account of the aftermath of the murder. Perhaps the most appealing aspect of Mink's wretched life is the loyalty of his wife to whom Faulkner does not give a name. Like Ruby Lamar in *Sanctuary*, Mink's wife does not hesitate to return to prostitution to provide the money for his escape; and when he is captured and taken to Jefferson, she follows him. Like Horace Benbow in *Sanctuary*, Ratliff, over the objections of his sister, takes the family into his house, provides clothes and food, and acts as the wife's "banker." Throughout the winter, while Mink remains in jail, his wife works to help support the family and to save for the legal expenses ahead at the trial. Mink waits anxiously for Flem to return and help, an act of faith that ignores the facts of Flem's character. In March, when Eula returns with her baby and without Flem, Ratliff knows that Flem does not intend to return until after the trial. Flem will deny the bond of kinship upon which Mink is depending.

The return of Eula and Flem's nonappearance, however, bring Book Three back to the plot line that Faulkner had begun in Books One and Two. Readers will remember that when Eula departs for Texas, Ratliff looks at her face: "It had not been tragic, and now it was not even damned" (p. 149); but when she returns, Ratliff looks again and thinks hers was not even a tragic face: "it was just damned" (p. 265).

Although it consists of two distinct and separate incidents—the horse auction and the treasure hunt—Book Four, "The Peasants," attains thematic unity through the exposure of human greed. In a single "trade" Flem defeats a considerable segment of the community, and in the final incident he even defeats Ratliff. This section of *The Hamlet* strongly reminds one of Mark Twain's "The Man That Corrupted Hadleyburg." In both stories, the corrupter may be the Devil himself, and the inhabitants are corrupted more by their own greed than by the Devil's machinations. Because of its humor, satire, pathos, and psychological accuracy, Faulkner's story of the spotted horses proves a worthy successor to Mark Twain's celebrated narrative.

At the outset, Ratliff warns the men of the community against trading with Flem. "So Flem has come home again," he says, "Well, well, well. Will Varner paid to get him to Texas, so I reckon it aint no more than fair for you fellows to pay the freight on him back" (p. 276). As the conversation continues, he repeats his warning: "A fellow can dodge a Snopes if he just starts lively enough. In fact, I dont believe he would have to pass more than two folks before he would have another victim intervened betwixt them. You folks aint going to buy them things sho enough, are you?" And before he leaves, he delivers a final warning: "You folks can buy them critters if you want to. But me, I'd just as soon buy a tiger or a rattlesnake. And if Flem Snopes offered me either one of them, I would be afraid to touch it for fear it would turn out to be a painted dog or a piece of garden hose when I went up to take possession of it" (p. 279). Ratliff leaves the group and refuses even to attend the auction.

Ratliff's warnings, however, fall on deaf ears because the men's greediness to obtain something for nothing overpowers their better judgment. They cannot resist the temptation to try their hand against Flem; neither can they suffer any member of their own group to get ahead of anyone else. When the Texas man gives Eck a horse, Henry Armstid cannot stand to see Eck get two horses for "a dollar a head" (p. 291) and rushes to bid the price higher. The ponies are soon sold.

The aftermath of the auction is both farcical and pathetic. Faulkner's description of the mad flight of the horses through Mrs. Littlejohn's house and across the countryside, particularly the encounter of Tull's wagon and its occupants with one of the ponies on the bridge, meets every requirement of hilarious farce. But the incident concludes with

Henry Armstid's broken leg, additional burdens being placed upon Mrs. Armstid, and assorted injuries to Tull. In addition, Mrs. Armstid's desperately needed five dollars of savings are gone. Because of Lump's perjury, Mrs. Tull's garrulousness, and the legalities insisted upon by the judge, the law cannot deal justly in the suits against Flem. As the episode ends, Flem's refusal to return any of Mrs. Armstid's savings to her provides convincing evidence of his total lack of any feeling of pity. The milk of human kindness and compassion does not flow in Flem Snopes.

Ratliff has little patience with the "peasants" who have allowed Flem to trick them. The sewing-machine agent points out that Eck did not have money to waste on wild horses and describes the additional labor in the field now the lot of Mrs. Armstid. Ratliff refuses to give Henry the money Flem has taken from the family. Ratliff would assist the helpless victims of Flem (for example, Ike Snopes), but he will not help those who have become willing victims through their own greed. "I never made them Snopeses," he says, "and I never made the folks that cant wait to bare their backsides to them" (p. 321).

The outcome of the horse auction serves as a prelude to the final contest between Ratliff and Flem. Ratliff's scorn of Armstid and others like him for their greediness heightens the drama of his own weakness. Ratliff, like the peasants, receives a warning. Will Varner cautions: "You got better sense than to try to sell Flem Snopes anything. . . . And you sholy aint fool enough by God to buy anything from him, are you?" (p. 353). The warning, however, likewise falls upon deaf ears because Ratliff has misread Varner's motive. The story of the buried treasure at the old Frenchman's place has persisted throughout the years. Varner must know, reasons Ratliff, that something is there. "If there wasn't, he wouldn't never bought it. And he wouldn't a kept it" (p. 335). Moreover, Ratliff cannot conceive of Flem Snopes taking it unless it were valuable. Thus, Ratliff's estimates of Varner and Flem form the basis of his decision to purchase the old Frenchman's place. Like the poker player who makes his moves in accordance with his understanding of his opponents' psychology, Ratliff acts from his own observations. He makes a fatal mistake, however, when he allows his own greed to influence his judgment; and in the end, he too suffers defeat from the same weakness that afflicts the peasants of the community. Perhaps the irony of the episode lies in the fact that very probably Flem never intended to catch

Ratliff with the salted mine. Flem set the trap to catch anyone who happened to come along. But the measure of the difference between Ratliff and Armstid lies in the fact that reason does return to Ratliff (and even to Bookwright), while Armstid continues madly digging. At the most, Flem has won only a temporary victory. Every man has a modicum of self-interest. Ratliff may fall a momentary victim, but he will rise again to continue the struggle. He is the Roland to whom Faulkner referred at the University of Virginia as representing "the impulse to eradicate Snopes." "When the battle comes," asserted Faulkner, "it always produces a Roland. It doesn't mean that they will get rid of Snopes or the impulse which produces Snopes, but always there's something in man that don't like Snopes and objects to Snopes and if necessary will step in to keep Snopes from doing some irreparable harm."[9]

For many readers, however, there may always remain a feeling that Faulkner has been too hard on Ratliff. He is a true wayfaring Christian who falls only to rise and fight onward. There is truth in the assertion that "couldn't nobody but Flem Snopes have fooled Ratliff" (p. 365). But one wonders if Faulkner sacrificed Ratliff to the demands of a "good story." The advantages, plotwise, of Ratliff's fall are considerable: his defeat not only proves that there lurks in every man a little of the Snopes greed but also allows for a "tables-turned" ending and provides a staging area for the scene of Flem's next triumph—Jefferson. The episode rounds out neatly the career of Flem in Frenchman's Bend, but an occasional reader asks if the manner is not a little too neat.

As Book Four concludes, Flem, Eula, and the baby are moving to Jefferson in the Varner wagon. They leave Frenchman's Bend by way of the old Frenchman's place. Ahead of them lie the adventures of Flem in the town. His character has already preceded him, for Mink, who has stubbornly clung to a faith that Flem would save his own kin, has at last learned the truth; and as he is being sentenced to life in prison, Mink interrupts the judge to say: "Flem Snopes! . . . Flem Snopes! Is Flem Snopes in this room? Tell that son of a bitch—" (p. 333). One day, forty years later, in *The Mansion*, Mink will deliver the message himself.

Of the numerous tribe of Snopeses, only Ike (if he can indeed be called a Snopes), Eck, who is not very bright, and his son, Wallstreet Panic, who plays a very minor part in *The Hamlet*, have any redeeming traits of character. The others—Ab, Flem, Mink, Lump, I. O., and Saint

Elmo—define collectively the meaning of Snopesism. Generally Faulkner describes them in terms of small, predatory rodents. The "head man" of the family, Flem embodies in his personality the essence of Snopesism. His name has an unpleasant sound, suggesting association with such repulsive words or ideas as *snake*, *sneak*, *sneer*, *snot*, and unpleasant bodily functions. As the novelist develops the character by constantly comparing him with hawks, wolves, frogs, and spiders, Flem emerges as a grotesque figure—a caricature—in whom the fundamental human traits of love, compassion, pity, integrity, fair play, conscience, and generosity are wholly absent. In their place there is a single overwhelming greed. *Snopesism* becomes another word for man's universal greed.

In attacking Snopesism in modern life, Faulkner seems to be trying to tell his readers that in the present century man's greed for material goods has become so great that it has almost obliterated the principles upon which right living must be based. The pursuit of happiness has become the pursuit of material goods, and the quality of life has in consequence notably diminished. Drawing upon the humanist tradition that extends back through Hawthorne, Emerson, Shakespeare, and Milton to Plato and the apostles, Faulkner affirms in *The Hamlet* that to defeat Snopesism a man need only reform himself from within. The good heart, the *bona natura* of Tom Jones and Huck Finn, the constant endeavor to practice honesty and charity are the weapons at hand against the evils of Snopesism. Faulkner would have his readers know that Flem seems to win easily, not because his way is efficacious but because the moral weaknesses of individuals or even entire communities leave his victims vulnerable.

Although *The Town* and *The Mansion* are beyond the scope of the present study of Faulkner's major novels, they carry forward to completion the story begun in *The Hamlet*. *The Town* covers events that took place between 1908 and 1927; and *The Mansion* ranges throughout the period between the murder of Jack Houston in 1908 and the murder of Flem Snopes in the fall of 1946. Thus, the trilogy, it may be said, deals with the first half of the twentieth century.

Having "traded" Ratliff for his part-interest in the Jefferson restaurant, Flem in *The Town* has little difficulty in obtaining a foothold in the community. From the restaurant, he leapfrogs to the power plant, leaving behind him, as he had done in Frenchman's Bend, another Snopes to take his place. Faulkner describes the process: "Snopes himself was out of it, replaced behind the greasy counter . . . by another Snopes accreted in from Frenchman's Bend into the vacuum behind the first one's next advancement by that same sort of osmosis by which . . . they had covered Frenchman's Bend, the chain unbroken, every Snopes in Frenchman's Bend moving up one step, leaving that last slot at the bottom open for the next Snopes to appear from nowhere and fill." [10] From the power plant, the froglike Flem leaps to the vice-presidency of the bank in 1927. Recognizing that further success depends upon his achieving respectability, Flem appears to become a champion of civic virtue and public morality.

Actually, Flem's methods have not changed. By planting whiskey in his kinsman's peepshow studio, Flem sends Montgomery Ward Snopes to the Parchman penitentiary, ostensibly so that the citizens of Jefferson will not be exposed as patrons of the pornographic show but actually to persuade Mink to make an escape attempt. In his climb to respectability, Flem creates a situation in which Eula must choose between suicide or elopement with her lover in an open scandal that she feels would ruin her daughter's life. She commits suicide. With Eula dead and her lover gone, the respectable Flem Snopes can move into de Spain's house and remodel it into an antebellum Southern mansion. Ratliff summarizes Flem's progress in Jefferson:

> [Flem] had ever thing now that he had come to Jefferson to get. He had more. He had things he didn't even know he was going to want until he reached Jefferson because he didn't even know what they was until then. He had his bank and his money in it and his-self to be president of it so he could not only watch his money from ever being stole by another twenty-two-calibre rogue like his cousin Byron, but nobody could ever steal from him the respectability that being president of one of the two Yoknapatawpha County banks toted along with it. [11]

At the end of *The Town*, Flem has gone about as far as he can in Jefferson.

In the final volume, *The Mansion*, Flem becomes a more or less static figure as Faulkner develops the stories of Mink Snopes, Gavin Stevens, and Linda Snopes. Nevertheless, Flem's presence is felt throughout the final novel. Even Mink, down in Parchman, acknowledges: "You cant beat him. There aint a man in Missippi nor the U. S. and A. both put together that can beat Flem Snopes." Flem does practice his old arts by outsmarting Jason Compson and obtaining Benjy's pasture for the Eula

Acres housing project. But throughout the novel, Flem is the focus of
Mink Snopes's long-plotted revenge. Mink has served fifteen years before
Flem sends Montgomery Ward to tempt Mink into putting on women's
clothes in an escape attempt. Caught as Flem knew he would be and his
sentence lengthened by twenty years as Flem knew it would be, Mink
serves until 1946, when he is pardoned through the efforts of Linda
Snopes and Gavin Stevens. Mink immediately obtains a pistol, slips into
Flem's Jefferson mansion, and murders the unresisting Flem. Faulkner
interprets Mink's character and actions in *The Mansion* with great compassion and sympathy. Readers disagree whether Faulkner has dignified
too much the unhappy career of Mink. Ratliff's final comment, "The
pore sons of bitches," [12] falls short of an adequate verdict.

The Hamlet is the finest of the Snopes volumes. Written close to the
height of Faulkner's creative powers, it contains a full measure of his
humor, storytelling art, and rendering of common speech. One could
describe it, in the words of Henry Fielding, as a comic epic in prose,
a masterpiece in the genre. In *The Hamlet*, perhaps more than anywhere else, Faulkner looked down upon his homeland and examined it
searchingly, critically, yet lovingly. He saw that it could be made a microcosm of modern life and thus a platform from which he could address
the world. His message reaches his readers couched in the humor, the
pathos, and the humanity of Frenchman's Bend: Snopesism, the individual and collective greed of man, has seriously corroded the quality of
modern life. He would have agreed with Thomas Carlyle that "cash
nexus" has replaced human brotherhood and goodwill. If man is to live a
meaningful life, he must constantly oppose that element of self-interest
that inhabits every man. In *The Hamlet*, man's greed is often seen as
comic, at times pathetic, but always a threat to man's well-being and
happiness. V. K. Ratliff, the shrewd, compassionate, sewing-machine
agent of Yoknapatawpha County, may falter upon occasion, but he lives
essentially a good life because he understands that greed and selfishness
are self-defeating. He stands at the opposite pole from Flem Snopes,
whose greed has destroyed his humanity. Flem has replaced the pursuit of
happiness with the pursuit of material goods, and in the race he has lost
his own soul. He becomes a startlingly vivid answer to Christ's question:
"For what is a man profited, if he shall gain the whole world, and lose his
own soul?" (Matthew, 16:20).

CHAPTER IX

Pensioners of History

Go Down, Moses

ALTHOUGH critics have staunchly defended the loosely knit structure of many of Faulkner's novels, the lack of controlling form and upon occasion even the absence of thematic unity continue to disturb readers. The individual parts often seem more strongly defined than the composite entities. *The Sound and the Fury*, for example, divides into four distinct sections that individually may seem more significant than their totality. Both *Light in August* and *Absalom, Absalom!*, moreover, appear to fragment into several stories that overshadow the individual work as a whole. After *Absalom, Absalom!* this tendency in Faulkner's work to break up into sometimes brilliant but not always well-unified episodes notably increases in *The Unvanquished*, *The Hamlet*, and *Go Down, Moses* and appears in *The Wild Palms*, which may have been written as a single work but has even been published as two separate novels.[1]

In part, this feature of Faulkner's writing may result from his practice of incorporating or adapting already written and already published short stories into the plot structure of his novels. Virtually every story in *The Unvanquished* Faulkner had either already published or intended to publish in a magazine. *The Hamlet* was put together in similar fashion; and in the instance of *Go Down, Moses*, the book not only was fashioned out of earlier written and published short stories, but also was first published with the title containing the qualifying phrase *and Other Stories*.[2] Years later, in 1949, when Random House planned to reissue *Go Down, Moses*, Faulkner wrote to Robert Haas: "Moses is indeed a novel. I would not eliminate the story or section titles. Do you think it necessary to number these stories like chapters? Why not reprint exactly, but change the title from *Go Down, Moses* and other stories, to simply: *Go Down, Moses*. . . .

We did *The Unvanquished* in this manner . . . and, for that matter, *The Wild Palms* had two completely unrelated stories in it. Yet nobody thought it should be titled *The Wild Palms* and another story."³ Although Random House dropped the offending phrase, the fact remains that in the years between 1936 and 1948, with the possible and very questionable exception of *The Wild Palms*, Faulkner did not write from original conception to final completion a single volume of fiction without borrowing heavily from the lumber in his artistic woodshed. Of the four works published during these years, *Go Down, Moses* suffers most from this method of composition by piecing together short stories.

The matter cannot be discarded merely as an academic argument about artistic form, because it bears directly upon the meaning and the implications of the entire work. Although the significance of this comment will become more apparent as *Go Down, Moses* is examined story by story, the overall proportions of the problem emerge from even a cursory examination of the contents of the book. As early as May 1, 1941, and probably even a year earlier, Faulkner had in mind the design of his book. On that date, he wrote Robert Haas:

> Last year I mentioned a volume, collected short stories, general theme being relationship between white and negro races here. This is the plan:
>
> Title of Book: *Go Down, Moses*
>   Stories:
> *The Fire and the Hearth*
>   Part One: published Collier's.
>   "   Two: Atlantic Monthly.
>   "   Three: Unpublished.
> *Pantaloon in Black*: Harper's
> *The Old People*:   "
> *Delta Autumn*: Unpublished.
> *Go Down, Moses*: Collier's.
>   I will rewrite them, to an extent; some additional material might invent itself in process. Book will be about the size and similar to *The Unvanquished*.⁴

Though by no means intended as a sequel to *The Unvanquished*, *Go Down, Moses* was, to a degree at least, designed to complement it by presenting an examination of the racial attitudes within a single family in the contemporary Southern community of Jefferson. The focus upon a single Southern family and the use of a point in history from which to measure or explain circumstances in the present are devices that have been prominent in Faulkner's fiction since *Sartoris*. That a considerable portion of the material that went into *Go Down, Moses* should relate to the past is not surprising. What is surprising, however, is that an even larger segment of the work consists not of stories about whites and Negroes in the McCaslin family but about hunting in the wilderness. As a consequence, the volume seems to divide into two parts. The long, novella-like story "The Fire and the Hearth" dominates the first part, while the second part consists almost entirely of the lengthy wilderness romance of "The Bear" and its related pieces ("The Old People" and "Delta Autumn"). The connection between the stories dealing with the relations between whites and Negroes on the one hand and the romance of the wilderness on the other never seems either logical or compelling. Regardless of the beauty and brilliance of both halves, Faulkner's failure to relate them convincingly becomes a crucial hurdle for readers.

Perhaps of lesser significance but certainly apparent to those who approach *Go Down, Moses* as a novel, the wide disparities among the stories also contribute to the weakness of the form. The initial story, "Was," for example, appears almost to have been written in the comic vein apparent in portions of *The Unvanquished*. Set during the days of slavery, "Was" features a make-believe manhunt and a poker game in which the loser wins the hand of an undesirable spinster. It is followed in "The Fire and the Hearth" by the lengthy analysis of the relationships between Zack Edmonds and Lucas Beauchamp, which in the present are also comic but in the past become deadly serious. Few readers, however, are astute enough to grasp any progressive treatment of white–Negro relationships between "Was" and "The Fire and the Hearth." The third story, "Pantaloon in Black," also set in contemporary time, bears no relationship to the McCaslin family and seems out of place in the book. The three stories that follow ("The Old People," "The Bear," and "Delta Autumn") constitute the romance of the wilderness. In "The Bear," Faulkner inserted a long section intended to link Isaac McCaslin's experiences in the wilderness to his sense of wrong and guilt over slavery, but most readers fail to see any necessary connection between them. The final story, "Go Down, Moses," narrowly avoids sentimentalism in the treatment of the need for white–Negro solidarity within the community. No one can doubt that Faulkner worked to connect these stories so that they would form a coherent whole, but in the end they proved too dissimilar. One cannot entirely dismiss the possibility also that the reason they could not be fused to become an organic whole lies in Faulkner's uncertainty about his own point of view. In 1942, when *Go Down, Moses* was published,[5] racial attitudes were in the process of change.

Between May 1, 1941, when Faulkner wrote Robert Haas about the proposed volume of "collected short stories," and the following December, when he finished the manuscript, the table of contents for *Go Down, Moses* underwent considerable revision. In June, 1941, Faulkner had finished a short story entitled "Almost." After the *Saturday Evening Post* declined to purchase the piece and Faulkner's agent could not sell it elsewhere, Faulkner changed its name to "Was" and used it as the initial story in *Go Down, Moses*. Faulkner revised "Almost" by substituting McCaslin Edmonds for the young boy named Bayard, shifting to a third-person narrative, and changing the name of Jason Prim to Hubert Beauchamp. The novelist also added the rather unusual introductory, almost fragmentary paragraphs relating to Isaac McCaslin that seem wholly unconnected to the remainder of "Was."

In Faulkner's original plan, the second story, "The Fire and the Hearth," would almost certainly have been the major story in the collection. For it, he would combine two already published stories, "A Point of Law" and "Gold Is Not Always," with a third work, "An Absolution," which had been retitled "Apotheosis" and was still unpublished. Each of these stories would be the core of a "chapter" in "The Fire and the Hearth." (The division of "The Fire and the Hearth" into chapters seems somewhat unusual in the light of the remainder of the stories in the volume.) In "A Point of Law" (first published in *Collier's*, June 22, 1940), Faulkner had told the story of the troubles between Roth Edmonds and his tenant farmers, including Lucas, who manufactured moonshine whiskey. The plot included the conflict between Lucas and his daughter Nat, and the title referred to the legal inadmissability of the testimony of one relative against another in a court of law. When he incorporated this story into *Go Down, Moses*, Faulkner added a great deal of new material, most notably the account of Lucas' relations with George Wilkins and the search for the buried treasure. Even more significantly, the author strengthened the theme of white–Negro relationships among the McCaslins; the entire present second section, for example, containing the long flashback in which he recounted the story of the birth of Roth Edmonds and the subsequent conflict between Zack Edmonds and Lucas, represented new material. Despite his extensive additions, however, "A Point of Law" remains the basic comic framework of Chapter One.

For Chapter Two of "The Fire and the Hearth," Faulkner used a story he had published in the *Atlantic Monthly* (November, 1940), entitled "Gold Is Not Always." This story of men's greediness for buried treasure seems heavily indebted to the similar incident in *The Hamlet*. Like Ratliff, Lucas allows his greed for buried gold to overcome his rational judgment, though he successfully utilizes the salted-mine trick, with which Flem Snopes defeated Ratliff, to gain ownership of the gold-finding machine from the city salesman. Lucas proves a sharp trader. In the end, the salesman's mad frenzy over the nonexistent treasure closely resembles the emotional state of Henry Armstid at the conclusion of *The Hamlet*. The basic material of "Gold Is Not Always" went into *Go Down, Moses* with very little change. For Chapter Three of "The Fire and the Hearth," Faulkner used "Apotheosis," a short story in which he developed the dual themes of Molly's concern for Lucas' obsession with the treasure and Roth's efforts to keep Lucas from getting a divorce. Faulkner's most notable addition to "Apotheosis" is again a flashback in which Roth Edmonds reviews the past relations of whites and Negroes in the McCaslin family.

Unlike "Was" and "The Fire and the Hearth," the following story, "Pantaloon in Black," has only the most tenuous connection with the other stories in *Go Down, Moses*. One wonders why Faulkner decided to use it, since the characters in it have neither kinship nor close association with the McCaslin family. Perhaps the best conjecture is that Faulkner may have decided that the moving account of Rider's suffering was too pertinent to the general racial theme to discard the story. In any event, he made very few changes in the original version, which was published in *Harper's* (October, 1940).

Although Faulkner planned to include it from the very beginning, he notably altered "The Old People" from the story that *Harper's* had published (September, 1940). The young, nameless narrator of the magazine story becomes Isaac McCaslin, and the relationship between Isaac and Sam Fathers becomes comparable to that between Lucas Beauchamp and Carothers McCaslin in "The Fire and the Hearth." The point of the story Faulkner shifted from hunting to the mystical initiation of Isaac

McCaslin in the wilderness. As the incident finally appeared in the volume, it served as a splendidly told introduction to the account of Old Ben in "The Bear."

In accordance with the table of contents that he suggested to Robert Haas in May, 1941, Faulkner next revised "Delta Autumn" (published in *Story*, May–June, 1942). In the original version, a Negro woman approaches "Uncle Ike" to inquire for Don Boyd, the father of her baby. Boyd has repudiated her and the boy and left her only a sum of money. Ike condemns Boyd's behavior but cannot believe that a marriage could take place at that time. In the hunt, Boyd kills a doe. As Faulkner revised this story for *Go Down, Moses*, he changed Boyd's name to Roth Edmonds and made the Negro woman the granddaughter of Tennie's Jim, thereby, many readers believe, making Roth commit the same sin that old Carothers McCaslin had committed generations earlier.

After revising "Delta Autumn," Faulkner decided that he needed additional material to supply a climax for the book.[6] The new material would be the story of the great bear of the wilderness, a story not a part of the original plan of the volume. Although a large portion of "The Bear" was new, for the second section he used a story that he had published earlier as "Lion" (*Harper's*, December, 1935). In "Lion," Quentin Compson is the narrator, and Isaac McCaslin appears as an old man. In the revision of the work for *Go Down, Moses*, the omniscient author becomes the narrator and Isaac appears as a youth of sixteen. To a degree, Faulkner shifted the main emphasis of the story from the dog to the bear. These changes make it fit into the pattern of "The Old People" and the opening section of "The Bear." As Faulkner wrote the remainder of "The Bear," he used other material from "Lion" in depicting the events at the end of the hunt. In the meantime, he wrote a magazine version of the bear story which the *Saturday Evening Post* published (May 9, 1942) shortly after *Go Down, Moses* appeared. The well known section four, in which Isaac explains his reasons for repudiating his inheritance, represented an attempt to connect the wilderness with the theme of racial injustice. This section was wholly new; later, when the bear story was reprinted in *Big Woods* (1955), section four was not included.

The final story, "Go Down, Moses" Faulkner had finished in July, 1940. As originally written, the young Negro about to be executed in Illinois for the murder of a policeman was named Henry Coldfield

Sutpen (grandson of Rosa Sutpen, a slave). In his manuscript, Faulkner changed the name to Carothers Edmonds Beauchamp, but ultimately decided to call the boy Samuel Worsham Beauchamp. Like "Pantaloon in Black," the story has only a tenuous connection with the white–Negro relations of the McCaslin family. Although the *Saturday Evening Post* rejected "Go Down, Moses," *Collier's* bought the piece and published it (January 25, 1941). With very little alteration, Faulkner used it for the conclusion of *Go Down, Moses.*

Because Faulkner himself stated that *Go Down, Moses* is a book about white and Negro relationships, readers are justified in approaching the work from this point of view. The white–Negro relationships are virtually all confined to the two branches of the McCaslin family. In the McCaslin genealogy the lineal progenitor of these people is Lucius Quintus Carothers McCaslin (1772–1837). This energetic but ruthless planter has a set of white descendants and a set of Negro descendants. The white line descends through Lucius Quintus Carothers McCaslin's son Theophilus (Uncle Buck, born about 1799) to Isaac McCaslin (born 1867), and through a daughter (Mary), who married Isaac Edmonds (Zack), to an unnamed son, to Carothers McCaslin Edmonds (Old Cass, born 1850), to his son "Zack" Edmonds (born 1873), to his son Carothers Edmonds (Roth, born 1898). Repeated references in *Go Down, Moses* are made to the fact that Isaac McCaslin descends through the male line, while the Edmondses descend through the female side.

The Negro branch of the McCaslin family descends through a male line.[7] Lucius Quintus Carothers McCaslin had a daughter, Tomasina (1810–1833), by his slave woman Eunice (died 1833). After committing incest with Tomasina, he had a son Terrel (Turl or Tomey's Turl, born 1833). Tomey's Turl and his wife Tennie Beauchamp had six children, three of whom died young and have no real part in *Go Down, Moses*. Of the other children, the most important is Lucas Beauchamp (born 1874), who married Mollie Worsham (born 1874); but the reader should also remember James (Tennie's Jim, born 1864), who became the grandfather of the woman who appears in "Delta Autumn" as Roth Edmonds' mistress, and Sophonisba (Fonsiba, born 1896), who moved with her scholarly husband to Arkansas.

In reading the book, one should be careful not to assume that the McCaslin Negroes who have prominent roles in it were born in slavery.

Of them, the most important is Tomey's Turl. In the fourth section of "The Bear," Isaac McCaslin recalls that immediately after Carothers McCaslin's death in 1837, some (what proportion is not given) of his slaves were freed. In the same story, Isaac also recalls that Uncle Buck and Uncle Buddy "during the two decades before the Civil War [accomplished] the manumission in title at least of Carothers McCaslin's slaves" (p. 256). No specific mention is made of the date or circumstances of Tomey's Turl's freedom. When Carothers McCaslin died, Tomey's Turl became an orphan (aged four), and at the age of twenty-one (1854) he was to receive the legacy of $1,000 from Carothers McCaslin's estate. In 1859, however, at the time of "Was," Tomey's Turl was still a slave. It seems rather unusual that while making no mention of Tomey's Turl, Faulkner would specify in regard to Tennie Beauchamp and her son Tennie's Jim that "her freedom, as well as that of her first surviving child [Tennie's Jim], derived not from Buck and Buddy McCaslin in the commissary but from a stranger [Lincoln] in Washington" (p. 271). Tennie's Jim, born December 26, 1864, almost two years after Lincoln's Emancipation Proclamation of January 1, 1863, would still have been a baby when Lee surrendered on April 9, 1865. Fonsiba, Lucas Beauchamp, and Mollie Worsham were never slaves. Faulkner has already written, in "The Fire and the Hearth," that Tomey's Turl also experienced "constitutional liberation" (p. 106) and elected to remain on the plantation.

To many readers, the title *Go Down, Moses* carries the implication that the work will deal with the setting free of the Negro. The original source of it is the biblical account of Moses' journey into Egypt to deliver the Israelites out of the bondage of Pharaoh that they might possess the promised land of Canaan. Exodus 3:7–10 contains the essential material:

> 7. And the Lord said, I have surely seen the affliction of my people which are in Egypt, and have heard their cry by reason of their taskmasters; for I know their sorrows;
> 8. And I am come down to deliver them out of the hand of the Egyptians, and to bring them up out of that land unto a good land and a large, unto a land flowing with milk and honey. . . .
> 9. Now therefore, behold, the cry of the children of Israel is come unto me: and I have also seen the oppression wherewith the Egyptians oppress them.
> 10. Come now therefore, and I will send thee unto Pharaoh, that thou mayest bring forth my people the children of Israel out of Egypt.

To these verses, one should add God's subsequent command to Moses that he say to Pharaoh, "Let my people go." The phrase is repeated again and again in the account of the plagues that were sent upon Egypt to force Pharaoh's compliance.

The other source, the Negro spiritual "Go Down, Moses," is also based upon the story in Exodus. The song, like the biblical prose, emphasizes the role of Moses in freeing the Israelites from the bondage of the Egyptians. Only the first verse and chorus are here quoted:

> When Israel was in Egypt's land,
> Let my people go!
> Oppressed so hard they could not stand
> Let my people go!
>
> Go down Moses
> 'Way down in Egypt's land
> Tell old Pharaoh
> "Let my people go"!

The song has often been interpreted as an expression of the longings of the Negro slave for freedom. The parallel with the Israelites, however, was never very exact, since America produced no Moses figure (Lincoln can hardly qualify), and the Negro's freedom involved no journey to a promised land.

In many respects the title seems scarcely appropriate to the volume. Except for the story "Was," the slaves in *Go Down, Moses* have been freed "at least in title" before the book opens; and if Faulkner intended to imply that the Negroes were to be led into a promised land, the title assumes a faintly ironical coloring. This inference is strengthened by Isaac's derisive question to Fonsiba's husband, "What corner of Canaan is this?" (p. 279). Moreover, the remark, never disputed, that "no man is ever free and probably could not bear it if he were" (p. 281) hardly seems consistent with the notion that the book will deal with the setting free of the Negro. The title, attractive as it is, applies to the content even less than the biblical story of David and Absalom applies to *Absalom, Absalom!*

"Was"

For the initial story in *Go Down, Moses*, Faulkner selected a comic yarn about a make-believe "manhunt" for a fleeing slave who is really not escaping and a poker game in which the loser has the most to win. Presumably, in order to give it some connection with the stories to follow, Faulkner wrote the curious opening paragraphs which affirm that Isaac McCaslin did not participate in "Was." That his participation would have been impossible, the reader learns at the end of the three paragraphs—the first and last of which are not even sentences and the second of which concludes with a sentence fragment—when Faulkner writes that Isaac McCaslin was not even born until eight years after the events of "Was." The title and date of the action, 1859, Faulkner may have intended to convey a suggestion of an old, legendary tale; but to some readers in 1941 (and probably to more today) the date 1859 signaled a story that took place in the days of slavery. "Was" seems to represent precisely the type of humor that thousands of *Saturday Evening Post* subscribers would have enjoyed in the days before Pearl Harbor, but it hardly represents a good choice for the beginning of a serious fictional treatment of white–Negro relationships.

The plot of "Was," narrated by an unnamed person who may have been Cass Edmonds but whose matter-of-fact, colloquial, adolescent tone reminds one of Huckleberry Finn, is patently absurd. About twice a year, Tomey's Turl "slips off" from Uncle Buck and Uncle Buddy's plantation to head for Mr. Hubert Beauchamp's place to see a slave named Tennie. Unless Uncle Buck can catch Tomey's Turl promptly, Mr. Hubert will return Tomey's Turl and bring with him Miss Sophonsiba, Mr. Hubert's sister, for a week's visit, an event the two bachelors consider a disaster. Before Uncle Buck can pursue Tomey's Turl, who has just "escaped" as the story opens, Uncle Buck must quiet the dogs who have just treed the pet fox behind the clock on the mantel, find his necktie, and eat breakfast. The romp of the dogs and the fox prefigures the human game of hide-and-seek that follows. In the subsequent pursuit of Tomey's Turl, dogs are brought out to find him; but since they regard him affectionately, he easily leads them into a cottonhouse and shuts them up.

The comedy continues when Uncle Buck, worn out from the night's run with Tomey's Turl, whom he never catches, climbs into bed only to discover that he has mistakenly gotten into bed with Miss Sophonsiba. For a time it appears as if he will be forced to marry her. To settle matters, Mr. Hubert and Uncle Buck resort to a hand of poker. The bet becomes $500 against "Sibbey," with the understanding that the lowest hand wins Sibbey and agrees to buy Tomey's Turl and Tennie. Because Mr. Hubert's "full house" (three kings and two fives) is high, Uncle Buck must buy Tennie and marry "Sibbey." But at this point, Uncle Buck sends for Uncle Buddy, a master poker player.

On the next evening, the three men agree that a game of stud poker will decide the matter. Faulkner must have enjoyed describing this game where both luck and psychological strategies become involved, though the issue seems finally decided by Tomey's Turl, who deals the cards. Uncle Buddy draws to an inside straight, while in the final moment of the game Mr. Hubert has three of a kind and knows that only the fourth trey in the deck could make Uncle Buddy's straight. But Mr. Hubert, glancing up at Tomey's Turl, ends the game by saying, "I pass, Amoedeus" (p. 29). Uncle Buck is thus free. Next day, however, Uncle Buck, Uncle Buddy, and Tennie ride home in the wagon while Tomey's Turl leads the pony. Back at the plantation, the fox has escaped again and the dogs are once more chasing him: like Tomey's Turl, the fox escapes.

Far from being a story about Moses demanding the freedom of the Israelites in Egypt or slaves longing for freedom, "Was" is almost a burlesque of the realities of 1859. Not many readers can forget the scenes: Mr. Hubert "sitting in the spring-house with his boots off and his feet in the water, drinking a toddy" (p. 9); the Negro boy sitting on the gate-post, blowing the fox horn until he is told to stop; the hounds; Miss Sophonsiba, with her roan tooth, her hair "roached under a lace cap" (p. 10), in her Sunday dress and beads and a red ribbon around her throat, engaged in her own private manhunt; and Tomey's Turl, holding the lamp shade and dealing the cards that will decide his fate and that of Tennie. If life in 1859 were anything like what appears in this story, it was mostly fun and games for all. Faulkner, of course, and his readers, knew better; this yarn was not supposed to be true.

"The Fire and the Hearth"

In the second story of *Go Down, Moses*, Faulkner writes a comic yarn about the adventures of the sixty-seven-year-old Lucas Beauchamp in 1941, but in two lengthy flashbacks that return the reader to events that took place in the nineteenth century, the novelist begins to examine very seriously the white–Negro relationships among the descendants of old Carothers McCaslin. The present-time of "The Fire and the Hearth" relates primarily to Lucas Beauchamp: his efforts to eliminate his competitor in the struggle for control of the unlawful manufacture and sale of moonshine whiskey; his slick trading practices that defeat the city salesman and give Lucas possession of the "divining machine"; and his marital troubles with Mollie because of his obsession with treasure hunting. Very skillfully, Faulkner unifies these episodes into a single story that is perhaps even more comic than the "manhunts" and poker games of "Was."

Within the almost tall-tale comic base of "The Fire and the Hearth," Faulkner defines the character of Lucas Beauchamp. Unlike most of the Southern rural Negroes of the period, Lucas considers himself financially independent because of the legacy old Carothers McCaslin left Tomey's Turl, Lucas' father. Tomey's Turl never claimed the legacy. Uncle Buck and Uncle Buddy, however, increased it three-fold, and Isaac McCaslin paid over to Lucas both his share and that of James or Tennie's Jim (Lucas' brother). Lucas thought about giving up farming; he "already had more money in the bank now than he would ever spend" (p. 33), and the buried treasure might make him rich beyond his wildest dreams. In 1941 Lucas is a hard, proud, even arrogant, selfish, greed-ridden man. He is ready to lie to his own advantage, to inform upon his daughter's lover in order to send him to the penitentiary, to break the law himself, and to drive harsh bargains with those who deal with him. Lucas is also a very foolish man, often unwilling to listen to those who would advise him in his own best interest. In fashioning his portrait, Faulkner seems to have combined many of the less desirable traits and activities he had used in *The Hamlet* to define white characters. Few can read "The Fire and the Hearth" without remembering the Pat Stamper–Ab Snopes horse trade, the legal technicalities of the lawsuits against Flem Snopes, the conflict between Ratliff and Flem, the salted-mine trick of Flem, and Ratliff's own greediness for buried treasure. Even Lucas' final gift to Mollie of a nickel's worth of candy reminds one of Flem's gift of a nickel's worth of candy to Mrs. Armstid "for the chaps." [8]

During the present-time sequences of "The Fire and the Hearth," relations between the white and Negro branches of the McCaslin family may not be so harmonious as they might be, but they are by no means hostile. Very conscious of himself as a descendant of old Carothers McCaslin by only two generations removed, Lucas has no special respect or even fondness for Roth Edmonds, the present owner of the land and head of the

McCaslin descendants. Faulkner records Lucas' thoughts: "He, Lucas Ḃeauchamp, the oldest living McCaslin descendant still living on the hereditary land, who actually remembered old Buck and Buddy in the living flesh, older than Zack Edmonds even if Zack were still alive, almost as old as old Isaac who in a sense, say what a man would, had turned apostate to his name and lineage by weakly relinquishing the land which was rightfully his to live in town on the charity of his great-nephew" (pp. 39–40). Privately, Lucas thinks the McCaslin line has deteriorated (Lucas' own descendants, one might observe, likewise deteriorate). Roth Edmonds is probably correct when he thinks that Lucas is *"more like old Carothers than all the rest of us put together"* (p. 118), but Roth's remark that Lucas, like old Carothers, is *"contemptuous . . . of all blood black white yellow or red, including his own"* (p. 118), seems wide of the mark.

For his part, Roth Edmunds, like Uncle Buck and Uncle Buddy, Isaac McCaslin, old Cass, and others in the family before him, acknowledges a responsibility for both Lucas and his wife Mollie. For the past twenty years, Roth has run the plantation; but, in 1941, as he looks back, "they seemed to him one long and unbroken course of outrageous trouble and conflict . . . with the old negro who . . . called him Mr Edmonds and Mister Carothers or Carothers or Roth or son or spoke to him in a group of younger negroes, lumping them all together as 'you boys'" (p. 116). "Impervious to time" (p. 116), Lucas has declined any advice, refusing to use such modern implements on the farm as tractors and airplanes for crop-dusting, "yet drawing supplies from the commissary as if he farmed, and at an outrageous and incredible profit, a thousand acres, having on the commissary books an account dating thirty years back which Edmonds knew he [Lucas] would never pay" (p. 117) and which Roth makes no effort to collect. Also vexing to Roth are the still, which Lucas had run for almost twenty years in Roth's backyard, and the three-hundred-dollar mule, which Lucas has stolen to use in the trade with the divining machine salesman. Presently, Roth is troubled by Lucas' behavior toward Mollie, his wife of forty-five years. Toward Mollie, Roth has special feelings; she has been "the only mother he, Edmonds, ever knew, who had raised him . . . teaching him his manners, behavior—to be gentle with his inferiors, honorable with his equals, generous to the weak and considerate of the aged, courteous, truthful and brave to all" (p. 117).

Although Roth does not say so in as many words, the fact is that Lucas has had land given him, unlimited supplies furnished free to him, and a legacy (increased three-fold and then doubled by the addition of his brother's share) provided to make him financially independent. And, as Roth implies, only Lucas' avarice has exposed his unlawful still, which he has operated in direct opposition to Roth's orders as well as those of the sheriff. Like old Carothers, Lucas has taken and taken, without any concessions or any evidence of even acknowledgment on his part. Yet despite Lucas' ruthless selfishness, Roth continues to feel a responsibility to intervene in Lucas' affairs at least to protect Mollie from Lucas and perhaps Lucas from himself. The endeavor proves difficult because of Lucas' uncompromising insistence that "I'm the man here. I'm the one to say in my house, like you and your paw and his paw were the ones to say in his" (p. 120). Stubbornly, Lucas refuses to bring the machine to Roth. Although at the divorce court Roth assumes responsibility for Mollie's welfare, he is relieved when Lucas declares that there will be no divorce. Finally, Lucas brings the machine to Roth and orders him to "get rid of it" (p. 130). Even then Lucas still persists in believing that the money is still buried, though, as he says, "I reckon to find that money aint for me" (p. 131). Lucas' grudging admission brings to a close the comic affair of his treasure-digging and "voce."

The racial tension of "The Fire and the Hearth" exists not so much in the present as in the past, and the account of it reaches the reader through two extended flashbacks that Faulkner added to the original stories of "A Point of Law" and "Apotheosis." These flashbacks are slightly disconcerting because of the sudden shift they make from the light, comic atmosphere of the present-time sequence to the dramatic confrontations, first between Lucas and Zack and second between Roth and Henry Beauchamp, Lucas' son. Faulkner's narrative technique at this point may also be confusing. The novelist introduces the flashbacks as "thoughts" in the minds of Lucas and Roth; but at some point, the reader is not certain exactly when, the narrative loses the "thoughts" coloring and takes on the immediacy of an on-the-scene recording of what happened. The reader is "there" as a silent spectator. When the narrative suddenly shifts back to the present time, the reader cannot be absolutely certain whether he is to understand the entire flashback as representing the attitude of Lucas or Roth towards those events—at least their version of them—or as a factual rendition of the events themselves.

256

Clearly, for Lucas, however, now sixty-seven, the crucial event of the past (history) relates to his encounter with Zack Edmonds in the first few months after the birth of Roth, forty-three years earlier. After the death of Roth's mother in childbirth, Mollie, Lucas' wife, who acted as midwife during the birth, remains in Zack's house to nurse not only Roth but also her own baby. Lucas keeps the fire going on his hearth for six months and then demands her return. At stake is Lucas' pride. As the two men face each other, Zack denies Lucas' unspoken accusation: "So that's what you think. What kind of a man do you think I am? What kind of a man do you call yourself?" (p. 47). Lucas replies: "I'm a nigger. . . . But I'm a man too. I'm more than just a man. The same thing made my pappy that made your grandmaw." Lucas will not even wait to hear Zack swear that he has not had sexual relations with Mollie. Later Lucas broods over his position. "*He* [Zack] *keeps her in the house with him six months and I dont do nothing: he sends her back to me and I kills him. It would be like I had done said aloud to the whole world that he never sent her back because I told him to but he give her back to me because he was tired of her*" (p. 49). He thinks: "*I got to kill him or I got to leave here.*" Just after daylight, Lucas enters Zack's bedroom to kill him for an act Lucas has no valid reason to believe Zack has committed and that Lucas has waited six months even to protest. In the heated discussion that follows, Lucas again asserts his McCaslin lineage. He beats Roth in a test of strength, takes the gun, and pulls the trigger. Only the misfire prevents the death of Zack—and also that of Lucas. Later, Lucas thinks that he would not have used the second bullet (for himself). "*I would have paid. . . . So I reckon I aint got old Carothers' blood for nothing, after all. Old Carothers*, he thought. *I needed him and he come and spoke for me*" (p. 58).

Although Roth Edmonds has had no dramatic confrontation with Lucas, Roth has not escaped the tension between the two races. In the second flashback, Faulkner records Roth's version of the family's history. Like Lucas, Roth cannot forget that while Lucas descends from old Carothers by a male line and in but two generations, he himself descends through a female line in five generations. To Roth, Lucas is "not only impervious to that blood, he was indifferent to it" (p. 104)—a serious misjudgment on Roth's part. Roth reviews the provisions of old Carothers and Uncle Buck and Uncle Buddy for Tomey's Turl, the transfer of the land from Isaac McCaslin to Cass Edmonds, and Isaac's efforts to pay the legacy to Tomey's Turl's children and to teach Lucas how to write his own checks. But what seems most vivid to Roth is his childhood. Mollie has been the only mother he has ever known. He has grown up with her son Henry as his "foster-brother" until one day "the old curse of his fathers, the old haughty ancestral pride based not on any value but on an accident of geography, stemmed not from courage and honor but from wrong and shame, descended to him" (p. 111). His consciousness of the differences between the races is foreshadowed in the sleeping arrangements but confirmed in the subsequent treatment he receives in Lucas' house. "So he entered his heritage," wrote Faulkner; "He ate its bitter fruit" (p. 114). Gradually Roth realizes that his father and Lucas have clashed over a woman and that Lucas has won, because "*if father had beat Lucas, he couldn't have let Lucas stay here even to forgive him. It will only be Lucas who could have stayed because Lucas is impervious to anybody, even to forgiving them, even to having to harm them*" (p. 116). Roth finally concludes that Lucas is "*more like old Carothers than all the rest of us put together, including old Carothers*" (p. 118).

Both Lucas' and Roth's memories of the past focus upon Lucas' pride and his dispute with Zack about a woman whose name Roth will never know. Later, when Faulkner presents Isaac McCaslin's account of the family history in "The Bear," he will concentrate upon old Carothers' moral sins of incest and miscegenation. Lucas has no moral scruples, and old Carothers' evils seem not to have greatly troubled Roth Edmonds. At the conclusion of "The Fire and the Hearth," the McCaslin past seems to have altered little in the present comic story. Lucas has salvaged most of his dignity, and Roth has protected Mollie by helping to end Lucas' compulsive search for a treasure he does not need and that probably does not exist. Both Roth and Lucas are descendants of old Carothers; but in the very ways that he is most like old Carothers, Lucas is least admirable. If anything, because of his concern for Mollie and his patience, even respect, for Lucas, Roth appears the better man. Faulkner's account, however, of the two branches of the McCaslin family has not been finished.

"Pantaloon in Black"

Of all the stories in *Go Down, Moses*, "Pantaloon in Black" is the least integrated into the series. Although it deals with the general theme of white–Negro relationships, it is connected to the McCaslin family only by the circumstance that Rider rents a cabin from Roth. Apparently, Faulkner made no real effort to fit it into the other stories, since in preparing it for inclusion in the volume he made very few changes in it. The story seems inappropriate because it departs violently from the tone of "The Fire and the Hearth" and provides no progressive approach to "The Old People," which follows it.

"Pantaloon in Black," nevertheless, is a powerful treatment of the failure of understanding between the two races in the community. In this story, the fault appears to rest upon the white people represented by the white deputy and his wife. The deputy begins his account of Rider's actions after the death of his wife with the callous pronouncement that Negroes "aint human" (p. 154) and proceeds, step by step, wholly to misinterpret the Negro's actions. Seen from the white deputy's point of view, Rider is an unfeeling, insensitive man, although the reader knows better. One must, however, be careful to resist the temptation to dismiss the deputy himself as the unfeeling, insensitive man. Every word he utters seems to convict him of the very lack of feeling that he finds in Rider; and in her acceptance of her husband's story at face value and impatience to dismiss it so that she can clear the table and get to the picture show, the wife appears as callous as her husband. The meaning of the story, however, is not the insensitivity of either Rider or the white deputy; rather, it is the lack of communication between them that makes each appear to be what he may not be in fact.

The Wilderness Romance

The three stories "The Old People," "The Bear," and "Delta Autumn" are so closely related by setting, characters, and theme that they should be read as a unit. Taken together, they form a romance of the American wilderness after the manner of James Fenimore Cooper, Nathaniel Hawthorne, and Herman Melville.[9] If a romance is defined as a story in which the writer seeks to reveal spiritual truths by blending with reality an element of poetry, the marvelous, and, often, ambiguity, Faulkner's stories properly belong to this form. The protagonist of this romance is Isaac McCaslin, and it focuses upon his experiences in the wilderness.

Although the poetic quality of Faulkner's prose has been widely admired, his use of the marvelous in the wilderness stories has received considerably less attention. "The Old People" contains an excellent example of his handling of it. As Sam Fathers and Isaac stand motionless against a tremendous pin oak, the wilderness breathes. "It seemed to lean inward above them . . . tremendous, attentive, impartial and omniscient" (p. 181), and somewhere in it moves the great buck "perhaps conscious also of the eye of the ancient immortal Umpire." For a moment, Isaac and the wilderness stop breathing; and, after hearing Walter Ewell's rifle, he turns to leave. Sam Fathers holds him back. Suddenly, Isaac sees the great antlered buck, "walking, tremendous, unhurried, slanting and tilting its head to pass the antlers through the undergrowth" (p. 184); and while Ewell's horn is still blowing, Sam Fathers rises and speaks to the great buck: "Oleh, Chief. . . . Grandfather." The vision of the great antlered buck is seen only by those initiated into the wilderness—Sam Fathers and Isaac (as will be seen, on another occasion McCaslin also saw it). Sam Fathers greets it in the secret language, thereby acknowledging his kinship with it. The entire incident has a transcendental quality that the nature-romance writers of the nineteenth century would have understood.

In "The Bear," Faulkner continues to add an element of the marvelous to his story. Old Ben, "an anachronism indomitable and invincible out of an old dead time, a phantom, epitome and apotheosis of the old wild life . . . widowered childless and absolved of mortality" (pp. 193–94), has preternatural knowledge of the hunters in the woods. When he dies, Sam Fathers dies, and the end of the wilderness fast approaches. In the final section, Isaac returns to the woods, leaves presents for the spirit of Sam Fathers, and greets the snake with the same words with which Sam Fathers had saluted the great buck. Throughout the romance, Faulkner emphasizes the occult mystery and wisdom of the wilderness. Sam Fathers, Joe Baker, Isaac, the great buck, Old Ben, and Lion participate in a world beyond the ordinary realities of life, a world close to the heart of nature itself. After Isaac has become one with this hidden world, he returns to actuality with special insights. His experience reminds one of Bryant's verses: "To him who in the love of Nature holds / Communion with her visible forms, she speaks / A various language." Sam Fathers and Isaac hear this language and gain access to her transcendental wisdom.

Much of the richness of Faulkner's wilderness romance stems from this transcendental quality. In addition, it gains depth and significance by its

connection with a historical concept that dates back to the very beginnings of American literature. Early in the seventeenth century, writers
had imaged America as either a desolate wilderness or a second Garden of
Eden. In New England, Puritans like William Bradford, who experienced firsthand the desolate wilderness of Cape Cod, thrilled to a vision
of themselves as God's chosen people being led out of a modern Egypt
(England) into a new Promised Land, a new Canaan. Conscious of their
place in history, they considered their migration, after the dispossession
of man from Eden and the atonement of Christ, the most important
event in the history of the world. Just as the Israelites had fought the
heathen dwellers in Canaan, so the Puritans knew they must master the
Indian aborigines, the rigors of the wilderness, and the wild beasts of the
forests before the Promised Land, the Garden of Eden, could be theirs. In
the South, the early American writer also pictured the new-found land as
a Garden of Eden and praised the incredible abundance of its forests,
streams, and rivers. In the South, too, the garden seemed threatened by
the Indian, and before long, men like Thomas Jefferson were aware that
another beast lurked in the garden—chattel slavery of the African.
Thus, the connection between the wilderness as a new Garden of Eden
troubled by both the Indian and the slave—two alien races—had been
established more than a century before Faulkner united them in his modern romance of the wilderness.

The American Revolution and, a few years later, the Louisiana Purchase gave new impetus to the wilderness romance theme. In the five
Leatherstocking Tales, but especially in *The Deerslayer*, *The Pioneers*, and
The Prairie, James Fenimore Cooper treated the potential conflict between the Edenic wilderness and the advancing frontier as one of the central problems of an emerging America. Although he utilized the romantic notion of the essential goodness of nature as the "handiwork" of God
and nature's role as teacher and guide to man's moral development,
Cooper saw clearly that the wilderness had within it the dual potential
for good or evil. Under proper circumstances nature or the wilderness
could reinforce God's precepts and educate a Natty Bumppo. But Cooper
also knew, just as Isaac McCaslin knew that there was not enough Bucks
and Buddies, that for every self-disciplined Christ-like Natty there were
hundreds of Hurry Harrys and descendants of Ishmael Bush. For every
Uncas and Chingachgook, there were many Maguas. Natty himself

had his limitations. Even more, Cooper knew—and approved the fact—that the wilderness was doomed before the march of civilization. Only through law, landownership, and fences could man live in a society where restrictions upon the individual's freedom were essential for the survival of all.

Although Faulkner's debt to Cooper's wilderness romances may hardly be overestimated, "The Bear" must also be viewed in the light of the development of the nature theme after Cooper. Among the transcendentalists, Emerson believed in the goodness of nature, but Melville speculated about the possibility that the heart of the universe might be evil rather than good. Hawthorne, conscious of his New England forefathers, recognized the necessity of evil in the garden as the paradox of the fortunate fall. In *The Scarlet Letter*, *The House of the Seven Gables*, and *The Marble Faun*, each man in each generation repeats the fall of Adam from Eden, thereby losing his own paradise. Moreover, as Hawthorne wrote in *The Marble Faun*, each sin "destroys more Edens than our own." This tragic concept of nature in relation to the individual and the descent of evil through the generations became part of the nature romance long before Faulkner alluded to it in Isaac's conversation in the commissary.

After the Civil War, the interpretation of nature underwent a radical change. The transcendental concept, as well as the literary form of the romance, lost favor because of the vogue of Darwinism and the ever increasing industrialization of American culture. The new approach to nature as "red in tooth and claw," as a vast chain of predators, and as a continual battle in which only the fittest survived destroyed any faith in its spiritual qualities. Stephen Crane's remark in "The Open Boat" illustrates the attitude at the turn of the century: "When it occurs to a man that nature does not regard him as important . . . he at first wishes to throw bricks at the temple, and he hates deeply the fact that there are no bricks and no temples. Any visible expression of nature would surely be pelleted with his jeers." No longer is nature a paradise garden or a guardian of one's moral being; at best it is a hostile force, at worst a matter of chance or apathy. In writing "The Bear," however, Faulkner ignored this modern view of nature and deliberately returned to the older romantic concept of the wilderness or nature as a guide or teacher of moral truths. In so doing, he was returning to the great literary tradition of the romance as practiced by Cooper, Hawthorne, and Melville and writing a story unlike any he would ever write again, perhaps the last nature romance in American literature.

The romance writer, conveying as he does spiritual truths through a blending of the literal with the symbolic or allegorical levels of a story, nearly always faces difficulties of communication. The author must take great care to make his meaning clear; and, in seeking the wider implications, the reader must also take care to confine his interpretations to what may be justified by the work itself without doing violence to the literal text or to the main "thrust" of the work. A certain amount of disagreement over meanings can probably always be expected. No one, for example, can be absolutely certain of what Old Ben and Lion in "The Bear" actually represent as symbols, though almost all readers will agree that they do have a symbolic function beyond the actual events of the story. Always, of course, the possibility exists that no specific allegory was intended, or that the work is not allegorically consistent within itself.

Few readers, however, would question that Faulkner attributes special qualities to Old Ben, Sam Fathers, and Lion that identify them as inhabitants of the world of romance. In the opening passage of "The Bear," for example, Faulkner places this ordinary forest animal entirely out of the class of any animal anyone has ever seen in the woods, while at the same time he retains enough of the actual features of a bear to keep him believable. Here Faulkner has superbly combined the real and the marvelous, the essential components of the romance, by taking a reality and developing it into a symbol that invites comparison with Melville's great whale. In a splendid passage, Faulkner relates that by the time Isaac McCaslin was ten years of age, he had already become involved with the bear and the wilderness:

> He had already inherited then, without ever having seen it, the big old bear with one trap-ruined foot that in an area almost a hundred miles square had earned for himself a name, a definite designation like a living man:—the long legend of corn-cribs broken down and rifled, of shoats and grown pigs and even calves carried bodily into the woods and devoured . . . a corridor of wreckage and destruction beginning back before the boy was born, through which sped . . . the shaggy tremendous shape. It ran in his knowledge before he ever . . . saw the unaxed woods where it left its crooked print. . . . It was as if the boy had already divined . . . that doomed wilderness . . . through which ran not even a mortal beast but an anachronism indomitable and invincible out of an old dead time, a phantom, epitome and apotheosis of the

old wild life . . . the old bear, solitary, indomitable, and alone; widowered childless and absolved of mortality. (pp. 192–94)

Thus, by 1877 (and even more so by 1883, when the events of the great bear hunt take place) Old Ben is a "phantom, epitome and apotheosis of the old wild life." He is also an "anachronism," that is, he has already lived beyond his time and should no longer be there. To Isaac, Old Ben seems "absolved of mortality." The old bear knows when a new person comes into the woods; he appears and vanishes mysteriously. As Sam Fathers says, "He's the head bear" (p. 198). He seems ubiquitous and omniscient. Such qualities accumulate until the reader finally realizes that Old Ben symbolizes the wilderness itself (to say he is God is to stretch the symbology too far, unless one views the wilderness or the universe as God).

Although Major de Spain's erroneous belief that Old Ben has killed his colt and thereby "broken the rules" (p. 214) becomes the pretext for the great bear hunt—Lion, as Sam Fathers knows, has actually killed the colt—the final conflict between the great bear (wilderness) and the ownership of property (civilization) has been inevitable. The conflict, in fact, began long ago. For many years, men have tried to kill the great bear, fired bullets at him, but Old Ben has been just "too big" for the horses, the dogs, and the shots directed against him (p. 193). Now what had been a yearly pageant or ritual has reached a point where to protect property (civilization) Major de Spain thinks that Old Ben must be killed. Thus, on a symbolical or allegorical level, the bear hunt is a conflict between civilization and wilderness in which the wilderness (Old Ben), as Isaac knows, is doomed.

Almost to the same degree as Old Ben, Sam Fathers likewise has affinities with the wilderness. As part white, part Negro, and part Indian, he unites all three races who have participated in the American Garden of Eden metaphor; and since he is heir to Old Ben or the wilderness, Faulkner may have intended to suggest through Sam Fathers that all races share in the legacy of nature. As he did to the old bear, Faulkner gives Sam Fathers a touch of the marvelous. A descendant of a chief, he answers to no one. With the old full-blooded chickasaw Joe Baker, Sam Fathers speaks in the "old tongue" and buries him with mysterious rites. Sam Fathers also greets the great antlered buck as kinsman and chief, apparently speaking a language the deer understands. He has fore-knowledge of Old Ben's appearances. After he has baptized Isaac Mc-Caslin as his successor and heir to the wilderness, Sam Fathers returns to the woods. His "let me go" (p. 173) recalls the title, *Go Down, Moses*, and echoes the Puritans' comparison of their flight from England, their Egypt. In the wilderness, Sam Fathers prepares for his death and that of Old Ben. Faulkner's description of Sam Fathers seems almost a predic-tion of Isaac McCaslin's old age: "*He* [Sam Fathers] *was old. He had no children, no people, none of his blood anywhere above earth that he would ever meet again. . . . It was almost over now*" (p. 215). His death, probably at the hands of Boon, and Boon's care in arranging the body on the platform in the wilderness facing west accentuate the mystical relationship that Sam Fathers bears to Old Ben and the wilderness. Viewed allegorically, the deaths of Old Ben and Sam Fathers may be understood as marking the end of the "old wild life," the wilderness, and man's right relation to nature. Only Isaac McCaslin and Boon ("co-heirs" of Sam Fathers and, by extension, Old Ben) now remain, Boon to endeavor futilely to protect his own and Isaac to live his life almost as futilely with the woods as "his mistress and his wife" (p. 326), according to the pattern set by his spir-itual father, Sam Fathers, but unable to make modern life conform to the way of the wilderness. Isaac will live to foretell the ultimate extinction of the wilderness as the economic system (industrialization) destroys it; but the wilderness will accomplish its own revenge because man will be de-prived of the spiritual values that it could teach him.

Although the allegorical roles of Old Ben and Sam Fathers may be interpreted with confidence, the symbology of Lion is much less certain. Actually, there is less of the preternatural about Lion than about Old Ben. From the outset, Lion resembles a gun: he is "almost the color of a gun or pistol barrel" (p. 216). Where this dog came from, no one save perhaps Sam Fathers knew: "part mastiff, something of Airedale and something of a dozen other strains probably . . . with cold yellow eyes and a tremendous chest and over all that strange color like a blued gun-barrel" (p. 218). About its eyes, "there was nothing of petty malevolence . . . but a cold and almost impersonal malignance like some natural force." His name is Lion, and, as Sam Fathers says, "He dont care about nothing or nobody" (p. 220). The association of Boon with Lion seems a natural affinity. "It was as if Lion were a woman—or perhaps Boon was the woman. That was more like it—the big, grave, sleepy-seeming dog which, as Sam Fathers says, cared about no man and no thing; and the violent, insensitive, hard-faced man with his touch of remote Indian blood and the mind almost of a child." As a plebian and Sam Fathers' huntsman, "Boon should have nursed the dogs" (p. 222). After predicting that "Lion would never cry on a trail," Sam Fathers adds, "He gonter growl when he catches Old Ben's throat. . . . But he aint gonter never holler. . . . It's that blue dog in him" (pp. 223–24). Faulkner's characterization of Lion repeatedly associates him first with a gun and then with the impersonality of a "natural force." The gun imagery suggests the impersonal, amoral, unemotional, motiveless yet fatal force that Lion represents in the story and contrasts with the ineffectiveness of Boon's man-made gun.

Isaac McCaslin supplies the clue to Lion's symbolical significance. Logically, Isaac should have hated and feared Lion, because Lion would be the means by which Old Ben or the wilderness would be destroyed. In suggesting the symbolical meaning of Lion, Faulkner also answers the question, why did Isaac not hate the dog. "It seemed to him [Isaac] that there was a fatality in it. It seemed to him that something, he didn't know what, was beginning; had already begun. It was like the last act on a set stage" (p. 226). Lion becomes the instrument of the fatality. Through him the inevitable will be accomplished; and Old Ben, Sam Fathers, and Isaac are powerless to oppose it, just as they are powerless to stop the destruction of the wilderness. Thus, artistically and allegorically, it is fitting that Sam Fathers, having returned to the wilderness to live out his final days and having foreknowledge of the death of Old Ben and the doom of the wilderness, should provide the instrument by which these ends are accomplished. Likewise, it seems fitting that Sam Fathers should have chosen for this purpose a natural force but one with the potency of a gun.

In "The Old People," "The Bear," and "Delta Autumn," Isaac Mc-Caslin's participation in the mystical, inexplicable life of the wilderness constitutes the principal motif of the romance. The great bear hunt, compelling as it is, takes second place to the developing commitment of Isaac to the wilderness itself. His actions after the hunt—that is, his return to the wilderness two years later, his efforts to deliver Old Carothers' legacies, his repudiation of his own inheritance, and his later life—are intended to result from his character formed under the tutelage of Sam Fathers.

Besides woodsmanship, Faulkner indicates that Sam Fathers taught Isaac "about those old times and those dead and vanished men of another race from either that the boy knew" and "gradually to the boy those old times would cease to be old times and would become a part of the boy's present . . . as if they were still happening. . . . And more: as if some of them had not happened yet but would occur tomorrow, until at last it would seem to the boy that he himself had not come into existence yet, that none of his race nor the other subject race which his people had brought with them into the land had come here yet" (p. 171). He learned also that his family's hold upon the land that would one day be his "actually was as trivial and without reality as the now faded and archaic script in the chancery book in Jefferson which allocated it to them and that it was he, the boy, who was the guest here and Sam Father's [sic] voice the mouthpiece of the host" (p. 171). In other words, even when Isaac was a boy, the wilderness had most reality for him when he thought of it as without slavery and as land not owned by anyone. The passage contains the origin of Isaac's later attitudes toward landownership and racial injustice.

Faulkner carefully traces the various stages through which Isaac passes in his wilderness experience. He enters "his novitiate to the true wilderness with Sam beside him . . . the two of them wrapped in the damp, warm, negro-rank quilt while the wilderness closed behind his entrance as it had opened momentarily to accept him, opening before his advancement as it closed behind his progress" (p. 195). The passage not only suggests that the life of the wilderness is a kind of religious experience but also that within it there are no distinctions of race. Already he has humility, and he learns patience while waiting on the stand for his opportunity to shoot. After he has seen for the first time the print of the bear's foot, he knows "what he had heard in the hounds' voices. . . . It was in him too, a little different . . . but only a little different—an eagerness, passive; an abjectness, a sense of his own fragility and impotence against the timeless woods"; and Isaac realizes too that the bear (wilderness) which has "run in his listening and loomed in his dreams since before he could remember and which therefore must have existed in the listening and the dreams of his cousin . . . and even old General Compson before they began to remember in their turn, was a mortal animal" (pp. 200–201). The bear has seen him; and although Isaac has not seen the bear, he remains motionless, "holding the useless gun which he knew now he would never fire at it, now or ever" (p. 203).

Although, with the aid of watch and compass, Isaac learns to be "better than a fair woodsman" (p. 205), Sam Fathers says he must put away these mechanical tools. In a passage that forecasts the shape of Isaac's life to come, Faulkner indicates the significance of these actions. "He had already relinquished . . . in humility and peace and without regret, yet apparently that had not been enough. . . . He stood for a moment—a child, alien and lost in the green and soaring gloom of the markless wilderness. Then he relinquished completely to it. It was the watch and the compass. He was still tainted" (p. 208). Only when he abandons them and becomes lost does he find himself, the bear, and the true wilderness. Only then does the vision, or the reality, appear to him. "It [the bear] did not emerge, appear: it was just there. . . . Then it was gone. It didn't walk into the woods. It faded, sank back into the wilderness without motion" (p. 209). On the last day in camp, he kills his first buck; and "Sam Fathers marked his face with the hot blood which he had spilled and he ceased to be a child and became a hunter and a man" (pp. 177–78). By this act, Sam Fathers "marked him forever one with the wilderness which had accepted him . . ." (p. 178)—"not as a mere hunter, but with something Sam had had in his turn of his vanished and forgotten people" (p. 182). Sixty years later Isaac McCaslin would still remember that moment when Sam marked his face with the blood "while he stood trying not to tremble, humbly and with pride too . . . : *I slew you; my bearing must not shame your quitting life. My conduct forever onward must become your death*" (pp. 350–51). As if in sign of its recognition and acceptance, "the wilderness ceased to breathe . . . leaning, stooping overhead with its breath held, tremendous and impartial and waiting" (p. 182) and almost at once Isaac and Sam Fathers see the vision of the great antlered buck.

Thus, Isaac ends his novitiate and begins his priesthood. In the years to come, he will continue to hone his woodsman's skills. At the age of sixteen, he will take part in the final hunt for Old Ben and read the ledgers in the McCaslin commissary. Five years later, at the age of twenty-one, he will try to explain why he wishes to relinquish his inheritance. Throughout his long life, he will maintain his communion with the wilderness and his rejection of the economic bondage that he believes results from landownership.

Added by Faulkner in 1941 to the already published story of "Lion," the long fourth section returns to the white-Negro relationship theme that the novelist began to develop seriously in "The Fire and the Hearth." That it has no compelling relation to the other sections of "The Bear," Faulkner himself recognized, as has been suggested earlier, by omitting this part in the reprint of "The Bear" in the volume entitled *Big Woods* (1955). The setting of this section moves away from the wilderness to McCaslin's commissary; the action takes place for the most part after the conclusion of the hunting story; and another character detracts somewhat from the prominence given earlier to Isaac. Furthermore, readers who have identified with Isaac in the account of his novitiate under Sam Fathers may doubt that the lessons Isaac learned in the wilderness can be applied directly to the actualities of the commissary ledgers and the management of the plantation.

Because of the abrupt shifts of time and place, section four makes difficult reading. It opens with a discussion between Isaac McCaslin and McCaslin Edmonds in the commissary where the ledgers which record the business affairs of the plantation are kept. This conversation takes place in 1888, when Isaac is twenty-one, five years after the great bear hunt and the death of Sam Fathers; but Faulkner blurs the "present-time" so that he may range backward and forward. At the mention of Uncle Buck and Uncle Buddy (p. 261), he interrupts the dialogue in 1888 to present in the following twenty pages (ending on page 282) an account of the McCaslin family derived largely from the old ledgers. Although the reader understands that he is seeing what Isaac saw at the age of sixteen, that is, in 1883, Faulkner does not hesitate to interpolate events that occur after that date. Two such events are specifically dated. When, on December 29, 1885, Tennie's Jim, then age twenty-one, vanished, Isaac journeyed to Tennessee to find Jim, returned without success, and gave his legacy to McCaslin on January 12, 1886 (pp. 271, 273); and when Fonsiba, age seventeen, married and went to Arkansas, Isaac, in December, 1886, found her and delivered her legacy (pp. 276–77).

In presenting the flashback scene with Fonsiba and her husband, Faulkner subtly shifts from Isaac's memories to the actual scene, a technique similar to that he had used in "The Fire and the Hearth" and that suggests the fade-out or fade-in of a motion picture sequence. At the mention again of Uncle Buck and Uncle Buddy (p. 282), the "present-time" begins again; but the conversation between Isaac and McCaslin is interrupted once more as Isaac remembers an occasion in 1881, when he and Sam Fathers, with the fyce, ambushed Old Ben but did not shoot (pp. 295–97). With the aid of italics, Faulkner also uses the motion picture camera technique for this flashback. The conversation between Isaac and McCaslin in 1888 resumes once more, but it actually concludes with Isaac's comment: "Sam Fathers set me free" (p. 300). The final two scenes of the fourth section—the opening of the legacy from Hubert Beauchamp to Isaac and the account of Isaac's relationship with his wife in Jefferson—take place in 1895. The next episode in Isaac's life will take place in "Delta Autumn," about forty-five years later.

Even more difficult for the reader than the time element is the substance of the argument between Isaac and McCaslin. Their talk ranges over the history of man, from his dispossession of the Garden of Eden, to the settlement of America, the Civil War, and Isaac's novitiate in the wilderness. If their discussion has a dominant theme, it is the justification of Isaac's repudiation of his inheritance. Even before the dialogue begins, Faulkner suggests two of its major lines of development, although the reader cannot be certain whether the passage is to be understood as a statement of truth from an omniscient author or as an expression of the thoughts of Isaac. In the passage, old Carothers is viewed as having purchased the land from "the wild men" and as having "believed he had tamed and ordered it for the reason that the human beings he held in bondage" (p. 254) had cleared the land and grown cotton upon it. For this reason, the passage continues, "old Carothers McCaslin, knowing better, could raise his children . . . to believe the land was his to hold and bequeath" (p. 254). Before the talk is concluded, the point is also made that despite the fact that the Civil War freed the Negroes, they were still bound to the land by "the slow outward trickle of food and supplies and equipment which returned each fall as cotton made and ginned and sold" (pp. 255–56). Thus, landownership and economic bondage become two focal points for the argument which follows.

At first, Isaac maintains that neither old Carothers nor the Indians before him owned the land, because God created man to be His overseer on the earth "to hold the earth mutual and intact in the communal anonymity of brotherhood" (p. 257). But McCaslin replies that ever since man was dispossessed of Eden, he has held the land and that God has condoned it. Shifting his ground somewhat, Isaac answers that God has merely watched the long history of man's injustices until "He used a simple egg to discover to them a new world where a nation of people could be founded in humility and pity and sufferance and pride of one to another" (p. 258). In this new world, old Carothers did own the land because God permitted it. God saw the land "already accursed . . . already tainted" by slavery before any white man brought it to the new world (pp. 258–59). Isaac suggests that "maybe" God chose old Carothers as "the seed progenitive of the three generations He saw it would take to set at least some of His lowly people free" (p. 259).

When, almost parenthetically, McCaslin identifies "these lowly people" as the "sons of Ham" (p. 260), Isaac, apparently in a reference to Noah's curse (Genesis 9:25) upon the sons of Ham as "a servant of servants shall he be unto his brethren," answers that the men who wrote the Bible were "sometime liars" even though they were trying to tell the truth, what "the heart already knows" (p. 260).

Returning to Isaac's remark that it would take three generations to set some of these lowly people free, McCaslin cites as exceptions Uncle Buck and Uncle Buddy and "a thousand other Bucks and Buddies" who knew the truth of the heart, "not to mention 1865" (p. 261). The conversation breaks off at this point and does not resume until twenty pages later (p. 282). In the meantime, Isaac thinks about the plantation ledgers kept by Uncle Buck (his father) and Uncle Buddy "in which was recorded the injustice and a little at least of its amelioration and restitution" (p. 261). Isaac knew that as soon as their father old Carothers was buried, they moved out of his unfinished "almost barnlike edifice" (p. 262) into a one-room log cabin, gave all the slaves their freedom at night, and gradually began to "amortize" the injustice to the Negroes. A group of these entries, contained in a long parenthesis, recounts the humorous story of Percival Brownlee.

Imperceptibly, Faulkner moves the reader to a point where he seems to be actually looking over Isaac's shoulder at the bare facts of McCaslin family history in the ledger entries that reveal the suicide of Eunice, old Carothers' slave, six months before the birth of her grandson Tomey's Turl. Abruptly, Faulkner writes about Isaac: "Then he was sixteen

271

[1883]. He knew what he was going to find before he found it" (p. 268). The reader moves backward in time with Isaac until both read the actual entry about the death of Tomasina and the birth of Tomey's Turl with the reference to old Carothers' will, that is, the legacy provided Tomey's Turl. According to Isaac's conjectures, which remind one of Quentin Compson's probing of history in *Absalom, Absalom!*, old Carothers had bought Eunice in New Orleans for immoral purposes and, a quarter of a century later, had forced their daughter Tomasina to commit incest with him.

After the reader has studied with Isaac the ledger entries about the birth of Tomey's Turl's children, he learns about Isaac's abortive trip into Tennessee in 1885 to deliver old Carothers' legacy to Tennie's Jim, an action recorded in the ledgers by Isaac himself. The reader also witnesses the confrontation between McCaslin and Fonsiba's fiancé and later between Isaac and Fonsiba's husband in 1886. Finally, the omniscient author informs the reader that in 1895, when Isaac was living in Jefferson, Lucas demanded his part of old Carothers' legacy.

For many readers, this long interruption in the conversation between Isaac and McCaslin seems needlessly confused narrative; but to those who pursue it with diligence and patience, it conveys the basic information that lies behind Isaac's attitude. If *Go Down, Moses* is to have any unity, a large measure of it must come from this recital of the tragedies in the McCaslin family. The horror and moral wrongs of slavery are brought home to Isaac through the sexual immorality of his grandfather; but no immediately satisfactory solutions to the problems created by the historical past for both white and Negro seem apparent.

The children of Tomey's Turl, each in his or her own way, seek to implement their constitutional freedom. Tennie's Jim simply vanishes northward. Fonsiba marries a Northern Negro who has come South and who considers himself free. Together they move to Arkansas to live off his pension, Fonsiba's legacy, and what they can earn from farming. When he meets Fonsiba, Isaac finds her no longer the person he has known all his life. "We are seeing a new era," her husband tells Isaac, "an era dedicated . . . to freedom, liberty and equality for all, to which this country will be the new Canaan" (p. 279). But Isaac instantly retorts: "Freedom from what? From work? Canaan?" (The sharp exchange between the two men reminds one not only of the persistence of the Puritan

272

analogy with the Israelites but also of Granny Millard's conversations with the Negroes fleeing towards their "homemade Jordan" in *The Unvanquished*.) Nine years later, in 1895, on his twenty-first birthday, Lucas demands his inheritance; and the reader already knows that his solution will be to remain on the plantation, manufacture and sell moonshine whiskey, and farm, charging his supplies and equipment to his account at the commissary, an account he never even thinks about paying. Like old Carothers, Lucas takes for himself whatever he can. What unites Isaac with Tennie's Jim, Fonsiba, and Lucas is that they have all endeavored to sever connections—repudiate?—with the past by proclaiming their "freedom." Their efforts to translate this freedom into action have alienated them from the society of which they are a part and from which, paradoxically, they all (except perhaps Tennie's Jim, about whom the reader has no information) receive support—Fonsiba by her husband's pension from his father and her own monthly pension from her legacy, Lucas by his legacy and the generosity of Roth Edmonds, and Isaac by his monthly income from McCaslin. But only Isaac has learned from the experience: as omniscient author, Faulkner writes that by 1895 Isaac "found long since that no man is ever free and probably could not bear it if he were" (p. 281).

When the conversation between Isaac and McCaslin finally resumes (p. 282), where it had left off (p. 261), McCaslin again reminds Isaac that there were men in the South like Uncle Buck and Uncle Buddy who had tried to right the wrongs of slavery and there was also "1865." But Isaac says they were not enough; nevertheless, if God could see the Bucks and Buddies, He could also see Isaac, "an Isaac born into a later life than Abraham's and repudiating immolation: fatherless and therefore safe declining the altar because maybe this time the exasperated Hand might not supply the kid" (p. 283). Although the allusion links Isaac with the biblical story, the link seems essentially negative. Actually, Isaac McCaslin's similarities to his Old Testament counterpart are very tenuous, for most of the biblical story applies to other characters. In the biblical story, Isaac is viewed primarily as the progenitor of nations. Genesis 25:23 is specific: the Lord said to Isaac's wife: "two nations are in thy womb, and two manner of people shall be separated from thy bowels; and the one people shall be stronger than the other people; and the elder shall serve the younger." Since Faulkner's Isaac is childless, the biblical story hardly seems to apply. It would apply to old Carothers. Moreover, it was Esau, not Isaac, who "despised his birthright" (Genesis 25:34) and became the "cunning hunter" (Genesis 25:27). Perhaps the only link to the biblical story is the negative one to Abraham's sacrifice, since it fits McCaslin's word for Isaac's action: *Escape.*

In Isaac's view of history, God saw that the continent He had created as a refuge and sanctuary for freedom was controlled by descendants of slaves, politicians, and manufacturers callous to the sufferings and injustices of slaves in the South. God might have repudiated the entire country except that one illiterate man was simple and crude enough to protest against injustice. Isaac refers to John Brown as the man who lifts "the long ancestral musket down from the deer-horns above the door" (p. 285). According to Isaac in his talk with God, Brown explained his action by saying: "*I am just against the weak because they are niggers being held in bondage by the strong just because they are white*" (p. 285).[10] Isaac concludes that "so He turned once more to this land which He still intended to save" (p. 285).

When McCaslin, in evident amazement, questions whether God had turned His back or turned His face to the South, Isaac answers that God had indeed turned back to the Southerners whose wives, he concedes, had helped the Negro in sickness and in want but that their help was not enough. "*Apparently,*" Isaac quotes God as saying, "*they [Southerners] can learn nothing save through suffering, remember nothing save when underlined in blood*" (p. 286). In reply, McCaslin cites instances of Southern military leaders killed or defeated or acting by chance and asks again if Isaac really thinks God turned his face back to the South. Isaac says, "How else have made them fight?" (p. 287).

Isaac defines *them* with a long list of groups of men in the North and central West, some who had no interest in the plight of slaves, others who sought only material gain for themselves, and still others who may have known the right but would do nothing to make it prevail. Isaac concludes that only the actions of such men as Jackson, Stuart, and Morgan could have made these men fight. "Who else," he asks, "could have declared a war against a power with ten times the area and a hundred times the men . . . except men who could believe that all necessary to conduct a successful war was . . . just love of land and courage—" (pp. 288–89).

Temporarily abandoning narration by direct discourse between Isaac and McCaslin, Faulkner chronicles with intense feeling the woes of the South during Reconstruction, "that dark corrupt and bloody time" (p. 289). The scenes and incidents in this long passage recall portions of *The Unvanquished*. Faulkner mentions the difficulties encountered by three separate groups of people trying to adjust to each other and to new circumstances: the white Southerners who had lost but were no less free to leave the land than those who had gained it; the ex-slaves "upon whom freedom and equality had been dumped overnight and without warning or preparation" and who misused freedom as "human beings always misuse freedom" (p. 289); and those who "followed the battles they themselves had not fought and inherited the conquest they themselves had not helped to gain" (p. 290). This last group, composed of the sons of middle-aged army quartermaster lieutenants, army sutlers, and army contractors would compete a generation hence with Negroes on "small sloven farms" and in the third generation would become barbers, garage mechanics, deputy sheriffs, mill or gin workers, and power-plant firemen and lead lynching mobs of hooded men. With them, Faulkner includes "that other nameless horde of speculators in human misery, manipulators of money and politics and land" (pp. 290–91) and the Jew who comes seeking a place to establish his descendants.

Although McCaslin had actually witnessed these men and events, Isaac, even when approaching eighty, would not be able to distinguish precisely which of them he had seen or merely heard about. In words that again remind one of *The Unvanquished*, Faulkner describes the South after the war as "a lightless and gutted and empty land where women crouched with the huddled children behind locked doors and men armed in sheets and masks rode the silent roads and the bodies of white and black both . . . swung from lonely limbs" (p. 291). McCaslin had seen men shot dead in polling booths and known an illiterate ex-slave named Sickymo who became a United States marshal (a slightly different version of Cassius Q. Benbow in "Skirmish at Sartoris" in *The Unvanquished*).

In the McCaslin commissary ledgers, the entries containing old and new names recorded the history of the entire South. Among the older names is that of Percival Brownlee. This "tragic and miscast" slave (p. 292), who could neither farm nor keep books, in 1862 conducted revival meetings among the slaves, disappeared, then reappeared leading a raiding party of Federal cavalry, and finally passed through Jefferson in the "entourage" of an army paymaster. Twenty years later, by chance, McCaslin heard of Brownlee as the wealthy proprietor of a New Orleans brothel. The ledgers also contained the names of Tennie's Jim, who disappeared; Fonsiba, who moved to Arkansas; and Lucas, who remained.

By 1888, twenty-three years after the surrender and twenty-four after emancipation, the ledgers can be read as a chronicle history of the entire South. More than anything else, they tell the story of the Negro's bondage to the land through the slow outward trickle of commissary supplies that returns each year during the fall as cotton (pp. 293–94); the passage repeats the observation made earlier (pp. 255–56). Isaac predicts that the Negroes will not always be bound to the land because "they will endure" and "they will outlast us" (p. 294). He adds: "They are better than we are. Stronger than we." Isaac names as Negro vices, "aped from white men . . . improvidence and intemperance and evasion" (p. 294), and McCaslin adds promiscuity, violence, instability and lack of control, and "inability to distinguish between mine and thine" (p. 294). Their virtues are seen as endurance and "pity and tolerance and forbearance and fidelity and love of children" (p. 295). Isaac implies that some of these virtues the Negroes had "already from the old free fathers a longer time free than us because we have never been free" (p. 295).

Instead of pursuing the idea of the white man's bondage, Faulkner, with only a slight transition, brings the reader back to an incident that took place seven years earlier and was recorded in section two of "The Bear." Confronting the old bear twice with guns in hand, Isaac and Sam Fathers failed to shoot (pp. 211–12). Afterwards, Sam Fathers told McCaslin about the incident. Now, in 1888, McCaslin endeavors to explain why Isaac did not shoot the bear; but for the most part, McCaslin's explanation explains little. In the lines that McCaslin cites from "Ode on a Grecian Urn," Keats is calling attention to the frozen motion of the figures on the urn. The youth cannot leave his song, the trees can never be bare of leaves, the lover though close to his goal can never kiss his beloved, and forever will he love and forever she be fair. Presumably, though one cannot be certain, Isaac wanted the yearly pageant of the hunt, the annual rendezvous with the bear, to continue on and on. To kill the bear would be to end the ritual. (He should have hated and feared Lion.) The figures on the urn have permanence, just as Isaac wanted the old bear (and the wilderness he symbolizes) to have permanence. Truth, says McCaslin, has permanence; like the figures on the urn, it does not change; and it covers all those qualities that Isaac learned in the wilderness: "*all things which touch the heart—honor and pride and pity and justice and courage and love*" (p. 297). At the end of the passage, McCaslin repeats this statement with slight variation: "*Courage and honor and pride, and pity and love of justice and of liberty. They all touch the heart, and what the heart holds to becomes truth, as far as we know truth.*" The passage recalls Isaac's earlier statement that "there is only one truth and it covers all things that touch the heart" (p. 260). Ultimately, Isaac's repudiation of his inheritance, as well as his priesthood to the wilderness, is a matter of the heart; but for most readers, Faulkner has not succeeded here in making Isaac's errand into the wilderness explain his rejection of the past. In the remaining paragraphs devoted to this lengthy conversation, Faulkner continues to wrestle with the problem.

The discussion approaches its climax. Once more McCaslin refers to the curse that Isaac has said (p. 278) lies upon the land and the people. The curse falls upon the "whole edifice intricate and complex and founded upon injustice and erected by ruthless rapacity and carried on even yet with at times downright savagery" (p. 298), yet that edifice is "solvent and efficient and . . . not only still intact but enlarged." Isaac repudiates it all. "I am free," he declares (p. 299). In the crucial passage that follows, McCaslin returns to Isaac's earlier idea of having been chosen by God to complete the work Uncle Buck and Uncle Buddy had only begun:

> "Chosen . . . out of all your time by Him. . . . And it took Him a bear and an old man and four years just for you. And it took you fourteen years to reach that point and about that many, maybe more, for Old Ben, and more than seventy for Sam Fathers. And you are just one. How long then? How long?" and he
>
> "It will be long. . . ." and McCaslin
>
> "And anyway, you will be free.—No, not now nor ever, we from them nor they from us. So I repudiate too. I would deny even if I knew it were true. I would have to. Even you can see that I could do no else. I am what I am; I will be always what I was born and have always been." (pp. 299–300)

For the moment at least, McCaslin appears to accept the notion that when Ikkemotubbe realized that he could sell the land "it ceased forever to have been his" (p. 300). Upon this assumption, McCaslin argues that the land belonged to Sam Fathers and that Isaac inherited from Sam Fathers; but this premise had already been refuted by the course of history after man's dispossession of Eden and by the specific statements of both men made at the very beginning of their long discussion that old Carothers did own the land (p. 258). To this strange line of reasoning, Isaac replies: "Yes. Sam Fathers set me free." Thus, since they have ruled out the inheritance of land, all Isaac could have inherited from Sam Fathers was a priesthood in a vanishing wilderness and a sense of freedom from participation in the "economic edifice" that is built upon landownership. To that degree, Isaac could be called the "spiritual heir" of Sam Fathers; but, as Isaac's subsequent life would demonstrate, this legacy would prove a rather empty affair. Isaac's errand into the wilderness should have prepared him for entrance into life rather than for a repudiation or escape from it.

The accounts of Isaac's legacy from Uncle Hubert and of his marriage seem widely removed from the explanation of his inheritance from old Carothers. The fact that his legacy proves to be a tin coffeepot full of IOUs and a handful of coppers instead of a loving cup filled with gold coins makes it hardly comparable to the plantation inheritance Isaac repudiated and the legacies Lucas and Fonsiba received at twenty-one. Rather, the pot and its worthless contents seem more a commentary upon the slow deterioration of a simple but indomitable old man than upon Isaac. But in the end, Faulkner through McCaslin offers the worthlessness of this legacy as the reason why Isaac must accept "as a loan" (p. 308) the monthly payment (or pension) from the economic "edifice" symbolized by the plantation which he has relinquished or repudiated but from which he continues to draw his sustenance. He resembles Fonsiba's husband, who, like Isaac, proclaimed his freedom but also drew his pension.

Isaac's marriage again forces him to choose between the plantation and his freedom. The wife, who now takes McCaslin's role, wants him to assume his position on the plantation; but Isaac, who has taken up the carpenter's tools after the manner of the Nazarene, refuses to go back, even at the cost of his wife and the possibility of an heir. As he concludes, "I cant. Not ever" (p. 314), he thinks: *"She is lost. She was born lost. We were all born lost."* The cry has much more in common with his earlier

278

verdict upon the land and the South than with his ringing declaration: "I am free." Here, at the conclusion of the long fourth section, Isaac himself seems more "lost" than his wife.

Throughout the long discussion between Isaac and McCaslin in the fourth section of "The Bear," the past, or history, remains the pivot upon which their thinking turns. Stretching so far back as the dispossession of Adam from the Garden of Eden, the only true paradise man has ever known, history—or their interpretation of it—shapes the attitudes of these two men as Isaac tries to explain his repudiation of his inheritance. Their talk focuses upon a single aspect of man's history—his freedom and his bondage. Quite properly, in view of the position he will ultimately reach, Isaac associates landownership with human bondage. The moment man assumed that he owned land, argues Isaac, that moment he was enslaved to it; yet without landownership, civilization or, for that matter, history, would be unthinkable. (Just as landownership may destroy Eden but create civilization, so the destruction of the wilderness becomes a prerequisite to civilization.) After some debate, both Isaac and McCaslin agree upon the fact of landownership.

They also agree that the Civil War and emancipation brought only partial freedom. The land was still owned, and the economic system, for which neither man has an alternative, inevitably binds man to the land. Although McCaslin does not make the statement explicitly, he could have observed, as he implies, that the plantation owner is no less bound to the land than the poor white and the Negro whose "furnishings" return as cotton.

At this point, Isaac begins to delude himself. Having a clear insight into the bondage inherent in the economic "edifice" of the plantation, he imagines that God—and Sam Fathers—has set him free from the entire system; he even goes farther to assert that God has chosen him to be a messiah to lead others to freedom. Like Fonsiba's husband, Isaac believes that he is forever free; though, unlike Fonsiba's husband, Isaac knows that the millenium will not arrive for a long time. But instead of becoming the messiah, Isaac seeks to escape from the economic system. Yet repudiate it as he will, he cannot free himself from either it or the past. Isaac's *"fifty dollars a month"* (p. 108), like the legacies, or pensions, or inheritances of McCaslin, Fonsiba, her husband, Tennie's Jim, and Lucas, testifies convincingly to the fact that the present is inextricably interwoven with the past. Not a single one of these characters is free from history, because they all depend for sustenance upon what was created in the past and continues into the present and future. In effect, they are all pensioners of history. Isaac's emotional cry "I am free" must give place to his more considered awareness that "no man is ever free and probably could not bear it if he were." He could not bear his freedom because he could not be free and live in society.

Isaac and McCaslin should be seen as two Southerners, men of good will, trying to analyze and perhaps to remedy the sufferings arising out of the legacy of slavery in the South. Upon many of the basic premises, they both agree. In "The Old People," Isaac is permitted to see with Sam Fathers a vision of the great antlered buck whom Sam Fathers addresses as "Chief . . . Grandfather." As Isaac matures, he becomes the idealist who has felt deeply, emotionally, imaginatively, personally, the sexual wrongs of slavery and seen the continuing economic bondage of the Negro. In his anger and frustration, he wants to wash his hands of the entire affair. Even before his cousin, however, McCaslin has also learned from Sam Fathers and seen the great antlered buck: "So did I. Sam took me in there once after I killed my first deer" (p. 187). And no less than Isaac, McCaslin has learned the importance of the heart, the *bona natura*, in right living. It is McCaslin, moreover, who explains to Isaac the relationship between the heart and truth and the importance in life of *"honor and pride and pity and justice and courage and love."* Though touched with a degree of Isaac's idealism, McCaslin seems to have his feet upon the ground as he views the present realistically. The wilderness experience may have taught Isaac the perception of the wrongs of slavery, but it did not lead him to an understanding of what must be accomplished in the present to eradicate injustice. The truths of the heart must be translated into the life of action.

In the end, McCaslin, not Isaac, utters the most profound truth that Faulkner asserts in *Go Down, Moses*. Speaking specifically of white-Negro relations but with application to the interdependence of man in society, McCaslin denies that Isaac will ever be free: "No, not now nor ever, we from them nor they from us." What McCaslin saw and Isaac did not see is that one cannot repudiate or relinquish his inheritance; like the past or history, a man's inheritance will always be with him, a burden for good or evil that he must bear. Although both men saw that evil and injustice cannot be eradicated overnight, McCaslin also understood that only by each individual shouldering his responsibilities is there any hope for the future. Race relations, better still, human relations, begin with the communication between one man and another.

Faulkner might appropriately have concluded "The Bear" either with the funeral of Sam Fathers or with the conversation in the commissary between Isaac and McCaslin. The deaths of Old Ben and Sam Fathers in section three "finished" the story of the great bear hunt, and in section four the novelist had done what he could to unite Isaac's errand into the wilderness with man's injustice to his fellowmen. But Faulkner may have felt that since the fourth section was, to a degree at least, an intrusion into the hunting story, he should return to the wilderness for the final scene. (The matter becomes even more enigmatic when one recalls that in "Delta Autumn" Faulkner brings the reader and Isaac back to the wilderness for yet another occasion.) Moreover, Faulkner's choice of the time-setting for the fifth section is equally puzzling. One wonders why he chronicled Isaac's return to the wilderness three years before the conversation in the commissary, since, presumably, anything Isaac experienced or learned in his visit to the woods in 1885 would have been reflected in his explanation of his repudiation of his inheritance in 1888. The fact is that for many readers, section five, which continues chronologically section three, seems in no way dependent upon section four. Possibly, Faulkner wished to have the commissary conversation take place in Isaac's twenty-first year, since at that time he would enter his majority and inherit the plantation. If this conjecture be true, perhaps Faulkner also felt that despite the date of the final episode, the reader would conclude the story with Isaac in the wilderness and, thus, in effect, ignored the time sequence and the problems it presents; but it is no wonder that Faulkner omitted the fourth section when he printed "The Bear" in *Big Woods*. Without it, sections of "The Bear" are mainly in chronological order.

More than anything else, the final scene of "The Bear" underscores the eventual destruction of the wilderness. Isaac, "co-heir" of Sam Fathers, moves unerringly to the dried mutilated paw of Old Ben above Lion's grave and to the tree which had supported the platform for Sam's body. Pausing only a moment, he quits the knoll "which was no abode of the dead because there was no death, not Lion and not Sam: not held fast in earth but free in earth and not in earth but of earth" (p. 328). But even as he realizes the immortality of nature, he encounters the snake, that ancient symbol of evil that first appeared in the Garden of Eden but has continued throughout the ages as part of man's ancestry. With the same words that Sam Fathers had used years before to address the great antlered buck (p. 184), Isaac greets the snake: "Chief . . . Grandfather" (p. 330). Isaac recognizes that the snake, as well as man's knowledge of it, remains a part of his heritage from Eden.

As Isaac moves through the woods, he hears the sound of Boon hammering the barrel of his dismembered gun, with which he has never been able to shoot anything, against its breech. Unable to grasp the philosophical significance of the doomed woods and the meaning of Sam Fathers and Old Ben, Boon, the plebian, nevertheless, instinctively knows what is happening to the wilderness. Coheir with Isaac to Sam Fathers, Boon sits with his back against the solitary old gum tree, protecting it and its population of squirrels and shouting: "Get out of here! Dont touch them! Dont touch a one of them! They're mine!" (p. 331). The tableaulike setting of Boon's outcry provides an artistically satisfying conclusion to the hunting and wilderness episodes of "The Bear."

In "Delta Autumn," Faulkner prolongs the earlier hunting stories by taking Isaac back into the wilderness for a final hunt, yet the only hunting that occurs takes place offstage; and the final comment, "It was a doe" (p. 365), has force mainly as a double entendre relating to the white-Negro relations theme. There seems no compelling necessity for the encounter between Isaac and the Negro woman taking place in a wilderness setting, and once again the doom of the wilderness and Isaac's memories of his boyhood experiences with Sam Fathers have only a tenuous connection with the racial problem presented by the Negro woman. Nearing eighty, Isaac himself cannot logically relate the two matters any better than he could at twenty-one, when he tried to explain to McCaslin why he repudiated his inheritance.

"Delta Autumn," nevertheless, may have been intended by Faulkner to serve as an epilogue to "The Bear." In that story, Old Ben and Sam Fathers died in 1883, and the commissary conversation took place in 1888, when Isaac was twenty-one. "Delta Autumn," however, takes place in 1941, almost the same time as "The Fire and the Hearth." Roth Edmonds has replaced McCaslin as the owner of the plantation. In the years intervening since old Carothers' death and even Isaac's boyhood, circumstances have altered considerably.

When he read the ledgers in the commissary, Isaac had been outraged by his mental picture of old Carothers' power to force his Negro slave woman into sexual relations with him and then to force their own daughter into incest with him. His crime was not only slavery and miscegenation but also incest. In 1941 Roth Edmonds, old Carothers' descendant, has a child by an unnamed Negro woman; and when she declares that her grandfather was Tennie's Jim, the white and Negro branches of the McCaslin family are again joined sexually. But the circumstances are vastly different. Incest is hardly an issue. The Negro granddaughter of Tennie's Jim would have been, by her account, a fourth cousin of Roth; and, since their great-great-great-grandmothers were not the same, even initially they would have been only half cousins. Unlike old Carothers, Roth had no knowledge of any relationship; in fact, if any incest is alleged in this instance, the Negro woman may be more guilty than Roth because she knew of the kinship and he did not. Moreover, whereas old Carothers had only to summon the woman to him, the relationship between Roth and his mistress has been a wholly voluntary affair. In her account of their liaison, she makes it clear that "I knew what I was doing" (p. 358).

To Isaac the woman reveals the whole sordid affair. She and Roth begin their relationship out of sexual desire, and for Roth it never becomes anything else. But the woman evidently wants it to be more than a temporary liaison. Though by no means an uneducated person, she has difficulty explaining her feelings and her purpose in coming. She knew "to begin with" (p. 358) that Roth would never marry her. They "agreed" again and again before he left New Mexico (p. 358). "I even wrote him last month," she says, "to make sure again and the letter came back unopened and I was sure. So I left the hospital and rented myself a room to live in until the deer season opened so I could make sure myself and I was waiting beside the road yesterday when your car passed and he saw me and so I was sure" (p. 359). But she has come to make "sure" again. In a reference to Isaac's wife, who wanted Isaac to resume his place as head of the plantation, Faulkner has already commented upon the situation of the Negro woman: "But women hope for so much. They never live too long to still believe that anything within the scope of their passionate wanting is likewise within the range of their passionate hope" (p. 352).

Although the woman's conversation with Isaac follows no logical sequence and several of her remarks seem to have no clear reference, she makes a case against Isaac. When Isaac asks her what she wanted or expected when she came, she replies, "Yes" (p. 359). After she has revealed her identity, Isaac repeats his question, and she answers, "Nothing" (p. 361). In the meantime, she has accused Isaac of spoiling Roth by giving his grandfather land that did not belong to him. Just how this act spoiled Roth she does not explain; neither does she explain how Lucas and Mollie also spoiled Roth. (Her judgment of Isaac may be as far off the mark as Lucas' earlier judgment had been.) She has also asserted that she would have made a man of Roth; but if Roth has not reached manhood at forty-three, he seems likely to be beyond reform. However vague her remarks may be, she scores a point when Isaac asks her if she does not have "folks" to look after her. She replies, "yes" and mentions her aunt (p. 360), who has been looking after her for the past two years since her father died in Indianapolis. Isaac (and Faulkner's readers) would know that "folks" might include the McCaslin family, even Isaac himself, though Isaac has never heard of her before. Her mention of her relationship to Tennie's Jim also awakens in Isaac's consciousness the memory of his unsuccessful journey into Tennessee to locate Tennie's Jim and deliver to him old Carothers' legacy—the legacy later put in Lucas' keeping. Against this background, her answer, "Nothing," to Isaac's repeated question, "what do you expect here?" (p. 361), reveals her hostility to the old man but still leaves unanswered her reason for coming.

Although she has not asked for help and Isaac has no power to alter her situation, he gives to her the hunting horn left him by General Compson. For him, it has great value; it symbolizes his lifetime devotion to the wilderness; and it is a symbolic fulfillment of his effort to deliver the legacy to Tennie's Jim. To the Negro woman, it means nothing, and she perfunctorily responds, "Oh, . . . Yes. Thank you" (p. 363). As he gives the horn, he suggests that she do what she has already said she was going to do, that is, go back North. He adds that she should marry a man of her own race and forget Roth. Her reply shows the intensity of her anger at Isaac's advice: "Old man . . . have you lived so long and forgotten so much that you dont remember anything you ever knew or felt or even heard about love?" (p. 363). Although from her angle of vision, Isaac has unfeelingly dismissed her love for Roth, from his perspective, he has suggested the best course of action open to her.

Despite Isaac's earlier statement that "most men are a little better than their circumstances give them a chance to be" (p. 345) and that at the moment of procreation the man and the woman "together were God" (p. 348), Isaac would repudiate both Roth and the woman. To a degree, he still is trying to "escape" the racial issue, but he has also learned some practical judgments. He knows that Roth has no intention of marrying her, a fact that the woman readily admits. Isaac knows too that in 1941, and "maybe for a long while yet," the mores of Southern society—and Northern too—do not sanction interracial marriages. For that, he says, "we will have to wait" (p. 363). In the long run, it would be best for her to forget Roth; and however much he deplored their conduct, there was little else he could say. Oddly enough, his practical advice sounds more like McCaslin than Isaac.

In terms of the white-Negro relationship theme in *Go Down, Moses*, "Delta Autumn" shows once more that no man can ever free himself from the burden of history. Despite Isaac's idealism and good intentions in renouncing his inheritance because of old Carothers' treatment of his Negro slaves, and despite the fact that had Isaac not repudiated his inheritance Roth and the Negro woman might still have carried on their affair, Isaac did make a mistake in thinking he could free himself from racial problems created before he was born or from an economic system upon which he and his society depended for the necessities of life. His conversation with the woman affirms the truth of McCaslin's prophetic remark that whites and Negroes are not now and never will be free of each other so long as they both live in the same society.

"Go Down, Moses"

In her old age, Mammy Callie Barr, who had been a member of the Faulkner family ever since the novelist could remember, continued to live in the small house behind Rowan Oak. Her age uncertain but surely more than ninety, her body frail but her hearing and vision still good, she had many friends of both races in Oxford. She took her meals in the kitchen of Rowan Oak, came and went as she pleased, and spent much of her time with Jill, Faulkner's daughter. Late in January, 1940, Mammy Callie suffered a stroke and a few days later died. On Sunday, February 4, a number of her friends, both Negro and white, gathered in the parlor at Rowan Oak for private services. At Faulkner's request, a choral group from Oxford's three Negro churches stood around the casket and sang several songs, including "Swing Low, Sweet Chariot," and Faulkner spoke feelingly of her life of devotion and service. After public services at the Negro Baptist Church, she was buried in St. Peter's Cemetery. Later Faulkner placed a marker above her grave with the following inscription: "Callie Barr Clark, 1840–1940, Mammy, Her white children bless her." In dedicating *Go Down, Moses* to her, Faulkner wrote: "To Mammy Caroline Barr, Mississippi, who was born in slavery and who gave to my family a fidelity without stint or calculation of recompense and to my childhood an immeasurable devotion and love."

Mammy Callie Barr is the prototype of Mollie Worsham in "Go Down, Moses." Written in the months following her death, the story, together with the dedication of the volume, is Faulkner's deeply felt tribute to Mammy Callie. Because he had experienced her in life before he realized her in fiction, Faulkner would have sharply resented those who would dismiss her as a sentimentalized "Aunt Jemima" stereotype. In 1940, out of his own personal experience, Faulkner would have vigorously affirmed that trusting and affectionate relationships could and did exist between whites and Negroes in the South. Just as he considered Mammy Callie a member of his family, so he probably felt that Mollie Worsham's place in Miss Worsham's home was both plausible and artistically acceptable because it had its prototype in the actuality he had known. Such racial relationships in the South, however, would change. Seventeen years later, during the integration crisis in Little Rock, he could write the editor of the New York *Times*, "this is the fact that white people and Negroes do not like and trust each other, and perhaps never can" (October 13, 1957). With allowance made for the emotions stirred by the Little Rock affair, the comment reflects the polarization of racial issues and their removal from private relationships to the more impersonal atmosphere of political forums and governmental programs. In the decades following Mammy Callie's death, the plot of "Go Down, Moses" probably would not have been possible, because not only were the Mammy Callies dying out but also the return of Butch's body would probably have been accomplished by some impersonal governmental agency. In 1940 Mammy Callie Barr and her fictional counterpart, as well as Gavin Stevens and the editor, may have been anachronisms, but they were still realities in small Southern towns like Oxford, Mississippi.

If in some private way Faulkner associated the song "Go Down, Moses" with Mammy Callie, his use of it for the title of the story and subsequently the book would be understandable. Otherwise, the title seems to apply only indirectly to the story. The primary biblical allusion is Mollie's repeated reference to her "Benjamin" having been sold into Egypt. Actually, Mollie confuses the accounts of Joseph and Benjamin. The sons of Jacob sold their brother Joseph to Pharoah for twenty pieces of silver (Genesis 37:27–28). Later, after Joseph had attained a high place in Pharaoh's kingdom, he demanded that the brothers bring Benjamin, their father's youngest son, with them when they return to buy corn; but Jacob was fearful to send Benjamin "lest peradventure mischief befall him" (Genesis 42:4) and "ye bring down my gray hairs with sorrow to the grave" (Genesis 42:38). Gavin Stevens starts to deny that Roth Edmonds has "sold" Mollie's grandson, Samuel "Butch" Worsham, but stops when the lawyer realizes that Mollie "*cant hear*" or, rather, is beyond convincing.

About the wider implications of "Go Down, Moses," readers have never fully agreed. In telling the story, Faulkner provides only a minimum of information about Butch's parentage, upbringing, and subsequent career in theft, the numbers racket, and murder; instead, Faulkner has concentrated upon the efforts of Mollie to locate the boy and the actions of various white characters to satisfy her wishes. Very plausible arguments have been made that Gavin Stevens, Miss Worsham, Mr Wilmoth, the merchants in the square, and even Roth Edmonds are motivated by a feeling that Butch was a member of the community and that their actions express community feeling. This interpretation receives powerful support from Miss Worsham's remark that "it's our grief" (p. 381), *our* being taken to mean the entire community rather than applying only to Mollie, Hamp, and herself. Perhaps influenced somewhat by later sociological emphasis upon "the black community" or "the white community," readers may have been perhaps too ready to read "community" into the action. Actually, there is not much interaction between whites and Negroes in the story. Except for Mollie and her brother, the characters are almost all white. Mollie talks only about "my boy" and "my Benjamin" (p. 371). Gavin Stevens does not make his plea for donations in terms of any regard of the community for Butch; rather, Gavin Stevens says, "It's to bring a dead nigger home. It's for Miss Wor-

sham" (p. 378). He acts primarily out of a sense of duty as county attorney and his regard for Mollie and Miss Worsham. The whole affair
remains an individual matter, and only in the widest sense can the story
be viewed as an interracial community action. Either interpretation,
however, would support the view that Faulkner intended the story not
only to honor Mammy Callie but also to exemplify the kind of goodwill
and respect, even affection, that could and upon occasion did exist in a
small Southern town. In writing the story, Faulkner may have idealized
somewhat the portrait of Mollie as he thought about the life of Mammy
Callie and his feelings for her, but his choice of the story to conclude *Go
Down, Moses* indicates that he was willing for this story to represent his
final word about white–Negro relations in this volume.

Chapter X

Yoknapatawpha
and the American Tradition

ALMOST forty years have elapsed since the publication of *Go Down, Moses*. During this time the literary reputation of William Faulkner has enjoyed a spectacular growth. From the unenviable position of a writer whose major works were out of print, he has become the most important American writer of this century. The record of his acceptance among academic critics has been without parallel. Admiration for his writing has become so fervent that to many of his followers every word he wrote has become sacred. His weaknesses have been ingeniously turned into virtues, and voices of dissent have been virtually silenced. In recent years, young scholars seeking dissertation topics have turned increasingly to the examination of the genesis and textual history and manuscript versions of even the most minor of his writings, while the academic press has made available many of the most ephemeral of his published and unpublished work replete with critical introductions that on occasion are longer than the pieces themselves. From the multitude of such publications, the uninformed Faulkner reader might well conclude that such pieces as *Mayday*, *Marionettes*, *The Uncollected Stories*, and *Mississippi Poems* are among his greatest works. For the Faulkner expert, the collector, and perhaps the literary historian, the publication of such materials is immensely worthwhile, but the attention given them should not even temporarily distract Faulkner's public from those works that form the heart of his genuine contribution to American literature.

In the preceding chapters of this volume, the discussions of Faulkner's nine major books published between 1929 and 1942 have suggested certain conclusions about his work as a whole. Viewed from today's perspective of literary history, Faulkner must be recognized as primarily a traditional novelist and not a radical innovator in the form. One has only to review the major novelists of the nineteenth century to find other writers who handled the same or similar themes and subject matter. Faulkner's use of fiction, for example, to dramatize problems of his native region in the perspective of the past has precedent in earlier American novels. James Fenimore Cooper had chronicled the settlement of upper New York state; Nathaniel Hawthorne had tested nineteenth-century transcendental philosophy in terms of the New England Puritan seventeenth century; and Ellen Glasgow had written brilliantly the social history of Virginia in more than a dozen volumes of fiction. In Faulkner's studies of the rise and fall of great families in the South, he had antecedents in such works as Edith Wharton's stories of little old New York and William Dean Howells' *The Son of Royal Langbrith*, *The Rise of Silas Lapham*, and his volumes recording the lives of the March family. Long before Sherwood Anderson counseled Faulkner to write about north Mississippi and its people, Hamlin Garland in *Crumbling Idols* (1894) had urged young artists to write about their own localities and to reach the universal through the local. Sarah Orne Jewett had taken Garland's advice and passed it along to Willa Cather, who returned to her native middle border to rediscover the Red Cloud of her youth very much as Faulkner later found his own Yoknapatawpha County. In his use of characters who appear in one work and reappear in others and in the creation of a fictional world corresponding to historical reality, Faulkner had American predecessors in James Fenimore Cooper's Leatherstocking Tales, in William Gilmore Simms's border and revolutionary romances, and in Francis Marion Crawford's multivolume *Saracinesca* series. About a century before Faulkner began to deal with racial injustice and miscegenation in his fiction, these themes appeared in the novels of Cooper, in James W. Eastburn and Robert C. Sands's *Yamoyden, A Tale of the Wars of King Philip* (1820), and in Lydia Maria Francis Child's *Hobomok, A Tale of Early Times* (1824). Likewise, Faulkner's concern with the tensions of adolescence and a young man's education or initiation into adulthood has a very lengthy American literary tradition dating back at least to Cooper's *The Deerslayer* (1841). To identify Faulkner's subjects and themes as primarily those of the American tradition in fiction is, of course, not to diminish his achievement, but rather to emphasize his "Americanness" as well as his "Southernness."

At the other end of the social ladder from Faulkner's Mississippi aristocrats—the Compsons, the Sartorises, the McCaslins, and the de Spains—are the backwoods farmers like the MacCallums, the "poor whites" like the Bundrens and Snopeses, and the Negroes—Southern characters whose prototypes Faulkner knew in the hills and small towns of his area. He depicted them with great insight, understanding, and, on occasion, compassion. Individualized as they are in Faulkner's stories, they yet have a very respectable literary ancestry dating back to the beginnings of the American novel. Undoubtedly, Hugh Henry Brackenridge in his *Modern Chivalry* (1792–1815) was the first to portray in a humorous and satirical fashion the backwoodsman and other "low-life" characters associated with rural communities along the Pennsylvania frontier. In the South and much closer to Faulkner are the poor whites depicted by the Old Southwest humorists who wrote in the decades before and immediately after the Civil War. Faulkner's Ab Snopes, Flem Snopes, Mink Snopes, Anse Bundren, the Armstids, and others like them may be recognized as the literary descendants of such rough-hewn fictional characters as Augustus Baldwin Longstreet's Ransy Sniffle (*Georgia Scenes*, 1835), William Tappan Thompson's Georgia "cracker" (*Major Jones's Courtship*, 1843), Joseph Glover Baldwin's varied portraits (*The Flush Times of Alabama and Mississippi*, 1853), Johnson Jones Hooper's Captain Simon Suggs and the Reverend Bela Bugg (*Some Adventures of Captain Simon Suggs, Late of the Tallapoosa Volunteers*, 1856), and George Washington Harris' Sut Lovingood (*Sut Lovingood Yarns*, 1867). Somewhat in a class by themselves yet belonging to the Old Southwest humorists group are the volumes by and about Davy Crockett, the most authentic being his autobiography (*A Narrative of the Life of David Crockett of the State of Tennessee, Written by Himself*, 1834). If one were to select a single story to illustrate the line of literary history from the Old Southwest humorists to William Faulkner, an excellent choice would be Longstreet's "The Horse-Swap," which bears comparison with Faulkner's tale of the Pat Stamper–Ab Snopes horse trade (or even the spotted horses story or the poker game for the hand of Miss Sophonsiba), but one could cite many other equally valid examples.

The Old Southwest humorists specialized in the realistic depiction of crude uneducated backwoods figures whose adventures and escapades, even cruelties, were seen as humorous. A central feature of their work was the tall tale, the comic yarn, the short anecdote, that made a "point." Originally the stories were probably transmitted orally, and to-day they are best appreciated when read aloud, a quality that Faulkner's work often shares. To the men who wrote them and to the planters who read them, these yarns about vulgar, low life were not respectable; they certainly did not belong in a lady's drawing room or on the library shelves with the works of such legitimate authors as Cooper and Scott. Often circulated in almost a clandestine fashion, when published they usually appeared first in William T. Porter's sporting magazine, *Spirit of the Times*.

After the Civil War, the local colorists, especially in the South, smoothed the rough edges and removed enough of the crudities of the Old Southwest humorists' material to make their stories acceptable to the editors of Northern literary magazines that became the main publishing outlets available to Southern writers. They added some new fictional types. Mary Noailles Murfree (Charles Egbert Craddock), for example, wrote stories about the Tennessee mountaineers; George Washington Cable featured the Creoles, the freed slaves, slave traders, and plantation aristocrats in fiction that explored racial problems of the Deep South; and Joel Chandler Harris created literary versions in dialect of Negro folklore in his multivolume series of Uncle Remus stories. In their efforts to refine the material of the Old Southwest humorists into stories of reputable literary quality and their expansion of its subject matter, the local-color writers made a valuable contribution to the literary origins of Faulkner's art.

Although recognizably different in social tone and artistic level, the literary traditions of the Old Southwest humorists and the local-color writers merged in the works of Mark Twain and William Faulkner. Both men took over the comic yarn or tall tale, types of character, vernacular speech, at times dialect, humor, and many of the narrative devices of their predecessors. What distinguishes Mark Twain and Faulkner is their ability to transform this kind of material into great literature. Both the Old Southwest humorists and the local-color writers failed to produce enduring literature in large part because they could not or did not embody in their work a profound commentary upon man's humanity. Ultimately, they offered readers a literature limited to the crudities and oddities of a specific area. Country bumpkins, the spiritually impoverished, stupid persons, idiots, degenerates, sexual perverts, and the like are not in themselves the genesis of lasting literature. Anse Bundren, for example, would be perhaps only a momentarily interesting object of literary curiosity had not Faulkner made him representative of the purely naturalistic approach to living; in similar fashion, in the work of a lesser writer than Faulkner, Flem Snopes would probably have remained a local oddity; but in Faulkner's hands, he becomes a splendid example of the impoverishment of man's spirit by the overwhelming power of human greed. One must never forget that Faulkner's worldwide appeal does not rest upon the realities of life in north Mississippi. More than anything else, Faulkner's contribution rests upon what his work says to men everywhere about the life of man in modern times; and just as long as his work has something of value to say to men, his fame and literary stature will endure.

Faulkner's fondness for the tall tale or anecdote, humorous or otherwise, has a bearing upon the form of his fiction. Throughout his fiction, the basis of his art is the single episode. As a result, his books seem to divide into brilliant but very loosely unified stories at times ingeniously yoked together. For example, after reading *The Sound and the Fury*, the reader is likely to remember the work not as a single story but as at least four separate stories relating to the Compson family. Such works as *Sartoris*, *Sanctuary*, *Light in August*, and *Absalom, Absalom!* similarly contain multiple plots, while there is serious question if *The Unvanquished*, *The Hamlet*, and *Go Down, Moses* may not be more properly called volumes of short stories than novels. In Faulkner's great outpouring of superb fiction during the 1930s, perhaps only *As I Lay Dying* was conceived and written as a single story. As has been observed earlier, this work, which Faulkner called a tour de force, is the shortest of all his books.

To see the differences between a novel written according to Faulkner's practice and a work artistically unified by the design of its plot, one has only to compare Nathaniel Hawthorne's *The Scarlet Letter* or Henry James's *The Golden Bowl* with one of Faulkner's Yoknapatawpha volumes. Hawthorne and James strive for a single effect by rigidly subordinating every incident or episode to the design of the whole. In Faulkner's work, an overall design is often difficult to identify, and many of the incidents are only loosely if at all contributory to the design. To phrase the matter in other terms, one could say that Faulkner's fiction in large measure lacks the organic wholeness that marks the novels of Hawthorne and James as well as a central, controlling philosophical idea that can be readily perceived by the reader as he moves forward in the work. In Faulkner's defense, it may be argued that no law of fiction exists to require that a novel possess unity of action or theme, though most American writers throughout the nineteenth century, from Cooper to James, respected this unwritten rule, which descends from their English forerunners of the eighteenth century.

Faulkner's attitude towards the form of his book-length fiction may have been influenced by the ideas of Sherwood Anderson. Although *Poor White* and *Dark Laughter* are fashioned somewhat after the same principles, *Winesburg, Ohio* is the best illustration of Anderson's theories and probably his book most influential upon Faulkner. Discarding conventional notions about a single plot developed organically through cumulative incidents, Anderson begins *Winesburg, Ohio* with a brief definition of the grotesque, which could be said to form a controlling theme for the work. The remainder of the book consists of twenty-three stories, many of which had already been published in *The Seven Arts*, *The Masses*, and *The Little Review*. In the majority of the stories, George Willard, a young reporter, can be said to function as a unifying device; but in the longest of the incidents, "Godliness, a Tale in Four Parts," which Anderson may have originally intended as the core of another novel, Willard is absent. The stories, when taken together as a whole, do delineate the community of Winesburg (in the same way that Faulkner's Yoknapatawpha volumes when taken together delineate the community of Jefferson and its vicinity), but in the sense that Hawthorne or James would have understood a plot of a novel, *Winesburg, Ohio* has no design. It is more a series of stories about a general theme than a novel. Anderson in effect discarded the organic development of a single plot from beginning through complication to conclusion. To a considerable degree, Faulkner's fiction from *Sartoris* through *Go Down, Moses* has affinities with Anderson's theory and practice of fiction.

The foregoing comments are not intended to suggest that Faulkner was wholly unconcerned with the artistic symmetry of his fiction; the much-discussed "counterpoint" feature of his plots, perhaps most notably seen in *Light in August*, does provide an artistic design that seems admirable to many readers. His use of flashbacks and the skillful withholding of information to heighten suspense have been highly praised. But Faulkner's fiction in the decade of the 1930s, particularly after *Absalom, Absalom!*, exhibits a marked tendency toward fragmentation after the pattern of *Winesburg, Ohio*. In his revisions of earlier published stories, Faulkner did work towards shaping the material into a more cohesive form, but in retrospect the revisions seem more in the direction of connecting a series of stories than toward the fashioning of a symmetrical work of art. One cannot but wonder if the pressures of his Hollywood experience and his ever-present need to make his literary work as financially successful as possible, that is, to get the maximum "mileage" out of a given story by selling it first to magazines and later publishing it in book form, did not color Faulkner's notion of what makes a novel. This inference receives support from his willingness to publish work containing internal inconsistencies and discrepancies that he could have easily resolved and his readiness to publish books before his revisions had completely fused his material. The fact is that *The Unvanquished*, *The Hamlet*, and *Go Down, Moses* are needlessly flawed by hasty, even careless workmanship. The blemishes of these volumes, which embody passages of Faulkner's finest writing, are all the more to be regretted, because in them he embodied much of what he had to say to his own time and to the future.

The perspective of literary history today helps Faulkner's reader to grasp the implications of his work far more clearly than they could have been understood in the author's lifetime. Presently, Faulkner's fiction seems more a continuation or logical development from the American nineteenth century than the outpouring of a radical innovator or experimenter. Currently, as in the future, his contribution to American literature rests not so much upon his ideas about artistic form, his narrative skills, the devices of his fiction, or even his stylistic accomplishments— important though these matters are—as it does upon the intensity and sincerity with which he has depicted the complexities of human experience measured by the progression of history. No other writer since Henry James has identified so directly and expressed so forcefully as Faulkner the truths that govern man's success or failure in right living.

As has been suggested earlier in this volume, Faulkner's Yoknapatawpha County, though distinctly Southern, rural, and agricultural, is actually a microcosm of modern times. In this representative fictional world, Faulkner has little to say about such urban matters as labor unions, employer associations, the municipal affairs of large cities, and, except for the production of moonshine whiskey, even less to say about manufacturing. Rather, the principal occupation of Yoknapatawpha County is farming, and its values are essentially agrarian. Although he was not invited to contribute to the attack upon the dehumanizing forces of industrialism launched in 1930 by "Twelve Southerners" in *I'll Take My Stand*, Faulkner would have been sympathetic to their position. Like them, he deplored the materialism that he felt had eroded human values. He saw with dismay the breakdown of parental responsibility in the home, the growth of religious bigotry in the churches, the failure of the courts to dispense justice evenhandedly, and the ever-widening racial division in the community. He chronicled with regret the decay of the leadership exercised by aristocratic men like his own ancestors and their defeat by the rising class of amoral businessmen. Although badly flawed by their arrogance and pride, the aristocrats were, in Faulkner's opinion, preferable to the Snopeses who replaced them in positions of power and influence in the community.

Like many other Southerners of the 1930s, Faulkner held the Southern economic system based upon tenant farming and sharecropping, legacies of the Civil War and its aftermath, responsible for much of the unhappiness and poverty of the South. When administered by dishonest and unscrupulous landowners, the "economic edifice" locked both races into bondage to the land, depressed their living standards, and stifled ambition. Although nominally free, the Negroes (and poor whites) were still bound in a vicious round of debt from which they might never be free. Although Faulkner had great admiration for the endurance and strength of the Negro race, in the 1930s, the decade of the Great Depression, he saw little evidence of immediate change in their prospects for the better.

Harsh and oppressive as the economic system of the South seemed to him and regardless of his awareness of the depths of man's folly and his propensity for evil, Faulkner yet asserted that man could "prevail." Like millions of his countrymen, past and present, Faulkner believed in the possibility of reform and progress. One has only to consider the lives of Jason Compson, Temple Drake, Gail Hightower, Thomas Sutpen, Flem Snopes, and others to understand that Faulkner believed that man's greatest enemy lay within himself and that man must reform himself from within before he can defeat those forces that undermine the quality of his life. Man's pride, hate, self-interest, greed, and willingness to purchase material possessions at the cost of private integrity inhibit his enjoyment of the good life. Insofar as he can, man must replace these traits with the virtues Faulkner names in his Nobel Prize Speech of Acceptance, "the courage and honor and hope and pride and compassion and pity and sacrifice which have been the glory of his past." To Faulkner, these are the verities of human experience. More and more, as time passes, Faulkner emerges as an advocate of traditional humanistic values. At the heart of Yoknapatawpha lies Faulkner's vision of man in a moral universe.

Notes and References

CHAPTER I
The Poles of Historical Measurement: *Sartoris*

[1] William Faulkner to Horace Liveright, October [16, 1927], November 30 [1927], in Joseph Blotner (ed.), *Selected Letters of William Faulkner* (New York: Random House, 1977), 38, 39.

[2] In discussing this essay, Joseph Blotner observes that Faulkner accepted Alfred Harcourt's proposal to publish the book if it were revised and substantial deletions made and that both Faulkner and Wasson made revisions. Near the end of this essay, which concerns the composition of *Sartoris*, Faulkner remarks: " 'The trouble is' he [Ben Wasson] said, 'Is that you had about 6 books in here. You were trying to write them all at once.' He showed me what he meant, what he had done, and I realized for the first time that I had done better than I knew." Although one cannot be certain, Faulkner's statement, taken in its context, suggests that Faulkner eventually saw that he did have six books in the *Sartoris* manuscript and that Wasson's cuts had helped the work. See Joseph Blotner, "William Faulkner's Essay on the Composition of *Sartoris*," *Yale University Library Gazette*, XLVII (1973), 121–24.

[3] Frederick L. Gwynn and Joseph L. Blotner (eds.), *Faulkner in the University: Class Conferences at the University of Virginia, 1957–1958* (Charlottesville: University of Virginia Press, 1959), 285.

[4] The foregoing account of the manuscript of *Sartoris*, is indebted to Stephen Neal Dennis, "The Making of *Sartoris*: A Description and Discussion of the Manuscript and Composite Typescript of William Faulkner's Third Novel" (Ph.D. dissertation, Cornell University, 1969).

[5] Quoted from Blotner, "William Faulkner's Essay on the Composition of *Sartoris*," 123. Material that Faulkner canceled in the manuscript and Blotner has printed in brackets has not been included here.

[6] Thomas Wolfe, *The Story of a Novel* (New York: Charles Scribner's Sons, 1936), 21.

[7] Henry Adams, *Mont-Saint-Michel and Chartres* (Boston: Houghton Mifflin, 1905), 377.

[8] Gwynn and Blotner (eds.), *Faulkner in the University*, 251.

[9] Sartre wrote: "Faulkner's vision of the world can be compared to that of a man sitting in a convertible looking back. At every moment shadows emerge on his right, and on his left flickering and quavering points of light, which become trees, men, and cars only when they are seen in perspective." Jean Paul Sartre, "Time in Faulkner: *The Sound and the*

Notes and References

Fury," in Frederick J. Hoffman and Olga W. Vickery (eds.), *William Faulkner: Three Decades of Criticism* (East Lansing: Michigan State University Press, 1960), 228. Sartre's article originally appeared in *La Nouvelle Revue Française*, June and July, 1939. The translation is by Martine Darmon.

[10] William Faulkner, *Sartoris* (New York: Random House, 1929), 91. Hereinafter, page references to this edition of *Sartoris* will appear in the text within parentheses.

[11] Joseph Blotner, *Faulkner: A Biography* (2 vols.; New York: Random House, 1974), I, 6.

[12] The account of William Clark Falkner's life that follows is based upon Blotner's biography of William Faulkner and upon Donald Philip Duclos, "Son of Sorrow: The Life, Works, and Influence of Colonel William C. Falkner, 1825–1889" (Ph.D. dissertation, University of Michigan, 1961).

[13] Memphis *Appeal*, August 7, 1861.

[14] Quoted by Alexander L. Bondurant in "William C. Falkner, Novelist," *Publications of the Mississippi Historical Society*, III (1900), 117.

[15] Quoted in Blotner, *Faulkner*, I, 220.

[16] Murry C. Falkner, *The Falkners of Mississippi: A Memoir* (Baton Rouge: Louisiana State University Press, 1967), 90–91; quoted in Blotner, *Faulkner*, I, 224–25.

[17] Faulkner's letters to his mother, Mrs. M. C. Falkner, contain several references to the scene in the gardens. "I came back toward home, stopping at the Luxembourg Gardens," he wrote on August 16, "to watch the children sailing boats on the pool. . . . And there was an old old man, bent and rheumatic, sailing a boat too. He hobbled along around the pool, but he couldn't keep up with his boat, so other people would very kindly stop it and send it back across to him." About two weeks later, he inquired, "I wrote you, didn't I, about the old man who sails his boat in the pool in the Luxembourg gardens? He was there bright and early this morning." Early in September, Faulkner remarked: "I have just written such a beautiful thing that I am about to bust—2000 words about the Luxembourg gardens and death. It has a thin thread of plot, about a young woman, and it is poetry though written in prose form." See Blotner (ed.), *Selected Letters*, 12, 15, 17. Echoes of these experiences are reflected in the closing paragraphs of *Sanctuary*: "in the Luxembourg Gardens as Temple and her father passed the women sat knitting in shawls and even the men playing croquet played in coats and capes, and in the sad gloom . . . the dry click of balls, the random shouts of children, had that quality of autumn. . . . They went on, passed the pool where the children and an old man in shabby brown overcoat sailed toy boats."

[18] Faulkner to Mrs. M. C. Falkner, postmarked September 6, 1925, in Blotner (ed.), *Selected Letters*, 18.

[19] *Ibid.*, September 28, October 7, 1925, pp. 26, 28.

[20] For the earlier "exiles," see Malcolm Cowley, *Exile's Return: A Literary Odyssey of the 1920's* (New York: Viking, 1951). For the later group, see Samuel Putnam, *Paris Was Our Mistress: Memoirs of a Lost and Found Generation* (New York: Viking, 1947).

Notes and References

CHAPTER II
The Collapse of Family: *The Sound and the Fury*

[1] Robert A. Jelliffe (ed.), *Faulkner at Nagano* (Tokyo: Kenkyusha, 1956), 103.

[2] Frederick L. Gwynn and Joseph L. Blotner (eds.), *Faulkner in the University: Class Conferences at the University of Virginia, 1957–1958* (Charlottesville: University of Virginia Press, 1959), 1.

[3] Several passages sound as though Faulkner may have glanced obliquely at the biblical account of the Garden of Eden. As the children return from the branch to the house while the funeral of Damuddy is taking place, a snake crawls out from under the house (p. 56; p. 45). Versh reminds Caddy that "your paw told you to stay out that tree" (p. 58; p. 46); and when Dilsey looks up into the tree that Caddy has climbed to look into the parlor window, she exclaims, "You, Satan" (p. 64; p. 54). For citation of the text of *The Sound and the Fury* used in this chapter and an explanation of the page references, see below, n. 14.

[4] Gwynn and Blotner (eds.), *Faulkner in the University*, 31.

[5] [William Faulkner] "An Introduction to *The Sound and the Fury*," *Mississippi Quarterly*, XXVI (1973), 413–14; quoted in Joseph Blotner, *Faulkner: A Biography* (2 vols.; New York: Random House, 1974), I, 568.

[6] Gwynn and Blotner (eds.), *Faulkner in the University*, 32.

[7] James K. Meriwether and Michael Millgate (eds.), *Lion in the Garden: Interviews with William Faulkner, 1926–1962* (New York: Random House, 1968), 147.

[8] The problems of the text of the novel have been examined in detail by James B. Meriwether in "Notes on the Textual History of *The Sound and the Fury*," *Papers of the Bibliographical Society of America*, LVI (1962), 285–316.

[9] James B. Meriwether (ed.), "An Introduction for *The Sound and the Fury*," *Southern Review*, n.s., VIII (1972), 705–10; and [Faulkner] "An Introduction to *The Sound and the Fury*," 410–15.

[10] William Faulkner to Malcolm Cowley [October 18, 1945], in Joseph Blotner (ed.), *Selected Letters of William Faulkner* (New York: Random House, 1977), 205.

[11] *Ibid.*, p. 220.

[12] Faulkner to Cowley [February 18, 1946], *ibid.*, 222–23.

[13] Gwynn and Blotner (eds.), *Faulkner in the University*, 77.

[14] William Faulkner, *The Sound and the Fury* (New York: Random House, Modern Library, 1946), 6. In 1966 Random House issued a hard-back reprint photographically reproduced from the first edition of 1929 (without the Appendix) and a Modern Library hard-cover reprint with the same pagination but including the Appendix at the end. In 1967 the firm issued the Modern Library College Editions paperback reprint having the first edition pagination and the Appendix at the back. For the convenience of readers, references to the novel will be placed in parentheses within the text to the first Modern Library edition of 1946 followed by a page reference that applies to the first edition of 1929 and to the other Random House reprints. Thus, the present reference would be cited (p. 6; p. 406).

[15] Gwynn and Blotner (eds.), *Faulkner in the University*, 3.

[16] Perhaps the best analysis of Benjy's monologue has been the study begun by an English class at the University of California at Berkeley and completed by two members of the faculty. The following analysis is generally indebted to the work of these scholars who

do not claim infallibility for their research; see George R. Stewart and Joseph M. Backus, "'Each in Its Ordered Place': The Structure and Narrative in Benjy's Section of *The Sound and the Fury*," *American Literature*, XXIX (1958), 440–56. Leon Edel has called the Appendix a way to read the novel "by a back door" and criticized the attempt to reassemble the events of Benjy's narrative in chronological order; see "How to Read *The Sound and the Fury*," in Stanley Burnshaw (ed.), *Varieties of Literary Experience: Eighteen Essays in World Literature* (New York: New York University Press, 1962), 241–57.

[17] For a discussion of the arguments advanced for these interpretations, see Hyatt H. Waggoner, *William Faulkner: From Jefferson to the World* (Lexington, University of Kentucky Press, 1959), 43–46; William R. Mueller, "The Theme of Suffering: William Faulkner's *The Sound and the Fury*," in *The Prophetic Voice in Modern Fiction* (New York: Association Press, 1959), 110–35; and Sumner C. Powell, "William Faulkner Celebrates Easter, 1928," *Perspective*, II (1948), 195–218.

[18] The amount of perceptive criticism of Quentin's monologue is substantial. In addition to the works of such scholars as Melvin Backman, Cleanth Brooks, Michael Millgate, Olga W. Vickery, Hyatt H. Waggoner, and James B. Meriwether, the following commentaries, though by no means a complete listing, have contributed generally to this discussion of Quentin Compson and *The Sound and the Fury*: Jackson J. Benson, "Quentin Compson: Self-Portrait of a Young Artist's Emotions," *Twentieth Century Literature*, XVII (1971), 143–59; André Bleikasten, *The Most Splendid Failure* (Bloomington: Indiana University Press, 1976); Lawrence E. Bowling, "Faulkner and the Theme of Innocence," *Kenyon Review*, XX (1958), 466–87; Carvel Collins, "Miss Quentin's Paternity Again," *Texas Studies in Language and Literature*, II (1960), 253–60; Carvel Collins, "The Interior Monologues of *The Sound and the Fury*," in *English Institute Essays 1952* (New York: Columbia University Press, 1954), 29–56; Louise Dauner, "Quentin and the Walking Shadow: The Dilemma of Nature and Culture," *Arizona Quarterly*, XXI (1965), 159–71; Martha Winburn England, "Quentin's Story: Chronology and Explication," *College English*, XXII (1961), 228–35; Wendell V. Harris, "Of Time and the Novel," *Bucknell Review*, XVI (March, 1968), 114–29; Perrin Lowrey, "Concepts of Time in *The Sound and the Fury*," in *English Institute Essays 1952*, 57–82; Mueller, "The Theme of Suffering," 110–35; Powell, "William Faulkner Celebrates Easter," 195–218.

[19] Jelliffe (ed.), *Faulkner at Nagano*, 104.

[20] Michael Millgate, *The Achievement of William Faulkner* (New York: Random House, 1966), 98–99. See also Cleanth Brooks, *William Faulkner: The Yoknapatawpha Country* (New Haven: Yale University Press, 1963), 339.

[21] Faulkner's critics have often remarked that the traffic pattern around the square would require Luster to turn right at the monument. Calvin Brown, however, has noted that this pattern was established after *The Sound and the Fury* was written. Earlier, traffic could flow in either direction from the monument. In any event, the point remains that Luster violated the practice to which Benjy had been accustomed, that is, Benjy's sense of order (and rightness). See Calvin S. Brown, *A Glossary of Faulkner's South* (New Haven: Yale University Press, 1976), 224 and note.

Notes and References

CHAPTER III
The Way of Naturalism: *As I Lay Dying*

[1] In the introduction to the Modern Library edition of *Sanctuary*, Faulkner wrote that he "shoveled coal from the bunker into a wheel-barrow and wheeled it in and dumped it where the fireman could put it into the boiler." In his biography of Faulkner, Blotner has suggested that this statement belongs in the realm of the imagination. See Joseph Blotner, *Faulkner: A Biography* (2 vols.; New York: Random House, 1974), I, 624. Similarly apocryphal are the stories suggesting that Faulkner wrote the novel on the back of a coal shovel by the dim light of the powerhouse furnace and that many young writers later sought the same job in the university powerhouse.

[2] Frederick L. Gwynn and Joseph L. Blotner (eds.), *Faulkner in the University: Class Conferences at the University of Virginia, 1957–1958* (Charlottesville: University of Virginia Press, 1959), 87, 207, 121.

[3] William Faulkner, *As I Lay Dying* (new ed.; New York: Random House, 1964), 141. Hereinafter, page references to this edition of *As I Lay Dying* will appear in the text within parentheses.

[4] Edgar Lee Masters, *Domesday Book* (New York: Macmillan, 1920), 20–21.

[5] See James Schevill, *Sherwood Anderson: His Life and Work* (Denver: University of Denver Press, 1951), 96–97; and Sherwood Anderson, *Sherwood Anderson's Memoirs* (New York: Harcourt, Brace, 1942), 289.

[6] For a discussion of the form of these novels, see the chapters relating to them. Neither Anderson in *Winesburg, Ohio*, nor Faulkner in the fiction that he wrote during his finest period seems much concerned with the creation of unified plots. In addition to the novels cited, the same tendency is apparent in *The Sound and the Fury*, *Light in August*, and *Absalom, Absalom!* In this respect, *As I Lay Dying* is exceptional.

[7] R. W. Franklin reaches virtually the same conclusion in his thorough examination of Faulkner's handling of time in *As I Lay Dying*; see his "Narrative Management in *As I Lay Dying*," *Modern Fiction Studies*, XIII (1967), 57–65. This problem, as well as many other aspects of the novel, has also been considered by André Bleikasten in *Faulkner's "As I Lay Dying"* (Bloomington: Indiana University Press, 1973).

[8] Perhaps the most notable exception is Dewey Dell's remark: "I feel like a wet seed wild in the hot blind earth" (p. 61). Brooks explains the incongruities between the characters' education and their sophisticated vocabulary and phrases as "one of the conventions which must be accepted in a reading of *As I Lay Dying*" and adds that "the language with which the author provides the character to express his innermost thoughts is not necessarily the same language the author has him use when he speaks to another character." See Cleanth Brooks, *William Faulkner: The Yoknapatawpha Country* (New Haven: Yale University Press, 1963), 160. The objection to the "convention" explanation is that the artificiality of the sophisticated vocabulary destroys the realism of the narrative and often brings a jarring note to a passage otherwise written "in character." Moreover, the novel contains many passages in which the sophisticated vocabulary occurs when the character is not relating his "innermost thoughts." Finally, many persons believe that a person's vocabulary has a direct relation to his thought, a point of view that Faulkner's practice in this novel would apparently support despite the damage to the credibility of the character that results from the vocabulary necessary to render the thought process.

[9] George Marion O'Donnell, "Faulkner's Mythology," in Frederick J. Hoffman and

Olga W. Vickery (eds.), *William Faulkner: Three Decades of Criticism* (East Lansing: Michigan State University Press, 1960), 87. The essay originally appeared in the *Kenyon Review*, I (1939), 285–99. Similar interpretations favorable to Anse have been made by Warren, who writes that "the whole of *As I Lay Dying* is based on the heroic effort of the Bundren family to fulfill the promise to the dead mother"—Robert Penn Warren, "William Faulkner," in Hoffman and Vickery (eds.), *Three Decades of Criticism*, 119, reprinted from the *New Republic*, August 12 and 26, 1946, pp. 176–80, 234–37. Brooks, despite some doubts about the Bundrens, believes that the novel deals with a heroic action; see Brooks, *The Yoknapatawpha Country*, 141. More recently, Melvin Backman has found the novel "a fable and poem which is simply and joyously alive" and adds that "anguish gives way to comedy, despair to duty, introversion to action, and obsession to love"; see his *Faulkner: The Major Years* (Bloomington: Indiana University Press, 1966), 177. A number of critics, however, have taken a more naturalistic position. Vickery has called the work "a travesty of the ritual of interment"—Olga W. Vickery, *The Novels of William Faulkner: A Critical Interpretation* (Baton Rouge: Louisiana State University Press, 1959), 52. Wasiolek describes Faulkner's tone as "bitterly ironic, resigned, and masochistically insistent not only on the bitter condition of man's life, but also on the obtuseness of man's awareness of it"—Edward Wasiolek, "*As I Lay Dying*: Distortion in the Slow Eddy of Current Opinion," *Critique*, III (Spring–Fall, 1959), 23. Volpe writes that the work presents "human existence as an absurd joke"—Edward Volpe, *A Reader's Guide to William Faulkner* (New York: Noonday Press, 1964), 126.

[10] The ages of Addie's children may only be inferred from information given at various places in the novel. Dewey Dell tells Moseley that she is seventeen (p. 190), and Anse says she has eaten his food for "seventeen years" (p. 246). Darl implies that Cash is two years older than he is (p. 11). Cash gives additional information: "me and him was born close together, and it nigh ten years before Jewel and Dewey Dell and Vardaman begun to come along. . . . And me being the oldest" (p. 224).

[11] The theme appears at frequent intervals throughout the novel from beginning to end. In the second section, Cora's daughter Kate complains that "rich town ladies can change their minds. Poor folks cant" (p. 7). Dewey Dell remarks bitterly, "We are country people, not as good as town people" (p. 58). Vardaman learns about the difference: "Because I am a country boy because boys in town. . . . 'Why aint I a town boy, pa?'" (p. 63). Anse thinks that townspeople do not work but live off "them that sweats" (p. 104). Addie remarks, "I know how town folks are" (p. 163). Vardaman hopes that "maybe Santa Claus wont know they are town boys" (p. 206). Jewel almost has a fight with a "goddamn town fellow" (p. 220). MacGowan notices that Dewey Dell is a "country woman" (p. 231) and remarks, "them country people. Half the time they dont know what they want, and the balance of the time they cant tell it to you" (p. 233). Dewey Dell promises Vardaman that the red train will not be sold to the town boys (p. 240).

[12] Addie's relationship with Whitfield and the name of their child seem to have a literary precedent in Hawthorne's *The Scarlet Letter*. Faulkner denied any conscious parallel and observed that "a writer don't have to consciously parallel because he robs and steals from everything he ever wrote or read or saw. . . . I took whatever I needed wherever I could find it." See Gwynn and Blotner (eds.), *Faulkner in the University*, 115.

Notes and References

CHAPTER IV
Spring's Futility: *Sanctuary*

[1] Frederick L. Gwynn and Joseph L. Blotner (eds.), *Faulkner in the University: Class Conferences at the University of Virginia, 1957–1958* (Charlottesville: University of Virginia Press, 1959), 90.

[2] See Joseph Blotner, *Faulkner: A Biography* (2 vols.; New York: Random House, 1974), I, 617–18.

[3] James B. Meriwether and Michael Millgate (eds.), *Lion in the Garden: Interviews with William Faulkner, 1926–1962* (New York: Random House, 1968), 123.

[4] Robert A. Jelliffe (ed.), *Faulkner at Nagano* (Tokyo: Kenkyusha, 1956), 64–65. Faulkner's revisions of the first manuscript of *Sanctuary* have been carefully studied by several scholars; see Linton R. Massey, "Notes on the Unrevised Galleys of Faulkner's *Sanctuary*," *Studies in Bibliography*, VIII (1956), 195–208; James B. Meriwether, "Some Notes on the Text of Faulkner's *Sanctuary*," *Papers of the Bibliographical Society of America*, IV (1961), 192–206; and Michael Millgate, *The Achievement of William Faulkner* (New York: Random House, 1966), 113–17.

[5] Blotner, *Faulkner*, I, 685.

[6] See, for example, Clifton P. Fadiman, "The World of William Faulkner," *Nation*, April 15, 1931, pp. 422–23. "By virtue of this book [*Sanctuary*]," wrote Fadiman, "he at once takes his place among the foremost of the younger generation of American novelists. He is an original."

[7] Henry Seidel Canby, "The School of Cruelty," *Saturday Review of Literature*, March 21, 1931, pp. 673–74. Wrote Canby: "I have chosen Mr. Faulkner as a prime example of American sadism because he is so clearly a writer of power, and no mere experimenter with nervous emotion. . . . In 'Sanctuary' I believe that sadism, if not anti-romance, has reached its American peak."

[8] New Orleans *Times-Picayune*, April 26, 1931, p. 26. The review of *Sanctuary* is the first of several reviews and other literary items printed under the title "Literature and Less: A Page on Books of the Day Conducted by John McClure." The final item, a review of Arnold Hoffriegel's *The Forest Ship*, is signed with the initials J.K.W.B. Blotner assigns the review of *Sanctuary* to Julia K. Wetherill Baker; see Blotner, *Faulkner*, I, 686. Although conceding that *Sanctuary* "lacks the precision, the intensity and the finality" of *The Sound and the Fury* and *As I Lay Dying*, the reviewer remarked that "it would be possible to quote from 'Sanctuary' . . . some of the most effective interpretation of emotion in American fiction." The reviewer called Faulkner "probably the best living novelist in America."

[9] Harry L. Martin, "Horrifying Tale Set in Memphis," Memphis *Evening Appeal*, March 26, 1931, p. 11. Martin called the novel "probably the most putrid story ever conceived in the mind of a southerner."

[10] Albert Camus to the *Harvard Advocate*, May 30, 1951, in *Harvard Advocate*, CXXXV (November, 1951), 21.

[11] Melvin Backman, *Faulkner: The Major Years* (Bloomington: Indiana University Press, 1966), 42.

[12] Cleanth Brooks, *William Faulkner: The Yoknapatawpha Country* (New Haven: Yale University Press, 1963), 138.

[13] The account of the origin of the story of Temple Drake is based upon Carvel Collins'

note about Faulkner's interview with the girl. According to Collins, "in the real, per-verted rape the implement was so fantastically unnatural that compared to it the imple-ment used by the fictional gangster . . . seems well along the way toward normalcy." Collins also implies that the famous corncob may have been suggested by the fact that the girl was born and reared in a little town called Cobbtown. See "A Note on 'Sanctuary,'" *Harvard Advocate*, CXXXV (November, 1951), 16. Since the only "Cobbtown" in the Southern states during the 1920s was a tiny village about sixty miles west of Savannah, Georgia, the girl's hometown may be an embroidered element in the story. Probably equally apocryphal but tempting for speculation is the notion that the "cob" may have been suggested to Faulkner by a sign on a general merchandising (and grocery) store on the Oxford Square indicating that it was "Cobb's Store." Every day Faulkner went to the Square; he must have seen this sign, which also included the phrase "Great Is the Power of Cash." Perhaps, and one can go no further, Cobbtown, Cobb's store, or the sign about Cash may have had something to do with *Sanctuary* and/or *As I Lay Dying*.

[14] As early as 1932, Professor Adwin Wigfall Green, at the University of Mississippi, identified the original of Faulkner's Popeye as "Popeye Pumphrey." Green also claimed that Temple Drake and Gowan Stevens were also "taken from life." See A. Wigfall Green, "William Faulkner at Home," *Sewanee Review*, XL (1932), 294–306. Green died in 1966, but among the still living longtime Oxford residents are those who insist that they know the identities of the real Temple Drake and the real Gowan Stevens. John B. Cullen, in *Old Times in the Faulkner Country* (Chapel Hill: University of North Carolina Press, 1961), 80–82, identifies Temple as Una Johnson, from Winona, Mississippi. For additional details of Pumphrey's career, see "Two Gangsters Dead after Five Battle," New York *Times*, June 24, 1929, p. 26; "Popeye Pumphrey Commits Suicide," Memphis *Commercial Appeal*, October 29, 1931, pp. 1, 3; and Robert Cantwell, "Faulkner's 'Popeye,'" *Nation*, February 15, 1958, pp. 140–41, 148.

[15] The account of the Memphis underworld of crime and prostitution is indebted to George W. Lee, *Beale Street: Where the Blues Began* (New York: Robert O. Ballou, 1934), 104–18; and William D. Miller, *Memphis: During the Progressive Era 1900–1917* (Memphis: Memphis State University Press, 1957), 87–103.

[16] See "Masked Man Kills Woman of Underworld," Memphis *Commercial Appeal*, Octo-ber 10, 1916, p. 8; and Blotner, *Faulkner*, I, 607.

[17] William Faulkner, *Sanctuary* (New York: Jonathan Cape and Harrison Smith, 1931), 185–86. The edition hereinafter cited in the text within parentheses is the Random House, Modern Library, issue of 1940 containing the introduction of four pages.

[18] Although details may vary, the main outlines of this well-publicized murder and lynching can be established from a number of accounts. See "Negro Brute Cuts Woman's Throat," *Lafayette County Press*, September 9, 1908; "Speedy Justice to Negro Fiend," Jackson *Daily Clarion-Ledger*, September 9, 1908, p. 1; "Brutal Negro Kills Woman; Is Lynched," Memphis *Commercial Appeal*, September 9, 1908, pp. 1, 8; "Sullivan's Hot Talk at Oxford Lynching," Jackson *Daily Clarion-Ledger*, September 10, 1908, p. 1; Cullen, *Old Times in the Faulkner Country*, 88–98; and Blotner, *Faulkner*, I, 113–14.

[19] See Cullen, *Old Times in the Faulkner Country*, 82–83.

[20] See Brooks, *The Yoknapatawpha Country*, 136. Michael Millgate has called attention to parallels and a possible source for the title in Shakespeare's *Measure for Measure*; see Millgate, *The Achievement of William Faulkner*, 119–21.

Notes and References

CHAPTER V
Life as a Journey: *Light in August*

[1] At Frenchman's Bend, as Popeye shoots Tommy, Temple starts to say "something is going to happen to me" and an instant later screams "something is happening to me!" (p. 122). In *Light in August*, Joe Christmas thinks, as he almost chokes Joe Brown, "*Something is going to happen to me*"—William Faulkner, *Light in August* (New York: Harrison Smith and Robert Haas, 1932), 97. Christmas repeats the remark with variations on several occasions; see 110, 129, and 261. Hereinafter, page references to this edition of *Light in August* will appear in the text within parentheses.

[2] "Fleeing Negro Shot by Officer," Oxford *Eagle*, March 13, 1919, p. 1. See also Joseph Blotner, *Faulkner: A Biography* (2 vols.; New York: Random House, 1974), I, 762–63.

[3] Frederick L. Gwynn and Joseph L. Blotner (eds.), *Faulkner in the University: Class Conferences at the University of Virginia, 1957–1958* (Charlottesville: University of Virginia Press, 1959), 74.

[4] *Ibid.*, 199.

[5] Herschel Brickell, "Mr. Faulkner Advances," *North American Review*, CCXXXIV (1932), 571; J. Donald Adams, "Mr. Faulkner's Astonishing Novel," *New York Times Book Review*, October 9, 1932, p. 6; Henry Seidel Canby, "The Grain of Life," *Saturday Review of Literature*, October 8, 1932, p. 153; Dorothy Van Doren, "More Light Needed," *Nation*, October 26, 1932, pp. 402–403.

[6] James B. Meriwether (ed.), "An Introduction for *The Sound and the Fury*," *Southern Review*, n.s. VIII (1972), 709. The introduction has also been printed in James B. Meriwether, "Faulkner, Lost and Found," *New York Times Book Review*, November 5, 1972, p. 7.

[7] Willa Cather, *My Ántonia* (Boston and New York: Houghton Mifflin, 1918), 398.

[8] Gwynn and Blotner (eds.), *Faulkner in the University*, 72, 97.

[9] *Ibid.*, 72.

CHAPTER VI
The Stubbornness of Historical Truth: *Absalom, Absalom!*

[1] William Faulkner to Harrison Smith [February, 1934], in Joseph Blotner (ed.), *Selected Letters of William Faulkner* (New York: Random House, 1977), 78–79.

[2] Frederick L. Gwynn and Joseph L. Blotner (eds.), *Faulkner in the University: Class Conferences at the University of Virginia, 1957–1958* (Charlottesville; University of Virginia Press, 1959), 76.

[3] Faulkner to Harrison Smith [August, 1934], in Blotner (ed.), *Selected Letters*, 84.

[4] Gwynn and Blotner (eds.), *Faulkner in the University*, 76.

[5] William Faulkner, *Absalom, Absalom!* (New York: Random House, 1936), 190. Hereinafter, page references to this edition of *Absalom, Absalom!* will appear in the text within parentheses.

[6] Ward L. Miner has offered several plausible suggestions about the significance of the differences between Faulkner's Yoknapatawpha County and Lafayette County, Mississippi. Miner suggests that Faulkner increased the size of the county (from the actual

679 square miles to the fictional 2400) to enable the reader to think of the county in larger terms and to accommodate Sutpen's hundred-square-mile plantation. Faulkner's population figures make the county more rural than it was in 1940 (or even in 1840 when the first census was taken) by decreasing the number of persons per square mile. Elizabeth Kerr has suggested that Faulkner made this change to emphasize the importance of the individual and the loneliness of life in the county. Faulkner also increased the proportion of Negroes to whites, possibly, as Miner believes, to make the fictional county reflect a racial mixture intermediate between Lafayette County and the Delta counties and to emphasize the presence of Negroes in the area. See Ward L. Miner, *The World of William Faulkner* (New York: Grove Press, Inc., 1952), 86–89; and Elizabeth M. Kerr, *Yoknapatawpha: Faulkner's "Little Postage Stamp of Native Soil"* (New York: Fordham University Press, 1969), 29.

[7] Clifton Fadiman, "Faulkner, Extra-Special, Double-Distilled," *New Yorker*, October 31, 1936, pp. 62, 64; "Southern Cypher," *Time*, November 2, 1936, p. 67; Mary Colum, "Faulkner's Struggle with Technique," *Forum*, XCVII (1937), 35–36; Herschel Brickell, "*Absalom, Absalom!*," *Review of Reviews*, XCIV (December, 1936), 15; Malcolm Cowley, "Poe in Mississippi," *New Republic*, November 4, 1936, p. 22; Joseph Blotner, *Faulkner: A Biography* (2 vols.; New York: Random House, 1974), II, 949.

[8] Faulkner's previously unpublished stories, including "Evangeline," "Snow," and "The Big Shot," discussed here, have been issued in a single volume; see Joseph Blotner (ed.), *Uncollected Stories of William Faulkner* (New York: Random House, 1979). The relationship of these stories, as well as "Elly" and "Mistral," to *Absalom, Absalom!* has been analyzed by Estella Schoenberg in her *Old Tales and Talking: Quentin Compson in William Faulkner's "Absalom, Absalom!" and Related Works* (Jackson: University Press of Mississippi, 1977). Like many of Faulkner's works, "Evangeline," which calls to mind Longfellow's poem, has no immediate connection with its literary ancestor. Both pieces, however, could be called, in Longfellow's words, examples of "the beauty and strength of woman's devotion." In Faulkner's "Evangeline," Judith's care for the insensitive Negro wife is the measure of her love and devotion for Charles Bon. Schoenberg points out that Faulkner probably took from Longfellow's poem the name Eulalia to use for Bon's mother in the chronology and genealogy of *Absalom, Absalom!* See Schoenberg, *Old Tales and Talking*, 46–47.

[9] "Elly" first appeared in *Story*, IV (February, 1934), 3–15. Faulkner included it in *Doctor Martino and Other Stories* (New York: Smith and Haas, 1934) and in *Collected Stories* (New York: Random House, 1950).

[10] Faulkner published "Mistral" in *These 13* (New York: Jonathan Cage & Harrison Smith, 1931) and in *Collected Stories*. The story is only partially summarized here.

[11] The waiter, for example, explains that the Big Shot "drops his axe in time to miss Brix with it." In the portion of the story not summarized here, the wife returns for the funeral of her husband, but leaves the village immediately afterwards. No explanation is given of her departure with the Big Shot. From the opening and closing paragraphs of "Snow," which have no necessary connection with Don and "I," the reader learns that a German general has been stabbed to death by the "Frenchwoman" who has been his companion for several years. The man reading the paper comments to his little daughter that the woman was not French but Swiss. The implication seems to be that the woman who stabbed the general was the guide's wife and the general the "Big Shot." The photograph and the news item under it recall the account of Caddy Compson which Faulkner gives in the Appendix to *The Sound and the Fury*.

Notes and References

[12] Papers discovered in 1971 in a closet at Rowan Oak, Faulkner's home in Oxford, Mississippi.

[13] Gwynn and Blotner (eds.), *Faulkner in the University*, 273–74.

[14] *Ibid.*, 275. Although Faulkner insisted that the novel was Sutpen's story, in the same passage he noted that Quentin was still seeking answers to the questions he had raised in *The Sound and the Fury*.

[15] Schoenberg, *Old Tales and Talking*, 4.

[16] Brooks strongly believes that in this meeting Henry Sutpen revealed to Quentin Compson the crucial facts of Bon's parentage. Although such a revelation would validate many of Quentin's statements and turn them from theory to fact, the explanation remains a reader's conjecture without explicit sanction in the novel. See Cleanth Brooks, *William Faulkner: The Yoknapatawpha Country* (New Haven: Yale University Press, 1963), 316–17, 440–41; and his *William Faulkner: Toward Yoknapatawpha and Beyond* (New Haven: Yale University Press, 1978), 320–25.

[17] Gwynn and Blotner (eds.), *Faulkner in the University*, 75.

[18] *Ibid.*, 274–75. In a lecture delivered at the University of Mississippi Faulkner Conference and published after the following account of the relationship between Quentin's role in *The Sound and the Fury* and in *Absalom, Absalom!* was written, Thomas Daniel Young has reached somewhat similar conclusions about Quentin. See "Narration as Creative Act: The Role of Quentin Compson in *Absalom, Absalom!*," in Evans Harrington and Ann J. Abadie (eds.), *Faulkner, Modernism, and Film: Faulkner and Yoknapatawpha* (Jackson: University Press of Mississippi, 1979), 82–102.

[19] Faulkner, *The Sound and the Fury*, 99; 98.

[20] *Ibid.*, 98–99; 97–98.

[21] *Ibid.*, 167; 185.

[22] Robert A. Jelliffe (ed.), *Faulkner at Nagano* (Tokyo: Kenkyusha, 1956), 46.

CHAPTER VII

The Civil War and Reconstruction: *The Unvanquished*

[1] Frederick L. Gwynn and Joseph L. Blotner (eds.), *Faulkner in the University: Class Conferences at the University of Virginia, 1957–1958* (Charlottesville: University of Virginia Press, 1959), 2. Asked at the final class conference more than a year later if there is "a particular order in which your works should be read," Faulkner replied: "I'd say that's [*Sartoris*] a good one to begin with" (285).

[2] Michael Millgate, *The Achievement of William Faulkner* (New York: Random House, 1966), 170.

[3] William Faulkner to Morton Goldman [probably late spring, early summer, 1934], in Joseph Blotner (ed.), *Selected Letters of William Faulkner* (New York: Random House, 1977), 80–81.

[4] Faulkner to Goldman [August, 1934], *ibid.*, 84.

[5] Joseph Blotner, *Faulkner: A Biography* (2 vols.; New York: Random House, 1974), II, 951.

[6] William Faulkner, *The Unvanquished* (New York: Random House, 1938). The text of the first edition, including the pagination, has been reproduced photographically by Random House and by Vintage Books, a division of Random House. Hereinafter, refer-

ences to this edition of the novel will be placed within the text in parentheses.

[7] Faulkner liked to provide seemingly exact time references in his fiction, but he appears not to have worried greatly if some references were inconsistent with others. Discrepancies of various sorts, including time, are involved in a number of Faulkner's novels and short stories besides *The Unvanquished*, most notably in *The Sound and the Fury*, *Absalom, Absalom!*, *Go Down, Moses*, and the Snopes trilogy. When preparing *The Portable Faulkner* for publication, Malcolm Cowley mentioned several problems of this nature to Faulkner, who took a cavalier approach to them. Somewhat of the same attitude Faulkner expressed in a prefatory note in *The Mansion*. The problems in *The Unvanquished* arise from Faulkner's fondness for mentioning historical events, Bayard's exact age, and placing dates on letters. In general, one can say that the first six stories take place between the outbreak of the Civil War and a time shortly after the end of the war, when Bayard Sartoris grew from a boy of approximately twelve to sixteen. Within these limits, the dates of the various stories may vary as much as a year. An example of the problem facing careful readers occurs in "Raid." In the original story published in the *Saturday Evening Post*, the General's order for the mules and Negroes is dated "August 14, 1864," but in *The Unvanquished* the date is "August 14, 1863." If this date is used as a key date to establish other chronology, confusion results. Particularly disturbing errors appear in "Skirmish at Sartoris." In that story, Bayard recalls that his father wrote home from Carolina in July, 1864, but Sartoris would have had no reason to fight in Carolina until Sherman captured Atlanta and moved into South Carolina in February, 1865. In "The Place of *The Unvanquished* in William Faulkner's Yoknapatawpha Series" (Ph.D. dissertation, Princeton University, 1959), James B. Meriwether has pointed out a number of inconsistencies in the work. Despite the headaches these matters present, Faulkner may have been correct in thinking that they do not interfere with the spirit of the work and do not bother most readers.

[8] See Joseph F. Trimmer, "*The Unvanquished*: The Teller and the Tale," *Ball State University Forum*, X (Winter, 1969), 35–42; and Hyatt H. Waggoner, *William Faulkner: From Jefferson to the World* (Lexington: University of Kentucky Press, 1959), 171. For a view more nearly in accord with that expressed here, see Joanne V. Creighton, *William Faulkner's Craft of Revision* (Detroit: Wayne State University Press, 1977), 74–75 and note.

[9] Faulkner, *Sartoris*, 195.

[10] Joanna's remark that her father would "understand that a man would have to act as the land where he was born had trained him to act" (*Light in August*, 241) has an interesting parallel in Cass Edmonds' assertion in *Go Down, Moses*: "So I repudiate too. I would deny even if I knew it were true. I would have to. Even you can see that I could do no else. I am what I am; I will be always what I was born and have always been"—William Faulkner, *Go Down, Moses and Other Stories* (New York: Random House, 1942), 299–300.

[11] Faulkner, *Light in August*, 218.

[12] Bayard imagines her as "the Greek amphora priestess of a succinct and formal violence" (252). Throughout the story, Drusilla bears comparison with figures in Greek tragedy. Critics have noted that verbena has associations with laurel (the reward of heroes and poets), myrtle (for Venus), and olive (a symbol of peace). The sprig of verbena Drusilla leaves on Bayard's pillow in the final section represents, of course, her acknowledgment of his courage.

[13] Gwynn and Blotner (eds.), *Faulkner in the University*, 256.

[14] If the next day Colonel Sartoris encountered Redmond, Faulkner does not recount the

incident; four months later, when Sartoris met Redmond, George Wyatt said the Colonel was wearing his derringer but did not touch it; and Ringo affirmed that the Colonel was smoking his pipe and had it in his hand when he fell. That Sartoris made no move to shoot Redmond, all accounts agree. The similarity of this portion of Faulkner's story to events in the life of Colonel W. C. Falkner is striking.

CHAPTER VIII

Materialism in the Country: *The Hamlet*

[1] William Faulkner, *The Hamlet* (New York: Random House, 1940). References to *The Hamlet* are cited within the text in parentheses, to the third edition, Random House, 1964. In comprehensive studies of Faulkner's fiction, such scholars as Joseph Blotner, Cleanth Brooks, Elizabeth M. Kerr, Michael Millgate, Peter Swiggart, Olga W. Vickery, Hyatt H. Waggoner, and others have written perceptively about *The Hamlet*. During the decade of the 1960s, particularly, Faulkner's critics examined virtually every aspect of the novel in considerable detail. Two full-length studies devoted to the "Snopes trilogy" are particularly valuable: Warren Beck, *Man in Motion: Faulkner's Trilogy* (Madison: University of Wisconsin Press, 1961); and James Gray Watson, *The Snopes Dilemma: Faulkner's Trilogy* (Coral Gables, Fla.: University of Miami Press, ca. 1968). A partial list of informative journal studies would include: Sherland N. Dirksen, "The First of the Snopeses," *Emporia State Research Studies*, XI (December, 1962), 5–45; Norman Farmer, Jr., "The Love Theme: A Principal Source of Thematic Unity in Faulkner's Snopes Trilogy," *Twentieth Century Literature*, VIII (1963), 111–23; Joseph Gold, "The 'Normality' of Snopesism; Universal Themes in Faulkner's *The Hamlet*," *Wisconsin Studies in Contemporary Literature*, III (1962), 25–34; Donald J. Greiner, "Universal Snopesism: The Significance of 'Spotted Horses,'" *English Journal*, LVII (1968), 1133–37; Elmo Howell, "Mink Snopes and Faulkner's Moral Conclusions," *South Atlantic Quarterly*, LXVII (1968), 13–22; Elizabeth M. Kerr, "Snopes," *Wisconsin Studies in Contemporary Literature*, I (1960), 66–83; Florence Leaver, "The Structure of *The Hamlet*," *Twentieth Century Literature*, I (1955), 77–84; William J. Palmer, "The Mechanistic World of Snopes," *Mississippi Quarterly*, XX (1967), 185–95; Ladell Payne, "The Trilogy: Faulkner's Comic Epic in Prose," *Studies in the Novel*, I (Spring, 1969), 27–37; and James L. Sanderson, "'Spotted Horses' and the Theme of Social Evil," *English Journal*, LVII (1968), 700–704. To this wealth of critical analysis, the discussion of *The Hamlet* that follows is indebted.

[2] Frederick L. Gwynn and Joseph L. Blotner (eds.), *Faulkner in the University: Class Conferences at the University of Virginia, 1957–1958* (Charlottesville: University of Virginia Press, 1959), 197.

[3] Faulkner, *Sartoris*, 172–73.

[4] *Ibid.*, 174.

[5] Joseph Blotner, *Faulkner: A Biography* (2 vols.; New York: Random House, 1974), I, 777.

[6] Oxford *Eagle*, May 17, 1934. See also Blotner, *Faulkner*, I, 849.

[7] William Faulkner to Robert K. Haas [received December 15, 1938], in Joseph Blotner (ed.), *Selected Letters of William Faulkner* (New York: Random House, 1977), 107.

[8] Faulkner to Bennett Cerf [received January 19, 1939], Faulkner to Saxe Commins [October, 1939], *ibid.*, 109, 115. Reviews of the novel, which began to appear in April,

1940, were generally favorable; reviewers in the *New York Times Book Review*, the *New York Herald Tribune Books*, the *New Republic*, as well as the Memphis *Commercial Appeal* and Memphis *Press-Scimitar*, placed the novel among Faulkner's best fiction. Writing for the *New Yorker*, however, Clifton Fadiman continued to find Faulkner's writing obscure, uninteresting, and tiresome.

[9] Gwynn and Blotner (eds.), *Faulkner in the University*, 34.

[10] William Faulkner, *The Town* (New York: Random House, 1957), 8–9.

[11] *Ibid.*, 347.

[12] William Faulkner, *The Mansion* (New York: Random House, 1959), 98, 429.

CHAPTER IX

Pensioners of History: *Go Down, Moses*

[1] William Faulkner, *Go Down, Moses and Other Stories* (New York: Random House, 1942). In the second printing, issued in 1948, *and Other Stories* was deleted from the title. In the present discussion, the shortened title will be used; references to the novel will be cited in the text within parentheses. The pagination of the Modern Library edition of 1955 and subsequent reissues by Random House coincides with that of the first edition.

[2] The attitude of the editors of Random House towards the form of the book is clear from a remark in a letter from Bennett Cerf to Faulkner, June 3, 1942. After noting that the volume was enjoying good sales, Cerf added that little could be done "with a collection of short stories in times like these"—quoted in Joseph Blotner, *Faulkner: A Biography* (2 vols.; New York: Random House, 1974), II, 1102.

[3] William Faulkner to Robert K. Haas [January 26, 1949], in Joseph Blotner (ed.), *Selected Letters of William Faulkner* (New York: Random House, 1977), 284–85. A portion of *The Wild Palms* has been issued as *The Old Man* (New York: New American Library, 1948) and in *William Faulkner: Three Famous Short Novels* (New York: Random House, 1958) and as *The Wild Palms* (New York: New American Library, 1948) without the parts called "Old Man." In 1954 the New American Library published both stories in a single volume but printed them separately instead of alternately as originally published. For a discussion of the textual history of *The Wild Palms*, see Thomas L. McHaney, *William Faulkner's "The Wild Palms": A Study* (Jackson: University Press of Mississippi, 1975). According to notes taken in the meeting of an English class at the University of Mississippi in April, 1947, Faulkner remarked that "I did send both stories to the publisher separately, and they were rejected because they were too short. So I alternated the chapters of them"—Lavon Rascoe, "An Interview with William Faulkner," *Western Review*, XV (1951), 300. In 1957, however, when talking to students at the University of Virginia, Faulkner said that "I'd write the chapter of one and then I would write the chapter of the other" to achieve counterpoint. He may have intended the story of the "Old Man" to underline the story of Charlotte and Harry Wilbourne in *The Wild Palms*. See Frederick L. Gwynn and Joseph L. Blotner (eds.), *Faulkner in the University: Class Conferences at the University of Virginia, 1957–1958* (Charlottesville: University of Virginia Press, 1959), 171.

[4] Faulkner to Haas [May 1, 1941], in Blotner (ed.), *Selected Letters*, 139–40.

[5] *Go Down, Moses* was published in the spring of 1942. Generally, the reviews were

more favorable and less harsh than those of his earlier books. Most critics took the title at face value and treated the work as a group of stories rather than a novel. Virtually all reviewers praised Faulkner's narrative skill and conceded him a high rank among contemporary novelists. Writing in the *New Republic* (June 29, 1942), Malcolm Cowley declared that "he is, after Hemingway and Dos Passos, the most considerable novelist of this generation." Subsequent criticism of *Go Down, Moses* has been abundant, varied in approach, and at times necessarily repetitive. In addition to the volumes surveying all or nearly all of Faulkner's fiction, a partial list of perceptive criticism relating to the novel would include Warren Beck, *Faulkner* (Madison: University of Wisconsin Press, 1976); H. H. Bell, Jr., "A Footnote to Faulkner's 'The Bear,'" *College English*, XXIV (1962), 179–83; Dale G. Breaden, "William Faulkner and the Land," *American Quarterly*, X (1958), 344–57; Lewis M. Dabney, *The Indians of Yoknapatawpha: A Study in Literature and History* (Baton Rouge: Louisiana State University Press, 1974); James Early, *The Making of "Go Down, Moses"* (Dallas: Southern Methodist University Press, 1972); Arthur F. Kinney, "'Delta Autumn': Postlude to *The Bear*," in Francis Lee Utley, Lynn Z. Bloom, and Arthur F. Kinney (eds.), *Bear, Man, and God: Seven Approaches to William Faulkner's "The Bear"* (New York: Random House, 1964), 384–95; Arthur F. Kinney, "Faulkner and the Possibilities for Heroism," *Southern Review*, n.s., VI (1970, 1110–25; Marvin Klotz, "Procrustean Revision in Faulkner's *Go Down, Moses*," *American Literature*, XXXVII (1965), 1–16; Kenneth LaBudde, "Cultural Primitivism in William Faulkner's 'The Bear,'" *American Quarterly*, II (1950), 322–28; R. W. B. Lewis, "The Hero in the New World: William Faulkner's 'The Bear,'" *Kenyon Review*, XIII (1951), 641–60; John Lydenberg, "Nature Myth in Faulkner's 'The Bear,'" *American Literature* XXIV (1952), 62–72; Herbert A. Perluck, "'The Heart's Driving Complexity': An Unromantic Reading of Faulkner's 'The Bear,'" *Accent*, XX (1960), 23–46; Henry Alden Ploegstra, "William Faulkner's *Go Down, Moses*: Its Sources, Revisions, and Structure" (Ph.D. dissertation, University of Chicago, 1966); David H. Stewart, "The Purpose of Faulkner's Ike," *Criticism*, III (1961), 333–42; Walter F. Taylor, Jr., "Let My People Go: The White Man's Heritage in *Go Down, Moses*," *South Atlantic Quarterly*, LVIII (1959), 20–32; Francis Lee Utley, "Pride and Humility: The Cultural Roots of Ike McCaslin," in Utley, Bloom, and Kinney (eds.), *Bear, Man, and God*, 233–60; Thomas J. Wertenbaker, Jr., "Faulkner's Point of View and the Chronicle of Ike McCaslin," *College English*, XXIV (1962), 169–78. See also below, note 9, for additional material relating to the wilderness romance in *Go Down, Moses*.

[6] As Blotner observes, Faulkner had reached the same conclusion in assembling *The Unvanquished*; see Blotner, *Faulkner*, II, 1080. In both instances ("The Odor of Verbena" in *The Unvanquished* and the great bear story in *Go Down, Moses*), the gain for the volume was substantial.

[7] The claim of the Negro branch to descent through the male line is slightly ambiguous. If Tomasina is considered as McCaslin's daughter, the descent would be through the female line in the third generation to Lucas; but if she is considered as McCaslin's "wife" (probably the correct interpretation), the descent would be through the male line (that is, from Tomey's Turl or Terrel) in the second generation to Lucas. Clearly in the text Lucas and Faulkner considered the descent was through the male line and in two generations (see 104).

[8] Faulkner, *The Hamlet*, 322.

[9] The following discussion of the relationship between the wilderness romance and Faulkner's stories about Isaac McCaslin and the great bear hunt has been adapted in part

Notes and References

from my article "Nature's Legacy to William Faulkner," in Evans Harrington and Ann J. Abadie (eds.), *The South and Faulkner's Yoknapatawpha: The Actual and the Apocryphal* (Jackson: University Press of Mississippi, 1977), 104–27; see also Ursula Brumm, "Wilderness and Civilization: A Note on William Faulkner," *Partisan Review*, XXII (1955), 340–50, reprinted in Frederick J. Hoffman and Olga W. Vickery (eds.), *William Faulkner: Three Decades of Criticism* (East Lansing: Michigan State University Press, 1960); Edwin Fussell, *Frontier: American Literature and the American West* (Princeton: Princeton University Press, 1965); Howard Mumford Jones, *The Frontier in American Fiction* (Jerusalem: Hebrew University, 1956); R. W. B. Lewis, *The American Adam: Innocence, Tragedy, and Tradition in the Nineteenth Century* (Chicago: University of Chicago Press, 1955); Leo Marx, *The Machine in the Garden* (New York: Oxford University Press, 1964); W. R. Moses, "Where History Crosses Myth: Another Reading of 'The Bear,'" *Accent*, XIII (1953), 21–33; Roderick Nash, *Wilderness and the American Mind* (New Haven: Yale University Press, 1967); William Van O'Connor, "The Wilderness Theme in Faulkner's 'The Bear,'" *Accent*, XIII (1953), 12–20, reprinted in Hoffman and Vickery (eds.), *Three Decades of Criticism*; Lewis P. Simpson, *The Dispossessed Garden* (Athens: University of Georgia Press, 1975); Henry Nash Smith, *The Virgin Land: The American West as Symbol and Myth* (Cambridge: Harvard University Press, 1950); Otis B. Wheeler, "Faulkner's Wilderness," *American Literature*, XXXI (1959), 127–36.

[10] Although this remark is confused and somewhat illogical, apparently Brown is trying to say that he is against the weak being held in bondage because they are "niggers" by the strong just because they are white.

Index

315

Index

Index

scribed, 95; motivating force of plot, 95; characterized, 95–100; treatment of his children, 96; desire for teeth, 97, 98, 99, 100, 109; "promise" to Addie, 97, 98, 100; remarks about love, 107; motivation similar to that of Addie, 109

Bundren, Cash: 91, 92, 93, 96, 100, 101, 102, 106, 107, 108, 109, 122; doubts about Darl's madness, 102; relationship to Darl, 102–103; understanding of Darl, 102–103; Faulkner's treatment of, 103

Bundren, Darl: 90, 91, 93, 94, 95, 96, 98, 99, 101, 107, 109; characterized, 101–105; relationship to Cash, 102–103; laughter, 102, 103

Bundren, Dewey Dell: 91, 93, 94, 95, 96, 98, 100, 101, 102, 104, 107, 109; dream, 92; desire for abortion, 100

Bundren family, 88, 91, 92, 99, 102, 103, 104, 105, 107, 109, 120

Bundren, Jewel: 92, 94, 96, 97, 99, 100, 102, 103, 104, 107, 108; characterized, 100–101

Bundren, Mrs., 92, 103, 104, 109

Bundren, Vardaman, 91, 92, 93, 94, 95, 104, 105, 107

Burch, Lucas, 135, 139, 141, 142, 152, 155

Burden, Calvin, 208

Burden family, 141, 142, 207, 208

Burden, Jim, 198

Burden, Joanna: 119, 136, 137, 138, 143, 144, 145, 146, 149, 151, 152, 212; characterized, 149–50; version of Burden killing, 208, 209

Burgess, Mrs., 53

Burt, Leonard, 136

Bush, Ishmael, 261

Butler, Birdie, 118

Byron, George Gordon, Lord, 60, 160

Cable, George Washington, 292

Calvinism, 136, 140, 146

Camus, Albert, 114

Canby, Henry Seidel, 113, 139

Capone, Scarface Al, 115

Carlyle; Thomas, 241

Cass. *See* Edmonds, McCaslin

Cather, Willa, 143, 198, 290

Cerf, Bennett, 191, 192, 193, 222

Cézanne, Paul, 20

Chance, 133

Charlie, 51, 56

Charlie, Bonnie Prince, 43

Child, Lydia Maria Francis, 290

Chingachgook, 261

Christ, 57, 58, 63, 88, 138, 261

Christmas, Joe: 113, 119, 135, 136, 138, 139, 156, 175, 234; as Christ symbol, 138; compared to Lena Grove, 140–43, 151; characterized, 141–43, 144–51; racial identity, 143, 144–46; Faulkner's comments about, 144, 145, 146; shoes, 145–46; freedom of will, 146, 151–53; relationship to McEachern, 147–48; troubles with women, 148–50; significance of his life, 150–51; unresolved questions, 151–52

Civil War, xii, 8, 9, 10, 13, 23, 25, 26, 44, 46, 160, 161, 168, 186, 189, 191, 192, 193, 198, 199, 201, 202–203, 217, 218, 223, 224, 250, 262, 270, 279, 291, 292, 296

Clark, Callie Barr. *See* Barr, Mammy Callie

"Clean Well-Lighted Place, A," 21

Clytemnestra (Clytie), 163, 173–74, 175, 176

Coldfield, Goodhue, 158, 173, 176, 179

Coldfield, Mrs. Goodhue, 158, 173

Coldfield, Rosa: 158, 161–62, 163, 169, 173, 174, 175, 176, 177, 180, 181; bias in account of Thomas Sutpen, 168, 171, 177; characterized, 177–78

Collier's, 244, 246, 249

Colum, Mary, 160

Commins, Saxe, 222

Compson, Benjamin (Benjy): 36, 39, 40, 42, 45, 46, 47, 49, 51, 52, 53, 55, 56, 57–58, 62, 63, 69, 71, 72, 75, 92, 121, 133, 187, 218, 240; mental traits, 39, 47–48, 49, 54, 57, 59, 60, 70, 83; association of ideas, 39, 47–49; change of name, 45, 48, 49, 50, 72; monologue analyzed, 47–59; drinks "sassprilluh," 52–53; preternatural knowledge, 53, 54; at the gate, 53, 56; sense of order, 54; voice change, 54; taken to cemetery, 54, 78, 81; birthday, 55, 56; castration, 55, 57; parallels with Christ, 57; humanity, 57–58; parallels with Billy Budd, 57, 58; parallels with suffering servant, 57, 58; need for love, 58; meaning of his suffering, 58, 78, 81; attitude toward Caddy, 70–71; described, 77; at church, 79, 80; knowledge of order, 81; character interpreted,

Index

Index

Index

Index

Index

Index

Index

208, 219, 221, 293, 294; publication, ix, 3, 4, 111; title change, 3, 4; cutting, 3, 4, 5, 220; defects, 3, 31–32; inception and composition, 5, 6; sources, 6; significance, 32–33; compared to *Sanctuary*, 129. *See also* Chapter I, 3–33; *Flags in the Dust*

Sartoris, Bayard (brother of Colonel John Sartoris), 23, 24, 25, 26, 28

Sartoris, Bayard (brother of Evelyn Sartoris), 5

Sartoris, Bayard ("old Bayard"; son of Colonel John Sartoris): 8, 11, 17, 26, 27, 44, 61, 193, 194, 195, 198, 200, 207, 208, 217, 218, 222; relationship to Henry Sutpen, 195; as narrator, 196–97, 198, 200, 202, 206; as central character in *The Unvanquished*, 198, 199, 201, 202; characterized in *The Unvanquished*, 201–202, 209–210, 211, 212, 213–15; memories of war, 202–204; revenge upon Grumby, 206; account of Burden killing, 207, 209; compared to Colonel Sartoris, 210, 214, 215

Sartoris, Bayard ("young Bayard"; great-grandson of Colonel Sartoris; grandson of "old Bayard"): 4, 8, 9, 23, 26, 27, 28, 29, 30, 31, 32, 35, 45, 61, 122; reaction to war, 6; marriage, 27; despair and disillusionment, 27–28; lack of self-discipline, 28

Sartoris, Benbow, 28, 35

Sartoris, Colonel John: 13, 17, 23, 24, 25, 26, 28, 32, 44, 75, 83, 174, 198, 201, 202, 205, 207, 211, 217, 218, 224; characterized in *The Unvanquished*, 195, 200, 208, 209, 212, 213, 214–15; compared to Thomas Sutpen, 213

Sartoris, Drusilla Hawk: 194, 200, 201, 202, 204, 206, 212, 213, 214, 215, 217; characterized, 207

Sartoris, Evelyn: 5; name changed to John, 6

Sartoris family: 8, 23, 25, 26, 28, 29, 32, 35, 83, 109, 186, 209, 211, 217, 218, 291; family traits, 29; decline, 120

Sartoris, John ("Johnny"; twin brother of "young Bayard"), 26, 27, 28, 29, 32

Sartoris, John (son of "old Bayard"; father of "young Bayard"), 8

Sartre, Jean Paul, 10

Saturday Evening Post, 190, 191, 193, 197, 206, 221, 246, 248, 249, 252

Saturday Review of Literature, The, 113, 139

Saul (biblical), 185

Scarlet Letter, The, 162, 262, 293

Schultz, Dutch, 115

Scott, Randolph, 192

Scott, Sir Walter, 10, 292

Scriabine, Alexander, 134

Scribner's (Charles Scribner's Sons), 192

Scribner's Magazine, 191, 195, 197, 206, 221

"Selvage," 166

Seven Arts, The, 294

Shakespeare, William, xiii, 82, 239

Shegog, Colonel Robert B., 161

Shegog, the Reverend: sermon, 78–79, 80

Shenton, Edward, 193

Sherman, Colonel William Tecumseh, 14, 15

Ship Island, Ripley and Kentucky Railroad Company, 16, 17

Shipp, Dr. Felix Grundy, 161

Sickymo, 274

Siege of Monterey, The, 13

Simms, William Gilmore, 290

"Skirmish at Sartoris," 190, 195, 196, 206–209, 212, 275

Slave Ship, 191

Smith, Dora, 117

Smith, Hal. *See* Smith, Harrison

Smith, Harrison (Hal), 3, 87, 111, 112, 157, 192

Smith, Major General Andrew J. ("Whiskey"), 15

Smith, Mary, 117

Sniffle, Ransy, 291

Snopes, Ab: 196, 201, 205, 217, 221–22, 234, 235, 238, 254, 291; characterized, 224–25; horse trade with Pat Stamper, 225, 227, 254, 291

Snopes, Byron, 4, 221

Snopes, Clarence, 126, 129, 132, 221

Snopes, Eckrum (Eck), 226, 236, 237, 238

Snopes, Eula Varner: 144, 218, 223, 232, 233, 234, 238; appearance, 220, 228–29, 235; as symbol of sexual desire, 228–29; as grotesque figure, 229; sexual experiences, 229–30

Snopes family, 44, 46, 217, 218, 219, 220, 221, 223, 224, 227, 228, 234, 237, 238

Snopes, Flem: 96, 99, 167, 217, 218, 219, 220, 221, 223, 224, 231, 232, 233, 234, 235, 254, 291, 293, 296; as grotesque figure, 225, 239; appearance, 225–26; career, 225–27, 239–41; trade with V. K. Ratliff, 227–28, 254; impotence, 230; in hell, 230; marriage, 230; spotted horse auction, 236–37; name, 239; as essence of Snopesism, 239, 241; defeat of V. K. Ratliff, 237–38, 247

325

Index

Index

bred," 179; characterized, 187; fatal defect, 188
"Swing Low, Sweet Chariot," 286

Tamar (biblical), 185
Tennie's Jim. *See* Beauchamp, James
Tennyson, Alfred, 88
Terrel (Turl; Tomey's Turl), 249, 250, 252, 253, 254, 257, 258, 271, 272
Thompson, Jacob, 15, 43
Thompson, John Wesley, 11, 12, 13
Thompson, William Tappan, 291
Thoreau, Henry David, 30
Thucydides, 229
Thurmond, Richard J., 15, 16, 17
Time, 35, 160, 193. *See also* History
Toklas, Alice B., 19, 22
Tom Jones, 180
Tomasina (Tomy; Tomey), 249, 272
Tomey's Turl. *See* Terrel
Tommy, 120, 124
Town, The: 220, 221, 222; plot, 239–40
T. P., 40, 52, 53, 54, 73
Tristram Shandy, 47
Tull, Cora: 92, 93, 96, 97, 107; judgments, 107–108; characterized, 108
Tull, Vernon, 91, 92, 93, 95, 97, 99, 101, 105, 106, 226, 236, 237
Turl. *See* Terrel
Turner, William, 161
Twilight, 35. *See also The Sound and the Fury*

Uncas, 261
Uncle Remus stories, 292
Uncollected Stories, The, 289
University Grays, 174
Unvanquished, The: ix, xii, 12, 14, 17, 24, 26, 44, 75, 88, 191, 209, 211, 221, 225, 273, 275, 295; as an introduction to Faulkner's fiction, 189–90; critics' estimate, 189–90; unity of, 190, 198–99, 243, 293; composition, 190–91; publication, 192, 193; revisions, 192, 193–97, 217; discrepancies in, 193–94; white-Negro relations in, 195, 200–201; as novel or collection of short stories, 197–99, 217, 293; essential subject, 201; desolation of war, 202–203; credibility of incidents, 202, 206; compared to *The Hamlet*, 217–19; relationship to *Go Down, Moses*, 244–45; weakness of form, 245. *See also* Chapter VII, 189–215

"Unvanquished, The," 190, 191, 196, 221, 222. *See also* "Riposte in Tertio"

Van Dorn, General Earl, 14
Vance, Lizzie (wife of William Clark Falkner), 13
Vardaman, James K., 220, 221
Varner, Eula. *See* Snopes, Eula Varner
Varner, Jody: 218, 226, 229, 230; characterized, 224
Varner, Will: 220, 225, 226, 227, 228, 229, 230, 234, 236, 237; characterized, 224
"Vendée," 190, 191, 196, 205, 206, 212, 221, 222
Versh, 40, 48, 50, 52, 53
Vidor, King, 192
Virginia, University of, 4, 8, 23, 37, 46, 87, 115, 128, 137, 144, 145, 157, 158, 168, 169, 180, 181, 189, 213, 218, 238
Volstead Act, 116

"Was," 245, 246, 250, 251–53
Washington (federal government), 207
Washington, George, 63
Wasson, Ben, 3, 4, 5, 29, 40, 220
Waste Land, The, 21, 36
Wharton, Edith, 290
White, Caroline (wife of Bayard Sartoris), 5
Whitehead (deputy), 136
White-Negro relations, 30–31, 160, 195, 245, 246, 247, 249, 252, 253, 257, 258, 259, 269, 280–81, 282, 285, 286, 288
White Rose of Memphis, The, 16
Whitfield, 92, 93, 105, 107, 108
Whiting, Brigadier General W. H. H., 14
Whitman, Walt, xiii
Wild Palms, The, 243, 244
Wilde, Oscar, 19
Wilderness Romance, The, 259–85
Wilkins, George, 246
Wilkins, Mrs., 21
Wilkins, Nathalie (Nat), 246
Wilkins, Professor, 212
Willard, George, 294
Wilmoth, 287
Winesburg, Ohio: xi, 89, 90, 198, 225, 294; influence on Faulkner, 294, 295
Winterbottom, Mrs., 208
Wolfe, Thomas, 7
Word, Caroline (wife of Joseph Falkner), 12
Word, Justiania Dickinson (wife of John Wesley Thompson), 12

327

Index